WHAT IS HAPPENING TO AMERICA?

The Hidden Truth of Global Destruction

Observations, Analysis and Commentary of a Soviet Attorney

Simona Pipko

Printed in the United States of America.

Library of Congress Control Number: 2022936308

ISBN	Paperback	978-1-68536-487-8
	eBook	978-1-68536-488-5

Westwood Books Publishing LLC
Atlanta Financial Center
3343 Peachtree Rd NE Ste 145-725
Atlanta, GA 30326

www.westwoodbookspublishing.com

CONTENTS

PART II

Socialism/Communism: The Enemy of Mankind

To the soldiers fighting
Soviet Fascism around the globe

And

For all those who survived Stalinism,
—and the millions who did not.

FORWARD

A World in Turmoil

Dear reader:

This book has been sabotaged and banned several times. Now it is the third try to bring the Truth to light.

If you want to understand what is going on in 21st century America and why America is so deeply divided—please, read this book.

If you are interested in knowing how "Uncle Joe" Stalin built the Chinese Communist State and married Islamism to Communist ideology—please, read this book.

If you want to know the origins of the Chinese COVID-19 virus—read this book.

If you want to know Vladimir Putin, his regime of Soviet Fascism and their war on Ukraine—read this book.

If you are ready to prevent a tragic future for America and defend her Constitutional republic—please, read this book.

If the leadership of American Military wants to know the real enemy and provide strong national security to the country, they should read this book.

Don't be shocked by the murder of FBI agents—all agents of the FBI should read this book.

I am a former Soviet defense attorney and am dedicated to share with you my experiences and knowledge that I acquired during the course of my life in Russia and America. It began in the Soviet Union during the reign of horror created by Joseph Stalin and his Communist apparatus. Those days influenced my entire life in a way that most of you will not be able to comprehend unless you read this book.

In these volatile times when the terms Socialist, Marxist, Communist, Racist, Radical Islamist and so many more are being applied to today's leaders, I would like to add a term that I have concluded fits the ideology that underpins it all—I call it Soviet Fascism.

Follow my experiences. Learn what I learned; and see if you draw the same conclusions. Please forgive my prose, which often reveals my very strong personal opinion and at times might contort phrases and offend those of you who love the flow of perfect English. I believe with every fiber of my body that this message must be heard, by you, by your family and friends, and by all Americans, before this great country, the last true bastion of freedom and Capitalism, falls under the influence of the destructive forces, persuasive schemes, fraud, and methodical programs that began many years ago. Here is my personal story, but above all, here is my alarming message for you:

Please heed it before it is too late to prevent the overthrow of this country we know and love by ever increasing, malevolent forces rising in America and across the globe. Knowledge of Russia and her Intel is a Must to secure global peace and tranquility—it is the deception of Socialism, an issue of vital national security…
January 2022

Simona Pipko

CHAPTER 1

1937—A Year of Infamy

If you have knowledge, let others light their candles in it.

Margaret Fuller

I was born in Moscow, the capital of what was then the Soviet Union. The only daughter of a medical doctor, I was surrounded by attention, love and adoration. I had been a lucky girl and felt I was the center of my mother's attention. Unlike other mothers, mine did not work—and I truly felt that she dedicated her life to me. From early morning to the late evening she was with me. Every morning she washed my face and hands, and then she combed my hair and tied up my bow. While my mother was washing my face and hands; I already knew what I would eat for breakfast. There were two choices: cooked semolina or hard-boiled eggs. Prepared semolina had a specific, pleasant smell, while hard-boiled eggs did not smell. And after washing I had my breakfast. My mother fed me, sitting in front of me and persuading me to eat, as I did not want to do that at all. Only by reading fairytales could she charm me into eating. My emotions during the reading were going up and down, and fascinated with expectations, I had opened my mouth waiting for the end of the story.

I remember one story in particular, because it made me so emotional that my mother was frightened. This was the story of "Ugly Dugley" and once while listening to it I cried and threw up my entire breakfast. My mother stopped reading and calmed me down while switching my attention to something else—she had such a patience in dealing with me!

Later on she finished reading the story, but I was crying again, and I still remember what a strong feeling of grief and joy I experienced during my mother's reading.

My mother made my life complete with a lot of love, new books and music. I loved everything about my mom: her black wavy hair, her kind brown eyes, the smell of her shoulders, her soft skin and the tenderness of her arms when they embraced me, and there was more than I can't put into words.

My father had no such time for me—he was working as a medical doctor, taught at the medical school and he also was writing his dissertation to get his PhD. Only on Sunday he could take out his beloved violin and play for awhile, but after 10 o'clock in the morning. We lived in a communal apartment where any instrument could be played only during a certain time frame. Another special feature of living in a communal apartment was the absence of lights in front of our front door—the bulbs had been stolen every time the management put new ones in. My parents learned to deal in the darkness with the keys that opened our front door.

After a few years, we moved from Moscow to Leningrad. In Moscow we shared a room with my mother's parents in a communal apartment. My father did not like it. At the time he was writing a dissertation and doing quite serious research on a new medication. He had received a position in the Erisman Hospital in Leningrad, but it was only half of the solution as we had no a residence in Leningrad—my parents had a stamp of *propiska*[1] in Moscow. The Erisman Hospital had no housing fund, so my father signed a contract with the October Railroad Administration in Leningrad to consult at their medical facility twice a month. For that he got rewarded with a room and *propiska* in their building. It was a very famous Pertsov's building; biggest in Leningrad. If I am not mistaken, 10,000 people lived in that building.

Pertsov was a successful Russian businessman dealing with railroad transportation, particularly with the first Russian railroad from St. Petersburg to Moscow. This was called the famous Imperial Government of Russia Nicolas Railroad built in 1869 in honor of Czar Nicolas. After the October Revolution it was renamed the October Railroad along with all the buildings surrounding it including the Pertsov's building which by then had become the property of the government with thousands apartments remade into communal ones. The building was constructed in a peculiar form, as if two capital "Es" were facing each other, connected at the top. A big yard in the center divided those "Es." The yard had never seen the rays of the sun, since the high buildings prevented them. The eight floors of the building had twenty-four front and back entrances. We had received a room in the communal apartment on the second floor of the Pertsov's building at 44 Ligovskiy Prospect, Apt. 232. Our communal apartment also had a telephone. I still remember its number: 596-46.

Although we had a pretty big room, there was not enough light—the only window at the corner faced the building's wall. We had to have electrical lights on all the time. There were seven families in the apartment, which had one kitchen, one bathroom, one lavatory and a long corridor. It had never been empty—each family had the right to locate some old items and boxes with laundry next to a door off their room. The kitchen was big and had seven tables with seven *kerosenka*[2] (an oil or paraffin-stove), one on each table. We had a table with our own *kerosenka* to cook on. The big kitchen also had a back door used to take the garbage out. All the neighbors threw their garbage down stairs to the back yard, where the big wooden boxes were constructed for garbage.

Our kitchen was the place for everyone to socialize. I had often been a witness to the different discussions between the neighbors, while my mother was preparing the meals. The kitchen was filled with various aromas from strong cabbage to fried fish. That did not bother me, since I had gotten used to the stink of an incredibly awful combination of vinegar with the stench of spoiled eggs. Nevertheless, at only three and a half, I remember one occurrence, but not for any aromas. It was a strange event that stayed with me my entire life.

It was the winter of 1934. I don't remember what part of the day it was—the light had always been on. Something very strange had happened in our communal apartment. My mother had not been in the room for a long time and went looking for her and in the kitchen I observed a pretty unusual scene. Several women, including my mother and one man, were standing in the middle of the kitchen, very close to one another, talking with troubled looks on their faces. I took a seat on my small chair at the corner close to the window and watched them. But I couldn't hear a word— they were all whispering. Some kind of concern or even anxiety emanated from them and it reached out to me. I did not know what it was, but the scene was so unusually alarming that I continued sitting still for so long that I was growing numb.

The back door of the kitchen was open and one woman was gesturing toward it with emotions… I couldn't hear her voice or make out any words, but suddenly several women began running to the door and then went upstairs along the stair case. I even heard their steps, though they tried to run quietly. My mother and the man remained in the kitchen and continued whispering and I lost track of time but I knew something threatening was happening and it kept me quietly watching. When the women came back, I couldn't hear their steps, so silent was their return. Their faces were pale and frightened, their arms crossing their chests. Breathing heavily, they joined my mother and the man. After a long pause the whispering conversation has resumed and I saw that my mother was very nervous. That made me scared—as if a huge cloud of fear came down from the sky and filled the entire kitchen.

When my mother saw me, she immediately took me in her arms, embraced me and rapidly walked to our room without saying a word. She did not talk for some time, embracing me to her chest, then she put me in my bed. That night the scary dreams tortured me and I was awakened by the conversation between my parents in the night's darkness and an absolute stillness…

"…they saw Stalin…" my mother said.

"…What?" Father was surprised.

"…Yes, they have seen Stalin. He was well-lit by the lampposts on the platform," Mother repeated. After a while Father asked:

"How could they see him from our kitchen?"

"They went to the seventh floor and saw him from the window on the staircase."

"And what did they see?"

"They saw Stalin walking back and forth in front of his car, continually smoking. There was no one else on the railroad platform. He was alone. The women even saw how he was dressed."

I knew the name Stalin. Our radio talked about him very favorably all the time and the children's choruses sang the loud songs about him. I did not associate his name with anything bad… certainly not enough to scare me. I went to sleep again and didn't hear the rest of the conversation.

In the morning, as usual, my mother read a book to me and I was listening and eating at the same time. The memory of the fear I felt during that kitchen episode had gradually subsided and my life of love, books, and music went on…

At the time, many people in our country had learned the German language. Approximately in 1936 my parents found a German teacher for me. I liked it. Soon she also started reading books to me, and the German books had wonderful illustrations, very funny colorful pictures. I liked them very much.

My German teacher had always worn the same white blouse, black jacket, black skirt, and seemed quite small. Her brown hair was pulled into a knot and her blue eyes looked at me with expectation and trust. She was a strict teacher in the presence of my mother. Yet when we were alone, she kissed me on my forehead after I counted to one hundred in German. She wasn't old, but her glasses were always on the end of her nose. I was afraid that she would lose them and be unable to read German books to me anymore. The most important thing for me was her character—she loved music.

As a matter of fact, my father also loved music very much. He composed music and played the violin. When we were in Moscow, he played in a group of young violinists together with David Oystrahk[3]. Some of his friends had moved to Leningrad as well and played in the orchestras of Mariinka (Mariinsky Theater) and the Conservatory Theater. Both were located on the same street, one across from the other. My father's friends had provided us with free tickets and my sociable German teacher was delighted and so was I. My father had no time to go with us. So, the three of us, my mother, my teacher, and I had become habitual visitors of both theaters. Some operas I knew by heart—we listened to them several times and the majestic influence of music penetrated my soul. It was also an excellent musical education—Tchaikovsky, Rimsky-Korsakov, Rubinstein, and Borodin had stimulated my enormous love for music and my musical taste.

My joy continued. My German teacher gave me lessons three days a week and on three other days she taught the twins girls in the apartment one flight down from me. What happiness it was when she introduced me to them! The girls were my age, Gerta and Truda. Although I did not have much free time, there are no words to describe the joy and delight we felt playing together.

By that time, my father had gotten his PhD and during his free time began teaching me to play the violin. I cannot say that I disliked the violin, but I had no love for it and my father had no patience for me. He wanted me to practice as much as possible. I did not like to do so.

For a couple of months my mother tolerated our arguments; however, her patience ended when she saw me crying. As a result, my mother brought me to the Musical School for Gifted Children. I passed several tests and had been admitted to the second class as I had already known the elementary lessons of the *School Berea*—elementary musical textbook for the violin. Three times a week my mother took me to the school by tram.

We had to get up early in the morning, as our trip could take more than an hour. Our tram went through the entire city to the Petrogradskay Storona. It was an interesting journey for me—I loved Leningrad, the city of palaces, historic monuments and beautiful bridges. Sometimes my German teacher took me to the Musical School and it was always very enjoyable viewing beloved Leningrad.

My twin friends studied piano. I often came down one flight of stairs to their apartment and the twins' mother organized our concerts. What a joy it had been! We could play there at any time, because the family had an individual apartment—they did not have neighbors! What a pleasure it was to play when you were in the mood to play music! Our building had only a few individual apartments for the top people in the October Railroad Administration. The twins' father was a Chairman of that organization.

By the year 1937, the three of us had achieved some successes and the twins' mother often organized our concerts. Both mothers were full of pride for their children and we also felt proud of our playing. I was a very happy girl—I felt fortunate; I loved my parents, I loved my friends, and I loved my Leningrad. My life was a beautiful fairytale; I was in seventh heaven, floating in happiness.

One morning we were going to the Music School, and when my mother opened the front door she suddenly stopped and put her hand to my mouth… it meant that I should not make a sound. As usual, there were no lights on our landing and nobody could see us while we stood there, stopped dead in our tracks. The twins' apartment's door was opened and we heard men's voices coming from there. Then, several plain dressed men brought out the twins' father, holding him under his arms. He was in his pajamas with a black long coat over them, and a cloth cap on his head, but his face was unrecognizable and very red. The group continued to down the main entrance. Then I heard the start of a car's engine and the sounds of it pulling away. Paralyzed, I stood quietly and I do not remember how long we were standing on our landing. Maybe it was only a couple of minutes, but for me it was an eternity. I knew that something terrible had happened, yet I could not perceive the real scale of the tragedy at the time. I was only six years old.

In silence we sat on the tram going to my Musical School. The palaces and monuments in my city did not bring any joy to me that day. My mind was running as I thought about the twin girls. Their father was taken away. How it is possible to live without a father? I was afraid to ask Mother about anything. Her beautiful face was also unrecognizable, but not red. On the contrary—her face was pale and she did not look at me. I felt that my grief was similar to hers and I did not know how to help my mother. My heart was bleeding, unable to do anything tangible to help.

I could not play violin at all in class. Mother told my music teacher that she didn't feel well and we went home. On the way back we did not talk. That night my parents were talking so quietly that I could not hear anything. In the morning, I ate while my mother read a new fairytale. After breakfast, I vomited up everything and began crying so loudly that my mother embraced and kissed me. But I saw that she was also distressed, and while kissing me drops of her tears touched my face.

"Simosha, my girl, don't cry. I love you very much, let's read a new fairytale. Look at this picture of a deer and a squirrel." Mother took a new book and showed me the pictures. Tears continued running down my cheeks and I could not see the pictures clearly. I do not know why I cried. But I did and I could not force myself to stop. Mother embraced me again, and took me in her arms and put me to bed. I slept for a long time.

That day, after I had awakened, Mother told me that my twin girl friends had moved to another city. I did not cry any more. But that was a time of real grief—I lost my dear friends. I was deprived of playing with them again, studying with them, having concerts, and enjoying their company. What an awful feeling it was! Yet in the back of my head the story of their father made me scared and confused, but I did not ask my mother about it. Something dangerous was obviously connected with all the events my twin friends had endured. That strange feeling stopped me from asking my German teacher about my experience. I could not trust myself to share my emotions with anybody after that—something stopped me.

My life continued along the usual schedule: reading books, taking German lessons, and going to Musical School. My mother was my best friend and my permanent tutor and teacher in life— she meant everything in the world to me. I loved her completely, however, after losing my twin friends, I desperately needed to play with other children. How jealous I was watching children playing in our big yard! But I did not have free time to play with them. We also had several children in our apartment and very seldom, when our neighbors did not object, we ran along our corridor. We would laugh and yell, but it was not allowed, and a neighbor would stop us. Even while playing hide and seek quietly, we couldn't restrain ourselves without laughing. My mother did not want to have a problem and she forbade me from playing in our corridor. I respected my mother's wishes and stopped going to play with children in our corridor. But playing with children had become a constant dream of mine.

One day, I got two A's in my violin studies and with eager anticipation, I wanted to get home to show them to my mother. By the time my German teacher and I got home my mother was not there, but my father was. He told me that Mother had gone into the hospital, and that he was going to take me to Moscow to stay with my grandparents. He did. I loved my grandparents, but that visit was different—I worried about my mom in the hospital. Our tiny room in a communal apartment in Moscow had a bed and an old brown sofa. My grandmother and I slept on a bed, my grandfather on a sofa.

Living in Moscow and longing for my mom, I slept night and day, my head covered with a blanket to block the strong smells of fried fish which occupied the entire communal apartment. Upon awakening, I'd ask whether my mother had come home yet and, receiving a negative response, would turn back to the wall and fall asleep again. Children grieve differently from adults. All that time in a room next to ours, a neighbor constantly played one record of music I did not like. It was Moldavanesca, a combination of sadness in allegro expressed by several whipping violins. Since that time, whenever I hear the music of Moldavanesca, a deep feeling of grief hits me again—my memory has not allowed me to forget that time of anguish.

My mother was not in the hospital; she was in prison. The events preceding her disappearance were simple. When our music school teacher told children about our kind and beloved Comrade Stalin, I had replied that he was wrong because my mother considered him a bandit and a butcher who was killing innocent people. By the time my German teacher and I got home that day, my mother had already been arrested.

She was charged with the attempted murder of Comrade Stalin… it was 1937, the year my childhood ended and I was just six years old.

When I grew older, my father told me another version of that story, that two of our neighbors had informed the police after a conversation in our communal kitchen. It was an everyday occurrence that women were discussing some topics while preparing meals. That day, Mother had voiced her strong contrary opinion, when several women in the kitchen expressed their admiration for the good deeds of Comrade Stalin. My father said that Mother not only disagreed with them but added that Stalin was a butcher because he had killed so many innocent people. Two of our neighbors were the informers. They went to the security agency to report my mother. Father also told me the end of the story—an incredible ending that I'll share with you now.

My father became a gynecologist after he had completed his PhD at Erisman Hospital. Once he dealt with a very tough labor—a woman of forty-two, pregnant with her first child, could not deliver the baby naturally. Compelled to deliver the child by Cesarean section, my father had saved both the mother and the child. At that time, the surgery had taken a lot of courage and skill on his part. Thanking him, the woman's husband had cried, as it had been his first and last chance to have a baby. He had told my father to feel free to call him if the need ever arose. That man was the city prosecutor.

When my mother was arrested, my father went to the city prosecutor, whose wife and baby he had saved. It was a dark time in the country when even being a city prosecutor meant little—the omnipotent NKVD[4] had installed its own system of law and order and nobody ever returned from prison. Yet a miracle could happen: my mother came back home, and so did I. The city prosecutor must have tried very hard to return the favor my Father had done for his wife.

Soon, however, I noticed a great change in my mother's behavior—she never kissed me after her return. She had become a completely different person—she seldom smiled, never laughed, and never participated in any political discussions. The prison experience silenced her for life. There was no more reading of the fairytales, no joyful chats and playing. Sadly, the impact of what had happened to us all had been engrained in our minds and never disappeared. It affected me in a very perceptible way—a small piece of smoldering fear had settled in my soul forever.

Living in a communal apartment had required a certain way of behavior for adults. For example, my parents had never talked about anything serious at the dinner table in my presence. They had to wait until it was night and then in a manner of prudent and cautious whispering. But life in our country had been invading our personal lives daily, with the subjects that nobody could avoid discussing. Very often I heard on the radio the word NKVD under the wise leadership of Comrade Stalin. Those four letters gave me the impression of people fighting our enemies and their accomplices—I grew to like people from the NKVD.

Formal schooling enhanced my learning experience. When I went to school for the first time, it was my birthday—September 1. And the first thing I saw in school was a huge portrait of Comrade Stalin with a smiling girl embracing him—the portrait was the embodiment of love between a father and a daughter. I appreciated it very much. At times like that my soul did not feel the smoldering sense of fear. On the contrary, I felt as if I were embracing my father and our life seemed as beautiful as a bouquet of flowers in Stalin's hand. The books we read about our wonderful country and our wise leader and teacher Comrade Stalin had started my political education. The war that began in 1941 had doubled my love for my country, for our Great Leader Comrade Stalin, for the people in our Red Army, and for the NKVD who fought our enemies and their accomplices.

It so happened that after the end of the war, I again heard the familiar four words—NKVD. At that time we lived in Minsk, where my father served. To save our room in Leningrad, I had to live six months there, while during the other six months my mother and sister lived there, while I moved to Minsk. Otherwise the neighbors would inform the housing administration and we could lose our room. Besides, Father had become sick, he had gotten a stomach ulcer and needed meals prepared at home. I have lived with him in a room of the communal apartment for six months, cooking and studying in Minsk's school.

Despite his illness, my father had started developing my musical and political education, during those months I lived with him in Minsk. As a matter of fact, Father was a pretty good musician, favoring the violin. He had never parted from his violin even during the siege of Leningrad during World War II. While defending that beautiful city of palaces and monuments, where a million people starved to death, he began composing music. His violin had become his friend and savior for all four years of the war. Usually, after dinner, Father would take his violin and play the melody he had composed, and after that I sang the melody and he accompanied me. I knew all of father's songs and quartets by heart. It was a wonderful time for both of us—I dearly loved music. One evening my father asked me: "Simosha, you are a big girl now. What do you want to be?" It did not take me even a second to answer:

"I want to be a singer!" Father started laughing hysterically for a while and when he stopped, his face become serious, and his eyes lost their warmth, as he said to me: "Take a seat, Simosha, I want to talk with you." He put his violin on the table and sat down. I also took a seat on the other side of the table—the violin between us. "We live in a very difficult time, Simosha," he began. "A woman in our country must have a serious career, otherwise there will be a lot of obstacles to overcome. I don't want you to be a singer; it is not a good profession in our country. You love history, so go and study it seriously in the university. You can go to law school, though it can be difficult to be a lawyer in our country." I didn't know what my father meant when he talked about the difficulties of being a lawyer. The events that followed our conversation had given me a hint of what it meant to be a lawyer and reminded me again about the NKVD as well.

One winter morning in January, 1948, I couldn't go to school—several streets were surrounded by police. I had to return home. As a matter of fact, by that time my attitude toward Comrade Stalin and the NKVD had radically changed. There were many causes why, but I wasn't lost in a dream world any longer. Living with Father had become another kind of education for me. I was older and Father slowly and intentionally started developing my political enlightenment. He told me that the girl in the picture with Stalin was not his daughter; she was the daughter of a man Stalin declared a Japanese spy and had executed. I was stunned and frightened. Slowly but surely Father was opening my eyes and mind to the real history of politics.

We discussed French Utopists San-Simon, Furrier, and Owen. My father had known history pretty well and our discussions opened my eyes also to the Soviet Socialist economic policy and anti-Semitism. He told me that the policy of anti-Americanism had created an image of the enemy, referring to "the Imperialist America" which was an evil presence in the world. Ai was already aware of the subject because I met with a real American man a few years earlier. I talked to him, and I was sure that America was for peace! I didn't believe the Soviet propaganda any longer, and I realized they were lying about America and about many other things as well.

So that January evening, when Father came home from the hospital, I asked him what happened on the street. He did not answer; his face showed me the indignation he was going through. Our friendship had allowed me to repeat the question; I wanted to know what happened there. It took some time for my father to respond, as if he hesitated to discuss the event.

"Let's eat, and then we'll talk," he answered. I saw he was very tired and upset.

I tried to calm him down, with no success. In silence I had prepared dinner, while Father read a newspaper at the table. We ate our dinner in silence, too. After we finished, I cleared all the dishes and sat at the table. "Can you can tell me now why you are so upset?" I said. After a pause Father spoke in a low voice, almost whispering:

"They killed King Lear!" he said, pronouncing every word slowly, his face getting red.

"What do you mean; they killed King Lear, I don't know what you are talking about."

"The NKVD killed Solomon Mikhoels!" he repeated with such a force that the drops of his saliva reached my hands.

"They killed Mikhoels in Moscow?" I asked.

"No, he was killed here, in Minsk." His face reddened even more.

"He is an actor, and why did they kill the actor?" I could not believe that a famous Jewish actor presented any threat to our country.

"I am tired. I don't want to talk about Mikhoels any more," Father said and went to the corridor to smoke. He was so upset that I did not insist on continuing our conversation. The next day, in school, I heard girls talking about the car accident, which had killed Michaels.

It was many years later, only after immigrating to the United States, that I learned the horrifying details of his death. He was assassinated on Stalin's personal orders by an agent of the NKVD. His death was masked by a car accident. He had been invited to an apartment where he was killed. After the murder, his body was brought up near the hotel where he stayed, thrown on the ground, and then a truck ran over his body several times....

It was the beginning of the Stalinist campaign against the Soviet Jews, which was started by the NKVD in 1948 with the assassination of Mikhoels. To perceive the depth of the Stalin's crime, I would like to give you a portrait of Solomon Mikhoels and a study of the policy of Anti-Semitism, which lasted many years and only ended with Stalin's death.

Mikhoels was the leading actor and director of the Jewish Theater in Leningrad. Marc Chagall was a decorator in his theater. Later on Mikhoels moved to Moscow and became a director and actor of the State Jewish Theater. His role as King Lear made him a celebrity in the entire country. People from all over the country came to Moscow to see him on a stage as King Lear. He did it in Yiddish. The Jewish Theater and its director Mikhoels had become a center of Jewish national identity. He had actively supported Stalin in his fight against Nazi Germany during WWII. In 1942, he was made Chairman of the Jewish Anti-Fascist Committee. In this capacity he traveled around the world encouraging the Jewish communities to support the Soviet Union in its war against Nazi Germany. While that stance served Stalin well during the war, once the conflict was ended he opposed Mikhoels' contact with the world leaders since the creation of "the Iron Curtain" had already begun. In 1946, the NKVD was divided into MVD and MGB divisions, a precursor of the KGB. With this act the system of oppression doubled. The Cold War had begun.

Just listen to this dialogue:

"Mikhoels must be liquidated," said Stalin. "But how can we do that?" asked Abakumov, the Chairman of the MGB. "By a car accident," answered Stalin. Mikhoels' fame had been so widespread that Stalin did not dare to organize a Show Trial against him. When I went on the internet many years later and read the essay *How Mikhoels Had Been Killed*, my hair stood up; I was horrified. Written by Gennadiy Kostyrchenko, it conveyed a secret conversation between Stalin and Abakumov. I had the impression that it was similar to the dialogue between two leaders of a criminal gang. Stalin said that it should be a car accident and gave permission to murder Solomon Mikhoels. The top secret documents have revealed the story of four gangsters, members of the Soviet Security, the MGB and their assignment to assassinate Solomon Mikhoels. The entire world should know that story to understand the real history and background of the MGB—a precursor of the KGB and current face of the Russian KGB's government.

This was the first murder in the anti-Semitic campaign undertaken by Stalin. Slowly but surely Stalin destroyed the entire Jewish cultural community. In 1949, by Stalin's order, the Soviet state media launched a massive propaganda campaign against "cosmopolitans" which was aimed directly at Jews. There were twenty-one Jewish theaters in 1939 but by the 1950s there was only one left. Jewish poet Peretz Markish observed at the time: "Hitler wanted to destroy us physically; Stalin wants to do it spiritually." The followed events had proved him wrong—physical deaths very soon followed spiritual ones.

After the campaign against the cosmopolitans was initiated, the Soviet authorities began the physical liquidation of the members of the Jewish Anti-Fascist Committee. They were arrested and charged with "cosmopolitism, nationalism, and serving the interests of the United States". On August 12, 1952, at least thirteen prominent Yiddish writers and poets were executed. They were liquidated by Stalin's order as "enemies of the people." Jews called it the "Night of the Murdered Poets." Many other prominent Jews were arrested, humiliated, tortured and imprisoned. A so- called "Doctor's Plot," had followed. The cream of the crop of the Soviet medicine (predominantly Jews) had been arrested and imprisoned. This was carried out by the MGB, a precursor of the KGB, with sinister plan to use the upcoming doctor's trial as an excuse for deporting all Soviet Jews to Siberia or the Far East.

Stalin's death in March, 1953, finally saved the surviving Jews.

However, it did not rescue the country, because Stalin's general policy of liquidation had never ended. He started his official duties as head of the country in 1927. He began with a three-fold agenda for the country. The first task was to build his personal power while brainwashing and fooling the general population. Secondly, he created a Communist Party of the yes-men dedicated to carrying out his agenda. Thirdly, he established punitive and security agencies to accomplish and complete the first two tasks. History proves that Stalin was successful in reaching all three objectives. An indoctrinated population adored him, Old Bolsheviks who opposed Stalin, had been liquidated, and the Communist Party faithfully carried out Stalin's agenda for many decades.

Central to all of Stalin's "accomplishments" of the punitive, intelligence, and security agencies was the Stalinist *killing machine*. The Soviet people called this evil group the *ORGANY,* which meant—*the Organs*. This title magnified the significance of the squad with every citizen of the country—nobody could exist without a heart or a liver. And the thinking went that we, the Soviet people, could not exist without *the Organs.*[8] Moreover, it was Stalin who had instilled the sense of superiority and omnipotence to *the Organs* to emphasize their role. It is with the help of the Organs that Stalin also killed his own old relatives who knew his past and therefore they must be liquidated as well.

The apogee of crime committed by *the Organs* came in the year 1937—The Year of the *Great Purges.*

No one will ever know how many Soviet people were arrested, tortured, deported and executed during that time. The numbers have to be in the hundreds of thousands, if not more, and all Soviet people lived in a climate of fear—terrorized by the constant, horrendous purge taking place across the country. The populace learned to be silent. I was one of the victims of that horror but I considered myself lucky that my parents were left alive and our family stayed in tact. Regrettably, our family was a very rare exception. Hundreds of thousands of other families had not been so fortunate—the arrested parents were tortured and executed, while their children were sent to orphanages across the eleven time zones. The children's names were changed to root out any information of the past from their memory. They lost track of their real names, as well as anything known about their parents. The writer Ehrenburg called them "the strange orphans of 1937."

The criminal process of liquidation, started by Stalin in 1927, had never ended. Though the world knows about Stalin's attempt to destroy Jews, they were not the only victims; other religions, ethnic groups and nationalities went through a real GENOCIDE perpetrated by Stalin. The United Nations has defined genocide as "any of the following acts committed with intent to destroy in whole or in part, a national, ethnical, racial, or religious group, as such; killing members of the group, causing serious bodily or mental harm to members of the group; deliberately inflicting on the group conditions of life, calculated to bring about its physical destruction in whole or in part; imposing measures intended to prevent births within the group, (and) forcibly transferring children of the group to another group." Stalin had perpetrated all of the above!

I would argue that the Soviets are guilty of the genocide committed upon many other groups of people. In 1944, the Stalinist *Organs* committed Genocide of the Crimean Tatars, Chechens, Ingushes, and other groups living in the Caucuses Mountains— their ethnic identity was the cause. They all had been deported to Siberia and Central Asia because of their ethnicity or religion. Predominantly elderly, women, and children, they were put in cattle cars and transported away. The lack of water and food, plus a variety of diseases caused incredible numbers of death—only one-third of deportees had reached the intended destination. I have described the deportation in *Baltic Winds*, Chapter 9, "Under the Banner of Socialist Morality," pp. 140-141.

Actions had been perpetrated against the people of the Baltic Republics—vast majority of them had been deported or killed as the Forest's Brothers while they were fighting the Soviet occupation. Of course, every crime should be investigated separately and identified in accordance with the UN's definition. Nothing has been done since by the United Nations, though the Ukrainian government and Ukrainian President Victor Yuzchenko has raised the issue of HOLODOMOR—manmade intentional starvation, a famine created and imposed by Stalin and the Communist government upon Ukraine. Not everybody agrees with the Ukrainian government calling Holodomor[9] in Ukraine—Genocide. Some argue that other ethnic groups had also been killed by the same starvation in many different areas: Russians in Ukraine, Kazakhs and Russians in Kazakhstan, and others. To me, it is Genocide against many others as well. It is certainly a crime against humanity.

All ethnic cases mentioned above have represented the term familiar to you today— *ethnic cleansing* of the civilian population. I had known the term since the year 1937, when I lost my friends, went through a tough time living without my mom for more than a year of her imprisonment—an enormous emotional toll on a child. Then I saw a crime scene where Solomon Mihkoels, a famous actor was assassinated in Minsk. I did not know the details of his murder at the time, but subconsciously going to school after the street was opened, I had always tried to avoid stepping on the place of the crime scene and crossed the street. Perhaps I am too passionate to be objective in identification of the Stalinist massive aggressions against many different nationalities. Time and further professional research will identify Genocide—the repressions of many different forms including deportation, and targeted categories of ethnic minorities. I will just try to give you the facts, the way I know them.

All activities against ethnic minorities undertaken by the Stalinist *Organs* had been aimed at certain ethnic groups and their territories.

People of the Baltic Republics had fought for their independence and Stalin hated them. He hated Muslims because they had been resentful to Russian domination on the Caucuses Mountains. Stalin hated Ukrainians for their national pride and had an eye on the fertile Ukrainian soil. As you can see *ethnic cleansing* has a long history because: Unpunished crime breeds repetition and the truth of these words is obvious in Russia today... political assassinations, wars against minorities especially on the Caucuses, attacks, and prosecution of critics of the government are similar to that of Stalin's regime.

Like a contemporary Russian regime, the Stalinist regime was not limited to liquidation of its own civilians—the aggressiveness and expansionism had stretched out to foreign countries as well. In 1950, the Korean War had started. It should be noted that Stalin hated President Truman. If fragile and frail President Roosevelt, a partner in WWII, appeased Stalin's ambitions, President Truman acted the opposite way. He dropped the atomic bomb to end the war and deprived Stalin of half of the Japanese territory. Vindictive Stalin could not forgive him. In 1945, WWII ended for all decent people, but not for Stalin. He had in mind his *second front*—Asia. Stalin viewed it as a strategic region of paramount importance for global domination. At that time a defeated Japan left a political vacuum in North Korea, and Stalin used it. A Korean Army was formed, and equipped to the teeth with Soviet arms, and, supervised by the KGB's advisers, sent to implement the Stalinist design in North Korea.

Stalin personally chose its leader, a captain of the Soviet Army and former policeman, Kim Il-Sung. Under his leadership, Stalin's design was implemented and the process of North Korea's Sovietization completed. Since then, the connection between the Soviet military, the KGB, and North Korea has never ended. "The Soviet General Staff worked out the plan for aggression in 1950, and the Soviets fully participated in the Korean War." That information had been revealed by one of the Soviet generals that participated in the Korean War in his speech in Seoul in 1992.

Maybe you do not remember, but the Soviets staged a bloody massacre of the civilian population in Budapest, Hungary, in 1956—civilians were crushed by the Soviet tanks. Then came a bloody massacre in Prague—Prague's Spring was strangled. By that time, Stalin had already been dead, but his creation of the *killing machine* that used to deal against the Soviet civilians was alive and well dealing against civilians abroad. It was Stalin who had established a political concept of Soviet Fascism using violence as the prime method of ideological expansion to obtain global power.

The new Soviet leadership had gotten *the killing machine* of Soviet Fascism as the ideological inheritance and invaded Afghanistan in 1979. Even before 1979, the Soviet Army participated in the war against Israel in 1973 on the Arab side. An enormous number of Soviet tanks and other arms had been delivered to Egypt and Syria. Besides that, the soldiers of the Soviet Army fought Israelis on the side of Egypt and hundreds of Soviet soldiers were killed in Yom Kippur War in 1973.

In 2006, at the time of this writing, *the killing machine* of Soviet Fascism is alive and well. Do you remember the Russian aggression in Chechnya?[10] Thousands of Chechens were killed, their houses destroyed, and the land of Chechnya burnt. As you know, the crime usually starts in the minds of the criminals; they transfer their ideas from one generation to another. The ideology of 1937 is alive and rules today. And this is the inevitable reason to conclude that the methods and the entire modus operandi of 1937, and crimes committed then, never ended—*the ethnic cleansing* in many places throughout our contemporary world testifies to that. All civilian deaths in different countries result in the same crime committed by the same *killing machine* of Soviet Fascism—the inheritance of the Stalinist ideology.

In addition to obvious violence, there was a non-military expansion of the ideology as well. During the Cold War we had talked a lot about Soviet expansion, even invented the policy of *Containment.* Regrettably the West has failed to contain expansion not knowing how Sovietization had been de facto implemented. Never playing by the rules, and having a global strategy, Stalin deceived and fooled the entire world talking about Socialism in a single country, while spreading his offensive design throughout the globe. Alas, nobody had identified his design then as Soviet Fascism.

To end this chapter, I would like to tell you about another tragic episode of my life that can explain the political transformation of my mind. It wasn't easy. Americans know Shakespeare very well, perhaps from studying him in school. My acquaintance with Shakespeare was a strange one if not mournful. I hadn't read King Lear; the Mikhoels' assassination made me read the play. My second connection with Shakespeare was almost a personal tragedy. Somewhere in the mid- 1960s, I was about to commit suicide. As matter of fact, living in Tallinn, a capital of Estonia, and working as a defense attorney for ten years I had become a witness of the crimes committed by Stalin against the Estonian people and many others as well.

After the revelation of Stalin's atrocities, thousands of people began returning from Gulags. All of them, eager to know their rights, flooded my law office. Crippled, physically injured, toothless, bald, emaciated, they looked at me with hope and anticipation— predominantly Estonians, they had already forgotten their native language and spoke only Russian. I heard horrifying stories from these victims of the thirties, forties, and fifties. At first, I didn't want to believe them, but new people were coming in to tell me of increasingly terrifying experiences. I could hardly cope with my emotions, afraid of weeping with a client. I couldn't sleep at night, so profoundly was I traumatized. I had found myself on a crossroad of criminal History. Powerless to change anything, I felt that I was guilty too. The conversation with one of my victims/ clients I described in *Baltic Winds*, pp. 22-23.

At the time of my agony, a group of cinematographers from Moscow came to Tallinn to produce a movie based on Shakespearean Hamlet. A huge majestic tower of Ellsinore had been built a few miles from the city—a spectacular picture from afar, and a bit gloomy as a harbinger of grief. The best view to see it was a cliff over the obis a mile from the tower. The cliff was so high, elevating over the ground that bare trees, which had already lost their green summer canopy on the slope of obis looked like human figures with raised up arms.

One gloomy autumn day, I took my two children and drove there. Standing on the cliff of my Golgotha, observing a foggy Ellsinore in total despair and fear, the thoughts of hopelessness flying through my mind overwhelmed me... I don't remember my movements and I don't know how long I stood there. But then a sudden frightened voice, almost a scream of my daughter had returned me to reality: "Mama! I want to go home...!" That was my second meeting with Shakespeare.

CHAPTER 2

My Hopes and Disappointments in America

In general, it was the ideology of Stalinism that forced me to immigrate—there was no future for my two children in our Motherland of Soviet Fascism. They became a primary force in driving me to leave the country. Our immigration to the United States in 1981 was an extremely difficult one, painful, and challenging. We did not have any relatives to help us. I had no money and knowledge of a new country and culture. But the toughest thing was my inability to communicate an elementary sentence—I did not know the language. Can you imagine a professional speaker doomed to silence? Hence my experiences and knowledge meant nothing. Immigrating to America and unable to express my opinion, I was doomed to non-existence and suffered immensely.

The language I did not know prevented me from being heard, (unfortunately I still do not have a gift of language. Sorry). Nevertheless, understanding the value of information America desperately needed, in a few years I started writing my first book with five dictionaries and two thesauruses. The main subject of my book was Stalinism and its Soviet System. It was my first attempt to speak out against the Soviet regime and the first identification of the regime as Soviet Fascism. I did it very delicately, without any details. The book was titled *Baltic Winds: Testimony of A Soviet Attorney.*

In 1984, I also got a teaching position at two universities in New York City. There are no words to express my happiness—I shared my knowledge and professional experiences with my students. They were very grateful to me for that. I had received hundreds of letters from my students during the years of teaching. As a rule, the student sent those letters together with their term papers. They were all working professionals, taking classes for continuing education in the evening and having little free time for the research, they were always late. However, their term papers were excellent, showing a great deal of their diligence. Their letters were a nice present for me.

Slowly but surely I have learned the American way of life: I attended classes to study the Torah in our synagogue, where I learned a lot about Americans and Jews. But my real teachers in America had become my students; they educated me a great deal. Our discussions had turned to the useful ways of presenting to them the truth about Russia, while their questions revealed the state of mind in America and the gap in the perception of the Soviet Union. I enjoyed my classes tremendously. That happiness of my life had brought me to the year 1992. By that time, *Baltic Winds* was in the state of completion, when I heard the name Bill Clinton for the fist time. He made me very nervous. His biography made me feel threatened—he has spent time living in Russia with the family of KGB members, a wife and a husband. Can you imagine my feeling towards Clinton? Watching him in the presidential campaign, I saw a carbon copy of the Soviet politicians. I disliked him intensely and could not believe in his presidential victory.

Each new fact about Clinton, moreover, pointed to the veracity of my first impression. He had been an activist in the antiwar movement, and once visiting Moscow lived with a Russian family. My God, he had lived with the family of a KGB member, or maybe even with two of them—a husband and wife. It was the only possible explanation—for nobody else in the '70s except the KGB members would have been trusted to accommodate a foreigner. Though, there was another scenario of Clinton's staying in Moscow—the Hotel National, my attitude toward him has not changed. Like the Hotel Astoria and Europeyskay in Leningrad, the Hotel National in Moscow served as a roof for the KGB to deal with foreigners.

I did not like Clinton's pictures of the '60s and '70s in Moscow either. He reminded me of a member of the Komsomol (Communist Youth League), that reservoir of human resources for the party and the KGB. The American media, busy with his womanizing activities, never opened thc curtain on the possibility that Clinton was affiliated with the KGB. When he, himself, explained his participation in the anti-war movement in Oxford, saying he "only organized teachers," no one from the media asked him who'd given him that assignment. I suspected the KGB had. I had known the KGB's modus operandi in using human weaknesses while recruiting foreigners—to supply "girls," obtain compromising pictures, and then blackmail. And that scenario generated in me an aggressive stance. I did not like Clinton even more.

The passport file story eventually validated my suspicions—it was well grounded, something beyond intuition. There were two critical aspects in the passport episode; first, the fact that pages from Clinton's passport were missing. Second, the information they contained. The concept of a passport, in America, differs totally from that in the rest of the world. An especially critical importance was attached to passports in all Socialist Bloc countries. Somebody in the State Department had had that kind of mentality, in removing pages from Clinton's passport. Or had he done it himself? Where had he traveled? And why had he concealed those trips? Taken together, the passport story revealed the typical KGB fingerprint to me—the handwriting on the wall. Where had our CIA and FBI been? Mr. Gates, Director of the CIA, kept silent though he was an expert of Russia. I was shocked.

What pain I went through when an attorney from the Bush Administration apologized for seeking information concerning Clinton's passport file! I could not believe it. People in the administration were not aware of the KGB's obsession with obtaining information about others and concealing its own! The Bush Administration gave up the presidency… I was crushed. But there was no alternative for me—I had to vote for Bush.

By that time, I had already driven pretty well across New Jersey and New York State. Sometimes I was even driving to Brooklyn to buy Russian food. As you know, we can physically move to another culture, but it is very hard to remove your culture from yourself. I loved Russian food, and despite heavy traffic, I went to the Russian store almost every month. Somewhere in 1992, I vented to the Russian store in Brooklyn. The store is a cultural scene you have to watch to know the Russian people.

Located on Briton Beach, the store did not have its own parking. To park the car took my nerves and twenty-five to thirty minutes. However, as soon as I entered the store, a familiar aroma of Russian food, a mixture of bakery, fried meat, and smoked fish immediately changed my mood. Frustration disappeared and the overcrowded place, full with loud voices, laughter, delight, and joy conversing in Russian, transformed me to an obedient admirer with my mouth watering.

The long lines did not change my mood—they are a part of the Russian culture. Standing in line, I studied the variety and amazing diversity of familiar cold cuts. Women behind me were talking about their family lives. They perhaps knew each other before coming to the store.

"My husband has just returned from Moscow," said a pretty blond, wearing a vivid red lipstick, which made her big strawberry- mouth even bigger. A fashionable green silk suit was showing her slim, good figure. "He wants to start a business in Russia," she added.

"You are kidding me, a business in Russia? We can't trust them. Tell him to wait a couple of years," warned the other woman, dressed modestly in black, and older than the blond. Laughing in return, the young blond pointed her finger to the face of her friend, continued smiling and said:

"Don't be so paranoid! Russia will be our partner for many years to come, I am sure. My husband told me that Clinton flew to Russia and had a meeting with the Chairman of the KGB."

"Who is the man and why he did fly to Russia?" asked the older woman.

"You haven't heard about Clinton? He is a young governor and he wants to be our President instead of Bush."

My mouth and throat instantly dried up. Clinton visited Moscow before the election? Russian culture taught us all about provocations with very negative consequences. Clinton and the KGB was not news to me, but the news about Clinton together with those three letters of the KGB in the Russian store in America, made me at once feel threatened and nervous.

Unfortunately, I couldn't discuss the matter at home. My friend, with whom I had been living with for five years, a good and decent man, was a Democrat. Stubborn and opinionated, he admired Clinton. I could do nothing. What an irony of life! The only person with whom I could trust such information was Michael, a young Republican man from the synagogue. The sense of duty burning inside drove me to talk to him.

Our synagogue's classes on the Torah continued to be a place for discussions and debates. I, however, no longer hoped to change anybody's mind. My experience, and time, had convinced me that my efforts would fail. It was beyond my ability to persuade people in the class that they had been supporting the wrong party and wrong policy. If Ronald Reagan could not change their minds, what could I do? The new ardor of the election year, however, brought our disagreements to the surface again. They were for Clinton and hoped that he would improve social conditions for the poor and cool down racial hostility between blacks and whites. They still had no understanding that social engineering breeds moral poverty and consequently exacerbates all the social and racial problems. Yet I was afraid to open my mouth. I planned to talk with Michael. Of course, we could not do it openly in the class. It was the last Wednesday in October of 1992. As soon as class ended, we left.

Slowly, he and I headed to our cars, talking. The air was fresh and pleasant. After sitting for two hours in the stuffy classroom, I enjoyed it. The cold October sun pouring out of a blue sky, gave us only its bright light, not warmth. I had already started to wear gloves. Michael, as usual, dressed very casually—in a suede jacket that almost mirrored the color of his reddish-brown hair. In class he always sat with that jacket on, never taking it off. His worn-out brown shoes, left over from the summer, deserved a rest. He seemed not to care about his appearance—his family and the computer occupied his entire life.

The huge parking lot with the rows of cars extending toward the green fence of trees, revealed all the activities the temple was involved in. The smiling and caring Mothers, who picked up their children from nursery school, were heading to their cars, talking loudly to their kids. Several people were bringing big brown bags of food to the temple, which would later be distributed to the needy. The cars came and went, accompanied by the ringing of children's voices, laughter, and faces radiating happiness. The other people from our class were all long gone, and only the two of us stood before Michael's burgundy Toyota, unable to end our discussion.

"I don't like Bush," he continued. "It shouldn't surprise you. He's imposed many new regulations that have crippled our economy. Maybe you have no understanding of how capitalism works, but Bush must know that. Yet he gave in to the pressure of liberals in Congress." I had never seen Michael so angry and categorical.

"Listen, he had no alternative. Besides, a cunning George Mitchell outwitted him."

"No, you're wrong. He might've vetoed the tax increase for many reasons, but primarily because he had promised 'no new taxes.' I'll tell you another thing; I'm going to vote for Clinton. He, at least, promises to get rid of regulations."

"Don't kid me, Michael. You'll never vote for Clinton, you're a Republican."

"I'm not kidding you. Bush is worse than a lot of Democrats. If Clinton does well as president, it will be good for the country. And if he's as bad as Bush, or worse, at least people will know to blame the Democrats."

I couldn't believe what he was saying. "Come on Michael, you know that most Democrats are hypocrites. Like the Soviets, they don't care about anything but power. They've manufactured an image of compassion for people, but in fact it's fiction—a ploy to stay in control. When Bush promised 'no new taxes,' he sincerely believed in the truth of his words. He didn't want to deceive anybody. He's a decent man." I still thought that Michael was kidding me and had intentionally overplayed his dissatisfaction with Bush. But his face was absolutely serious.

"You're wrong again, Simona. Bush could have vetoed those spending bills just like Reagan did. I can't think of any domestic policy of George Bush's that would have surprised me if it had come from Dukakis instead." He despised Bush, but I had to warn him about the alternative.

"Forget the past, Michael. We're electing our own future. Please be serious." I tried to calm down. It didn't last long—my passion prevailed. "Clinton is a liar. Don't you see it? You won't get a word of truth from his mouth." I said it in such a subdued but high pitched way that my voice broke. I didn't know what to do and how to explain to Michael what I knew about Clinton. There were fewer cars left in the lot, and not many people to hear our words, yet I was still afraid to discuss the subject in such an open space. But when Michael pulled the car key from his pocket, I realized that I would not have another chance—the next class would be on Wednesday, the day after the election. I had to start immediately.

"Do you know who Clinton is?" I asked. He gave a dismissive grimace.

"Certainly I do. But perhaps you don't, and his philandering has preoccupied your mind, Simona. Forget it. We need a leader with a clear vision of the future."

"You're mistaken. I don't care about his womanizing activities or his personal life. I can tell you even more. His love affairs serve him pretty well—they divert people's attention from the main issue." And I repeated the question. "Do you know who Clinton is?"

"He's a Democrat, so what?"

"He's *not* a Democrat," I paused. "He is playing the role and the real Clinton will bring the KGB into the White House!"

"What, the KGB in the White House…? You are *crazy*, Simona! What an insane idea! As usual you're exaggerating the situation." His anger against Bush evaporated as he began to openly laugh at me. The bright sun laughed with him, so that even Michael's hair sparkled. I didn't know how to begin.

"I'm *not* crazy, Michael. The only difference between us is that I know who Bill Clinton is and you don't. If he wins, I can predict today what he'll do to America." My words changed nothing. With a self-righteous smile, he looked at me, his brown eyes squinting.

"How can you do that?"

"Very simple—I have already been there."

"I don't get it. Where have you already been, and what's wrong with Clinton? Who is he in your assessment?"

"He's a crook, Michael!"

"Oh, you make me laugh. A crook in the White House is no novelty in America."

"Michael, he's a *Soviet* crook! He's an American Stalinist!" I said, lowering my voice but staring intently at him.

"I don't know what you're talking about. What does American Stalinist mean? Tell me. What he's going to do to America?" He asked with an element of patronage. I didn't like it—he was ten or fifteen years younger than I and should have maintained a basic respect. But the situation forced me to talk.

"I'll tell you what. He'll do the same things the Soviets were trying to achieve for many years: he'll fool the American public and demoralize and destroy the American military. He hated it twenty years ago, and as president he can do a lot of harm to our military, if elected," I almost whispered.

Michael's mouth stretched into a big smile. "OK. Tell me about the kind of harm we can expect."

"I don't know exactly, but there are different ways to undermine our military—to weaken its morality and fighting ability, to expose it to dangerous predicaments. He may allow the Russians to acquire critical military technology, which they have been spying on for decades. That I know for sure. Can you perceive the damage our national security will suffer?"

"Give me a break, Simona. Why would he destroy his own army? Don't you hear the absurdity of your words? And what's wrong with the Russians? They're trying to democratize their country. Am I correct?"

"Forget about democracy in Russia. It's not even in the embryonic stage yet. Clinton's victory will adversely affect the process itself and Yeltsin personally. He's an old and sick man." Michael stared at me and then whispered, "I don't want to debate anymore."

I had to get straight to the matter. "Listen, the situation is very complex indeed, but the secret is that Clinton's dossier is in the hands of the KGB, and that will help the Soviet mafia to regain power. That correlation could drastically reduce the chances of building democracy in Russia."

To my surprise Michael didn't get the significance of this information. The concept of a "dossier" had different meanings to us. He also knew nothing about the Soviet mafia.

"Oh, Simona, you're exaggerating the matter again. How could the American president negatively affect the building of democracy in Russia or elsewhere?"

"Clinton can. You don't know him. If he's elected, it'll embolden the communists and thugs like Zhirinovsky. The Soviet cronies around the world will strive for power again. They know who Clinton is. They are all 'brothers-at-arms' in every fiber and are bound forever. If the Democrats in America have been building 'a great society' for several decades, Clinton will complete the task, and implement the 'social engineering' globally." Michael, seeing that I was nervous, no longer smiled, but was not serious either.

"How exactly can an American president be connected to the Soviet thugs you're talking about?"

"Very simple, he belongs to their camp, and his dossier—" "What?" Michael didn't grasp the word dossier.

"His file is in the hands of Primakov. Do you know that man?"

"No."

"He is a spymaster with forty years of experience working against America, primarily with the Arabs and Chinese. All the files of Soviet collaborators are 'diligently safeguarded' by the KGB. Primakov is the person who keeps an eye on them. Believe me; he knows how to manipulate people. If Clinton wins, Primakov will micromanage American foreign policy. Do you understand that? Clinton will do whatever Primakov orders!" I hissed angrily, not knowing how to get inside his head. He couldn't grasp the matter. I saw it. But the conversation, perhaps, intrigued him, especially the Russian connection.

"Listen, Simona. I'm not an expert on Russia and trust you in that. But what kind of a linkage is there between Clinton in Arkansas and that man in Moscow?"

"I've already told you—Clinton's file is in the hands of Primakov."

"So what? Maybe your file was there as well."

"Maybe, but it is in a different department, because we belonged to different camps and adhered to different ideologies."

"You know, I don't like conspiracy theory. I believe in vigilance, not paranoia. The Cold War is over. Please, don't complicate your life and mine, too." Once again he began opening the door of his car... I was losing. He still didn't get it. I almost screamed, to catch his attention.

"It's *not* a conspiracy theory; it's the reality of conspiracy in life, a conspiracy of evil. If you care about your children, you should think now about their futures."

He turned his head toward me. "My children have nothing to do with our conversation."

"Yes, they do. National security is our main parental concern," I shouted in his face. "If Clinton is elected, terrorism will come to America."

"What's the *connection* you're making up again? Why will Clinton invite terrorism?" Confused, Michael looked at me quizzically, leaned on his car, and shrugged.

At that moment it occurred to me that he did not know anything about the passport story, or the substance of Clinton's file. Besides, he had never heard about Stalinism that had successfully corrupted some American intellectual's decades before, or the KGB's involvement in terrorism, and therefore could not perceive the seriousness of the issue.

Though we were both Republicans, we saw the problems through a different prism according to our life experiences. I had to be more specific.

"This election is a matter of life or death for America. The connection between Clinton's election and terrorism is as follows. All terrorists respect only strength. President Reagan won the Cold War because the Soviets respected only real force. It cost us trillions and we won. But we are unable to change the old mentality overnight. The international terrorism did not happen in a vacuum. It had been sponsored, coordinated, and controlled by the Soviets for several decades. The old connections and psychological patterns are still alive, and so the terrorists in different countries, united by common hatred of America. They respect only strength. Their leaders know who Clinton is. They're all tied by the same rope—their files are in the hands of the KGB." Michael listened to me as I went on.

"Clinton's election will trigger the return to power of the communists in the former socialist block countries. It'll reverse what we won in the Cold War. Make no mistake about it. All thugs around the world will be welcomed in Clinton's White House if he wins. Especially watch the Chinese and Arabs and their boss, Primakov. Saddam Hussein is alive, and the KGB is still obsessed with oil. Don't you understand that the future of our America is on the line?"

"If I'm not wrong, Simona, you're confusing two issues. Terrorism in American is one thing: terrorists in the White House are quite another."

"No, Clinton unites the two. If he is elected, his file in the KGB will become a world treasure overnight, and Clinton himself, a target of blackmail. He'll do everything he can to prevent its disclosure."

"Why? What's in there that we don't know? He dodged the draft. We all know that. He had mistresses. We don't care. What's so precious in the file?"

"The information about his collaboration with the KGB for decades."

"How do *you* know? You saw the file?"

"No, I just know the KGB. I've lived through its activities and know its signature. That's why I can predict what will happen in America if Clinton wins."

"OK, tell me what?"

"Have you heard how the apparatchiks are fighting against the reforms in Russia? The same war against capitalism will come to America. The onslaught of Sovietization will proceed by means of the usual KGB

same way that the American people had and, not knowing the truth, had to attract the public by sensations. In doing so, our media had become a twin brother to the former Soviet media—empty in substance. It had always irritated me when a reporter called Zhirinovsky a hard-line nationalist. Wouldn't it be more appropriate to call him a Stalinist? At least the word would bring a sense of reality and a warning.... What could be worse than the deceived media in democracy!

One person who stood out from the chorus of American deceived believers was Rush Limbaugh, a real American patriot. I should call him, I thought. And I did. It was not an easy matter to get through, but God was with me and finally after twenty or so minutes, I got the opportunity to talk to Rush. I was so nervous to speak to him that I am afraid he did not understand the significance of my information; I was talking about the Soviet involvement in the anti-war movements around the world and about Soviet Health Care, that was worth nothing. I also told him that Clinton was a member of the anti-war movement and that gave me the suspicion that he worked with the KGB. You can read our conversation on the last pages of *Baltic Winds*.

Clinton has won and all my prediction has become a reality of life. He fired all U.S. Attorneys at once to instill his own law and order. With habitual Soviet aggressiveness Clinton destroyed the government of Haiti. Then Waco came about with the death of innocent children and people brainwashed by the scoundrel masking as a priest. Seeing the scenes of Waco's burning have brought the old smoldering burden of grief to my heart surfacing with incredible pain like in 1937, when I lost my mother. Yet there was something else in Waco nobody paid attention to: several former bodyguards of Clinton had been killed there. For me it was a sign of crime, premeditated crime to get rid of the witnesses. Those actions were very familiar to me as a special operation— people who know too much must be liquidated... killing children and the aftermath of the crime had brought the stench of 1937 back to me. It was not the America I loved.

But what had stunned me completely was Clinton's invitation to the White House of a known terrorist, Arafat. If I, an average individual, knew the real activities of Arafat as a terrorist, how was it possible that the President of the United States and his CIA did not know that? And what followed had become an international scandal. Clinton helped Arafat to commit fraud against Israel— the Oslo Agreement. He practically twisted arms of the Prime Minister Rabin and forced him to sign that fraud, designed by the KGB and maybe by Primakov himself. As a matter of fact, fraud was a landmark of the Soviet life. I had known then that the Agreement would bring Israel to the brink of destruction. I was right. But I could not predict the events that followed—Mr. Rabin was assassinated, by a man married to the Russian psychiatrist. And that told me a lot about Clinton and his Administration. I was terrified. But I could not do anything except write my books and warn my America. I did.

With horror I had watched how Clinton twisted arms of the next Israeli Prime Minister, Barrack. Arafat was invited again to the White House and a plan or proposal that definitely limited the Israeli ability to exist, had been announced. Arafat rejected that proposal. For me it was clear that Clinton and Arafat were playing a game of buying time, the same way they were successful with the Oslo Accord years ago. Meanwhile, the neighbors surrounding Israel were receiving high-tech military equipment with the staff managing it from Russia; the Russian government had obtained a strategic domination in the Middle East through its friends- terrorists Arafat, Hamas, and Hezbollah. The oil conspiracy had been developing through Clinton's entire term. Please pay attention to Clinton's activities—he had suddenly pronounced our coal reserve in Wyoming or Utah a State National Park. Clinton had also blocked drilling oil in the Arctic Ocean in 1995. I wonder what Clinton's motivation was for doing all of that. What about you…?

I felt great pain watching Clinton skillfully seduce ill-informed and naïve Americans. Surprised how inattentive to the events and trustful to Clinton the American public had been, I watched with anguish. People did not pay attention to his personal behavior vis-à- vis Middle East. The American Jews especially surprised me—the vast majority had supported Clinton… I was shocked. The decision in my mind had come immediately: in my second book I must write about Carlos the Jackal and the Soviet oil conspiracy against the West. As a matter of fact, the Middle East was a Soviet target for many years and if the Arabs collaborated with the Soviets, it was Israel like a bone in their throat which prevented the Soviets to complete the domination of the world's oil resources.

But that was not the end of the surprises—I later found out that Clinton had redistricted Jerusalem offering a part of the city to Arafat! Disgusting—Jerusalem has been the capital of Israel for 3, 000 years! Israeli Prime Minister Barrack had agreed with all of that. I suspected him of some ties with Russia then, and was stunned by Clinton and Barrack's conducts and their policy of retreats. I knew that it would not work in dealing with the terrorists, but only bring new conflicts and casualties. And when Clinton had bombed the aspirin factory in Sudan to divert attention from his Monica-gate, I stopped being astonished—my worse predictions had become a reality.

A few years ago, when I became acquainted with the internet, I found the description of the event in December 1934, I had witnessed in our communal apartment—the assassination of Sergei Kirov. The article was incredible the way it presented Stalin's character, the techniques he used in crime and the quality of the analysis of the tragedy. I have dedicated many pages to Stalin and the perpetration by him of a variety of different crimes. The article "A Tale for Our Times," by Gavin Gatenby surpassed all my knowledge about Stalin. November 30, 2004, *Deep Geopolitics.* It was such a detailed and documented observation of Stalin's plot to murder Kirov that even I was stunned by the author's competence and his comparison of Kirov's assassination with Kennedy's. Let me give you one paragraph to show the significance of the piece.

"Kirov was shot to death on the 1st December 1934, certainly on the orders of his mentor, Joseph Stalin. His assassination was a textbook 'false flag' operation and certainly did more to divert the current of human history into regressive channels than the assassination of John. F. Kennedy. Both in its style of execution and its ramification it set a benchmark for the cynical manipulation of the public and the falsification of history..."

The article showed the etalon political technology of assassinations. This brilliant article should be read by all Americans to understand the lethality of the world we live in. Remember the term "a textbook 'false flag' operation," you will hear again and again about such operations implemented in different countries. Just remember the terms and watch the world's events. Please, read the piece in its entirety to understand completely what was going on in Russia then and is going on in our Earth today in America...

Returning to Clinton's presidency, I had news for myself as well. Information about my book, *Baltic Winds: Testimony of A Soviet Attorney* had been blocked. I understood that Clinton himself or his CIA did not want the truth about Stalin and his crimes against humanity to get out and be known. Or maybe Clinton did not like and did not want the information in the book about him to be known? It's quite possible. What could I do? I was unable to fight them all... I did what I could—I started to write my second book. By that time, constantly discussing Russia with my students, I came to the conclusion that they did not know elementary facts about Soviet life.

It was obvious that the field of political science researching Russia did not work productively and was filled with incompetent and ill-informed people. Meeting those "experts" in some conferences, I have observed the field of Sovietology and Kremlinology in a state of complete disarray. Once at Colombia University several professors admitted that they did not know what the word "Troika," means and they could not perceive the universal meaning of Show Trials. I was stunned to hear that and felt I had an obligation to continue the subject of Soviet Fascism to present the whole record of Soviet mendacity to the American public—the record, description, and application of distortions, fraud, deceit, hoaxes, and assassinations, let alone the Soviet arsenal of criminal activities.

In my first book, I just mentioned the term Soviet Fascism— my task was to show the facts of real life under Soviet Socialism, I also identified the ideology of Stalinism. I decided my second book should be dedicated to the specific presentation and analysis of the term Soviet Fascism and the Soviet mafia that drove it. I had a task;, to identify the real conception of Soviet Fascism as an aggressive and militant ideology of violence and war to obtain CONTROL and POWER. To do all of that was not easy; lacking good command of English and being dependent on dictionaries and several thesauruses made it a tough job. The sense of danger for my America had forced me to do so—I wanted the American public to be acquainted with all the patterns, techniques, and tricks of the enemies coming to our land. I had no doubt that they would come to harm my naïve and trustful America and its people.

If you read *Baltic Winds*, you will see that I have titled the last chapter "*The Soviet Mafia* is Coming." Maybe the Clinton Administration did not like the title and information in the book because I had received a letter from the Dean of the New School for Social Research, which had devastated me. It was 1993 and she, like Clinton's Administration, also did not want the truth about Russia to get out—she had cancelled my course, *Russia in Transition*. I have no words to express my despair—teaching had been my vocation, my joy, and happiness. Something similar to the harassment and attacks against the opposition in Russia had found me in America.

Life proved me right in many of my suspicions. Though I had expected some kind of unprovoked and unexplained killings to appear on American land, the murder of young boys in Arkansas and the arrest of innocents had threatened me by its familiar design—the arrested had been witnesses of the prior crime or knew something that was not supposed to become public. It was a quintessential Soviet technique of fabrication of the case in Arkansas—framing innocent to prevent the truth to be known. The next killing came soon; when the story of Kathleen Villey, Clinton's attention towards her, and the suicide of her husband appeared in the press. I knew that her husband had been killed by somebody—he did not commit suicide. I could not do anything at the moment, but I decided to write about the Soviet technique of getting rid of dispensable people the same way they have acted against the opposition—via manufactured suicides. The next action familiar to me had become the files of the leadership's members of the Republican Party that were brought from the FBI to Clinton's White House! What a clear demonstration of KGB's style it was! A typical KGB special operation!

The next couple of years brought even more signs of similarity with the same Soviet methods and more suspicions. I will never forget the scene of Clinton and Yeltsin's press conference, where a strange situation occurred before the entire country. The journalists were asking Yeltsin questions, but he responded with one phrase: "You failed, you failed, you failed…" He stood like a rock, with stern seriousness on his face while he repeated several times, "You failed." As an obvious contrast to him, Clinton was dying of laughter, banded, swaddling in laughter, his face down, he even dried his tears. Some journalists laughed with him, some stood confused—it was a very unusual situation, but not for me. Yeltsin warned the journalists to watch closely, he could not say openly what was in his mind; however, a dramatic expression on his face must have been alarming to the media. Alas, fooled media remained confused. Meanwhile Clinton continued laughing hysterically, protecting himself with the laughter, diverting attention from Yeltsin and his attempt to expose the fraud—a typical Soviet maneuver to prevent an upcoming dangerous information from being exposed. Evasiveness is one of the Soviet methods of public behavior in the open arena of debates or discussions.

Another example of Clinton's behavior that was familiar to me was that he created a clan of yes-men; mediocre and obedient politicians carrying through his policy—clan analogous to the Soviet mafia. The yes-men had built a kind of defense to prevent any exposure of their activities—a Soviet-style political machine, acting in complete secrecy, to attack and fight the Republican opposition. To expose this political machine you need to investigate only some members of the mafia-machine to have the big picture of their activities—Hubbell, Richardson, Berger, and of course General Wesley Clark the vivid representatives of Clinton's political clan. There you will find all the attributes of the Soviet falsehood described by me on the preceding pages— disinformation, deceit, fraud, and crime—a triangulation. In addition to that, Clinton's performance during Y2K in the year 2000 seemed to me a bit strange—maybe it was just a special operation to infiltrate the entire American cyber system? I am afraid we will pay a dear price for that in the future.

The situation in the country had become so dangerous that the impulse of self-preservation had driven my consciousness to complete my second book as soon as possible and present the chronology of the Kremlin's oil conspiracy from Arafat and Carlos the Jackal, recruited by the Kremlin, to Putin's contemporary administration… I must show all of the Kremlin's tactics and strategies in a war against America and Western civilization! I knew that ahead of us lied a lot of troubles—economic and political crisis and disasters of different kinds as we had never seen before, the American people would endure. They had no idea of what was coming their way. They were not ready for 9/11 and they were unaware of what they are up against now. I must warn them! The image of the Twin Towers collapsing before my eyes into the dust has been engraved in my mind forever…

The next few years brought some satisfaction and some troubles to me and my desire to educate the American public. I wanted to show them how Sovietization is slowly but surely devouring our America, exposing Sovietization as political correctness that is destroying common sense in America. In my second book I have also described Stalinist Socialism, identified the ideology of Soviet Fascism, and connected Al-Qaeda's activities with the KGB. The title was *The Russian Factor: From Cold War to Global Terrorism*. My girl-friend edited the first three chapters; I hoped the publisher would do the rest. Despite some difficulties I have published both books after the election of President George W. Bush.

It did not help me. And again, the information about both my books has been blocked. Besides that, the second book was purposely sloppily copy edited by the publisher and that virtually sabotaged the book. I was embarrassed and ashamed to promote it. I suspected our intelligence agency's involvement by "working" in cahoots with my publisher to kill the book—the truth shouldn't be known! In fact, they suppressed critically important information needed by the American public and Western civilization. That attempt to silence me had reminded me of the old Soviet time and devastated me enormously. I was stopped again in my desire to educate Americans, to tell them the truth about Russia, to prevent another tragedy. For me my beloved America and our national security has faced an imminent threat and danger on a variety of different fronts. That real threat motivated and drove me to write the third book to warn you. I did. You are reading it now.

CHAPTER 3

Lessons from President Harry Truman

The last several decades have turned the term "Liberal" into a hostile word in America. Have you ever thought why and who is responsible for that in the twenty-first century? The word Liberal derived from Latin, *Libber*—freedom. The term "Liberals" came to life as a representation of the people with strong principles and beliefs, embracing a certain philosophy in a conception of liberty. It describes and indicates various types of individual freedom, such as religious liberty, political liberty, freedom of speech, right of self-defense, and the like. This is a very positive identification of the "Classic Liberals" in history during the nineteenth century. They are for all the liberties plus they are the patriots of their country, pursuing national security along the path of the truth. They are self-sufficient and love the flag, country, and religion. I love them and share their ideas and feelings.

I do not like the "Modern Liberals." They have usurped the honorable term of liberty that has nothing in common with their activities and agenda. Lacking a grasp of reality, they are actually soft on Soviet Socialism and now soft on Soviet Fascism. They had some kind of romantic sentiments towards Russia in the past. Perhaps Tchaikovsky, Pushkin, or Rachmaninov had created that perception and image a century ago at the time of "Classic Liberalism." It was primarily a social and cultural term. At the time, Russian literature and the Arts had been the stewards of the country's morality, and Tsarist Russia and America had a mutual respect for each other. That time has passed and ended—the October Socialist Revolution of 1917 in Russia had drastically changed the relation between the two countries.

Today we are dealing with the far-left "Modern Liberals," the carrier of political correctness. The term has become purely political. And the situation has become even more confusing, because for example in Russia, some fighters for the truth opposing the Russian KGB's government are called "liberals," which is not correct. Therefore, the task of this book is an attempt to identify and distinguish between the terms "Classic Liberals" and "Modern Liberals," and between "Modern Liberals" and "Conservatives." The term Conservatives also comes from Latin and means traditions, protection, and safety. The clear identification of the terms Liberals and Conservatives can help to expose the forces responsible for a substantial shift within the liberal paradigm of America and the world during the twentieth and twenty-first centuries.

As you know I lived for fifty years in the Soviet Union and knew very little about liberties, yet researching the subject, I found an interesting point of view in the Second Edition of the Columbia Encyclopedia on how to defend Liberties: "Liberties need to be defended against encroachment, and sometimes populations have to submit to their temporary curtailment. In time of national danger rights are sometimes suspended, as was the rights of habeas corpus by President Lincoln in the Civil War, and the struggle for rights not yet acquired may have to be discontinued." p.1129. In fact, the Encyclopedia refers to the "Classic Liberals" of the nineteenth century. Deeply respecting those who are in a time of national danger still, I would like to give you a vivid example of them in 2006.

Have you ever heard a Conservative praise a Liberal? Watch me; I am going to do just that—some Classic Liberals have deserved it. According to Orwell's utopian Big Brother, "peace is war and war is peace." Following that concept, Hollywood has created hundreds of spy thrillers; some good, some not so good. The year 2006 produced an exceptionally good one, a significant and vital film: *The Good Shepherd*—a great movie. More than a thriller; it contains historical substance, a reflection of the past critically important for the present and the future.

The movie combines most of the requirements for a historical drama in the background of the highly secretive CIA creation: human bravery and tenacity in achieving objectives for national security, great personal sacrifices, and endless love for America. It is in that spirit of love for our country that the film was made. The cast is suburb, the film is timely, and its lessons are clear and crucial. Let me give you some history.

Many historians consider Ronald Reagan the president who *defeated the Evil Empire.* It is partially true, but only partially. Sixty years ago, another American president, Harry S. Truman, provided us with the means and ideas to survive and win the Cold War by establishing the CIA.

American foreign policy is the first echelon of our national security. Every American president is a custodian of foreign policy; therefore, every American Presidency is consequential. However, the presidency of Truman was more consequential than others.

President Harry S. Truman created the CIA by signing the *National Security Act of 1947* in direct response to Stalin's creation of the KGB a year earlier. President Truman's action is the crux of the matter; the core action that both specifies and determines an appropriate response to the horrors of both the twentieth and twenty-first centuries.

Everyone has known the KGB; just hearing those three letters triggers fear and anxiety in many people. Although Soviet security and intelligence agencies have existed under different names since the Russian Revolution in October 1917, Stalin formally established the KGB in 1946. He did so by dividing the notorious NKVD (People's Commissariat for Internal Affairs) into two parts: the MVD and MGB. At the time, the entire Soviet Government was receiving new designations. The term People's Commissariat was changed to Ministry. The divided NKVD gave birth to the MVD: Ministry of Internal Affairs and the MGB: Ministry of State Security—all of them have the Para-military status.

We called it the "notorious" NKVD intentionally because the NKVD tortured and killed millions of innocent people. Among other functions, its responsibilities included management of the Secret Police, regular police Militia, and forced labor camps known as Gulags. A small footnote: When Hitler came to power in 1933, he sent his emissaries to Moscow to learn the structure and management of Soviet security and intelligence, the internal and external agencies within the NKVD. The top German officers were admitted to the Soviet military Academy. There was not only a military collaboration between Nazis and the Soviets, but also a close cooperation of their Gestapo and the Soviet NKVD. Besides that, the two countries had close economic and political ties—52 percent of the Soviet's exports went to Germany. The Nazi-Soviet Non-Aggression Pact of August 23, 1939 had divided Poland between the two and by doing that initiated WWII. Please, keep in mind that Hitler and

Stalin had been allies and partners, sharing the same view on the world until the summer of 1941.

It should be said that Germans considered the Soviet intelligence agency as the best organized and most efficient in the world. Walter Schellenberg, Hitler's chief of Counterintelligence during WWII, in his memoirs acknowledged the excellence of the effectiveness and efficiency of the KGB's methods of operation and organization. Learning from the Soviets, the Germans, however, had been more direct and open in their violent activities—they had a Death Squad, while the Soviets called it the *Special Forces or Speznas* and never used the words "death." Moreover, Stalin made a deal with Hitler to divide Europe; then one of them violated the deal and incited the start of WWII. The war revealed the deadly face of the NKVD even further. The resemblances to Gestapo are stunning—the NKVD's *barrage squads* moved behind the Soviet soldiers with machine guns to shoot in the back those who intended to surrender to the Germans. That was even worse than interrogations, torturing, and managing the Gulags.

Do not be confused by all the changes of abbreviations and acronyms; these are the hallmarks of the Soviet secret police apparatus to cover-up crimes prior committed. The Soviet people tired and confused with the constant changes in the agencies' name and abbreviations were absolutely right giving them all a collective designation—the *Organs.* The KGB had a long line of precursors: the Cheka,[15] GPU,[16] OGPU,[17] NKVD, and MGB. The name Committee for State Security (KGB) came to life after Stalin's death in 1953. The reason for changing the title of Ministry to Committee is obvious—to cover-up the crime committed by the MGB under its Chairman *Lavrentiy Beria.*[18] To reduce the power and image of the agency before the world, the term Ministry was replaced by *Committee:* literally *Committee.* As you know today, it was not the last cosmetic change of this notorious agency. Today instead of the KGB, Russia has the FSB.*19* The substance and intent of this agency has not changed *—the Organs* have the same agenda and objectives. It should be noted that *the Organs* also comprise the KGB's big twin-brother the *GRU*[20]—a military foreign intelligence apparatus, which has a tremendous number of agents.

What we know as a fact today, President Truman foresaw nearly sixty years ago the identical objectives of all Soviet agencies, like the Soviet people did. Despite the long line of name changes within the Russian intelligence and security apparatus, President Truman had known that the 1946 division of the NKVD into MVD and MGB was a highly significant act. First, it doubled the Kremlin's power and control over Soviet society by the security forces. Second, it revealed and demonstrated Stalin's desire for the Russian Intelligence machine to operate with deep international involvement. That is why the creation of the CIA in 1947 was a must. President Truman was right.

Like President Truman, our other President, Ronald Reagan, also acted promptly and decisively in the 1980s. He was very vocal calling a spade a spade in identifying the Soviet Union as *The Evil Empire.* His words were extremely important for the people of the world and no less important for the Soviet people. It was President Reagan's courage, confidence, firm belief in his action, and love for America that furthered the collapse of the Soviet Union—the truth is the best disinfector. His presidency helped Yeltsin a great deal in his fight against the Communist Party and the KGB. Ronald Reagan's call for freedom in his speech at Moscow University had been heard by all Soviet people. Unfortunately, President Clinton acted the opposite way in the 1990s and as a result we have instability across the world in the twenty-first century.

People of many different nationalities and races know the three letters KGB because of the KGB's extensive global reach. Its main operational objective is recruitment and infiltration of foreign governments, institutions, and organizations. That exact type of infiltration took place in the heart of our intelligence agency sixty years ago. *The Good Shepherd* presents to us a Russian mole that knows our secrets and because of him, a decent individual is wrongly identified and ends up committing suicide—a horrifying scene. It doesn't matter whether the episode is fiction or a real account of events sixty years ago. All Americans should see the film, because the aggressive infiltration into foreign governments, institutions, and organizations by the Russian Intelligence apparatus is a stark reality today.

A December 16th, 2006 article titled "Don't Mess With Russia" published in *The Economist,* seriously analyzes Russian behavior in the field of energy. The article states, "Mr. Putin's use of energy as a weapon is only one instance of Russian assertiveness that nowadays seems to border on gangsterism." The term is exactly appropriate. The murder of former Russian agent and dissident with polonium-210 in London is another instance. This is more than gangsterism; it is nuclear terrorism.

Litvinenko[22] was murdered ostensibly because he spoke out about the war in Chechnya and the murder of a prominent government critic, journalist Anna Politkovskaya.[23] For your information she is not the only journalist killed—twelve other journalist critics of the KGB's Russian government speaking the truth have been assassinated in the last several years. Please, consider the rule of the KGB—a former agent or informer should be liquidated at any time for the benefit of the agency, let alone critics of the KGB.

Reportedly, eighty-eight bankers and journalists have been shot or stabbed for the last several years. A human rights activist Alexei Simonov, the son of famous Russian poet Konstantin Simonov, told CNN's journalist Amanpur that 220 journalists had been assassinated and only five cases investigated… I have already written in chapter 4, *Messages From the Grave*, p. 89, *The Russian Factor*, the story about a brave man Yuri Schekochikin, a member of the Russian parliament, who was one of the first openly reporting criminal activities of the Soviet mafia in the beginning of the 1990s. As we found out later, he was poisoned and had symptoms similar to those Litvinenko had experienced before his death. Please, listen to his words: "While organized crime in the West traditionally is engaged in fields such as drug peddling and prostitution, the Soviet mafia… is ubiquitous. The very nature of the Soviet sociopolitical and economic system gives rise to all sorts of criminality and corruption, making it very difficult for Westerners to comprehend the extent of crime… a discussion of the mafia is above all a discussion not of the criminal, but of the political." Isn't it clear now why he was poisoned?

However, Litvinenko and Politkovskaya are both special cases. I believe that Anna Politkovskaya and Alexander Litvinenko had been murdered because they knew something more than Chechnya only. Perhaps they had a piece of information about either the KGB's connection to Al-Qaeda or evidence of a special operation with nuclear materials brought to Iran or another country by the KGB. I believe the former, and I expressed my opinion in chapter 11, "Perestroika and Bin-Laden," *The Russian Factor*: *From Cold War to Global Terrorism*, Xlibris, 2006. Please, keep in mind that the KGB is functioning through the chain of special operations— Spez. Operazia. And remember that Anna Politkovskaya was assassinated on Putin's birthday, October 7, 2006. The old KGB's traditions are alive and well in the twenty-first century.

There is another troublesome point. During the last ten to twelve years we have witnessed an enormous number of missteps and failures by our security and intelligence agencies, as if they are unaware of what is going on in the world. I have already written about systemic and structural problems within both. The unstable situation in Iraq and Iran is a result of some of them. The time span is very suspicious and coincides with the KGB led by Putin gradually but surely coming to absolute power in Russia. In 2000, the KGB became the government of Russia with former KGB Chairman Putin as its President. In fact, as with Viet Nam thirty years ago, Russia had a close relationship with Iraq and Iran as well. The KGB had trained Saddam Hussein's intelligence and security agencies during three decades. Today the same type of infiltration continues in Iran—the KGB organizing and training intelligence and security forces of Iran the same way it had done training in Iraq. Iran's military has also been reorganized like the Soviet style offensive force. Please, keep in mind that cooperation of Iran with Russians implies the establishment of covert military programs in Iran the way Russians had done in North Korea. Remember the special operations. You will hear about them soon. Sixty years ago, President Truman gave us the tools to survive and gain knowledge of a dreadful part of the world that hates us. Nothing has substantially changed since then in Russia. Moreover, after the collapse of the Soviet Union in 1991, Russian envy and hatred of America has doubled. Then President Truman realized the threat, acted promptly and decisively, and enabled our victory in the Cold War fifty years later. Unfortunately, a strong presidential character and decisiveness, let alone competence, are not fashionable nowadays in America. Unlike in America, in Russia the same aggressive evil agenda and activities against the West and especially against America continue today with mounting intensity.

In this respect, another quotation is in order. Mr. Putin once said the following: "There is no such thing as a former KGB man..." His recent arrogant anti-American speech in Munich proves that. The historical parallel with Munich of 1938 is stunning! In addition to the provocative speech, his native agency FSB (former KGB) organized a huge anti-American campaign among Russian youth at the end of March. The campaign portrayed America as the major threat to Russia, including possible danger of American involvement in the upcoming Russian presidential election. Wow! Have you heard about that?

Simultaneously, Putin is waging an aggressive war against a pro-democracy coalition known as "Other Russia" and "United Civil Front." The opposition's peaceful Dissent's Marches in Nizhniy Novgorod, St. Petersburg, and Moscow have been causing a lot of blood on the streets, as Russian Militia dispersed marchers with application of exceedingly brutal force. Do you remember the NKVD, its Militia and the *Organs?* They are still in power. People in the opposition suffered severe injuries, some of the leaders were arrested, among them Garry Kasparov, the former chess champion of the world.

A couple of months later; the anti-American propaganda had doubled in Russia. What do you think now about the Russian campaign depicting our country as an aggressor? Are you ready to mess with Russia? I can help you to make a decision. After writing about the new anti-American campaign, I have researched to find out who the young Russians were that incited and organized by the FSB or by *Organs* in a propaganda speech against America. I would like to share some information with you. The name of this new political force is NASHI,[25] which means OURS. The pro- Putin movement Walking Together in total secrecy and with a lot of money from the Kremlin, has created a new youth movement NASHI announced on March 1, 2007. The goal is to keep the Motherland from being colonized by the United States. The founder of NASHI, Vasiliy Yakemenko is traveling across Russia and speaking before students, calling Ukraine "an American colony." I want to remind you that the Orange Revolution in Ukraine in 2005 has created in the Kremlin a paranoid fear that of what happened in Ukraine might happen in Russia.

Knowing old Soviet propaganda machine completely inherited by the Putin administration, I would rather rely on the objective information received from the witnesses. The leader of Yabloko's[26] youth movement, Ilya Yashin had managed to sneak into the meeting held in a building owned by the Putin administration, but he was recognized and Yakemenko ordered his security guards to throw him out. Yashin suggested that "one of the tasks of the 'Nashists' is to intimidate the opposition youth so that they are afraid to attend public meetings." He is partially right— intimidation is an important instrument of power, which is used the same way Stalin did. Today, however, the political predicament in Russia is more complex—President Yeltsin's inheritance has left opposition, which did not exist and was completely absent in

Stalin's time. Today there are two types of the opposition in Russia. One is the real opposition like the SPS—Union of the Right Forces. Another is the controlled ones. There are several controlled opposition parties in Russia; creation of Nashi by Putin's administration is the example of the next one—the movement is officially independent, but in reality coordinated and controlled by the Kremlin. Reportedly, the NASHI had been formed as "a paramilitary force to attack Putin's harshest critics." All of that is the Kremlin's preparation to the election of thc Russian Duma (parliament) in December 2007.

It is important to have a clear understanding of the title NASHI's meaning, because it also exposes the agenda of the movement. In Russian culture and later in the Soviet culture there always was a division between who the enemies were thought to be. The Soviets usually used the words of the opposite notions like WE and THEY, US and THEM. The title NASHI means OURS and intends to carry that exact opposite feeling to THEY and THEIR. OURS identifies antagonism and hostility, animosity, and defiance to THEIR. The term NASHI warns you to be ready for confrontation; it means the primacy of OURS over the outsiders. That is the explanation of why President Putin is shown in highly positive aspects only—he is OURS! The Russian media and print is practically in the hand of his party. People are bombarded with the scripted spins agitating for Putin. Just watch how they all praise Putin, working like a mafia-rocket to fight for power and grab it.

A member of the Communist Party, Putin has never formally resigned from it, but nobody dares to ask him the question. The media and print are creating a hard-core dedication to their leader Putin in the hearts of the youth including HASHI. The same way the Stalinist Communists created dedication to them Comsomol (Communist Youth League) in the past. It was a major Stalinist credo of divisiveness—US against THEM. Watch the HASHISTS; they will be the banner of the anti-American campaigns organized by the Russian KGB's government in the future! Also watch how the Stalinist credo has been spread throughout the world, especially throughout the Islamic one.

Now the Kremlin is maneuvering the old and known way, using youth movements to antagonize the youth and Russian population against dissidents and America—they are not OURS. The agenda and modus operandi is the old and usual one— violence in suppression of dissent in concert with anti-American propaganda. Watch HASHI, thre breeding hate and violence movement, subsidized by the Kremlin.

Remember the unspeakable violence at the building of the Estonian Embassy in Moscow during the Russian official protest concerning the monument of the Soviet soldier in Tallinn (capital of Estonia), and carry out by the NASHI. The monument was moved to the cemetery and by HASHI's activities you can judge the Kremlin and its modus operandi. By the way, the attack on the foreign embassy is viewed as a declaration of war. Analogous violence by the young Russians in Tallinn took place there; the stores had been vandalized, innocent people and policemen on the streets injured, the normal life of the city disrupted. Moreover, the Estonian cyber space and its entire cyber system have been infiltrated by the Kremlin and its normal function blocked! Please, remember that infiltration into the cyber system of the independent countries is one of the elements of the asymmetrical war for world domination, waged by the Kremlin…!

For your information, I was practicing law for twenty-five years in Tallinn. The location of the monument in the center of the city was very inconvenient for many reasons and especially for the traffic concerns. Maybe it was not the proper time for the relocation of the monument, but it was a legitimate action taken by the independent country for the well-being of its citizens and the reconstruction of the streets in its capital. The unspeakable violence of the Russian youth in Tallinn is a real demonstration of hostility and animosity—the vivid division on OURS and not OURS, which in this case was the Independent Estonian government.

The attack on the Estonian Embassy in Moscow was not unique; on the contrary, similar violence took place at the Ukrainian exposition of Holodomor in Moscow. It was destroyed with an exceptional meanness—Stalin's crime and his legacy cannot be demonstrated, the exposition should be destroyed…

The same kind of destruction policy had been employed against Estonia. An unprecedented cyber-attack by the Kremlin had been launched against independent Estonian cyber space violating and paralyzing all activities of the Estonian government and its people. I would like to remind you that the first hacker breaking into America's City Bank many years ago had resided in St. Petersburg, Russia. Pay attention to the Russian youth, the Kremlin exploits the movement in many different fronts for its advantages.

In December 2007, there will be an election to the Russian Duma (parliament), and that is why I am trying to warn you about continuation of violence and fraud. The peaceful demonstrations of the opposition in different cities of Russia will be violently suppressed by the forces familiar to you: the Militia, *the Organs,* or Special Forces. We can also expect an application of a variety of fraud. As a matter of fact, I have written my first two books to acquaint you with the term Soviet Fascism and its global activities in the strife for global domination—infiltration, fraud, and corruption are the major tools and components of the ideology. I completed my second book *The Russian Factor*: *From Cold War to Global Terrorism* in 2004. For many different reasons a part from me, you have not read my books. And this fact obliged me to try again with the presentation of more detailed facts with a sense of Russian history to give you a complete understanding of what is going on in Russia today.

If you read *Baltic Winds*, you know the Old Russian policy of Russification used and emphasized by Stalin. I have ended *Baltic Winds* with excruciating pain and a sense of upcoming danger—danger to Russia itself and to the world. The policy of Russification, usually carried out by an ideological department of the *Organs*, plus subordination to the government media at the time of Stalin. There were 170 nationalities and ethnic groups in the Soviet Union; Russification forced them all to study and speak Russian. Contemporary Russia has more than 100 different nationalities and ethnic groups. What is going on in Russia today the ruling party would not call Russification, but in reality it is even more dangerous than Russification, it is nationalism with a fascist underpinning in a country with nuclear missiles. The Nashists' movement, in all its activities glorifying Russia testifies to that.

From my two previous books, I had considered the Yeltsin government as the best Russia could dream of, though he practically lost the fight with the KGB. So somewhere in the 1990s, I noticed the similarity to Russification, but nobody pronounced the word Russification. Considering that United Russia's party of power with its leader Putin has the KGB's background, we can expect a complete Stalinist revival with even more dangerous consequences for the world. Only people with knowledge of that background can identify that menacing tendency today. I did at the end of the 1990s, noticing the old, familiar predicament in Russia created by Putin's KGB—predator is always a predator. The policy of ethnic majority or nationalism is a direct avenue to the totalitarian rules. The Columbia Encyclopedia Second Edition identifies the predicament:

"...a strong nationalism naturally leans to defensive and even to offensive measures and to continuous hostility toward some other nation or nations. Such state nationalism is also frequently linked with IMPERIALISM, as shown obviously in Fascist Italy and National Socialist Germany. Those and the other fascist powers showed, too, the value of nationalistic propaganda in giving individual citizens a feeling of status of belonging to a great and glorifying whole," p. 1360. This is a description of National Socialist Germany and today's Russia. I would only add to the description the creation of the loyal youth movements by the ruling power—Hitler's Jugent in Germany and NASHI and others in Russia.

Remember the meaning of the name NASHI—a youth antipode to THEY—a motto to distrust others. This was a Stalinist motto in the process of molding the youth's mentality in the tenets of Soviet Fascism—the Stalinist inheritance. The Russian KGB's government is doing just that in the twenty-first century. I am very much aware of the direction of current Russian ruling elite and know that you are not aware of it. Hence, the rest of the book will be an attempt to acquaint you with the patterns and activities of this ruling power, which is called the Russian KGB's government today.

Dear reader; I know, you wonder why I am telling you about the events going on in Russia. There is a reason, a serious one. A huge devastating trap is ahead of you. The trap is plotted by both internal and external forces to destroy you and our country. Nobody warns you—I must. To keep our land free, you should see the world through the point of *good* vs. *evil*, face reality, and be ready to fight *evil* successfully. It is the Russian intelligence that is plotting this trap and I do not want you to fall into it. The information about my two books published in 2002 and 2006 was suppressed and you have not read them. I am again giving you the truth and warning you in 2007. The truth addressed in this book should never leave you mind—be aware of and be prepared to defend Liberty. Do not trust and rely on mass media—it will betray you.

Devastating troubles are coming our way. To grasp the threat, here is a story to remember. A decent Russian man, whose name was well known in Russia, came to the American Embassy in Moscow in the summer of 2001. He warned people in the Embassy that several planes would attack America soon. People in the Embassy did not believe him.

You know the rest of the story… please, believe me.

CHAPTER 4

And Evil is Alive and Well

It is with a direct purpose that I have written my first chapters to acquaint you with the chronology of the Russian intelligence and security services, the Russian security forces—the NKVD and its offspring the KGB and FSB—*the ORGANS*. The reason is simple—to give you a big picture of Russia today, as the concept of security forces have not changed since their inception. The Russian KGB's government is the carrier of that old concept today. There is some history. The NKVD came to birth on December 20, immediately after the October Socialist Revolution of 1917—its first name was the Cheka. The abbreviation means the Extraordinary Commission (The All-Russian Extraordinary Commission for Combating Counter-Revolution and Sabotage). I found a lot of terms identifying the word extraordinary in the Roget's Thesaurus. These two described it completely—monstrous and unaccountable.

This is a recounting of the Cheka from Wikipedia:

"The Cheka is reported to have practiced torture which rivaled that of the Spanish Inquisition. Victims were skinned alive, scalped, 'crowned' with barbed wire, impaled, crucified, hanged, stoned to death, tied to planks and pushed slowly into furnaces or tanks of boiled water, and rolled around in internally nail-studded barrels. Some of the atrocities were truly invented." One of the interrogators ran from the Cheka to the West and published a book. I read it. His description of the Cheka's activities was analogous to the description presented above by Wikipedia.

For the period July-December 1918 the Cheka killed more than 6, 000 people. During the period 1918-1920 the death toll rose to 12,733 killed. And though all of that happened on a piece of land in central Russia within only twenty provinces, experts consider these semi-official figures as an understatement. Some suggest 250, 000, some—500, 000 killed. But even these stunning numbers are only half of the truth. The other half is an unlimited investigative power of the Cheka and its members—the Chekists who investigated, interrogated, and tortured the way it mentioned above. There was a system or a special order and line for those who were to be liquidated. First was the political opposition, next landlords and industrialists, then the technical intelligencia, and after that the cultural one. There was no mercy for their families.

Obsessed with investigations and liquidations, Cheka's atrocities and executive power have applied to women and children as well. Wikipedia describes it this way: "Women and children were also victims of Cheka terror. Women would sometimes be tortured and raped before being shot. Children of eight to sixteen were imprisoned and occasionally executed." The policy of *The Red Terror* had no mercy on anybody in the mass arrests, deportations, and executions.

I would like to give you one example of the execution of those days. The Communist's Cheka had murdered Tsar Nicolas II, his wife, and their five children. It was a horrendous killing of innocent people, where blood was pouring out like the streams of the river in the dark, tiny basement of the Old Russian monastery in Siberia. After the execution, the corpses of the Russian Royal family were thrown into a pit with hydrochloric acid. Do you get the picture? I have read a book about the entire ordeal and the man named Yurovsky,[27] who by order from Moscow was responsible for the execution. Finishing his bloody assignment in Siberia, he got a powerful position to administer the Russian Gold Reserve in Moscow. The description of the bloody murder of the Royal Romanoff's family remains in my memory.

In 1922, a Chairman of the Cheka Felix Dzerzhinsky[28] had changed its name to GPU—the State Political Management. Pay attention to a combination of two words which characterizes the secret police—Political Management. Since then the name of the Soviet Intelligence apparatus has been changed many times, the next name was the OGPU; however, its political agenda and objectives remained the same. The changes were always cosmetic to cover-up the crime against humanity prior committed. In 1934, the OGPU had also gained a sinister reputation and was renamed. The next name was the NKVD, which had combined control over all three branches of the secret police—political, economic, and regular police. They were fighting their own population.

Needless to say, Stalin had quadrupled the crime against humanity. Reportedly, under the reign of his Chairman of the Cheka Yezhov, three million people had been killed or vanished during one year. Stalin had untied the hands of the secret police with an absolute absence of accountability, which was very conducive to falsifying and manufacturing the cases. Stalin used to produce a list of people to be annihilated, the manner and methods were the job of the secret police. It could be assassination, kidnapping, or investigation and interrogation with torturing for preparation to the show trials.

The list of practicing tortures in the '30s has been enlarged: pulling out teeth one after another, applying electrical waves to genitals, or putting needles under nails had become preferable methods. As a rule, all accused victims had pleaded guilty and been charged with espionage. Although innocent, they, however, admitted their guilt, because they left their families behind in jeopardy. I know one case where the accused had not pleaded guilty—his name was Yenukidze, he did not have a family.

The vast majority of accused had been charged with espionage on behalf of England, France, or America. Stalin's paranoia of espionage had no end. He had also invented several ways of securing his leadership as the First Secretary of the Communist Party. If brutal violence was the first undertaking in fighting for power, silencing others was the second one. He had also created the most long-lasting third one—a manufactured search for the enemy, to find a scapegoat. As a matter of fact, the economic situation was so bad, that someone, but not Stalin, was supposed to be blamed. Security and Intelligence agencies were working days and nights searching for enemies. The waves of repression were spread throughout eleven time zones; the yes-men in the government, an army of provocateurs, agitators, and informers helped—millions of innocent people were annihilated.

For this reason I called the search for the enemy or creation of the enemy's image, the third and most long-lasting method of fighting for political power in the Soviet/Russian behavior. It is a historically known fact that Stalin hated private ownership and private business—he preferred collectives, a communal ownership under the centralized government. The result was dreadful. All Stalin's agricultural programs were disastrous for the country. By official Soviet statistics: "In 1927, about 25 million individual farms comprised 98.3 percent of all agricultural units in Russia." A successful agricultural country, feeding a part of Europe, Russian agriculture was ruined, its farms destroyed, farmers— "kulaks-exploitators" *the Fists,* and "enemies of the people" arrested or killed. As a result—mass starvation resulted in the death of millions. Central Russia and Ukraine suffered the most, and even today in the twenty-first century every Ukrainian remembers the word—*Holodomor*—man-made mass starvations and deaths. On the bodies of the dead people and confiscated property, Stalin's collectivization had wiped out the agricultural middle class, which had been growing since the beginning of the twentieth century. Russia had paid dearly for finding the "enemy." The Soviet agriculture has never recovered.

To grasp the economic disaster and people's misery, please, keep in mind that in addition to ruined agriculture, by a stroke of a pen, Stalin abolished NEP (New Economic Policy) and nationalized private businesses and banks. The industrialists and owners of the private banks had shared the fate of the farmers— they were arrested, killed, deported, some immigrated. The Soviet government had become the unique owner of the country's entire economy and its natural resources. Regrettably, the world is still unaware of the devastation created by Stalin in the country —no movie or an emotional narrative to expose the man-made human tragedy extended throughout eleven time zones has been made.

Another disaster was Stalin's policy of forced Industrialization—millions vanished or were killed. One example is the Belomorkanal (White Sea Canal), a link between Leningrad and the White Sea. Hundreds of thousands of the "enemies of the people"—farmers, political prisoners, and some criminals were digging thirty- seven km. of the canal through hard rock with primitive working conditions and little mechanical equipment. Living in brutal cold under inhumane conditions they died like flies by the hundreds. Those who survived were sent to other penal labor projects. This way Stalin was shaping the Soviet Socialist economy on the corps and bodies of the Soviet citizens. The casualties were in vain— the first Five-Year Plan had failed. I should repeat that all Stalin's undertakings had been carried out by the Cheka, GPU, OGPU, and the NKVD—the nucleus of the Soviet Power and the Soviet Socialist System—*the ORGANS...*

To see the big picture of Soviet life under Socialism and Stalin's design for the society, I have to introduce another menacing institution, which was established to fight civilian population—the *Gulag*[29]—*The Chief Administration of Corrective Labor Camps and Colonies* of the NKVD. As you can see the name can be used in plural as well—*Gulags*. Anne Applebaum, in her book *Gulag: A History*, gives an excellent definition, "The word Gulag has also come to signify not only the administration of the concentration camps but also the system of Soviet slave labor itself, in all its forms and varieties: labor camps, punishment camps, criminal and political camps, women's camps, children's camps... Gulag has come to mean the Soviet repressive system itself... the set of procedures that prisoners called the 'meat-grinder': the arrests, the interrogations, the transport in unheated cattle cars, the forced labor, the destruction of families, and the years spent in exile, the early and unnecessary deaths."

Every Soviet family was affected by Stalin's crimes, every citizen bore psychological scars. Foreign writers and journalists could not conceive the reality and praised Stalin, the Soviet people. Yet some honest foreigners knew a lot. Brave voices began accusing Stalin. And that is why the third and long-lasting method of searching for the enemy came to life—the accuser must be immediately accused back, the brave voices must be shut down! As usual this method was also carried out by the state security agency and secret police. And again a new wave of oppression and the liquidations of millions of innocent swamped the country, and a socialist society of the collectives had no instrument or vehicle to stop that fly-wheel of repression.

For your information, the long-lasting method of obtaining or maintaining power, Stalin had created a mechanism of "defense," a pattern of Soviet/Russian behavior, which is alive and well today: "Confronted with problems you should attack an adversary or manufacture the crisis to hide behind, diverting attention from the real problems." That behavior of looking for the enemy, attacking adversary, or manufacturing the crisis is alive and well in twenty- first century Russia, it had been returned to practice by the KGB. Just watch Putin's government and its activities.

In addition to all of that, Stalin had armed the Soviet security agencies and secret police with an ideological foundation, a platform and a banner under which all crimes were committed—the theory of Marxism-Leninism. He preached Marxism-Leninism for building Socialism and Communism, but instead spread Stalinism throughout Russia and the globe with all the elements Cheka's DNA, its genes, and chromosomes. The West had been fooled by Stalin, talking about building Socialism in only one country. In fact, Stalin had had just the opposite agenda—world domination under the slogan: "Proletarians of the world unite!" A lot of Jews were also fooled and enthusiastically served in the party, institutions, and organizations created by the system. The people of the country were cut off from the objective information—the censorship of the entire media had prevented the truth from getting out—Stalinist ideology had reigned.

Talking about the Cheka's DNA, its genes, and chromosomes, I cannot avoid showing you the similarity with their creator. Stalin had transferred to all Soviet intelligence and security apparatuses elements of his own character and habits. Brutality was the major one—he destroyed his old family members to cover up his past and preserve his power and titles. He used to send to death millions by signing a list then submitted it to the Cheka, and after that he watched a movie. By the way, there are a lot of resemblances I have found in the characters of Stalin and Hitler. Both loved their mothers and respected, if not hated, their despotic Fathers. Both started their political career very early and manifested aggressive ideas in their writings, sitting in prison. Both strived for power using deceit, fraud, and other low and treacherous tools and devices. The only difference is that Hitler was elected in a quite fair election, while Stalin initiated a bloody revolution.

It should be noted that Stalin's theory of Marxism-Leninism was a skillfully designed and well structured FRAUD. First, Marxism speaks about a certain location—the countries with advanced conditions of European civilization and therefore with a more developed proletariat. Second, though Lenin was not a paragon of virtues, he was right admitting the absence of a proletariat able to lead the revolution in Russia. In fact, Stalin actually manipulated labels of Marxism and Leninism, creating his own dogma under the cover of that title. As you can see, the FRAUD was possible and brought to life in the country and later on in the rest of the world, by brutal violent force. (Read *Baltic Winds*: *Testimony of A Soviet Attorney*, the chapter "The Fraud of the Century.")

For decades, the radicalization of the state security, intelligence agencies, and police was going on as "The Great Terror," had approached its apogee in 1937, the year of "The Great Purges." "Not only Old Bolsheviks, but many Stalinist party leaders were eliminated. Purged were 70 percent of the Central Committee members. At the eighteenth Party Congress in 1939, only 35 of 1,827 rank and file delegates were present! From the party and army the purges reached downward into the general populace as friends and relatives of purges were arrested." All Soviet people know the terror and tragedies of the year 1937, where besides unlawful arrests, kidnappings, and shootings of innocent people, children of the killed, arrested, or deported parents were taken to the special orphanages; concentration camp style.

Along with brutal force and horrible purges, Stalin had also invented a sophisticated propaganda machine to defend crimes committed. Public radio (there was no private one) and every printing unit in the country had a sensor—the *Department of Agitation and Propaganda*. By machinery of moral relativism, the Department had blended the borders between moral and immoral, producing social falsehood that affected a nation's psyche. The major components of its operations had become deceits, fraud, distortions, deceptions, perverted language, and sometimes hoaxes. As a result, despite all of the crimes, purges, and terror, the *Department of Agitation and Propaganda* had been extremely successful in its disinformation and fraud—criminals had become heroes, heroes had become criminals. The Soviet intelligence, secret police, and their activities were romanticized in the Soviet literature and cinematography creating a culture of perverted justice among Russian youth and ill-informed population throughout the world. The mighty traditions of Russian literature were serving a totalitarian regime on a mass level.

When I call the *Department of Agitation and Propaganda* Stalin's sophisticated propaganda machine to defend crimes committed, I have in mind certain standards or tricks Stalin invented in approaching the issue. For example, in his war against peasantry of Russia and Ukraine, Stalin had never used the word peasant or farmer. To win that war, Stalin inspired all the people to fight against peasantry and farmers for "the bright future of Communism" by a trick. He created the enemies, by giving them pejorative nicknames *the Fists*—"kulaks" or "enemies of the people," both are highly negative. And the trick of perverted language had worked miraculously—all Soviet people were brought up to fight "enemies of the people." The words had very well affected starving, intimidated, and tired out by the revolution people. Words have mattered. By demonizing people Stalin established a method of an ideological character assassination; personal destruction to get rid of his adversaries. Since then Stalin had armed the *Department of Agitation and Propaganda* with this and many other tricks based on lies, hoaxes, fabrications, fraud, deception, and falsifications.

Under the name of Marxism-Leninism Stalin had created his own body of work—A Short Course, a compellation of deceit, fraud, and revised and perverted history. A Short Course had been studied in all schools and universities throughout the country. Like the secret police, the print, radio, and their *Departments of Agitation and Propaganda* with other thousands of affiliations were the watchdogs of Stalin's creations. Agitation had influenced people's minds and consciousness—propaganda raged their emotions. That way the image of the "enemy" was concocted. The indoctrination of the next generation has continued by the same manipulations—the end justifies means. That way a Socio- ideological movement with imperial objectives and an agenda of the Communist ideology was born, its name—Stalinism, a system of total control, unprecedented large bureaucracy, and permanent terror.

Information is power and it has always been an indispensable commodity for the Stalinist state—no information should come in, none should go out. Like in Nazi Germany listening to a foreign broadcast was illegal and sometimes treasonous. It is for that reason the Iron Curtain was built to prevent objective information from the West from coming in. For the same reason the hunt for honest clergymen and journalists has never ended—they were the messengers of the truth, but Stalin labeled them also as "Enemies of the People," and "Enemies of the People" must be killed! Assaults, arrests, and exiles of honest clergymen, professional journalists, writers, and poets had completely eliminated the truth from media, print, and publications. Those who attempted to expose the regime had paid with their lives: They had been interrogated, tortured, and executed. Read the story of a Great Russian poet Osip Mandelstam." *The Russian Factor: From Cold War to Global Terrorism*, p. 206, Xlibris, 2006.

The Russian Orthodox Church was also practically destroyed and only the priests that collaborated with the secret police could survive and serve. Empty churches were used as the stables for horses and storages. Religion had become substituted by the Communist ideology; the infiltration into the houses of faith by the KGB had become the norm. The Russian Orthodox Church was the first target. And though Stalinism had disseminated hatred to all religions, he at the same time used all of them for his political advantages. The landscape of the Old

Faithful Russia had been dramatically changed. A few synagogues that survived in the big cities could function only under supervision of the secret police. In fact, Stalin had turned religion into an instrument of subversion and propaganda, politically managed to serve him and the Communist Party.

No political dissent was allowed and those who attempted were investigated, interrogated by the secret police and sent to Gulags or shot. The world should remember how the best minds, millions of the Russian intelligencia, salt of the Earth, had been targeted by the Red Terror and Purges. They appeared before Show Trials, were sent to Gulags, kidnapped, assassinated, or sent to psychiatric medical facilities run by the NKVD. The Soviet Judiciary was used to officially implement the method of a character assassination—show trials testify to that. Stalinist dictate of extremism and a pyramid of hatred had been built—all that terror lasted for several decades.

Hence, Stalin had institutionalized brutal violence and mass-repressions as a major form of activities within the Soviet body politics—the ideology of Soviet Fascism. In the rim of ideology the Soviet judiciary was used as an instrument of fear for the entire population. We all knew well Article 58 of the Criminal Code30—Counterrevolutionary Agitation and Propaganda with severe punishment. Article 58 was applied pretty loosely—a joke could cost you a long trip to Gulags, imprisonment for years, often for the entire family. An unprecedented scale of social engineering had a tremendous impact on the Russian traditional values system. As a result of the social changes, life was cheapening, violence and fear prevailed. Living under constant psychological terror the traumatized people of Russia changed even more—they gave in. Opposition has ceased to exist. Stalin had achieved total victory over his own people.

The state's rights dominated over individuals. The latter were practically subordinate to the Soviet government—the notion of human rights or civil rights did not exist. Yet it was not enough for Stalin. As the outstanding individuals among clergy or writers had tried "to violate" Stalin's victory over the Russian people by opening their mouths and telling the truth, the special psychiatric medical facilities within the Gulags had been set up for them. The leading role in the development of the mechanism of terror and political repression as the medical abuses had been taken by the Serbsky Institute in Moscow:

"Serbsky was established in 1923. By the mid-thirties, its emphasis shifted from being a research establishment... to an uncontrolled monopoly over who could be committed and involuntarily committed—even if they were not insane. ...By the beginning of the 1950s a very fine-tuned mechanism of political repression with the application of psychiatry had been established. This was based on the Criminal Code and departmental regulations ordering the clampdown of 'anti-revolutionary' activity and the use of forensic-psychiatric examinations to determine which 'insane' persons had committed dangerous crimes against society and required safe keeping in special prison psychiatric hospitals (gulags). ...Psychiatric repression...affected practically every sector of Soviet society..."

Summary of the Report on the Findings of the Investigation by the Commission on Rehabilitation of Victims of Political Repression During the Soviet Era to Boris Yeltsin, President Russian Federation.

I would use much stronger words to characterize medical abuses by the legal system, because psychiatric abuse did not end in the prisons, it was applicable to the people outside prisons as well—the jurisdiction of all courts throughout the eleven time zones of the country. I had met experts from the Serbsky Institute in courts and Military Tribunals on the side of prosecution, but a defense attorney was powerless—I had lost those cases. The Soviet legal system served only the Soviet State, not the individuals. And though I have studied the forensic psychiatry under the care of wonderful professor Sluchevsky, I couldn't win the arguments against the experts of the Serbsky Institute—psychiatry or abuse of it was their profession.

In the midst of medical abuses, show trials, purges, executions, and forced collectivization the next Soviet Constitution had been enacted on December 5, 1936. It was called *Stalin's Constitution.* Just before December, in November 1936, Stalin assured the Eighth Congress of Soviets because the rapid industrialization and collectivization had eliminated landlords, capitalists, and kulaks. "There are no longer any antagonistic classes in the Soviet society, which consists now of two friendly classes, workers and peasants." The Stalin Constitution, he claimed, would be "the only thoroughly democratic constitution in the world."

Reading that had brought to me an understanding of how deeply I myself was brainwashed and fooled—the word "friendly" did not exist in the Soviet lexicon—hypocrisy and lies run the Soviet society. And what existed in the lexicon was aimed at the Soviet people to deceive and indoctrinate them by covering up the crime committed. When I was a teenager, I often heard the word "psyhushka"[31]—slang for a psychiatric institution. In law school we joked laughingly, verbally sending students with the weird ideas to "psyhushka." We consciously called "psyhushka" the medical, psychiatric facilities I was describing before, because we were sure that only crazy people were contained there. The Soviets had such sophisticated methods of propaganda that it was very easy to fool us all. There were a lot of "false flag operations" nobody was able to detect. Like to me, the clarity of the crime committed by the government came much later to many other youngsters as well. We were fooled, but unfortunately we had company from the West: Roman Roland and Bernhard Show had also been deceived—they liked the Constitution. Unlike Lenin, Stalin operated by hypocrisy and pleasant words fooling everyone and nobody could expose deceit or hypocrisy, and reveal the truth—fear had chained us all.

The Communist Party and the Stalinist state had paid special attention to the growing young population of the country. Indoctrination had started from kindergarten to the membership in the Communist Party: Octoberists,[32] Pioneers,[33] Youth Communist League, and so on. Toddlers and teenagers knew Stalin very well— his portraits were in each kindergarten, school, and in all public facilities. Literature and songs glorified him. His personality played a major role in the youngsters' upbringing and their minds' development. Children were pit against their parents like Pavlik Morozov, and were practically taken away from the culture of their household. By 1938, Stalin became an all-powerful father figure, a saver. The scale of brainwashing had approached an epidemic proportion—some children loved Stalin more than they loved their parents! Our multinational psyche had drastically changed at a mass level and I was among those who went through that Soviet brain-grinder of a socialist experiment. Meanwhile, the regime of permanent terror had become ubiquitous. This observation is a personal reflection on past events—I have lived through them.

In this respect, I would like to give you the predicament Soviet women had experienced in their lives. The Stalinist system practically excluded women from any participation in the politics of the Soviet state—men ran the country. Women had to accept the dirtiest, lowest-paying, most physically debilitative, and socially denigrating jobs. They repaired the streets in the cities and worked fourteen to sixteen hours cultivating the land with their own hands in the countryside. Men no longer accepted that kind of work— they were busy building the Communist state and the Socialist economic system to succeed in the process of world domination. Windows of opportunity for women simply didn't exist in the country building Soviet Socialism,

However, there was another tragic angle in women's lives— every one of them had permanently undermined her health with numerous abortions. They had no other options—three to five abortions were considered a normal fact of life in Soviet society; some had eight to twelve, or even more all were paid for by the government. In a society where a sex life, typically taboo, rarely appeared on the agenda and abortion served as the only method of birth control. Hardship generally prevailed over all human feelings, and women were doomed to serve men obsessed with power and busy building a military empire. From kindergarten to higher education, girls and boys were brought up under the Stalinist culture of treating women as second-class citizens. Due to that culture, the Stalinist system had turned women into the mules of the society serving the state.

As a founder of the Soviet System and its bureaucracy (*cadres decide everything*), Stalin understood the significance of the leadership in the country and created a clan of new leadership, conducive to his vision of the world and his ideology—no women could apply. He preferred loyalty to decency and obedience to competence. And though the Communist Party had an absolute power in the country, it was able to maintain power only by being secured with its loyal police, security, and intelligence agencies. Stalin knew that. His model for a leader was the blend of political operatives with a security background. It took several decades to eliminate natural development within Russian leadership. Some leaders according to Stalin's list were liquidated by the secret police. Finally, Stalin's vision has molded and produced the type of yes-men with lust for power, he would be satisfied. I will give you a few of them—Uri Andropov, Eugenie Primakov, Vladimir Putin, and Sergey Ivanov— they are the Chekists. Vladimir Putin has often publicly called himself a Chekist.

To fully understand the mentality of the Russian public I have to give you some historical events of the past. The Cheka was the Soviet's first violent state' institution, but not the first Russian one. The first Russian precursor and analogous program to the Cheka had been established 500 years ago. It is not an accident that world history called the Russian Czar Ivan IV, Ivan the Terrible. The son of Vasilyi III, he took power in 1544 and favored the common people, warring against the nobles. Then, everything changed with the death of his beloved wife Anastasia, allegedly poisoned. The paranoia of treason and fear of the enemies had transformed the character of the Czar Ivan since then. In 1565, he created a special corps to fight treason—its name *Oprichnina.*[35] The corps, responsible and accountable to the Czar alone, instituted a period of terror, executions, and exiles from Russia. Many boyars were executed and many exiled.

A contemporary Russian historian and dissident Valeria Novodvorskaya, wrote dozens of essays on Russian History. I would recommend to all professors of Russian History in America to use the material—the only objective representation of Russian's past. Her work can help the world to perceive a contemporary Russia as well. She told an interesting story about Czar Ivan. He had seven wives and once sent his ambassadors to Queen Elizabeth of England with a marriage proposal. The Queen had replied, saying that she had to have a permeation of English Parliament to get married. Czar Ivan was outraged and furious. In his response he wrote that in Russia he, Czar of Russia is the only one who judges and pardons his people. Marriage to the Queen of England never happened.

The paranoia of the plots to kill him led Czar Ivan to war. For an alleged plot he had destroyed Novgorod, Tver, and other Russian cities; their citizens had experienced unprecedented cruelty from the hands of the *Oprichniks,* the violent corps created by the Czar. And finally, Czar Ivan had even killed his own oldest son. For all of that history has given him the name Ivan the Terrible. He practically revived the ancient barbarian motto—*Submit or Die.* The same motto *Submit or Die* was revived in the sixteenth century, then again by the Chekists in the twentieth century and by Putin in the twenty-first century. However, there is a difference—Ivan the Terrible did not have radio, TV, internet, and… Polonium-210. I can't omit another significant feature of the Soviet Socialism— pseudo-science. Have you ever heard about Academician Lyssenko? To perceive all the agricultural troubles of the Soviet Union and the essence of the pseudo-science you have to know that name. A mediocre intriguer, a biologist from Ukraine, Trofim Lysenko[36] had been building his career on the corpses of civilians dying from starvation in 1930. He led the campaign against geneticists of the world and exploited the ideological tenets Stalinists had undermined the entire Soviet agriculture. In cahoots with the party bosses on the wave of Stalinist repressions and using the Marxist-Leninist ideology, he had begun a slanderous and vicious campaign against the geneticist's scholars worldwide who proclaimed, "No ideology and politics in science." Of cause, the first were the Soviet Geneticists of the Soviet Academy of Science. Academician Vavilov was the main target of Lysenko's campaign.

I have read a book about Academician Nikolai Vavilov[37] and his struggles with Lysenko. There is no end to my respect and admiration for Academician Vavilov. He continued his research of the fruit flies even after being arrested. He died in a Gulag. Lysenko had done everything possible to silent him, using the Soviet state security apparatus at the time when scientists were arrested, jailed, and shot. To perceive the ideological situation in the Soviet Academy of Science and understand Lysenko's attacks against genetics, let me give you one quote:

> "Lysenko made the most of this image... in attacking geneticists and contrasting their 'useless scholasticism' with his own great 'practical successes.' He began to speak of class struggle in science and declared in his speech at the 2nd all-union congress of shock collective farmers in 1935 that 'a class enemy is always an enemy whether he is a scientist or not.' Stalin, who was present, exclaimed at the end of his speech, 'Bravo Comrade Lysenko, bravo.'" *Marxism and the Philosophy of Science: A Critical History*, by Helena Sheehan, Humanities Press International, 1985 and 1993. A very informative book about Stalin and the political mafia and the clans around him is written by Miklos Kun[38]—*Stalin: an Unknown Portrait.* Analyzing Stalin's tyranny we should also acknowledge that the Global Financial Crises of 1930 had also untied the hands of another dictator—Hitler.

Only with the knowledge of the past can we appreciate the opportunities which arrived in the 1990s. Yeltsin's appearance on the world stage in the 1990s was a phenomenon in Russian and Soviet history. The press and the entire media had become really free. He has brought the historical changes not only to Russia, but to the world: the KGB was reformed and its Chairman Vladimir Patanin offered to abolish the KGB all together. Yeltsin gave freedom to all Russian colonies, dissolving the USSR. As soon as he became president of Russia, his government canceled all textbooks on History (Social Science), new textbooks reflecting factual events and the collapse of the Soviet Union were ordered. Yet Yeltsin had his enemies as well—the Chekists. And the Old Stalinist Guard of the security agencies, the ORGANS immediately started the underground battles against Yeltsin. Slowly but surely the Old Guard has been undermining Yeltsin's credibility, prestige and health, at the same time they used him to grab power (the methods used require separate research).

The war against Yeltsin started in September 1991, when Gorbachev appointed Eugenie Primakov the first deputy chairman of the KGB and later on as the head of SVR—Foreign Intelligence Service (the Spy Agency). *The Organs* were "working" tirelessly sabotaging Yeltsin's power and prestige. The election of Bill Clinton in America was the last nail in Yeltsin's political coffin— the KGB won. Coming to power as the first President of Russia, Yeltsin made a colossal mistake by not acting promptly and decisively to pronounce the KGB and the Communist Party the outlaw organizations—the criminal ones. He hesitated.... And you know the rest and the end of the story.

Until the 1990s, the Russian educational system had carried on the design of the Stalinist era. Marxism-Leninism was mandatory in all colleges and universities—for law schools and judicial institutes the subject was studied during the entire four years of schooling. The interesting fact is that investigative power of the secret police is almost unlimited today and unlike within the Cheka, all the investigators are the graduates of law schools. And during the first few years of Yeltsin's presidency the security agencies had worked underground; however, the concept of security within those agencies has never changed. Like at the time of the Cheka, security meant nothing else except ATTACK to CONTROL, attack of the adversary on all fronts possible for obtaining or maintaining power and control. This exact concept is alive and well in twenty- first century Russia—progression and continuity of it you will see soon.

It is alive in its evil spirit of attacking the advisories, but it is also alive in the letter of the law. In 1946, it was the MGB, then the KGB, and in the twenty-first century it is the FSB. You can see the continuity of the letter "B" in all three abbreviations. The letter "B" means Security—Bezopasnost. And this is the crux of the matter—in the mentality of the Russian apparatus; security can only be obtained upon attacking and controlling the advisory. The Russian concept of security remains the same, regardless of the time passed and changes in Russia.

In my first articles, I have already described the significance of the creation of the CIA and Truman's response to Stalin's creation of the KGB in1946. Unlike Yeltsin in the 1990s, President Truman acted promptly and decisively in 1947: perhaps he knew the Russian concept of security. It is for this reason I have described in my articles a dispersal of the "Dissenters March" by Russian security forces with blood on the streets in April 2007, sixty years after President Truman's decisiveness in handling Russia. It took another sixty years for Europe and election of the Chancellor Merkel, who grew up in East Germany and knows the concept of security to have "ten exchanges with Mr. Putin over human rights and other contentions issues at a Europe-Russia summit meeting."

It was a strong response by Chancellor Merkel's to manipulation of the law and brutal application of force by the Militia at the "Dissenters March," which has been spread to other Russian cities in May 2007. The old Soviet concept of security meant and still means nothing else but ATTACK to CONTROL. Moreover, the brutal methods of Militia often remind us of the Check's old habits. By the way, have you seen the recent Al-Qaeda's torture chamber and methods it practiced on the Iraqi civilians? I was stunned by Al-Qaeda's methods of torture in Iraq—they are reminiscent of the old methods practiced by the Check a ninety years ago!

If Harry Truman was a great American President aware of the coming danger of the Soviet Socialism, the world was blessed to have another great man as well—Winston Churchill. Can you imagine, he warned us then, in 1945 about Soviet Socialism's inability to manage without a "kind of Gestapo?" He was so right that fifty years later, through my personal experiences, I had arrived at a new term—Soviet Fascism. I did it in my previous two books by showing the Soviet Fascism that is still talking about security while invading other countries. As a matter of fact, the Russian concept of security had been spread and applied to all the advisories outside the Soviet/Russian Borders, destabilizing the entire world. The manner and method of it, spread across the world will be discussed in the next chapters.

But to complete the main idea of this chapter, I am about to tell you what has happened on May 19, 2007 in the Red Square in Moscow. In honor of the 85th anniversary of the Pioneer organization, several thousands of school children had been gathered in the Red Square to take an allegiance to the behests of their grandfather-Lenin.

CHAPTER 5

Tell Me Something I Don't Know!

Hardball MSNBC

Dedicated to Jimmy from Brooklyn

I am a Republican political junky and I like to watch *Hardball*—it shows incompetence. Dear Chris Matthews, you do not know a lot, but don't be discouraged—Warren Buffet also has no idea of the events and issues I am going to narrate in this book. I will try to tell you the most important story of our days—the story of our foremost enemy—The Russian KGB's Government.

It is for a reason I have discussed Russian secret police, security and intelligence agencies in the preceding pages, the agencies long bloody path to become the Russian Government. I wanted you to know the reign of terror that ruled Russia by those agencies—they are the nucleus of Soviet Power and the Soviet Socialist System. Reportedly one dissident said that we must hate the Soviet Power and fight it to the end of our life. I agree. Do I have the credentials to examine the agencies that constitute the nucleus of the Soviet Power? Yes, I think, I do. As matter of fact, the year 2007 is a very sad reminder of the year 1937—the year of The Great Purge, executed by those agencies submerged eleven time zones of the Soviet land seventy years ago.

You know that I am a graduate of a law school. For a long four years I sat next to the future members of the NKVD, MVD, KGB, and FSB. We all listened to the same lectures, read the same textbooks, other materials, and had passionate arguments on the same topics.

We all watched the same propaganda movies, read the same books of Social Realism teaching intolerance and hatred. All of that has given me imminent knowledge of the makeup and mental outlook of those students. Some of them have become my friends, and after graduation we worked in the same city. There was another crucial common feature for us all—none of us knew the term "Human Rights." There was no such a subject in the law schools we attended. There were 200 students in our course. After graduation, in accordance with national service policy, approximately 70 percent were sent to the MVD, prosecutor's office, and the courts, 10-15 percent to the KGB, the rest to other governmental organizations. Almost all Jews including me went to the Bar Association, the only non-government entity to be defense attorneys—there was no option for us. The Bar Association is comprised of only defense attorneys.

Perhaps the structure of the security and intelligence agencies is not my expertise, yet the mental outlook, mindset, mentality, and character of the people serving there is my exact expertise. Thousands and thousands of my clients, people visiting my office have added that picture with their personal stories and cruelty of the people within those agencies and the secret police. I believe my forth chapter fully detailed the matter of repressions and violence within the Soviet/Russian territory—to a certain degree you are familiar now with the Cheka. I did it because the topic of this chapter is the implementation of the same violence by the same agencies throughout the world—the objective or agenda is also the same—world domination.

As usual, history will provide us with documents and the state of events in those days. "From the first days of the revolution (1917) Lenin did not believe that he would be able to maintain power in Russia. He hoped for either the world revolution or the Bolshevik's upheavals in the largest European countries. The Comintern (Communist International) together with the GPU (State Political Management) worked hard to create their affiliates in Europe."

I stopped translating here purposely. Please, pay attention to the agency called GPU. It is the second changed name of the Cheka. Do you remember the crimes it has committed in its own territory?

Now I will continue the translation: "We were taught that Jacque Duclo,[40] Marcel Kashen, and Morris Torres had established the French Communist Party. In reality everything was designed and done in Moscow. In France, the group of GPU's agents and emissaries was headed by the native Austro-Hungarian, Eugene Freed. Degot, Sokolovsky, and Anna Pauker at the time Rabinovich, were members of the group. The documents, decoded instructions, and texts of the reports from the archive of the CPSU listed all these names. The group spared no expense to recruit the French agents and in accordance with Moscow assigned them as the leaders of the French Communist Party. The group had never worked openly—always disguised, staying in a shadow."

Considering the recent murders of journalists in Russia, I cannot disclose the name of the author who wrote the mentioned above quotations. However, I can give you the names of the authors who practically told the same story taking place in another part of the world, in China. I am doing that to enlighten you with the information from the twentieth century to better understand what is going on around the world now in the twenty-first century.

So, if during Lenin's time the recruitment and infiltration into the foreign governments had started, it had quadrupled under Stalin. His ferocious appetite for real world revolution and the enormous scale of the Communist's expansion he undertook should frighten any decent individual in the globe today.

Of course I knew that Stalin had helped Mao and Communist China to defeat Chiang-Kai-shek and his Nationalist force, but I did not know how it had been done. I learned it and you should also know it to grasp the reality of the twenty-first century. For this reason, in our discussion, I am going to use a lot of words and several quotations from the book titled: *Mao: The Unknown Story* by Jung Chang and Jon Halliday. It is a monumental study, an enormous volume of thorough historical research and an account of the Chinese Communist Party and its leader Mao-Tse-tung. We will analyze the text in details. The long list of people inside and outside China interviewed for the book is a good sign of the book's authenticity. There is no more voluble information than the observation of the people who lived their life through the events described. Look at this.

"The idea of forming this Communist Party did not stem from the professor, or from any other Chinese. It originated in Moscow. In 1919, the new Soviet government had set up The Communist International, the Comintern, to foment revolution and influence policy in Moscow's interest around the world. In August, Moscow launched a huge secret program of action and subversion for China, starting a commitment of money, men, and arms three decades long, which culminated in bringing the Communists under Mao to power in 1949—Soviet Russia's most lasting triumph in foreign policy."

To grasp the unique predicament in China in the beginning of the 1920s, it should be noted that the great upheaval was taking place ten years before in the country—China, the Empire for a thousand years has become a Republic. Those changes were going on in the background of the Japanese expansion holding Chinese territory. Even after the WWI settlement, Japan continued staying on the territory it had seized from Germany during the war. Many Chinese were disappointed in a Republican government, national sentiment infuriated. It was a time when political parties grew and expressed more radical solutions.

"The Nationalists' Party had been founded in 1912 by the merger of a number of Republican groups. Its leader was Sun Yat-sen,[43] who had briefly been the first provisional president of the Republic." But he lost his position and had been trying to overthrow the Peking government since then. This objective led Sun-Yat-sen to embrace Moscow. The Soviet government shared this goal of subverting the Peking government. Sun-Yat-sen wanted to establish an army with military material supplies from Russia. The Soviet Politburo gave full backing to the Nationalists with money and advisors. The decision was signed by Stalin, who had begun to take a close interest in China.

At the time, the Civil war between the Reds and the Whites in Russia was going on and by the 1920s the Bolsheviks took Central Siberia, the land which border China. The Comintern sent a representative to China, to set up the Communist Party. The other agent was reporting to Moscow that he was contacting "revolutionaries in various cities." Under Russia's supervision the Chinese Communist Party was founded in 1920 and Moscow's emissaries organized its first Congress.

To understand how easy the process of establishing the party was done, let me give you some ideas. The charter of the Communist Party was copied from the Soviet one. The actions are very simple. First you have to have three members of the party to establish a political cell—one Communist can recruit another two and you have an official Communist party cell. If it is a city, then the district unites all the cells. This way you have a District Communist Party Committee. Several districts could be amalgamated into the City Party Committee, then to Provinces or

Regions and then to the top. The Russian emissaries had organized all of that and the first and extremely important order had followed.

Though young and small, the Chinese Communist Party had received an assignment from Moscow—the Russian double-game had started. To be sure that Sun Yat-sen served Moscow's interests the Chinese Communists got an order to join the Nationalist Party. Stalin spelled out the design of that double-game in a secret session of the Politburo: "we cannot give directives out of here, Moscow, openly. We do this through the Communist Party of China and other comrades in camera, confidentially..." The Chinese Communist Party had been used by Moscow as a Trojan horse to manipulate the much bigger and older Nationalist Party.

Reading the book you will learn that at the time Mao was not a Communist, he was a radical romantic. Once, in the magazine *New Youth*, an advertisement was issued about the bookshop. He wrote: "There is no new culture in the entire world. Only a little flower of new culture has been discovered in Russia on the shores of the Arctic Ocean." Writing a letter to his friend in France, Mao expressed his admiration for Russia again. He declared that he "deeply agreed with the idea of using the Russian model to reform China and the world...when Moscow decided to set up an organization... called the Socialist Youth League, to create a pool of potential Party members, Mao was contacted to do the job." Hence, it was not a coincident.

In his love for Russia, Mao was not alone. The predicament can be easily explained: "For now, Communist Russia was actually in vogue....a Russian Study Society was being founded, with no less a personage than the county chief as its head. Russian popularity was in large due to a fraud perpetrated by the new Bolshevik government—the claim that it was renouncing the old Tsarist privileges and territory in China, when in fact it retained them. Russian-controlled territory covered over a quarter of a million acres, and constituted the largest foreign concession in the country." Those who know the patterns of the Soviet Power and the Soviet/Russian propaganda machine can immediately recognize them—their tentacles have maneuvered slowly but surely.

Do you remember the Soviet *Department of Agitation and Propaganda?* It was the most important part of the Communist's activities around the globe including China. To me propaganda is a system of influencing human emotions and Stalin had found the "best" ways to do that by inventing slogans and labels—false slogans and labels to create false impressions and brainwashed the public. In fact, false slogans and labels bring an illusion of morality and helped Stalin to spread his dogma. For example, the farmers had never been "the enemies of the people," on the contrary they had feed the country. But for political reasons Stalin had presented them as "the kulaks exploitators;" annihilated them all and destroyed Russian agriculture.

Something reminiscent to that had happened in China. Like Russia, China was an agricultural country with the peasantry in millions. Moscow had coached both the Chinese Nationalists and Communists in dealing with peasants: they must be coerced into doing things that left no way back into normal life to make compromises later with gentry and bourgeoisie. Fights emerged with the landlords and had started under the Nationalists: "But the landlords had always made sure that the social structure was preserved… as long as they were not caught in the crossfire. Now, because the Nationalists were following Russian instructions aimed at bringing about a Soviet-style revolution, social order broke down for the first time. Violence erupted…"

The Communists went further using the labels "the kulaks exploitators" and "the enemies of the people"—rural China was sinking in blood of "…the landed tyrants, bad gentry, landlords, capitalists, with no need to report to anyone…. The regime called on people to disembowel and slice off heads… slaughter on the spot with no hesitation. Have absolutely not a shred of feeling… kill, kill freely. To kill is the topmost important work in an uprising. Children were praised for automatically killing reactionaries. … One of the Russians had reported to Moscow that everything had been given over to fire and sword and people were shot right and left." Do you feel the Stalinist terror in China's air?

Mao was Stalin's diligent student. With time he had become a cruel and brutal leader of China. But he was not the same person I called a romantic radical in the beginning of his political career. An interesting episode from the beginning of his political education is presented by the authors of *The Unknown Story:* "When Mao first told the troops that they were about to become Mountain Lords— bandits—they were dumbfounded, that was not why they had joined a Communist revolution. But, speaking in the name of the Party, he assured them that they would be special bandits—part of an international revolution. Banditry was also their best chance, he argued: Mountain Lords have never been wiped out…" Reading it, I did not know whether to laugh or to cry. What a "wonderful" perspective for the World!

It did not take a lot of time for the diligent and zealous Chinese students to act the way their teachers taught them and exhibit the same brutality. I would like to give you an episode from *Mao: The Unknown Story.* As a matter of fact, the Chinese Communists who often were called the Reds had been trying to reach Russian- controlled borders in the North, in order to receive arms—an operation later known as "to link up with the Soviet Union." The Nationalist forces to prevent that pursued the Reds and forced them to retreat. Prepared for the evacuation, the Reds screened all proposed evacuees.

"Those rated unreliable were executed. They totaled thousands. Among those killed were most of the teachers in army school, who were often captured former Nationalist officers. The execution took place in a sealed-off mountain valley, where a huge pit was dug. The victims were hacked to death with knives, and their bodies kicked down into the pit. When this pit was full, the rest were made to dig their own holes in the ground, and were then hacked to death, or buried alive. The massacre was carried out by the state security system…" I believe that the Chinese state security system reminds us of the Soviet one.

As you can see, in its usual strategy Moscow has been infiltrating both contesting political forces; the Communists and the Nationalists. The Nationalist army had Russian advisors and there were several KGB stations in China. "With close Russian supervision, the new Nationalist authorities in Human gave peasant associations their blessing—and funding—and… the association had sprung up in much of the countryside in the province of 30 million people. The social order was turned upside down."

You should know that Stalin was personally dictating policy on China, especially after the split between the Communists and the Nationalists. It was Stalin who had ordered the Communists to form their own army and conquer China with the gun. "… the use of force to bring the Chinese Communists to power— had been Moscow's favored approach ever since the Commintern was founded in 1919. As long as the Nationalists were in play, Moscow's strategy had been for CCP (Chinese Communist Party) members to infiltrate and subvert the Nationalist armed forces. Once the break came, Stalin ordered the Communists to pull out those units they were able to control, and 'form some new corps." Nobody could compete with Stalin in the art of intrigues, perfidy, and treachery. All these "qualities" he implanted into the cadres of the agencies I discussed in the previous chapters. I would say that the authors of *Mao: The Unknown Story* has described it much better than I did. Judge for yourself, here it is: "Planting moles was one of the priceless gifts that Moscow bequeathed to the CCP. Mostly these moles joined the Nationalists in the first half of the 1920s, when Sun Yat-sen, who was courting the Russians, opened his party to the Communists. Infiltration worked on several levels. As well as overt Communists working inside the Nationalist movement, as Mao did, there were also secret Communists, and then a third group, those who had staged fake defections from the CCP." Please, remember this description—Soviet/Russian agencies had used the same methods and tactics on multiple levels around the globe.

Let me give you another crucial term invented by Stalin and his operatives that is extremely important in the twenty-first century. This term has been practiced in China since the 1920s. Do you remember three levels of the Soviet/Communist agents infiltrated into the Nationalist forces? Listen to the details and the consequences of the Soviet activities:

"When Chiang-Kai-shek split from the Communists in 1927, a large number of these secret agents stayed as 'SLEEPERS,' to be activated at the appropriate time. For the next twenty years and more, they were not only able to give the Reds crucial intelligence, they were often in a position to have a substantial influence on policy, as many had meanwhile risen very high in the Nationalist system. Ultimately, the agents played a gigantic role in helping deliver China to Mao." It is an incredible revelation for the understanding of politics in the twenty-first century. Of course I knew that infiltration aimed at destruction of an adversary from within, before reading this book. Yet the authors of *The Unknown Story* have exposed the mechanism of infiltration, which is inculcation of the moles to organize defeat, *to organize defeat from within.*

In my preceding chapters I had tried to describe the predicament inside Soviet Russia only and never mentioned the GRU: the Soviet/Russian military intelligence. As this chapter attempts to demonstrate the patterns of the Soviet infiltration outside Russia, I have to bring to light the GRU—(Chief Intelligence Management), Soviet Military Intelligence. Like the Cheka, the GRU was created by Lenin in 1918. Unlike the Cheka, the GRU had never changed its name, perhaps, because of the Soviet's main priority of secrecy, very few people knew of its existence. And so the GRU is Russia's largest intelligence agency, operating the residences all over the world. The name of the GRU came to light thanks to perestroika and the writings of the agents defected to the West. The GRU and the Cheka often cooperated. For your information, the GRU deploys six times as many agents in foreign countries as the successor of the KGB—SVR—Foreign Intelligence Service responsible for intelligence abroad. I have to go back in time for you to grasp the significance and scale of the Russian Intelligence abroad to organize defeat from within. Let me give you the story of Jacob Blumkin for that reason.

A young Jew from Odessa, Jacob Blumkin, was a member of the gang among other sixteen to eighteen-years-old boys like him in Russia seething with the Revolution of 1917. There is no doubt of his Socialist inclinations. Reading Blumkin's biography, I found him in Moscow as a member of the Cheka in 1918. Moreover, he was not a Bolshevik, but a Left Socialist Revolutionary—SR (Essers). "Blumkin, a nineteen-year-old youth, was the Cheka official deputized (by Dzerzhinsky) to guard the foreign representatives." *Give us the Head of Dzerzhinsky*, by David Tenner. On July 6, 1918 Jacob Blumkin assassinated the German Ambassador to Russia Count Mirbah. Blumkin did it as the Left-SR to discredit the Party. Besides the political intrigues within the new Bolshevik's government, the story reminds me of the communist techniques of infiltration into the Nationalist Party of China to organize defeat from within. But Chekist-Blumkin's story goes further....

After the assassination, Blumkin disappeared from Moscow and soon appeared with his gang in Azerbidgan, which was bordering Iran. Using political instability and agitating local people Blumkin had organized the Persian Soviet Socialist Republic in Iran—the Soviet Republic of Gilan in 1920. Blumkin's next location was Mongolia, and the movement for Mongolian independence from China had begun—Mongolia became independent in 1921. It took only three years and Mongolia became a Communist State in 1924. It is no coincidence that all Soviet security agencies called themselves the Chekists. Following Blumkin's biography and his activities as the official member of the Cheka, I found a close coordination between all of the security agencies. I also came to the conclusion that the creation of the Communist State in China had only been a part of a huge global master plan to CONTPOL and have POWER over all of South Asia. North Asia had already been under Soviet territory.

Now, when you are familiar with the cooperation between the major spy agencies, the GRU with the Cheka, let me tell you how the Red Army in China was established, by reading my main source *Mao: The Unknown Story*: "A huge secret military advice and support system for the Chinese Communists was set up in Russia. The GRU had men in all the main Chinese cities, providing arms, funds, and medicine, in addition to intelligence that was often critical to the CCP's survival, Moscow also sent top-level advisers to China to guide the Party's military operations, while greatly expanding military training for CCP cadres in Russia." That way the Chinese Red Army was established in 1927.

In all chapters, I am exposing a major modus operandi of Moscow—deep infiltration and control from within. I believe that the examples of events in France and China have clearly illustrated my point—Moscow's total supervision. I would say even more— in the Chinese's case it was a mere subordination to Moscow— the process of Sovietization was substantially speeding up. But infiltration was only one of the methods in the fight for global domination inextricably connected to the other one—the multiple levels of recruitments. One cannot exist without the other—*Mao: The Unknown Story* presents dozens of portrayals of the Soviet moles from all three levels infiltrating the Nationalist force.

I have to admit that Stalin and his operatives from the Commintern, mostly European Communists, had talent for spotting talented people. Paying close attention in forging the Soviet leadership, with no less persistence Stalin had forged the leadership of other Communist countries. You are familiar with the creation of the French Communist Party, the same story had happened in other countries and in China. One of the outstanding individuals was Chou En-lai —unquestionably Stalin's success!

"Tenacious and indefatigable, even impervious to cold, Chou was a good administrator and a brilliant organizer. Moscow spotted him, and gave him the crucial task of creating the Chinese Communist Party. … Chou's secret responsibility was to plant Communist agents among the higher ranks, with a view to taking over part of the Nationalist army when the time came—which he did… …His domain was vast: he set up the Chinese KGB, under Moscow's guidance, and ran its assassination squad. But organizing the Chinese Red Army was his main job. …He proved to be a genius at operating in clandestine conditions, as people who worked with him testify. ...Chou's loyalty, combined with undoubted ability, was the main reason Moscow picked him to be chief Party leader from 1928..."

I agree with every word they characterized Chou En-lai with. I have obtained identical information about him from other sources. Life proved his extraordinary ability as a political leader, he was also well known in the world and prime minister of China for a quarter of a century under Mao. I hope that he finally recognized the fraud of the Stalinist dogma in the 1970s and made possible cooperation with President Nixon. This split with Russia had been a landmark for China's history, enormously important for the entire world. Knowing the vindictiveness of the Soviet mentality, I would like to know the real cause of Chou-En-lai's death. The Soviet vindictiveness cost Richard Nixon the presidency. I hope World History will finally uncover the Kremlin's crime against both.

The defeated Chiang-Kai-shek had also been a victim of Stalinism—he lost his country and fled to Formosa. Unlike Chou-En-lai he did not trust the Soviets from the beginning, but cooperated with them in hopes of outwitting them. It was a very risky undertaking! He had underestimated the Soviets and paid a dear price. There is more similarity between Chiang-Kai-shek and Richard Nixon—both had been outwitted by the Soviets and destroyed. Unfortunately, the current American president does not know the history and is repeating the same mistake.

Dear Chris Matthews, there is good and evil in the world. Unfortunately, the virus of Socialism had infected your brain and the real world history of evil escaped it—you became immune to the truth. I believe I have proved my main point, exposing the real agenda and objectives of the Kremlin's government— achievement of world domination. But you are still immune to the truth. For others the issue is also complicated to grasp in its entirety, I need another chapter. As a matter of fact, the Soviet government had a two-fold strategy to achieve the objectives. One was aimed at the capitalist countries to weaken their system. The other was to help the Communist Party take over power and establish a Socialist/ Communist regime. Those who lived through the twentieth century would remember the major point of contest: which economy is more productive, the Socialist or the Capitalist one—the crux of the matter.

Hence the Stalinist fight against Capitalism had become a landmark of the Cold War and a substantial part of the twentieth century.

You have already been acquainted with some of the tools, methods, tactics, and tricks of Stalinism, but you do not know the entire script of the double-game yet. I will continue to acquaint you with it in the next chapters. But now, let me explain why I dedicated this chapter to Jimmy from Brooklyn.

I came to the United States in 1981. At the time, I knew a couple of English words and that was it. I couldn't construct an elementary sentence in English. Perhaps some of you know about the difficulties for newcomers in adjusting to a new country, new culture, and a new language. I was one of them. And to adjust to the world around me, I had to know the language. I studied English with diligence. In an attempt to absorb every bit of knowledge as quickly as possible, I drilled myself day and night. I stopped reading in Russian, and slept with the radio on, so the English words might enter my subconscious mind, but my mind seemed unable to absorb the language. Having always considered myself reasonably intelligent, I was profoundly frustrated at my inability to learn quickly.

Listening to the radio day and night, and enjoying the eloquence of the hosts, I had chosen two talk show men, Barry Farber and Bob Grant, for their incredibly vivid and rich English. What a pleasure they gave to me by their wonderful command of English—I enjoyed listening to them and… envied them a bit. One night I was awakened by an unfamiliar voice that delivered a brilliant speech against Chinese Communists, working throughout the world to undermine the United States. I was listening to the speaker perplexed—the American man knew the subject well and demonstrated the examples of the Soviet's and Chinese Communists' subversive activities in Chinatown, Manhattan, New York City—the city I lived in.

The man's knowledge had surprised me—an American was versed well in the Soviet strategy! Who is he, how does he know such important details? My pulse was rising as I listened to him—he knew even more than I about the events of subversive activities in America. At the end of his speech the host thanked the speaker, and acknowledged his deep interest in the subject. The host addressed the speaker as Jimmy from Brooklyn. The man called regularly to radio 77, WABC and every time he spoke I learned a lot from him. Jimmy from Brooklyn knew about subversive activities of the Kremlin as well. He hated Russian Communists and often exposed their longing for world domination. He is still very vocal at the radio station and I learn a lot from his monologues. The dedication to him is only a small token of gratitude to a man who has been tirelessly spreading the truth for the last twenty years— Jimmy from Brooklyn.

CHAPTER 6

Stalin and Mao—Friendship Forever

The Old Soviet slogan of the 1950s

The idea of Socialism is highly attractive and contagious as a virus for those who do not know Socialism and admire it. That is the reason I spent time analyzing the masterpiece of contemporary historical research in the development of the Chinese Communist Party—*Mao: The Unknown Story.* It is a monumental work that exposes the core of the Communist ideology, its modus operandi, tools, methods, devises, and techniques, a textbook of the entire system that was designed for teaching and coaching how to cheat, deceit, and indoctrinate human psyche, regardless of nationality, race, religion, or ethnicity—all of that for world domination.

That is why I analyzed the material in such detail. I do not know another book that gives us such a broad historical landscape of the ideology from its inception to successful development throughout the world. I had been writing about the policy of infiltration and recruitment in all my articles, but the book *Mao: The Unknown Story* had given us brilliant images and terms to conceive and memorize forever. The first one is *The Trojan Horse.* These three words delineate activities that are always associated with deception, tricks, fraud, and death. And this is the essence of the Communist Ideology and Socialism invented by Stalin. I express my sincere gratitude to the authors of the remarkable study *Mao: The Unknown Story.* Constantly writing about the Soviet/Russian modus operandi I never used that basic term *The Trojan Horse.* Alas!

Another term is no less significant than the first one. In my earliest articles I had already used a term "sleeper cells" in regards to the terrorist plot in Buffalo, New York. I knew those sleeper cells also existed in Europe and both Americas. I did not know that they had been around in China since the 1920s—a remarkable story. When Chiang-Kai-shek broke with the Communist Party, "a large number of these secret agents stayed as sleepers to be activated at an appropriate time." The Soviet script of infiltration had never been changed. I would like to remind you that analogous policy for victory in the Russian Revolution was undertaken by Lenin[46] in his master plan—small political units were spread throughout Russia, their name—*the Soviets.* They played a major role in Russian defeat during WWI organized by the Bolsheviks and in victory during the Bolshevik Revolution of 1917 in Russia.

The book gave us the third term with an image to remember, especially today in the year 2007. It is the term of the new Communists' forces characterized in the 1920s by Mao as "special bandits—a part of international revolution." There are two main elements or factors in the sentence to consider: First is "special bandits" that symbolizes violence, and the second is "international revolution," which speaks for itself and identifies Mao's thought process. In other words it simple means—world domination with application of force—Moscow's school of thought. As we are watching the world today, both of these elements are at play on all continents of the globe. And that condition of the world forces me to present my explanation of the predicament.

To do that, I would like to go first to the time of World War II and the situation in Asia. As I have already mentioned Stalin was offended by President Truman and hated him. If fragile and frail President Roosevelt, a partner in WWII, appeased Stalin's ambitions, President Truman acted the opposite way. He dropped the atomic bomb to end the war and deprived Stalin of having half of the Japanese territory—the symbol of Stalinism—division. Vindictive Stalin could not forgive him. In 1945, WWII ended for all decent people in the world, but not for Stalin. He had in mind his *second front—Asia.* China was close to establishing the Communist State and Stalin viewed Asia as a strategic region of paramount importance for global domination.

Stalin's *second front* meant a war, and considering the Asian military theater, a war against America. You have to know Stalin's character to conceive the meaning of the war designed by him. That war meant using all possible tools, manners, and methods. Besides military forces, it meant sophisticated deception, tricks, hoaxes, and a variety of techniques—nobody could compete with Stalin in the art of intrigues and perfidy. Those who think that Winston Churchill's speech in Fulton started the Cold War are mistaken. Before his speech in 1946, the Soviet *Department of Agitation and Propaganda* had launched a familiar three words, a symbol of the Cold War, *The American Imperialism.* It should be noted that if in the 1930s an anti-Western propaganda was directed against England, France, and America, after WWII it was primarily the anti-American one.

After WWII, a defeated Japan left a political vacuum in Korea, and Stalin used it. Korean Army was formed, trained, and equipped to the teeth with Soviet arms, and supervised by the KGB's advisers, and sent to implement the Communist regime in North Korea. Stalin personally chose its leader, a captain of the Soviet Army and former policemen, Kim-Il-sung. Under his leadership the Stalinist regime was implemented in North Korea and the process of Sovietization completed later on. Like defeated Germany, Korea was also divided into two occupation zones, the Russians north and the Americans south on the line along the 38th parallel in 1945. The policy of division is a landmark of Soviet Fascism.

Though, by mid-1949 all Soviet and American troops had been withdrawn from Korea, Stalin's vindictiveness had no barrier. "The Soviet general Staff worked out the plan for aggression in 1950, and the Soviets fully participated in the Korean War." That information had been revealed by one of the Soviet generals participating in the Korean War in his speech in Seoul in 1992. It should be noted that the connection between the Soviet military, the KGB, and North Korea had never ended since Kim-Il-sung came to power in 1945.

So by 1950 both China and North Korea represented two Stalinist states as the carbon copies of their Soviet precursors. The social infrastructure, especially judicial and legal systems, in their regulation of population, labor and housing allocations, mirror the Soviet state with striking similarity. In Communist Vietnam and Cambodia, the same scenario of Sovietization was repeated later. Controlled by Moscow, all these countries were built by Stalinist political troops on three main pillars: a strong leader supported by omnipotent party apparatus and security forces—the Formula for Power with no personal accountability.

It was not only Stalin's vindictiveness, but a combination with sinister aggressiveness for world domination—a clear political motivation. Because Stalin's further destabilization of non- Communist Asian countries proceeded in a systematic manner with a diversified policy, the Communist or Marxist insurgency in the Philippines and Indonesia became infiltrated with Soviet intelligence agents into the business and government institutions in India, Japan, Indonesia, and so on. In two decades, Stalin's *second front* "achieved" a great deal. Do not be surprised by brutality and an exceptional cruelty in the countries discussed above, just recall the Cheka.

To give you a more descriptive characteristic of Stalin's *second front*, I have to return to The Unknown Story. A top French adviser in Indochina had described it in these words: "... the Russians are looking for one billion human beings, human beings from Asia, a sort of human livestock, to get them to fight the West." As you can see, the idea and threat of war in Europe visited several officers. A French adviser was not alone; Major General Barr had a similar view: "... the Russians could organize a Chinese division and take it over to Germany or in that area... I am afraid that idea would appeal to some of the Chinese Communists."

There were other American officials giving strong warnings. The head of the U.S. mission in Yenan had opened his final report with a three-word alarm: "Communism is International!" Our ambassador in Moscow, Averill Harriman, felt that Marshall was not sufficiently aware of the "Russian danger." I could have given you many other words of well-informed and competent people to prove my point, but unfortunately, there were even more Americans ill-informed and unaware of the "Russian danger." Just read the conclusion of the authors of *The Unknown Story* in this respect:

""The Moscow-Mao double act deceived many into suggesting for decades that Mao could have been won over by the U.S., and that the U.S. had lost the chance to detach Mao from the Soviet camp. In fact, in secret, Mao always told his Party that the friendliness towards America "is only a tactic of expedience in our struggle against Chiang."" This quotation I took from the chapter titled *Saved by Washington of The Unknown Story.* I would say the Red's deception had saved Communist China.

The book is such a rich source of information that it helps me to prove the ideas I had expressed and discussed in my earliest chapters.

I did not know anything about George Marshall, except the fact that he was the author of the *Marshall Plan. The Unknown Story* gave me additional data. President Truman had understood that the civil war in China should be stopped. Yet he did not have a clear picture of who was who. The Moscow-Mao deception act was in progress and Mao even floated the idea to change the name of the Party "of calling it not 'Communist' but something else. Then the situation… will be more favorable, especially with the Americans… Molotov[49] fed the same line to Roosevelt's then special envoy to China."

So President Truman sent America's top general, George Marshall, to China. As a matter of fact, Marshall knew China because he served in China in the 1920s. He did not like Chiang-Kai-shek because of the corruption of his relatives and "was susceptible to CCP claims that it and the N.S. had a lot in common." Chou-En-lai had charmed Marshall by telling him that "the CCP desired a democracy based … on the American style." Later on, Chou-En-lai told Marshall that Chairman Mao preferred America to Russia. Marshall had no idea of Mao's relationship with Stalin. He told Chiang-Kai-shek in December 1945: "it was very important to determine whether or not the Russian Government was in contact with and was advising the Chinese Communist party." This unawareness borders incompetence! And there is something even more dangerous.

Listen to this: In February 1948, being a Secretary of State, George Marshall told the U.S. Congress that "in China we have no concrete evidence that the Communist army is supported by Communists from the outside." This is more than incompetence, it is ignorance! The Pentagon and State department had a strong disagreement with Marshall's opinion. Now we have to admit that Averill Harriman had been right when he felt that Marshall was not sufficiently aware of the "Russian danger." As usual Mr. Harriman expressed his feeling very politely, considering the upcoming danger for the National Security of America.

While rolling towards victory, Communist China and Moscow had another diabolic plan for aggression. Though the personal relationship between Stalin and Mao was not always a good one, the fear and hate of America, common drive for expansion and desire for world domination had united them. You have to read *Mao: The Unknown Story* to see how scrupulously and diligently they had planned and prepared for the war in Korea in the words of a Commander, of the Soviet Air Force in Korean War, Lt. General Georgiy Lobov. "So it was that out of the global ambitions of the two Communist tyrants, Stalin and Mao… China was hurled into the inferno of the Korean War on 19 October 1950…" I would say even more: The old slogan *Proletariat of the World Unite* has been changed to *The Left of the World Unite Against America and the West!* It was the beginning of WWIII. Read *The Russian Factor* for the details.

I am trying to maintain the chronology of the world events and *Mao: The Unknown Story* has helped me enormously. North Korea was only the first step for the two tyrants in their Asian expansion. In 1950, Mao was in Moscow and discussed another topic with Stalin—Vietnam. As a matter of fact, Ho Chi Min had lived in China for a decade and spoke fluent Chinese. Mao had been training, arming, and funding Ho. The design for Communist Vietnam had been communicated and decided in Moscow. But Russia did not have a common frontier with Vietnam which made it difficult for Stalin to command from afar. China had the border with Vietnam and Stalin gave Mao custody of Vietnam, passing on to China the enormous expense of sustaining the Indochina insurgences.

China had become the Asian outpost for infiltration of Japan, Indonesia, Pakistan, and Malaysia and for igniting violent insurrections abroad. Reading *Mao: The Unknown Story*, you will find Mao's design for infiltration of these countries which was the carbon copy of Stalin's secret, intimate relationship with Communist China before the country had been conquered. Interviewing the head of the Japanese Communist Party at the time, Kenji Miyamoto, the authors of the book give us Mao's instruction to him: "Whenever there is a chance to seize power, you must rise up in armed struggle." That same instruction was given to the Communist Party of Indonesia—PKI, the largest one in Asia, with some 3.5 million members. In addition to that, China, Vietnam, and the Laotian Communists had coordinated military strategy in Indonesia with the war in Indochina. "Mao tried to ignite violent insurrections wherever he could."

I have found something even more stunning in the book: "In 1965, China began talking about transferring nuclear know-how to Pakistan—or more accurately, dangling the prospect. Pakistan had grown more and more useful to Mao as a staging post to the Middle East, and Peking aggressively backed Pakistan's ambitions over Kashmir, training Kashmiri guerrillas for what China presented as a 'national liberation' war." Wow! Please, read it again slowly, analyze and compare it with the events that have happened since. You will find how the fraud of the Communist ideology has been spread throughout the Asian continent and its inextricable connection with the Middle East of 2007. If you look back on the world hot spots, many of them were so-called "National Liberation Wars." In fact, all those wars around the globe had been waged by the Communists to take power away from the legitimate governments.

After reading about Mao's interest to Pakistan, I have another even more intriguing issue for you to research. While discussing the source of nuclear bombs in Pakistan a few years ago and knowing the Soviet style of dealing within the world, I have doubts about A.Q. Khan's ability to be a provider of the nuclear design. Now, after reading Mao's interest in Pakistan in 1964 and his inextricable connection to Moscow, I am sure of the source—it is Moscow again. I have to leave the research of the matter to the experts of our intelligence in the Pentagon. My suggestion would be the following: 1. Look closely at the Bhutto government and corruption within it. 2. Research the connection of A.Q. Khan with Moscow, Peking, or North Korea. 3. Corruption is one of the devices in the mechanism of infiltration used by the Soviet/ Russian intelligence.

Please, remember the *Organs* and, the Cheka's DNA, its genes and chromosomes passed to all Soviet satellites. Perhaps China was the first one working hand in hand with the KGB and GRU, while the world had been deceived and unaware of that criminal cooperation aimed against Western civilization. Please, also remember that the Cheka is not the only agency which had been copied by China—the entire Soviet Socialist system, with all its DNA, genes, and chromosomes had been copied by China. The authors of Mao: The Unknown Story are making this issue the cornerstone of the book—its sine quo none!

You would not believe it, but the idea to make China a superpower came to Mao's mind very early after the establishing of the Communist State. My impression is that the major cause of that was Mao's desire to be freed from Stalin and after his death from the Soviet tutelage-patronage. The diplomatic arguments between Moscow and Peking started in the 1960s. They soon turned into small clashes. There had especially been many clashes along the 7,000-kilometers of Sino-Soviet border. I knew about one big collision on the island Damansky. In 1970, my friend returned and said that hundreds of Chinese people were killed by the Russian artillery on Damansky Island. I believe that Mao has never trusted the Soviets since.

Mao definitely was not an ordinary man—a prolific reader and journalist, he was well versed in world history, philosophy and knew very well the culture of his native China. Due to the unpredictable historical tapestry or cacophony of events and a will of others, particularly Stalin, Mao has become "Chairman Mao." It was his fate to be at the crossroad of a transformed Asia and the world. Reading Mao: The Unknown Story, you will agree with me. Of course, Mao himself tried to make it possible, but the circumstances put him in the position of second violin—Stalin was the first.

Knowledge of Soviet History has helped me to arrive at the conclusion. Reading Mao: The Unknown Story helped me to compare Soviet and Chinese History. You will see in the book the progress of events and the ideas that were realized during decades of the Chinese Communist development. It was not Mao who found Stalin. On the contrary, it was Stalin who was coaching Mao, shaping his mentality, and supervising all the activities within the Chinese Communist Party for several decades. Stalin had made Mao Chairman Mao. Just recall the events in the beginning of the Socialist Revolution in Russia and compare them to what *The Unknown Story* narrates in the incredible details of Chinese history during the first decades of Communist development. Not only the events, but the methods, arrangements, techniques, and the entire modus operandi are identical!

Do you remember Stalin's man-made starvation causing the death of millions in Ukraine and Central Russia? The same happened in China with millions perishing. Do you remember the terror and purges in the Stalinist Soviet Union? The same happened in China where millions of innocent people died. The influence of the Soviet Union and their leaders was unquestionable in all respects. When you read *Mao: The Unknown Story*, it is hard to find a page where Moscow, Russia, or Russians is not mentioned. The ideological impulse has been transferred in its fullest capacity. The world knows the Soviet military expansion; however, there was an ideological expansion implemented by the Stalinist *Department of Agitation and Propaganda*. The connection of teachers and students is the crux of the matter of the twentieth century—an ideological historical pattern. I called this precedent a *diabolic ideological expansion—Stalinism*, a Socialist arrangement designed by Stalin. He had never been a Marxist; he just used the Manifesto's terms Communist or Socialist model to cover up his ideology of Stalinism. Both terms, adjectives, which are highly used in political literature and print, present a clear Stalinist fraud that has nothing to do with Marxism. People were lost in the jungle of political jargon, yet fraud remains fraud. I have already researched the issue in my book *Baltic Winds: Testimony of A Soviet Attorney,* in the chapter *The Fraud of the Century.*

Let me give you an example of a *diabolic ideological expansion* within Stalin's *second front.* As you know, Stalin made Mao a custodian of Vietnam, during their meeting in Moscow in 1950, and Mao had become a real Stalin's heir within Indochina later on. This is Mao's quotation from the assignment and order to the Vietnamese in 1964: "Don't be afraid of U.S. intervention... at most, it's no worse than having another Korean War. The Chinese army is prepared, and if America takes the risk of attacking North Vietnam, the Chinese army will march in at once. Our troops want a war now." He also asked the Vietnamese to escalate fighting in the countries neighboring China like Laos and Thailand. This speech was very familiar to me: aggressiveness and defiance, instigation of war and hostility to America. Mao just reflected the speech of his mentor—Stalin. This is the best example of *diabolic ideological expansion!*

As s child, I heard many of Stalin's hateful speeches and they deeply affected me and increased my love for him. Stalin spoke very slowly, his tone monotonous without emotion voice, he had an accent, but Stalin's ability to communicate was so impressive that the country's heart sank listening to him. Even after WWII his speeches carried on an incredible sense of truthfulness, protection, a call for vigilance, justice, and hate against our enemy. Those speeches stayed with me every day of my life. It took many years for me to grasp mentally the reality of the predicament I lived in and Stalin's propaganda intertwined with emotions to brainwash the youth of the country. As an experienced lawyer I came to the conclusion that it was an aggressive medieval intolerance, turned into action throughout the world later on.

Stalin once said that the Soviet people were the little screws of a big machine called the State. The Soviet Socialist State had always been a priority over the people. The Soviet propaganda had been constantly developed during the decades. Regardless of nationality, all Soviet people were fed with a special package of ideological phraseology, labels, and symbols sitting firmly in our brains even today. *A diabolical mental expansion* was the well constructed ideological weaponry, which besides us, has wounded millions throughout the globe—the second most effective after military expansion or the tactic of infiltration. Just look at the world in 2007…

Mao has been one of Stalin's first students since the 1920s— quite a term! Reading the book about China I compared the Chinese political environment with the Soviet one, and found that Mao was a very diligent student—he had built China copying the Soviet Union completely. I have already written about Stalin's *Formula for Power*, before I read the book. Now I am delighted to have confirmation of my ideas from the Chinese authors. Reading further I found even more information about Mao's aggressive poster so peculiar to Stalin's and the Soviet lexicon. Another order to the Vietnamese urged them "to help build up a guerrilla army in Thailand, where America had military bases." Mao's words in 1964 had echoed those exact methods of the global instability in 2007.

The term *guerrilla* army, mentioned by Mao, deserves detailed discussion. It was not him who invented the term; please remember that he was surrounded by the Soviet military experts in his war against the Nationalists forces for several decades. Though the *guerrilla* war has a history of many centuries back, only in the modern time was it called *guerrilla* war and identified as the operations of terrorists, insurgent or revolutionary groups. Reading *The Unknown Story,* I have met the events and tactics of revolutionary groups familiar to me from Soviet/Russian History. Practically, the Soviet/Russian experiences had been completely transferred to the development of the Chinese Communist State, Communist Vietnam and later on even further—around the globe. Listen to Mao's theory in his fight against the Nationalist forces presented by Wikipedia: "Mao Zedong, during the Chinese Civil War, summarized the People's Liberation Army's principles of warfare in the following points for his troops: *The enemy advances, we retreat. The enemy camps, we harass. The enemy tires, we attack. The enemy retreats, we pursue.* Guerrilla Warfare… (was) part of an integrated continuum aiming towards a final objective.

…Mao's seminal work On *Guerrilla Warfare* has been widely distributed and applied, successfully in Vietnam, under military leader… closely follows the Maoist three-stage approach." I would like to repeat again that Mao's initial knowledge came from the Soviet/Russian military experts. It is another example of Stalinist *diabolic ideological expansion.*

All Soviet/Russian immigrants know well the term *guerrilla war*, a war inside the enemy's territory, insurgency. In Russian it is called the *Partisan's War*—a predominant notion of Russian History. There are, however, some differences in the Russian approach to guerrilla war before the Revolution of 1917 and that of the Soviet time. Russian pre-revolutionary culture, its literature, poetry, and even music were full with glorification of the Partisans. Russian composer Ivan Glinka has written the opera *Life for the Tsar,* glorifying an ordinary peasant Ivan Susanin in 1812, who had brought the enemy squadron to the dense forest and refused to show them the way out. We see the wrath of the ordinary people and their typical Russian response.

This is how Wikipedia describes Napoleon's invasion of Russia in 1812 as another pre-revolutionary event: "…two actions could be seen as initiating guerrilla tactics. The burning of Moscow after it had been occupied by Napoleon's Grand Army, depriving the French of shelter in the city, resembled guerrilla action insofar as it was an attack on the available resources rather than directly on the troops. …In a different sense, the imperial command that the Russian serfs should attack the French resembled guerrilla tactics in its reliance on the Partisans rather than on army regulars. This did not so much spark a guerrilla war as encourage a revengeful slaughter of French deserters by Russian peasants." Pay attention to the words "a revengeful slaughter" by Russian peasants—it is a cultural feature of the Russian population. That exact events took place in Soviet Russia one hundred years later during WWII.

The difference in methods, structure, and command, however, was drastic. By WWII, the Soviet government had already has quite an experience in the war of the *Reds* against the *Whites*, where the Soviet intelligence and security forces had played major roles. The *Whites* had been defeated with the active role of the Stalinist Cheka and its brutal methods. That exact structure has remained during WWII. All the activities of the *Soviet Partisans*[51] inside the enemy's territory had been coordinated and supervised by the Soviet/Russian military intelligence. The Partisan's War was massively organized throughout the entire European part of the Soviet Union, occupied by the German Army. (The term the Soviet Partisans has a unique historic meaning, which is foreign to other languages.)

Due to closed supervision by the military intelligence, the Partisans had often been used in the offensive operations together with arm forces, especially in the second part of WWII. Their everyday activities were well known: ambush the Germans, sabotage in many different forms, explosions of bridges and derailment of trains, arson, and small-scale confrontations. However, the most important operations under the military intelligence were that of gathering information for the Soviet armed forces and intensive propaganda campaigns. Knowing the *Department of Agitation and Propaganda* you can recall all their methods of operation.

The Partisans had been one of the contributing forces in the Nazis' defeat. And that was acknowledged by the German military experts. Considering all Stalin's mistakes before the war and during it, the Partisan's War in Belarus, Ukraine, and other regions of the Soviet Union played a significant role in the victory over Germany. Look at the old Soviet movies showing how the Partisans derailed trains, blew up buildings, and damaged planes on the ground. Don't you see a similarity between the Partisan's actions in the twentieth century with the activities of the insurgency in Iraq and Afghanistan in the twenty-first century? I do.

Another factor in the victory of WWII was the variety of American help. After the end of WWII, Stalin and the Soviet officialdom had forgotten all American help and started projecting the image of America as *The Imperialist America-the enemy.* That change reflects Mao's thinking as well—the teachers were continuing to share their fighting experiences with their student- associates in China through the Soviet military expert. Whatever differences between the Partisan's War of the nineteenth century and twentieth century both had been wars of liberation from the aggressors Napoleon or the Nazis.

After the end of the WWII, the Soviet officialdom resumed its AGGRESSIVE power around the world, which began in the 1920s. Besides known infiltration in France, building of the French Communist Party, participation of the Soviet intelligence and its military advisors in Spain added to a lot of unnecessary death in the 1930s, *The Russian Factor*, pp. 93-94. After Spain it was the *North War* against peaceful neighbor Finland waged by Stalin to conquer the territory in 1939. Yet the major aggression took place against three small Baltic Republics, they were occupied by the Soviets as a result of the Stalin-Hitler Pact just before WWII. After the war, Stalin returned to his usual hostile and aggressive policy towards the entire world of capitalism—infiltration, killing, and vandalism.

If you remember, I took this excursion to the past for a reason—to prove my point that while writing his *On Guerrilla Warfare;* Mao used knowledge received from his teachers, the Soviet military intelligence. His three-stage approach was widely used in the Vietnam War by Viet Cong. Let me give you what Wikipedia says once more to prove my point: "Guerrilla tactics are based on intelligence, ambush, deception, sabotage, and espionage, undermining an authority through long, low-intensity confrontation. It can be quite successful against an unpopular foreign or local regime, as demonstrated by the Vietnam conflict..." In both my books since the 1980s I have tried to describe the Soviet/Russian supervision of the war within Indochina...

There is another issue to show you the major role of the Soviet military intelligence in WWII, and the illegal methods implemented by them. Let me give you one very notable example for our future. And again, we have to make an excursion to the past. Have you ever heard the name Raoul Wallenberg?[52] He was a real hero during WWII—he had saved thousands of Jews and people of other religions from the Nazis. A famous Swede, he had been working under the noses of Nazis in Budapest and other cities helping people to escape. His activities cannot be called anything other than heroic. The entire world was grateful to him for his courage and bravery. As soon as the Soviet Army entered Budapest in 1945, Raoul Wallenberg disappeared! He was kidnapped by the Soviet intelligence. For many years nobody knew his fate.

Immigrating to the U.S. in 1981, I by chance came upon material explaining at least where and how Raoul Wallenberg died. And this is another story connecting us again with the Soviet intelligence. In 1946, the man named Victor Abakumov was appointed head of the ministry for State Security—the MGB, a precursor of the KGB. "Abakumov was a notoriously brutal Chekist who tortured people with his own hands." PWHCE. He had worked under the general supervision of Beria. After Stalin's death in March 1953, Beria was overthrown; Abakumov was charged and tried for his role in the case known as the *Leningrad Affair* and executed in December 1954. I have read a protocol of his interrogation and there he mentioned Raoul Wallenberg. Abakumov alleged that Raoul Wallenberg died of a heart attack in 1953. A small footnote: The NKVD, MGB, and KGB had practiced the injections, which were provoking heart attacks. This story can show you the face of Russia today, run by the heirs of the Checka and KGB, the contemporary FSB.

Telling you the story of Raoul Wallenberg, I thought that he was the first victim of modern kidnapping. I was wrong. Reading *Mao: The Unknown Story*, I have found that the son of Chiang-Kai-shek was kidnapped by the Soviets a decade earlier and lived in the Soviet Union. Maybe that was the reason Chiang-Kai-shek could not break up with the Soviets. To illustrate modern kidnapping, I will give you another horrific event. The Italian Prime Minister Aldo Morro was kidnapped by the Italian Red Brigades and later he was assassinated. The Red Brigades had been the military force of the Italian Communist Party. For your information 20 percent of the Italian police were Communists in the 1970s. I hope the issue of modern kidnapping and its origin is clear to you.

Now I would like to continue my acquaintance with the book that opened my eyes, I hope yours too. Stalin's *second front* in Asia was not the end of the Communist objectives. *Mao: The Unknown Story* has revealed other stunning information—the Communist's connection to Africa to establish a dominant role in the Third World! Research the biographies of the African leaders and you will find that all of them had primary connections with the Soviet Union, some educated there. I am wondering whether France knows who had instigated the revolt in Algeria. Or maybe the French Government knows who had attempted to assassinate President De Gaulle and destabilized the French Republic? General De Gaulle had saved France twice: first from the Nazis, then from the Communists by refusing to give them arms.

The partial answers to two questions asked above can be found reading *Mao: The Unknown Story.* I had known before that the Soviet Union infiltrated the African continent by many different ways: the heads of the states had been trained by the KGB in the Soviet facilities and had Soviet advisors; an enormous number of African students were studying in Soviet educational facilities, and so on. This subject was fully discussed in *The Russian Factor*. I had no idea of the Chinese leadership engaged in the same policy of infiltration into Africa. As I found out, the Chinese leadership, besides associates in Asia, had a close relationship with President Nasser of Egypt, Ben Bella of Algeria, Julius Nyerere of Tanzania, and many others. Therefore, despite some discord between China and the Soviet Union, we can conclude that both had the same final objectives—exporting the Communist ideology, furthering world domination.

If you read *The Russian Factor*, you are already familiar with the Soviet activities in Africa and the Middle East that began in the 1950s—the objectives to control natural resources, especially oil, of the two areas. Yasser Arafat had been recruited by the KGB in 1957 and since then the Middle East has been destabilized. President Nasser of Egypt had 20,000 Soviet military and intelligence advisors. With the help of the Communists in South Africa, the Soviets practically had influence on all countries of the African continent through the leaders educated in the Soviet Union and the Soviet advisors there. You also must be familiar with the Soviet design to obtain power in the countries rich with oil and other natural resources to suffocate the West. *The Russian Factor*: *From Cold War to Global Terrorism* has researched the issue in detail. I gave you an example of Zimbabwe, formerly Rhodesia. When you see what Soviet henchmen Mugabe has done to the country, you will grasp the scale of disaster in the entire continent of Africa. I can guarantee that if Mugabe loses in the up-coming election, he will never relinquish the power like his masters in Moscow. Watch him.

Africa was not the last destination for the Communist infiltration and invasion. And again, the Soviet Union initiated the policy and played the role of a leader in subverting the Latin America's governments. Mao also tried to be involved simultaneously with a fight against the Russians. *Mao: The Unknown Story* narrated an interesting episode illustrating Mao's attempt to outwit the Russians. "Castro described Mao as 'a shit,' and then went public in front of a large international audience… accusing Peking of applying economic pressure to try to lever him away from Moscow.…Mao called Castro 'a jackal and a wolf.' Mao had placed high hopes on Castro's colleague Chee Guevara. On Guevara's first visit to China, Mao demonstrated uncommon intimacy with him… fulsomely praising a pamphlet of his. …When Guevara returned to China in 1965, just before going off to try to launch guerilla ventures in Africa, and then Bolivia, Mao did not see him… But in the end, Mao could not get Guevara to take his side against the Russians… When Guevara was killed in 1967, Peking privately expressed delight."

It is obvious to me that the Soviet Union was the primary aggressor—China secondary. Stalin was the initial cold, calculated, predator-expansionist, Mao the follower not always successful. And this fact has compelled me to do something you could not expect from me. Reading *Mao: The unknown Story*, I was surprised by Mao's attitude to his alleged enemies at the end of his life. I interpret this change of heart based on my own experiences. You can say that I am not going to die from modesty comparing myself to Mao. I agree. However, nothing is more valuable in life than experience. And we share the life experiences of being deceived and fooled along with millions throughout the world. As I am not of Mao's statute, the circumstances for being deceived were different—I personally paid a dear price, millions others paid for Mao's mistakes.

The book I am researching, I took from the library and was supposed to return it in three weeks. But the book was so saturated with information that I prolonged the term four times. Reading and writing at the same time, I have ended the preceding chapter not knowing the circumstances surrounding Mao's death. It was my opinion that both President Nixon and Chiang-Kai-shek had been the targets and victims of Stalinism. Can you imagine my feelings when I read that Mao had drastically changed his attitude towards those two? It was not a coincidence. I believed Mao learned his lesson. Listen to this:

"Around the time of Chiang's funeral, Mao mourned the Generalissimo for an entire day, in private. On that day, Mao did not eat or speak. He had an eight-minute tape of stirring music played over and over again all day long to create a funeral atmosphere, while he beat time in his bed, wearing a solemn expression. The music was set specially for Mao to a twelfth-century poem, in which the writer bade farewell to a friend who bore an uncanny resemblance to Chiang—a patriotic high mandarin whose career ended tragically and unfulfilled, and who was being exiled to a remote part of China. The writer told his friend:

"You and I are men of history
No little men chattering about minor affairs!

"This was exactly how Mao felt towards Chiang. Days later, Mao rewrote the last two lines of the poem so that they read:

"Go, let go, my honored friend,
Do not look back.

"This change turned the poem into an unmistakable valediction. Mao was writing his own envoy to a fellow thwarted giant."

I do not want to comment on Mao's final action toward Chiang-Kai-shek. You can judge his conduct by yourself. The only thing I would like to remind you of is that after signing a list of 345 old Bolsheviks to be shot, Stalin went to see a movie. Do you see the difference between the two? Mao had changed his attitude towards President Nixon. Perhaps in the end of his life Mao grasped the Soviet treachery and recognized the victims. The above mentioned poem was re-recorded to music, and was one of the poems sung to Nixon, "When Mao brought the former U.S. president over to say personal goodbye. ...The state of mind led him to an extraordinary sense of fraternity with those who regarded as 'fallen kings' around the world. Top of the list was former U.S. president Richard Nixon, who had been forced from office by Watergate in August 1974. Time and again Mao went out of his way to proclaim his profound feelings for Nixon. Weeks after Nixon had been ejected from the White House, Mao asked Imelda Marcos... to pass on his good wishes and invitation to Nixon to revisit China."

It is incredible to read what Mao did to bring former president Nixon to China. "...in February 1976, Mao sent a Boeing 707 to Los Angeles for him, complete with the protocol chief of the Foreign Ministry, another unheard-of gesture. The fact that the plane ran the risk of being seized as collateral against U.S. assets expropriated in China was immaterial for Mao. When he saw Nixon again, Mao clinked teacups with him, and when Nixon took his leave, Mao struggled to the door, standing unaided, to see him off, looking melancholy. Mao had invited him to China for what was, in effect, a private farewell.

"...Nixon's daughter Julie and her husband David Eisenhower were given an astonishing welcome in December the following year. Mao told Julie: 'write to your father at once; tell him I miss him.' When Julie got back to America, Peking's envoy told her that Mao 'considers you part of his family'—a remark that was absolutely unique." Reading this brought tears to my eyes: it was a moment when Mao's Chinese cultural wisdom had triumphed over ideological injustice.

I have another issue to discuss in order to complete the portraits of Mao and Stalin. After Stalin's death there were several attempts by the remaining leaders to take over. Fortunately, only Beria and his henchmen were assassinated and three other Russian leaders run the country together for a while. The situation in 1991 was more serious—the young Russian Democracy was at stake. Do you remember the coup of Russian military and security against Yeltsin's government in August 1991? Stalinist Socialism has always fought to survive. Something similar to that took place in China—the system has its patterns. *The Gang of Four* was fighting the Alliance of Deng Xiaoping, Chou-En Lai, and Marshal Ye who tried to save China from stagnation and introduce a free market to the country.

As a matter of fact, Deng Xiaoping had been a founder and had started bringing forth his ideas of free market even some years earlier. He had never betrayed his ideas—even repressions and arrests of his relatives and his own arrest did not break him. He had even argued with Mao, and… won. "In April, after Mao returned to Peking, Deng gave Mao a piece of his mind… On May 3, in front of the Politburo… Mao said he had 'made a mistake.' This was an unprecedented climb-down…" Have you ever heard Stalin say, "I made a mistake?" Never! This is the difference between the two!

In the last year of Mao's life, Deng had confronted him many times and every time Deng was winning. Can you imagine anything reminiscent to that at the Soviet Politburo in Moscow during Stalin's time? Do not get me wrong—I am not defending Mao, I am just giving you information to find a proper stand Vis-à- Vis China in the twenty-first century.

To put it in appropriate historical context for China, I have to admit that the Soviets were not the only force guiding the building of Stalinism. The Chinese history played a role as well. We all know Confucius and wise and highly moral Confucianism with its system of "ethical precepts for the proper management of society." We also know the power of his smart and ethical sayings. Unfortunately, China had the dark side in its history which could have helped to shape unethical behavior.

For many decades Chinese military had been trying to invade Japan in the past. It sounds laughable in the twenty-first century, but the wooden floats or rafts were built to reach Japan and conquer it centuries ago. An Emperor of China once had a slogan, which can be translated close to "I want my people to have full stomachs and empty hearts." The slogan incredibly resembles Stalinism. Deng Xiaoping definitely belonged to the Confucius part of Chinese history. His legacy of implementing a free market economy had damaged the Stalinist economic stagnation in China and changed in some quarters the old Chinese/Stalinist mentality.

The events which happened at the end of his life resembled those of the Yeltsin demise. Yeltsin was sent to retirement by the old apparatus of the Chekists, who are holding power in Russia today. The Chinese Chekists did almost the same to Deng Xiaoping. Let me give you an example. Chou-En-lai died in April 1976 and popular protest broke out all over China, as a volcano erupted to express loathing for Mao's policies and to denounce the Cultural Revolution. In Peking, the enormous crowd filled Tiananmen Square to mourn Chou-En-lai. *The Gang of Four* was trying to disperse the demonstrators violently. "Even more amazing, in the heart of the capital crowds destroyed police vehicles broadcasting orders for them to clear the square."

The crowd set fire to the headquarters of the militia who were organized by *The Gang of Four* with much bloodshed. It was the first bloodshed in Tiananmen Square. At that time in 1976, Dang Xiaoping said that people have the right to express their feelings. During the events of 1989 in Tiananmen Square, the Chinese Chekists had spread false information about the bloodshed, alleging that it was Deng who gave the order to shoot students. I do not believe a word coming from the Chinese Chekists accusing Deng, besides, his mental capacity at the time left much to be desired. We have to understand the inside of the Chinese intentions and policy to act effectively in the future. For this reason I am trying to give you some pros and cons of their history.

The Olympic Games of 2008 will take place in China. I have already heard voices calling for boycotting them. It will not change the Chinese government. The only lesson from history we have gotten from President Nixon is that of detaching China from Russia. His policy has helped a leader like Deng Xiaoping to change China for the better. This is the only way to secure peace in the future. And knowledge of the pathological Stalinist system must be spread throughout the world to fight it successfully. Intelligent, hardworking Chinese people with high entrepreneurial spirits should be targeted as well—they have a horrifying national memory of the past and as soon as we revive that memory, we have a chance for success. Some of freedom-loving Chinese will tell us about the Olympic Games—to participate or to boycott them.

Meantime, the Russian government should be the focus of American Foreign Policy—exposing it we will lead the world to peace, collaborating with it we are doomed to destruction. I do not know how we can identify the current Chinese leaders, whether they are the heirs of Dang Xiaoping or the heirs of *The Gang of Four*. I am still sure that the Kremlin's influence has played and is playing a major role in the contemporary Chinese policy towards the West. It can be changed by exposing the Stalinist fraud. President Nixon was right trying to detach China from Russia and for many other reasons he was right, too—in the twenty-first century it is to detach China from Iran, Russia's front-man. I hope to explain my view in the next chapters.

CHAPTER 7

WWIII: Recruitments and Drugs, Infiltration and Assassinations

You perhaps noted that the words "spy" and "espionage" I seldom use. It does not mean that Russia stopped spying, on the contrary—business is booming. However, after the James Bond adventures known to everybody, a spy's craft has become romanticized. The reality of the Communist's agenda of world domination and WWIII requires different and more precise concepts as the war has no main frontline, but multiple fronts and franchises. With my ample knowledge, but limited vocabulary, I have chosen four essential terms: recruitments, infiltration, assassinations, and drugs to emphasize the Russian connection. Recruitments and infiltration, in this particular case, means destruction of the target from within. The world has been experiencing both for decades and you will realize it in the years to come. As Africa was not the last destination in the Communist's design, I would tell you another story about infiltration and something even more dangerous connected to it. Now it is the proper time to move to Europe and both Americas.

Sometimes the names of people and words identifying the objects can tell you many other different things, helping you to understand the big picture. When I immigrated to the United States, I did not know the language and to learn it, I listened to the radio day and night. The first surprise was that of listening to the Russian first names used in America. I found many Russian first names like Tanya and Natasha among the relatives of The Black Panthers. I was surprised but I did not pay attention to that. Later on, when I could understand the meaning of the reports in the radio, I became even more surprised.

As you know for example, the name of the car Jeep is one of the most popular in America. You hear this name often and are used to it. In Russia, almost the same car had another name and we, the Soviet people, were used to that name for decades. The Russian name of the car was Willis—almost a carbon copy of the Jeep, with another name. Willis was a car also widely used on roads with tough conditions. It was the time when America seriously started its fight with drugs—the war on drugs permeated media's headlines. Once, while listening to the radio, I heard an interview with two drug-trafficking gangsters from Columbia— they were talking about Willis. In the beginning, I was surprised how the Russian name could pop out in South America. Of course, I knew the Soviet tendency to infiltrate the bordering countries in Europe and Asia, but South America...! The more I listened and read, the more I learned.

In 1991, I got the information about the infiltration of South America by the Soviets in detail. It was a steady and substantial study-research cataloged and documented in a reputable and reliable book: *Red Cocaine*: *The Drugging of America, by Joseph D. Douglass Jr.*, Clarion House, 1990. Some of the facts presented in the book were familiar to me; however, the abundance of data and evidence, illustrated with documents, stunned me. It was a catalog of the crimes perpetrated by International Communism led by Moscow. The last page of the book was addressing the reader. It did not help. In my opinion the book was blocked from worldwide distribution by the force that is blocking my two books a decade later. Judge for yourself reading the Clarion House's address:

> Publisher's note from Red Cocaine
>
> When discussing the importance of what you are about to read, it is difficult not to sensationalize.
>
> The message of Red Cocaine is one of the most vital of our lifetime.
>
> It is no exaggeration to say that the lives of millions of people depend on whether sufficient attention is paid to the evidence revealed here.

> We at Clarion House are very pleased that Red Cocaine is the first work issued by our new publishing company. We intend for Clarion House to become a leading publisher of Americanist material, and we are proud to make such a significant start.
>
> For more information of what you might do to help reach others with the vital Information Red Cocaine contains, please see the last page of this book.

I immediately run to the last page. It was addressed to the reader and urged to act promptly. Can you imagine what I felt reading this call for survival? Discussing the book in the class, I found out that none of my students even heard about the book. And that raised a red flag. As an American citizen, I believe that an enemy force inside our country was responsible for blocking information about the material exposing the crimes committed by the Soviet Bloc countries. I hope you will agree with me in the end of this book.

So let's read and discuss what *Red Cocaine* has narrated for us. We will discuss and analyze information from *Red Cocaine*. As you already know, the Chinese Communist State had been built with major Soviet involvement and supervision. You would think that the Soviet/Russian Communists were so engaged and occupied by the Chinese case that they had no time for others. Wrong! In 1955, the Soviet leader Nikita Khrushchev gave the idea to the members of the Communist Party—drugs and narcotics trafficking should be viewed as a strategic operation that would directly weaken the enemy. "Accordingly, he ordered a joint military-civilian, Soviet- Czechoslovak study to examine the total effect of drug… on Western society; its effects on labor productivity, education, the military (the ultimate target at that time), and its use in support of the Soviet Bloc intelligence operations." WWIII was marching on through Europe to the West…

The effects of drugs were analyzed by scientists from the Soviet Academy of Sciences and the conclusions were that the drugs trafficking would be extremely effective and the most vulnerable countries would be the United States, Canada, France, and West Germany. This study was approved in 1955 by the Soviet Defense Council. It was the first formal Soviet decision to launch narcotics trafficking against the bourgeoisie and especially against the American capitalists:

"Soviet strategy for revolutionary war is a global strategy... narcotics strategy is a sub-component of this global strategy. ... First was the increased training of leaders for the revolutionary movements—the civilian, military, and intelligence cadres. The founding of Patrice Lumumba University in Moscow is an example of one of the early actions taken to modernize the Soviet revolutionary leadership training. The second step was the actual training of terrorists. Training for international terrorism actually began as 'fighters for liberation.'...The third step was international drug and narcotics trafficking. Drugs were incorporated into the revolutionary war strategy as a political and intelligence weapon to use against the bourgeois society and as a mechanism for recruiting agents of influence around the world."

Just listen to the rest of the quotation: "The fourth step was to infiltrate organized crime and, further, to establish Soviet Bloc sponsored and controlled organized crime syndicates throughout the world. The fifth step was to plan and prepare for sabotage throughout the whole world. The network for this activity was to be in place by 1972.. ...The decision on organized crime... was to be a global operation targeted against... the United States, along with France, Great Britain, Germany, and Italy... The main reason for infiltrating organized crime was... information on political corruption, money and business, international relations, drug trafficking, and counter-intelligence—was to be found in organized crime. ...A secondary reason was to use organized crime as a covert mechanism for distributing drugs." Wow!!!

As a matter of fact, I have already discussed the Soviet operation on drug trafficking in my first book: *Baltic Winds*: *Testimony of A Soviet Attorney.* At that time I discussed the Soviet and Cuban intelligences and their activities in cahoots with drug cartels drugging America. *Red Cocaine* described in detail the concealed operations of the Cuban DGI and the Soviet KGB, using a powerful drug syndicate in Colombia and Panama against America. I wrote the book in 1992 and for the first time I also gave the notion of Soviet Fascism in the 1990s. Certainly *Red Cocaine h*elped me to arrive to that conclusion. Now at the time of global terrorism, writing the third book, I have a duty to give the reader a detailed explanation of all the terms I used in my first two books and all the avenues the Soviets organized to drug America. *Red Cocaine* provides me with needed information and data.

In the Soviet operation of drugging America, besides Cubans, the central role was given to Czechoslovakia as well. The first plan was put into action in 1956; it instructed Czechoslovak strategic intelligence to infiltrate seventeen different organized crime groups including the Mafia in France, Italy, Austria, Latin America, and Germany. I have already mentioned that 20 percent of the Italian police were members of the communist party and the Italian Communist Party used them heavily in the infiltration operation. "These members helped the Soviet Bloc intelligence agents infiltrate the Mafia. War criminals, e.g. Germans were also coerced into assisting the Soviet Bloc agents in this endeavor, especially throughout Latin America."

You can ask why the leading role in the drugging operation had been given to Czechoslovakia. In my opinion it was not a coincidence—Czechoslovakia was the most industrial country of the Soviet Bloc in Europe. In both my books, I had warned that the Soviet application of drugs to prisoners started in the beginning of the 1950s. I met a person who was drugged in a Soviet Gulag, *Baltic Winds: Testimony of a Soviet Attorney*, chapter 18, "The Yellow Pills and a Message from Captured American Pilots." If you read the book you should remember my opinion on application of drugs to the American soldiers as well by the medical doctors from Czechoslovakia in the Korean War. *Red Cocaine* confirms it. "CIA concern about Soviet, Chinese, and North Korean use of LSD and other drugs in mind-bending experiments became real during the Korean War… during the late 1950s, a research program was undertaken to obtain data on the actual effect of different drugs on soldiers, which involved the use of Soviet soldiers as guinea pigs. As part of this research, an espionage program was initiated to penetrate Western medical and science centers, especially those of a military nature, to determine how much the West knew about the effects of drugs on people—particularly the effect on military combat-effectiveness…"

Let me add more to that information: In the book *Red Cocaine* there is serious research of the issue and answer to the role of the Czechoslovak research and doctors. During the studies the use of narcotics and drugs was recognized as a special dimension of chemical warfare and was formally added to military planning of Czechoslovakia as a part of chemical warfare research.

There were two civilian intelligence-managed training centers in Czechoslovakia; one on the border with Austria and another on the border with West Germany. Both centers were jointly planned by GRU (Soviet military intelligence) and its Czechoslovak counterpart, Zs. (Do you remember GRU's activities in China?) The following instruction from the Soviet Defense Council took place in 1959 0r 1960. There is no doubt that like in China the Soviets have the leading role, the execution was assigned to Czechoslovakia. Look at this instruction:

"Each course consisted of three months of intense training. While Marxism-Leninism indoctrination was present, thc cmphasis was strictly on the drug business. The Soviets provided the Czechoslovaks with a copy of the Soviet schedule and lesson plans, which Czechoslovaks copied. The course including instruction in:

> The nature of the drug business, type and quality;
> Means of production;
> Organization of distribution;
> Drug markets and buyers; Security;
> Infiltration of existing production networks;
> How to use the experience of intelligence networks;
> Communications within drug organizations;
> How to pass intelligence information; and
> How to recruit intelligence sources."

If we assume that each training center was the minimum size, the number of graduates would exceed 25,000 by 1990. But this is only the tip of the narcotic iceberg. Many other similar centers were established in the Soviet Union, Bulgaria, and East Germany. The students in the Czechoslovakia centers were predominantly from Latin America, Western Europe, Canada, Middle East, and the United States. Bulgaria handled the Middle East, Turkey, Afghanistan, Pakistan, Lebanon, and Syria. East Germany's focus was on Western Europe and Scandinavia.

"The graduates returned to their respective countries and applied their skills. Some built independent operations, other cooperated with ongoing operations. Those who deviated and attempted to 'change sides' were killed." There is information from a witness that two graduates from the Czechoslovak center were killed when they switched sides. More amusing information concerning the drug money would confirm again who is who: All earnings went to the Soviet Union directly and after that each intelligence service of the satellites performing the training was reimbursed. The study of Soviet intelligence concluded that U.S. intelligence and counter-intelligence were blind, which made the Soviet narcotics operation much easier.

Red Cocaine tells us another interesting story about how drug money was used for weapons and military supplies. The First Secretary of the Communist Party of El Salvador was told directly by the Czechoslovak official that in return for the weapons and military supplies, it was their responsibility to help the Czechoslovaks pay for the weapons through drugs. When the First Secretary responded that El Salvador had a limited market, but if it extended to the United States and Canada there would be no problem with money. The Czechoslovak official answered that the United States and Canada *were* the primary targets.

Czechoslovakia was a very active party in the narcotics enterprise; in addition to that, its capital, Prague, became a city where the KGB and GRU's handlers met with their agents working in the West. Czechoslovakia had another assignment to establish the same training centers in North Vietnam, North Korea, and Cuba. At the same time, the Soviet did everything possible to hide the narcotics operations from the West to avoid upsetting their strategy of peaceful coexistence—a usual Soviet policy of deceit, distortion, and defiance.

It was the Chief of the Soviet General Staff, Marshal Zakharov who said that Soviet intelligence had concluded that U.S. intelligence and counter-intelligence were blind. He was right— the U.S. and British intelligences were busy in Asia, watching narcotics trafficking activities through Thailand and Hong Kong, let alone China, known for its history of narcotics trafficking. There is the big picture of the entire globe before us—a globe under attack by the Soviets and the Communist Bloc countries—a confirmation of the communists established drug-trafficking networks of warfare against Western Civilization.

Red Cocaine is a truthful and brilliant book written in the 1980s which warns us about upcoming narcotics warfare with striking details and documentation. Its summary is equally impressive: "Narcotics, terrorism, and organized crime were coordinated and used together in a complementary fashion. Narcotics were used to destroy the society. Terrorism was used to destabilize the country and prepare the revolutionary situation. Organized crime was used to control the elite. All three were long-range strategic operations, and all three were incorporated into Soviet Bloc planning by 1956." Look at our world now fifty years later and you will find incredible "achievements" of the Soviet fatal design. *Red Cocaine* was a harbinger of our future and we missed it.

Yet, narcotics warfare was only a part of a more sinister and more enormous conspiracy against the entire Civilization. And again infiltration and recruitment were playing a major role. Though I do not like to violate the chronology of events, I want to give you some examples for your better understanding; therefore, I have to go a few years back. At Yalta Conference, Eastern Europe was practically given to the Soviets. Though Stalin had promised Roosevelt and Churchill a free election there, the Soviets as usual disregarded their promises and acted their usual way—they liquidated "disloyal" leaders.

The first victim, besides Poland itself, was Stanislaus Mikolayczik[57], a Polish Prime Minister in the Polish Government in exile at London. He held regular contact with the leaders of Polish resistance, who were regularly supplying the Allies with intelligence information about the Eastern Front, helping the Soviets to fight Nazis—the common enemy. Polish underground movement has provided information about the V-2 rocket to Britain and also been involved in the sabotage and destruction of the German supply trains and communication centers. It was the largest underground resistance army during WWII—300,000 patriotic men and women. Its name was the *Polish Home Army.* If you know about the revolt of the Jews in the Warsaw Ghetto in 1943, you know only a part of the Polish national tragedy. The other part of the tragedy is the destruction of the *Polish Home Army and the Warsaw Uprising*—usual Russian treachery....

In 1944, the Polish government in exile in London made a decision to increase armed fighting against the Nazis as they retreated under Soviet pressure. The Polish units and regiments within the occupied country fought dozens of battles with Germans, especially in the area close to the Eastern Front, helping the Soviets to beat German's resistance. But as soon as the Soviets captured the area they imprisoned Polish officers and soldiers then transported them to the camps in Russia. But nothing could stop the Polish people from fighting for their independence.

Knowing about the Soviet offensive on Warsaw, the Polish units attacked the Germans simultaneously in the entire city. The Nazis suffered considerable losses; almost the entire city of Warsaw was occupied by the Polish Army. After three days of battles, the Germans started a strong counter-offense using tanks and heavy artillery. Immediately after fighting started in Warsaw, the Soviets halted their offense and watched battles and the destruction of the city. For two months the betrayed and abandoned Poles fought the Nazis. Warsaw lay in ruins, 250,000 civilians that fought heroically were left without shelter, water, food, and no hope for outside intervention, while the Soviets calmly watched the Polish tragedy from the shore of the river Vistchula. Twenty thousand Polish soldiers and officers went to prisoner-of-war camps in Germany. Only when it was clear that the Warsaw Uprising was crashed by the Nazis, did the Soviets resume their move. They "liberated" the destroyed capital of Poland and Pole-witnesses of the tragedy.

Prime Minister Stanislaus Mikolayczyk, like many other Polls, could not forget the tragedy—he became an outspoken anti-communist. Retuning to Poland he joined the new Polish government as vice premier and the only center of opposition to the Communists and the Polish leaders, Socialist-stooges, trained by the Soviets within Russia during WWII. Then together with the Soviets they adopted the new procedure in the election of 1947, which resulted in Mikolajczyk defeat. To stay in Poland, under the Soviet-Socialist government was risky—the former Prime Minister fled to the United States. The Polish Home Army was no longer available to defend independence.

The Soviets became the masters of his Motherland-Poland. Can you imagine the inflictions left by the Soviet betrayal in the memory of the Polish psyche?

It definitely affected my psyche. If you read *The Russian Factor* you should know the story about my father—he hated Communists and called them "the bandits in power." Every night under his blanket, he listened to the BBC. He did not know that I was listening, too. Mikolajczyk story and the election of 1947 in Poland were discussed every night by the BBC. The name Mikolayczik was ingrained in my mind for the rest of my life…

Similar things happened in other countries of Eastern Europe as well. The situation in Czechoslovakia is another vivid example of the Soviet reign in Eastern Europe, showing the brutality, treachery, and crime they committed. In 1940, Germany occupied Czechoslovakia, a government-in-exile was established in Britain and Jan Masaryk was appointed Foreign Minister. He was a son of the first President of Czechoslovakia Tomas Masaryk and his American wife, Charlotte Garrigue. Jan Masaryk, well educated in Prague and the United States, made regular broadcasts over the BBC to occupied Czechoslovakia. After the liberation of his country, he remained Foreign Minister as part of a multi-party National Front government. In February 1948, Czechoslovakia was practically occupied by the Soviets and as a protest the non- communist members of the cabinet resigned from the government to force a new election.

They did not know the Soviets' tricks and acted as though they lived in an independent country. The Soviets seized the opportunity and formed a government under Communist Klement Gottwald. Masaryk remained Foreign Minister. At the time, he was reportedly planning to marry American writer Marcia Davenport. You know how Stalin forged the leadership in his country; due to a total subordination to Moscow, all communist governments of the Soviet Bloc were run from there. Masaryk had no chance to be Foreign Minister in Gottwald's cabinet, the Soviets hated him. In March 1948, Masaryk was found dead, dressed in his pajamas, in the courtyard of the Foreign Ministry Building below his bathroom window. The initial "investigation" stated that Masaryk had committed suicide by jumping out of the window. It is now commonly believed that he was murdered by the ascendant Communists. A Prague police report in 2004 claims that Masaryk was murdered. The highest-ranking Soviet Bloc intelligence defector, Lt. Gen. Ion Mihai Pacepa described his conversation with Nicolae Ceausescu who told him about "ten international leaders the Kremlin killed or tried to kill." Jan Masaryk was one of them. *The Kremlin's Killing Ways*, by Ion Mihai Pacepa,[59] *National Review Online*, November 28, 2006.

I knew many criminal deeds committed by the Soviet Communists and their KGB, yet my hair stood up when I read the essay. By the way the essay has a sub-title—*A Long Tradition Continues*. And that criminal tradition was described by the author as vividly and reliably as only a former highest-ranking member of the intelligence community could do. I did not know that it was a whole department responsible for assassinations abroad. And the revelation about Kennedy narrated so openly stunned me. ("Among the leaders of Moscow's satellites Intelligence services there were unanimous agreement that the KGB had been involved in the assassination of President Kennedy.") The second revelation was about an attempt by the Kremlin to poison Mao Zedong. Wow! Look at Mao's rise in power and his distrust of the Soviets. He was right. It is impossible to retell this report—you have to read it.

Sometime in the 1980s, in my first book, I discussed John Kennedy's assassination with my dissident friend from Moscow, who, as I found out later on was a member of the KGB. At the time of our conversation I was not well versed in geopolitics and did not know the term "false flag operations." He told me that several assassinations in America were organized by the Soviets in the 1960s. Only coming to America, could I figure out the meaning of his accusations. Take for example four assassinations at the time: President Kennedy, Martin Luther King, Jr., Senator Robert Kennedy, and Malcolm X. Holding their breath, terrified people were watching their leaders assassinated one after another. The series of murders had catastrophically affected "domestic tranquility" of America and its vision of the world in the 1960s. It was also an onslaught of unidentified dark forces on America's psyche, but nobody identified those dark forces. By the way, the author of the term "false flag operations" had compared the John Kennedy assassination with Kirov's committed by Stalin.

Today, forty years later, we are not sure that we know the whole truth. Looking closely, we can find that these four murders had two common features. First, we are not sure it was just alone assassin, or more. Second, researching the details of each of the four assassinations, you will see there are many similarities as if the operational techniques had been designed by the same source. The absence of credibility and assurance in a complete and overwhelming truth is still in the minds of Americans. My personal suspicion is the fact that the Warren Commission Report was published in the Soviet Union for the top echelon. I have read it—my friend from the Estonian Communist Central Committee gave it to me.

By the way, I liked the movie *JFK*, by Oliver Stone; a lot of the questions raised are logical and to the point. Several coincidental disappearances and mysterious deaths of people are questionable and suspicious, too. I just want to remind you of the principal part of Soviet activities, which are recruitments and infiltration into foreign governments, institutions, and organizations—the major task is the creation of a network of loyal cadres in foreign territory to implement the agenda. In addition to that, assassinations were becoming an integral part of the Soviet Foreign Policy—foreign leaders who disagreed with the Kremlin were to be liquidated. Stalin had written two lists of the leaders to be assassinated: one of domestic leaders, the other one of foreign leaders to be assassinated. Once more I recommend that you read the essay by

Ion Mihai Pacepa, *The Kremlin's Killing Ways*, National Review Online, November 28, 2006.

I called the Communists and Socialists in foreign countries the Soviet stooges or henchmen. I know what I am talking about—I have met some of them. It was well known that the Soviets were preparing pro-Soviet governments inside the Soviet Union for all East European countries, constantly training the cadres of comrades. Some members of the cabinet in the German Democratic Republic had been trained in the prisoners-of-war camps in Russia. The members of "*The Estonian Korpus*"[60] had fought on the Soviet side in WWII and after "liberation" of Estonia; some of them became the Estonian Government in Tallinn. I knew a few; they all took marching orders from the Kremlin.

Another grave case of assassination is worth mentioning. The first United States Secretary of Defense was James Forestall,[61] a Democrat with a strong military background. In early 1945 he advocated a softer approach to Japan, because his primary concern was "the menace of Russian Communism and its attraction for decimated, destabilized societies in Europe and Asia." His opinion was so strong that it bordered on insubordination towards President Truman. Forestall had a say in the Chinese issue as well—he supported Chiang-Kai-shek while Truman's Administration supported the Communists. He was a very strong advocate of France, defending it from a Communist takeover.

It was May 22, 1949, the first United States Secretary of Defense James Forestall was found dead on the grounds of Bethesda Naval Hospital. The official report stated that his death resulted from a fall out of the hospital's window. Do you believe it? I don't. The year before a politician who was about to marry the love of his life, was also found dead after falling out a window; Foreign Minister of Czechoslovakia in the Communist government which did not share his anti-communist view. Doesn't it resemble the situation of the death of our Secretary of Defense who was also an outspoken anti-communist? His death led to a lot of speculation and controversy within the media. Later on, the poem written by him as a suicide note was found to not be written in his handwriting.

Throwing out the window the leaders of opposition was a usual method implemented by the Cheka. Just read about the OGPU *Trust Operation* and the fate of Boris Savinkov who collaborated with Sidney Reilly, an Englishman. Savinkov was thrown out from the

Lubyanka prison's window, in Moscow. There is a list of senior U.S. government officials who were assassinated or died under mysterious circumstances—General Patton among them. There are other methods of killing implemented by *the Organs*— car accidents, plane crushes, and so on. If you read *The Russian Factor* you are familiar with the death of Walter Krivitsky[62]—the former head of Soviet Military Intelligence in France, defected to the U.S. He had already testified before several state institutions and was about to testify before the New York legislative committee investigating Communist infiltration in the state's educational system, when he was assassinated on February 10, 1941. You can also find a list of some U.S. officials assassinated in the document I am going to give you a quotation from. The document is titled *Misconduct.org. Anti-Christian Discrimination At Indiana University.*

"Krivitsky was naming persons who had been assassinated and said he could prove that many peculiar death were bona fide assassinations. He indicated that many assassins were medical personnel... which allowed for the deaths being attributed to natural causes. Krivitsky claimed that assassins used a complete series of chemicals that produced symptoms of liver, heart, and kidney failure, and cancer, leukemia or blood cell diseases." We are talking about crimes committed sixty years ago! Can you imagine the "development" in this respect in the country called Russia, run by the KGB's government and former KGB agent as its President? Mr. Pacepa answers the question: "Vladimir Putin appears to be only the latest in the long line of Russian tsars who have upheld the tradition of assassinating anyone who stood in their way."

For good reason, I told you about the techniques of the Soviet infiltration and as an example mentioned the GDR's government and the *Estonian Korpus*. The same techniques are still used around the world today, including the United States—forged by Stalin a spy network comprises the cadres of loyal comrades. It is at work presently! In this respect, I would like to add the information I have received lately. Some Russian journalists and witnesses are talking about Stalin's intent to unleash World War III in the 1940s-1950s. I believe he did just that and the actions undertaken by Stalin's intelligence corroborate their assertion. The war was brought into as well. To know the Stalinist cadres in America, just go to the online site *History of Soviet and Russian espionage in the United States* and you will have a long list of the Soviet/Russian spy rings. To grasp their motives, just read again the Soviet Defense Council's document:

"Soviet strategy for revolutionary war is a global strategy... First was the increasing training of leaders for the revolutionary movements—civilian, military, and intelligence cadres. The founding of Patrice Lumumba University in Moscow is an example of one of the early actions taken to modernize the Soviet revolutionary leadership training." Our academia had become one of the targets for training the leaders for revolutionary movements— molding Soviet-style leaders on our soil—the actual agenda. And though the infiltration into our Unions, Hollywood, and other institutions and businesses has continued, the indoctrination of our youth remains the main target, like it used to be in my time in the Soviet Union under Stalin. Please, read the list of the Soviet's cadres in America and you will see that the vast majority of them have taught our youth the system of Soviet Socialism—typical Soviet propaganda. The result of that we are experiencing in the year 2008. Moreover, the methods of reprisal to the ideological opponents are also brought to our land. The demonized name and fate of Senator McCarty, testifies to that. He was right warning about the Soviet penetration into our State Department and the Military. With typical Stalinist venom of personal destruction he was politically assassinated. Watch the repetition of that policy against the Republicans by the Democrats in 2008.

In my opinion, WWIII for world domination started in the 1920s when the clear Soviet policy began building the Communist State in China, and became determined to create Communist States in Europe. Though the first steps were not military, especially in Europe, they expose a clear strategic design for world domination. I displayed all the arguments in *The Russian Factor*—the strategic design was replicated in America. In that book you will find the definitions of the terms "Stalinist terror ideology," "Sovietization," and "Soviet Fascism." My opinion has not changed since. On the contrary, the events of the last seven years vividly testify to my predictions coming true. It was 2002 when I wrote that "Putin's Russia is an underreported ticking time bomb." Was I right!

I am writing this page in the middle of the discussion between Republicans and Democrats about the surge in Iraq. The Democrats in Congress have already stated that the surge will fail and we have lost the war. I am not a military expert and I have no opinion on the subject. What I know for sure is the consequences of the surge, because I know who is behind the insurgency. I have already analyzed the sources of insurgency in chapter 11, *Perestroika and Bin Laden*, pp. 222-237, *The Russian Factor.* Today, five years later, the source of the insurgency has not changed; it is the Kremlin's students. However, the result of the surge can modify and alter the Kremlin's strategy in Iraq. If the surge succeeds, the Kremlin's strategy will change. Instead of military action, the Kremlin will use its infiltration and penetration strategy. The Iraqi's government will be infiltrated if it has not been yet. I do not believe in the reliability of the Iraqi government—we are dealing with the Middle East's politicians—I do not trust Nouri Maliki.

Let me give you a story that can illustrate a possible future for Iraq. Holding its breath the world was watching events in Moscow, where Yeltsin's victory brought to the Russian people the freedom they had been longing for, for decades. People were running with enthusiasm to the statue of the first Chekist, Dzerzhinsky, to crush it. My own joy had no barrier watching from New York the scene of the falling statue in Moscow. To make a long story short, I can tell you that fifteen years later Putin's government is discussing restoration of the menacing figures—the symbol of oppression, torture, and death. Do you remember Saddam's statue and the people of Iraq crushing it? History can repeat itself sometimes... God forbid!

In Iraq, the key issue is still the oil conspiracy and the Kremlin will fight to the end to have at its disposal Iraqi oil, like they had at the time of Saddam. Like Arafat, Saddam is a link, a very important link in the Kremlin's long-range chain of oil conspiracy. Nobody is talking about the history of the Soviet/Russian design and an aggressive continuation of the master plan under Putin's presidency—a lot of trouble is ahead of us. Yet the field of political science called the Kremlinology is silent like it was in 1938. I see it as a sign of incompetence and acquiescence with the status quo. Or, maybe infiltration into the field prevents the truth from getting out. Infiltration's prime task is the politization of democratic institutions and organizations, indoctrination of their leaders in the tenets criticizing capitalism by using deception, fraud, bribes, manipulations, and many other machinations.

There is another angle in the war against Western civilization—infiltration into the financial institutions to destroy them from within and to discredit the capitalist's economic prospect and developments. Several years ago I wrote about the Enron crash as an example of the Soviet scheme and plot to infiltrate, manipulate, and cripple world economic growth. I believed then in the beginning of the twenty-first century that the world's economy was a Soviet target as well. Moreover, for me it was a criminal arrangement between domestic and foreign crooks to undermine the American capitalist economy and through it the world economy. Taking into account the globalization of the world's economy, it is possible to destroy it by crippling the American economy. I did not like Clinton's friendship with Enron's CEO in the 1990s. I believed that Enron's scheme would be repeated many times in the future to achieve the agenda and destroy our capitalist economy. I also did not like Clinton's deregulation of the banking system and investment institutions to increase the homeownership of low-income Americans, especially Blacks. To me it was social engineering Soviet-style and could be deadly for the future housing market. I thought that Clinton's administration prepared and left a lot of potential troubles for the Bush administration. Unfortunately, my views are not known to the American public— the CIA in cahoots with my publisher was suppressing information about both my books—hiding the truth.

Meanwhile, World War III is going on—infiltration or penetration, drugs, recruitments, and assassinations are marching on across the globe. Yet people of the world are unaware of that— to my frustration, they know nothing about WWIII. They are kept in the dark, deprived of the opportunity to learn the truth by reading my books, warning them about the war going on during the last decades. It is especially dangerous for my America. The vast majority of young Americans do not know about the Cold War, let alone all the history of the Stalinist ideology and the KGB. God, help them to learn the truth about our foremost enemy and survive WWIII.

CHAPTER 8

The Red Menace: From China to Jihad

In accordance with my habit, I would like to return to the chronology in the Kremlin's Foreign Policy of the 1950s-1960s. The next target in the agenda after China had become the Middle East—to control oil reserves and suffocate the West. It was Stalin's idea. He was the first to acknowledge a new Jewish State in 1948, hoping for another satellite now in the Middle East. When Israel turned her face to the United States, the Stalinist foreign policy had drastically changed—the intelligence forces, a second echelon, came to achieve world domination by hook or by crook. Stalin had tremendous experience as a commissar for the nationalities in the country of more than one hundred different ethnic groups. He knew how to deal with them, and pitted them against each other— it had been his paramount agenda. Now it was the Middle East's turn to experience Stalinism.

A compulsive obsession with world domination by hook or by crook within the Kremlin leadership is understandable. As a matter of fact, a leader with the best ideas and best mechanism for implementation of them is coming to power in the democratic regimes. The Soviets/Russians knew only Stalinism, and therefore violence as the only mechanism for implementing an idea. The arsenal to achieve it besides military force, but by a second echelon that contains: deception, fraud, perversion, tricks, hoaxes, and so on. You have already been acquainted with several patterns of the Soviet/Russian activities in the world based on the way they acted toward China. The creation of a leader obedient to the Kremlin within foreign territory was one thing—molding a Soviet-style leader was another pattern.

In the culture of the Middle East deceptions and lies are values; therefore, recruitments can be done much easier. In 1957, Arafat became an agent of the KGB. When I was talking about world domination by hook or by crook, I had in mind, for example, the fraudulent transformation of Arafat's background performed by the KGB. A homosexual Egyptian and well-off bourgeois, he was recruited by the KGB foreign intelligence that turned him into a Marxist. The KGB destroyed the official records of his birth in Cairo, replacing them with fictitious documents, fraudulently locating his birth in Jerusalem. That is the way Arafat became a Palestinian and the constant destabilizing factor on the Middle East.

Arafat and several Soviet henchmen of the Muslim Brotherhood like al-Zawahiri and Sheikh Yassin had been trained in all the Soviet's recruiting tools and methods of propaganda to organize groups of the West's haters. The Soviet henchmen had established terror-gangs and became the leaders in the Middle East, carrying out the Kremlin's design of destabilization. The Soviet motives had been laid out in details by *The Russian Factor*—it is oil. This Soviet design to suffocate the West goes back to Stalin's overall foreign policy, a strategic design aimed at world domination. Just read the conversation with my communist-husband *Baltic Winds*, pp.252-253, and you will see the true motive for oil in his sincere arguments with me forty years ago. He was the Communist Party Secretary of the Bar Association, a mouth-piece of the Soviet policy—the strategy of obtaining oil's resources goes back decades.

I have written several pages in *The Russian Factor* to show that the Soviet long-range design for oil was a part of the Soviet foreign policy against the West. I told the story of a young man giving an interview on TV in a Moscow hotel. Coming to America I found out that the young man turned out to be Carlos the Jackal[66] and a leader of the terror-gang that seized seventy hostages at a meeting in Vienna of oil ministers from OPEC in 1975 and killed several of them. Carlos's connection to Moscow is not known by many, especially in America. He is currently in a prison in France. I hope my friend from France, a professor at Sorbonne who is researching the issue and the role played by Carlos the Jackal will soon publish a conclusion.

The Middle East is a knot of the countries with enormous reserves of oil and the Soviet design had in mind all those countries. The long-range strategy is having pro-Soviet governments in the countries with reserves of oil. But this is not the end of the strategy—the countries with sea ports located on the navigation line should also be pro-Kremlin. The task is huge—to have the means of transportation for oil in the Kremlin's hands as well. Look at the countries along the shore line: Egypt, Libya, Lebanon, Yemen, Somalia, Ethiopia, and so on. There you will find political forces and groups fighting each other for power: assassinations of the legitimate leaders, chaos, and enormous casualties among civilians, destruction of land, and a real threat to the neighboring countries. Doesn't it remind you of the predicament in the early Soviet Union and Stalinist modus operandi? It reminds me of the past—Stalinism had come to the Middle East.

If Arafat and the Muslim's Brotherhood's[67] henchmen had a task to destabilize the area, there was another huge Soviet program implemented in Syria, Iraq, Libya, and Iran—the model described as *The Formula for Power.* It was a copy of the Soviet policy of infiltration applied in North Korea, China, and Eastern Europe. The only difference was the absence of the word Communist's— the Middle East did not use the term. It was a kind of camouflage not to frighten the world and cover-up the Soviet expansionism. You can read about it in *The Russian Factor*, chapter 7, *Evildoer: The Formula for Power.* In short, the Stalinist formula consisted of three major components: 1) a strong leader, 2) a powerful political party, 3) omnipresent intelligence and security services apparatus. The latter part had regular help from the Soviet/Russian apparatus of the intelligence and security agencies.

The Soviets were very successful in Iraq and Syria: Soviet advisors, predominantly from the military and the KGB had trained intelligence and security agencies of both countries. I had a client who worked in the terrorist's training camp in Syria. Several similar camps had been established in the Soviet territory. However, the main "work" to destabilize the West took place outside the country by the Kremlin's intelligence. With its help, *The Formula for Power* had been later implemented in Iran with the similar three components. Do not be confused by the religious forces in Iran—infiltrated Islam, with some Ayatollahs' camouflage was used and is used as a tool in the fight against the West. *The Formula For Power* was working the same way. Look at secret nuclear cooperation between North Korea and Iran—they are strong allies and their activities are coordinated by Russia. As a matter of fact, Pacepa's essay listed the Shah of Iran as a target of assassination by the KGB. The Soviet forces won—in 1979 the Shah was thrown out by the Ayatollahs and died of cancer.

The illness and death of the Shah is quite suspicious. Reading Pacepa's essay, I found an interesting statement, which is based on his conversations with the Communist leaders: "I know for a fact that the Kremlin has repeatedly used radioactive weapons to kill political enemies abroad." His words coincide and corroborate testimony of another defected Soviet agent Walter Krivitsky who was assassinated by a bullet to the head—execution style. Prior to his death, he testified before the U.S. House Committee on Un-American Activities and before the British Government, stating that many peculiar deaths were bona fide assassinations. I hope that young researchers will find interest in the issue and we will finally know the names of those assassinated and the truth about Soviet/Russian activities concerning oil in the Middle East including Iran.

It is for that reason in *The Russian Factor*, the chapter 7; I have introduced the man responsible for the building of the anti- American forces in the Middle East since the 1950s—an agent in the Middle East, and later on a head of the KGB, Eugeniy Primakov. To me Primakov is a sinister individual, who activated the Kremlin's evil deeds. I will give you the opinion of a senior policy analyst of the Heritage Foundation, Ariel Cohen, PhD. "Primakov was befriended and supported Saddam Hussein of Iraq, Hafez al-Assad of Syria, Muammar Qaddafi of Libya, and Yasser Arafat, leaders of the anti-American camp in the Middle East. He maintains close personal relationship with these leaders to this day. … Primakov played an important role in the 1970s and 1980s in formulating the Soviet Union's policy in the Middle East and South Asia." December 15, 1997.

That document Mr. Cohen titled as "The Primakov Doctrine." This Doctrine confirms the Kremlin's long-term strategy for world domination. It also brings to memory the Cheka, and other intelligence and security agencies in past Soviet experiences which I have described in the preceding chapters. In addition to that, please remember that those Soviet agencies had the contracts to train security forces of all above mentioned countries in the Middle East. Do not be surprised by inhumane practices of the security and intelligence agencies in those countries. Also try to perceive the enormous distraction traced to their activities.

Yet a part of the strategy—fostering and molding the leaders of the countries that embraced and practiced *The Formula for Power* took place within the Soviet/Russian territory as well.

The Soviets had not always moved its army or gangs into foreign territory, they fooled the West, inviting young people of the world, especially Arabs of the Middle East to "study" in the Soviet universities and institutes. That had been a well-thought-out policy based on Arab's behavior, their historic inclinations, and facts. Besides Arabs, young people from Asia and Latin America were very welcome to enroll and attend the Soviet educational facilities for free. Many accepted the invitation, flooding available educational institutions and dormitories. Returning home, the former students have become prime ministers, presidents, and chancellors of their native countries.

Do you remember the Patrice Lumumba University in Moscow? It was the place where students from all inhabited continents had "studied" under the KGB's supervision. The Soviet molding of the "students-leaders" later resulted in the bloody confrontations around the world. I dedicated several pages to the issue in *The Russian Factor*, chapter 9, *The Mysterious Aggressor: Soviet Fascism*. The point is to show and prove the inextricable connection between the past and present forces destabilizing the world. The Patrice Lumumba University changed its name; it is now *People's Friendship University of Russia*—the substance and the agenda is still the same—indoctrination of youth against the West. Of course you have to know the Soviet educational system with its extensive study of Marxism-Leninism, which means Stalinist Communism or Socialism, to see the design clearly. Let me give you some quotations about the University to demonstrate the continuity and scale of the Soviet undertaking:

"Currently over 4,000 international undergraduates, graduates, postgraduates from over 130 countries of the world study here." Special features of the University are: "Multi-nationality of the collective of teachers, students, post-graduate students and trainees—representatives of 450 nationalities and tribes from more than 130 countries of the world." Please add to the description the reality—all the above exists under the close supervision of the KGB, which is called today FSB. Can you now make a connection between the past and our presence? Maybe now you can perceive the result of destruction in Africa administered by the tribes' leaders studying in Moscow? Just go to Congo or Sudan and you will see that the destruction is still going on.

At this point, I can't help but give you another source for the world's destabilization and destruction. There was the Institute of Social Science in Moscow. In fact this "Institute" was a center for terrorists' training with several affiliated training camps in the outskirt of Moscow. This so-called "institute" was teaching military programs to people from around the world, but predominantly those from the countries with a long line of shores. I believe that General Ai did from Somalia and his officers had been studying courses on navy military operations; because the Soviet navy officers and even generals were teaching there. The building close to the metro station *Airport* had a deep basement several floors down. I also believe that the top people from Al- Qaeda were studying there, too.

Writing *The Russian Factor*, I made some observations and conclusions based on my knowledge of the Soviet/Russian mentality, behavior, motivations, and their past practices. For example, I suspected that it was al-Zawahiri who persuaded Bin Laden to switch sides and turn to the Soviet camp. What a surprise it was, when I read in the first paragraph of Pacepa's essay that al-Zawahiri, number two in Al-Qaeda, was trained by the Soviets! Can you now connect the past with our terrible present? It was al-Zawahiri's gang that assassinated President Sadat in a bloody terror attack in Egypt. The handwriting was so familiar to me in 2004, because in chapter 11, *Perestroika and Bin Laden*, I was trying to make that connection and prove that behind al-Qaeda is Soviet/Russian intelligence and possibly Putin personally. Today, after the terrifying murder of the Russian dissident Litvinenko in London; it is inevitable for the past to finally blend with our horrifying present and opens our eyes even wider.

The plan to make oil a major weapon against the West was conceived by Stalin in the 1950s. Do you remember Stalin's meeting with Mao in Moscow? They planned a long-range strategy within Asia. But it was not only Asia. By that time Israel had already turned her face to America, and the Muslim world with oil had attracted Stalin. Mao, in his ambitions, proved it: "Pakistan had grown more and more useful to Mao as a staging post to the Middle East and Peking aggressively backed Pakistan's ambitions over Kashmir, training Kashmiri's guerrillas for what China presented as a National Liberation War," taken from *Mao: The Unknown Story.* There are two main violent ideas: "training guerrillas" and "a staging post to the Middle East" which are covered up by the words "National Liberation." The totalitarian Communists had adored the words National Liberation in 1950s. It resulted in real life later on—the KGB's agent Arafat had established the Palestinian Liberation Organization—a terrorist formation.

As we know today the guerrilla warfare or insurgency had started after the creation of Pakistan in 1947 and still goes on today. Considering what was said above, I see two main points in deliberating the connection between the past and the present. The first is the Muslim's warfare against civilized India supervised by international communism. The second is the bridge in time and space from guerrilla warfare or insurgency in Asia to the Middle East, as a continuation and implementation of a long- range strategy. This bridge had been built by the same forces of international communism—the agenda was to form a clan of supporters to take over and set up the oil terror conspiracy against the civilized world. Common extreme hate of the West had united plotters under the Soviet guidance and banner of Stalinism. As you now know, I called the ideology of Stalinist Communism, Soviet Fascism—an ideology of terror, the cruelest prosecutions, and wars, human suffering, and deaths. Hence, we can make a conclusion—the notion of international terrorism based on the experiences of the partisan-guerrillas during WWII had been discussed by Stalin and Mao at their meeting in Moscow in 1950. A small note: Reportedly, Al-Qaeda trains the Muslim insurgency in Kashmir—an ideological circle has closed.

All countries which were run by the Soviet henchmen, gravitated to that system, adhered, and operated accordingly. I called those countries the countries of Soviet Fascism. To perceive the matter, its significance, and fully comprehend the world we are living in, you have to read *The Russian Factor*, chapter 9, *The Mysterious Aggressor: Soviet Fascism.* Only then can we discuss war in Iraq. And to do so, I have to give you another term— *The Soviet Mafia*. It is not my invention; it is the title of a book written by another Russian lawyer, a brilliant journalist and writer, Arkady Vaksberg,[69] St. Martin Press, 1991. The author called the entire Soviet/Russian officialdom-establishment the Soviet Mafia. I agree with him.

There are three main concepts in the book. First, the evil empire may be dead, but not the evil that drove it—the Soviet mafia. Second, the book gives us a new definition of political forces and their leaders previously known as the Communists, the KGB, and the Soviets. Vaksberg redefines those old terms with a new collective identity: the

Soviet mafia, the nucleus of organized crime. Third, the Soviet mafia is a multinational political force with no limit to any ethnicity, religion, or race. Considering the arguments presented above, I believe that Islam and Jihad are the instruments of the Soviet mafia used against the West—it unites all the countries of Soviet Fascism with a common agenda aimed against the West.

Islam had not been reformed since its birth in the sixth century. Yet, history had recorded its aggressive and expansionist tendency with killing as a part of the training since then. Living under a strict Shariah-Islamic law, all Muslim countries had been lacking social and cultural development happening within the Judeo-Christian world during the centuries of Renaissance and Enlightenment. Infiltrated by the Soviets in the twentieth century, Islam was politically managed by them since then. The Muslim countries, their Mosques, and especially the Arabs of the Middle East had been indoctrinated and provided with the contemporary ideology close to the Arab's historical character. It is an aggressive and expansionist ideology of Stalinism—Soviet Fascism. Many countries and leaders of the Middle East therefore constituted the *International Soviet Mafia,*[70] which included Saddam Hussein.[71] That was the world we lived in, in 2003. Doesn't it remind you of the world with the countries of Axis (Germany, Italy, and Japan) in the end of the 1930s? Do not expect departure or retreat of the contemporary Axis countries—the multi-faceted body with its venomous tentacles is growing up under the Russian umbrella and the motto "only ahead and never surrender." Keep in mind this huge umbrella geographically—besides South Asia, it is the Middle East: Iraq, Iran, Syria, and others through which acting terrorists are receiving enormous amounts of arms, weaponry, and constant coordination with the Kremlin. The KGB, by using Arafat and other leaders had created a snake pit, the foundation of a Muslim terror-university armed with the ideology of Soviet Fascism, shaping a militant force in the Middle East since the 1950s. The Russian connection is alive and well in the twenty-first century.

After Arafat, his heirs Hamas[72] and Hezbollah[73] continue fighting Israel by all means with the ideology taught to them: violence, deceit, fraud, and so on. They are firing rockets to Israeli towns, destined to kill civilians and terrorize the entire population. In our increasingly interdependent world, they permanently destabilize the region and Saddam helps them. Arafat's heirs are true disciples of Stalin's modus operandi: violence, intimidation, deception, fraud, game with words, and so on. As Stalin, in the midst of total terror, claimed that the Soviet Constitution is "the only thoroughly democratic in the world," the same way Arafat's heirs fooled their population living in total deprivation. They are deceiving and misguiding their own people using the terms "democracy" and "freedom," perverting the real meaning of the words. Look at Hamas; it won an election in Gaza using these terms. And nobody in the West has exposed Hamas' fraud. Democracy is "the capacity of a people to control their institutions for their own best ends," a concept of universal human liberty within the population mentally ready for it. Neither Hamas nor the Palestinians are familiar with the concept. As a result, Hamas has achieved Control and Power, a regime of permanent terror— continuation of the Soviet design for war and instability in the Middle East. There is nobody in Hamas to talk about peace— Moscow's henchmen do not want peace, they want war and are fighting together with their masters for world domination…!

I have to repeat that there is no nationality called Palestinians. The term Palestinians (Arabs) did not exist before WWII. Palestine is an administrative territory and 5,000 years of Jewish history makes them more Palestinians than Arabs coming from the Arabian Peninsula. I have already discussed the subject, *The Russian Factor*, pp. 151-162. I am not alone "Whereas recognition has been given to the historical connection of the Jewish people with Palestine and to the grounds for reconstituting their national home in that country," The League of Nations Declared on July 24, 1922. The term Palestinians (Arabs) was initially proclaimed by President of Egypt Gamal Abdel Nasser in the 1950s. Keep in mind that Gamal Abdel Nasser had been decorated with an Order of Hero of the Soviet Union by the Soviet leader Khrushchev.[75] A Soviet friend, President Nasser had received enormous quantities of arms and weaponry from the Soviets in 1956. At this point, I would like to remind you of another episode in the same direction: the year 1957, when Arafat was recruited by the KGB and by forgery made a Palestinian. The same fraudulent scenario was used to create contemporary Palestine and Palestinians (Arabs)— both terms are fraud. Though the Middle East was not a peaceful area at the time, different countries were involved to bring stability to the region then.

The situation in the entire region has changed drastically since the Soviets became interested in the area. If you trace back the events since

1956-1957, you will find the coordinated actions on the part of Arafat and the Muslim Brotherhood to destabilize the region and establish a constant state of war with Israel. The region was targeted by the Soviets for oil, using Islam as a tool— the design created by Stalin. His henchmen had rooted into the soil of the Middle East the cells of cancer, a disease of the Soviet mentality to achieve CONTROL and POWER, investing in hate and brutal violence—a concept developed by Stalin. There won't be peace in the Middle East until terrorists and their ideology of Soviet Fascism are exposed.

Another example is Syria. Thanks to the Kremlin's henchmen in Syria, Lebanon has been in fire for more than thirty years. The tragedy of its capital Beirut, the Middle East's Paris, is going on now. Look at another part of the world, at Nigeria. It has oil and because of that the rebels there are blowing up the pipe lines to create uncertainty in the world's oil market. I have found that Russian businessmen paid money to the terrorist-gang for blowing up the pipe lines—the oil conspiracy directed at crippling the world's economy, especially airline and auto-industries. Islam as a tool of war has been spread throughout the globe. The International Soviet mafia is on the march around the world, using Islam to instill the ideology of Soviet Fascism.

Besides the ideology, we also have to remember the second part of the Soviet mafia's agenda;, conspiracy of oil terrorism. Needless to say, oil is the blood of the world industries, the source of energy and progress in the civilized countries and their capitalistic economy. The Soviet mafia, as a driving force of the conspiracy made oil a weapon in the war to stop all the positive developments in the West. This war has been going on for many decades on many different fronts. The 9/11 attack on the World Trade Center was just one link in a long chain of battles against Western civilization. But it was the most menacing, dreadful, ominous, and fateful attack—the West could not tolerate the attacks any longer—response had become a moral imperative...! Looking at the activities of the Soviet mafia and its "accomplishments" throughout the world during the last sixty years we ought to view the war in Iraq through the prism of the ideology of Soviet Fascism which was exported and enforced by the Soviet mafia in Iraq. Moreover, Saddam had presented the largest double sword tentacle of Soviet Fascism—ideology plus oil. Saddam was constantly destabilizing the Middle East, inciting Palestinians to suicide missions by paying them money. The time has come to react to Saddam's criminal activities—a moral imperative, let alone America's security and prestige. Where and how do you start? Afghanistan is obvious—Al-Qaeda had a training camp there. And what should we do after that? It is clear to me that Iraq became the second step for a reason.

First, it is clear that all Saddam's security and intelligence agencies had been trained by the Soviet/Russia forces. When I heard that Saddam's representative had a meeting in Prague the situation became more obvious: as a matter of fact, the top officers of the KGB regularly met their agents in Prague—the city designated for high level meetings. Second, the members from Saddam's government had transported eight to ten of their children to Moscow; the Iraqi ambassador in Moscow initiated the operation. Third, if you know the *International Soviet Mafia* and intend to start fighting it, Iraq geographically is the best location to start with. Please take the map and see it—it is impossible to participate in this discussion without a map of the Middle East. And take into account that recruiting Arafat in the 1950s; the Soviets have spread their influence to the rest of the Middle East since then. Iraq, as the center, presented the best opportunity for success. In this respect it was one of Bush's correct decisions.

If you read *The Russian Factor* you would know that Stalin was Saddam Hussein's idol, but his godfather was Mr. Primakov. Following his maneuvers in the Middle East, his background and biography, you will read even more about the Kremlin's long- range strategy for world domination. Today, you can find the evidence for Soviet/Russian determination in this direction. Look at Hamas, Hezbollah, Syria, Libya, Iran, North Korea, and their relationship with Russia—they are all on the same camp against the civilized world. This is the best evidence of the rightness of all my theories and terms—*International Soviet mafia, The Formula for Power, and Soviet Fascism.* The conclusion was obvious—we did not have an option—Iraq, having the third largest reserve of oil, was the right country to start with in response to the attacks by the Soviet Mafia. And Justice was served—Saddam Hussein had been tried by the Iraqi Tribunal and hanged as a War Criminal.

This is a milestone of the international politics of the twenty- first century—the first member of the *International Soviet Mafia* fighting against humanity appeared before the court and was identified as a War Criminal. Saddam Hussein is the first, but not the last, member of the international conspiracy against the West tried by the Tribunal. I have no crystal ball to show the next Soviet henchman, but I have an idea. My father gave me the idea in 1980. It was around the time when I was about to immigrate to the United States and came to say goodbye to my father in Leningrad. We had a conversation I reproduced in my first book *Baltic Winds*: *Testimony of a Soviet Attorney*, pp. 315-316:

"Separation from you will be one of the most difficult experiences of my life. It's even more painful that I can't help you. But the thought that you and your children will be free at last gives me some comfort. Yet you have to promise me one thing." He glanced at me and waited as I dried me eyes.

"What should I do, Papa?"

"I want you to promise me that no other country will ever seduce you—not England, not France. You must go to America... there won't be peace in Europe... you're entering an unfamiliar world, and I want you to understand the transformation going on in it. Have you heard about the American hostages in Tehran?"

"Well, I've heard something."

"It's not *something*. Young people... students brainwashed by Marxist ideology, took those Americans and humiliated them. The only crime of those hostages is that they're *American*.

Do you know who's behind that ordeal?"

"No, I don't."

"The Soviet bandits, who are spreading the plague of hatred against America because they can't destroy it the way they're destroying Europe."

"What do you mean, destroying Europe?"

"I mean just what I said. In our age, ideas run the world, and the wrong ideas destroy it. You... are leaving because the country adhered to a wrong idea. That's why I want you to go to America.

...Did you meet the KGB agents recruiting students in your law school?"

"Yes, we had them every year. They asked for cooperation."

"You see how easy it is—first indoctrinate and then recruit. Remember, the KGB uses the same strategy in major universities around the world. It gets its payoff when youngsters become professionals. In the Middle East some of them join terrorist groups trained by the Soviets, in Europe they join the government. Let me tell you about the results of that. In the thirties, the KGB recruited five students from Cambridge in England, and later on it had the entire British counterintelligence in its pocket. You are not staying in Europe... you must do your utmost to get to America." My father's words had never left my mind, they stayed in my subconscious. He was talking about a danger of staying in Europe. He had foresight and vision of the future. I had not. Now, many years later, I can see the overall dynamics of the events in the world—the Stalinist ideology is moving from one country to another like a plague. It contaminates the land and the human psyche. I saw it by my own eyes. I felt it. And with time a more complete idea and identification of Soviet Fascism had been growing and ripening in my head. Soviet Fascism[76] has become the ideology of different political groups, an amalgamation of Marxists, Communists, Socialists, Anarchists, radical Islamists, and other left-wing groups around the globe, united under the Kremlin's umbrella to fight Western civilization. Be prepared— different types of violent extremism even a revolution will become an instrument of official policies of the countries adhered to Soviet Fascism... WWIII is marching around the globe...

CHAPTER 9

The Evil Empire of Global Terrorism

The conversation with my father took place thirty years ago in 1980. I have learned a lot since then—our globe experienced even more. Stalin was looking forward when he molded leaders of his ilk. All the latter Soviet regimes completed his motto—the masses must be organized. They had followed Stalin's precepts in the process of molding the leaders, including the leaders of the outside world to acquire world domination through them. And every day of America's unawareness was bringing Soviet Fascism closer to victory. You know the *Axis of Evil* in the twentieth century, the twenty-first century will surprise you tremendously—Jihad merged and blended with Latin America's Socialism. Do you remember narcotics warfare against the West under the Kremlin's guidance? Though it continues, now it is warfare on another front developed by the Kremlin—the oil terror conspiracy against Western civilization.

You perhaps have already learned that the Kremlin's intelligence to serve its interest often doing the covert operations by the hands of others—the front men and front leaders. I have my experiences, knowledge of the Soviet System, Stalinism, and awareness of the arsenal of Soviet behavior and their modus operandi. Like in the case of the narcotics warfare against the West in the twentieth century, in addition to that, we are now dealing with the front men in the case of the oil terror in the middle of 2007. You saw the pictures of the three front men in all our news papers—they are the Troyka of the Soviet mafia doing the job of extending the ideology of Soviet Fascism. The Kremlin has practically delegated the job to its Moscow stooges. Like Arafat and

Saddam, they are also the War Criminals who should be appearing next before the International Tribunal. The next faces of Stalinism and Soviet Fascism are the President of Iran, Mahmoud Ahmadinejad,[77] President of Venezuela, Hugo Chavez,[78] and President of Bolivia, Evo Morales. Yet the Iranian President Ahmadinejad is perhaps the first in line.

Though I did not find documents showing his training by the Soviets, I would argue that he was trained in Stalinist's precepts. I have arrived at that conclusion while researching his biography, activities, deeds, and the words spoken by him. It was many years ago that I wrote my suspicions that behind the Islamic revolution in Iran stood the Soviet regime. My suspicions were based first on the Soviet oil-conspiracy against the West, and second on their activities within the Middle East—Arafat, al-Zawahiri, and others trained by the Soviets. I also knew that the founder of Islamic Republic Iran, Ayatollah Khomeini,[79] living in France had a group of advisors and assistants who were shaping the regime, preparing for the Islamic Revolution in Iran. They had produced thousands of cassettes with Khomeini's appeals to the Iranians calling for revolution. There was no DVD at the time, but the use of technology by the religious leader was very suspicious to me—I suspect the Soviets were behind it.

The time, events, and Ahmadinejad himself has proved my suspicions. The article titled "Ahmadinejad? Who's he?" has shared my suspicions and given documented information about him. "After finishing high school Ahmadinejad went to Elm-o Sanaat University in 1975 to study engineering. Soon the whirlwind of Islamic revolution led by Ayatollah Ruhollah Khomeini swept him from the classroom to the mosque and he joined a generation of firebrand Islamic fundamentalists dedicated to the cause of an Islamic world revolution." Before giving you the rest of the article, I would like to focus your attention on the similarity within any mafia of molding and bringing a new leader to the surface after the clandestine meeting of the bosses. Do you remember how in the 1990s we asked each other "Putin? Who's he?" Think about those similarities, please. Only now we can continue reading the article "Ahmadinejad? Who's he?"

"Student activists in Elm-o Sanaat University at the time of the Iranian revolution were dominated by... Islamic fundamentalists. Ahmadinejad soon became one of their leaders and founded the Islamic Students Association in the University after the fall of the Shah's regime.

In 1979, he became a representative of Elm-o Sanaat students in the Office for Strengthening of Unity Between Universities and Theological Seminaries, which later became known as the OSU.[80] The OSU was set up by Ayatollah Baheshty, who was… a key figure in a clerical leadership.

"Beheshty wanted the OSU to organize Islamists students to counter… the opposition among university students. The OSU played a central role in the seizure of the United States embassy in Tehran in November 1979. Members of the OSU central council who included Ahmadinejad were regularly received by Khomeini himself. During the crackdown on universities in 1980, which Khomeini called the 'Islamic Cultural Revolution, Ahmadinejad and the OSU played a critical role in purging dissident-lectures and students many of whom were arrested and later executed. Universities remained closed for three years and Ahmadinejad joined the Revolutionary Guard." Please, pay attention to Ahmadinejad's complete copying of the Soviet-style activities against dissent in the analogous Cultural Revolution taking place in all targeted countries cooperating with the Soviets. Do you remember the Soviet *diabolic ideological expansion* and *the Organs* that implemented it? Just note to this:

"In the early 1980s, Ahmadinejad worked in the 'Internal Security' department of the IRGC (the Islamic Revolution's Guards Corps) and earned notoriety as a ruthless interrogator and torture. According to the state-run website Baztab, allies of outgoing President Mohammad Khatami have revealed that Ahmadinejad worked for some time as an executioner in the notorious Evin Prison, where thousands of political prisoners were executed in the bloody purges of the 1980s." Please, pay attention to the methods used to take over—they are identical to the methods of the Communist Party used around the world—an ideological army. Your attention should also be focused on the incredible similarities with the criminal activities of the Cheka described in the first chapters of this book. The similarity will continue as we read the article further.

"In 1986, Ahmadinejad became a senior officer of the Special Brigade of the Revolutionary Guards and was stationed in Ramazan Garrison… in western Iran. Ramazan Garrison was the headquarters of the Revolutionary Guards' 'extra- territorial operations,' a euphemism for terrorist attacks beyond Iran's borders. …Ahmadinejad became involved in the clerical regime's terrorist operations abroad and led many 'extra-territorial operations of the IRGC.'

"With the formation of the elite Qods (Jerusalem) Force of the IRGC, Ahmadinejad became one of the senior commanders. He was the mastermind of a series of assassinations in the Middle East and Europe, including the assassination of Iranian Kurdish leader Abdurrahman Qassemlou, who was shot dead by senior officer of the Revolutionary Guards in Vienna flat in July 1989. Ahmadinejad was a key planner of the attack, according to sources in the Revolutionary Guards." And again, I would like to remind you of the structural similarity of the elite formation Qods or the Revolutionary Guards with the KGB. Please, also watch for a contemporary situation in Russia and Putin's actions directed toward the youth, their preparation, and virtual involvement in the upcoming Duma parliamentarian election. Do you remember the youth movement NASHI? Stalinism is their religion in the twenty- first century!

Now we can return to the article. "In 1997 . . .Ahmadinejad returned to Elm-o Sonata University to teach, but his principal activity was to organize Ansar-e Hezbollah, a radical gang of violent Islamic vigilantes. Since becoming mayor of Tehran, in April 2003, Ahmadinejad has been using his position to build up a strong network of radical Islamic fundamentalists organized as 'Abadgaran-e Iran-e Islam' (literary, Developers of an Islamic Iran). Working in close conjunction with the Revolutionary Guard's, Abadgaran was able to win the municipal elections in 2003 and the parliamentary election win 2004. They owed their victories as much too low turnouts and general disillusionment with the 'moderate' faction of the regime as to their well-oiled political and military machinery.

"Abadgaran bills itself as a group of young neo-Islamic fundamentalists who want to revive the ideas and policies of the founder of the Islamic Republic, Ayatollah Khomeini. Ahmadinejad's record is typical of the man chosen by Khamenei's entourage to put a new face on the clerical elite's ultra-conservative identity. But beyond the shallow façade, few doubt that the Islamic republic under its new President will move with greater speed and determination along the path of radical policies that include more human rights abuses, continuing sponsorship of terrorism, and the drive to obtain nuclear weapons." *Iran's New President Has a Past Mired in Controversy*, Tehran, June 25, 2005—"Ahmadinejad? Who's he?" Iran Focus Special Wire News. Wow! The article is right on the money and confirms many of my points.

I purposely took time to present this article to convey the opinion of the Iranians about their new president. What I found surpassed my expectations—the biography of Ahmadinejad is a carbon copy of a Soviet mafia member. I have found all the components emanate from the Stalinist regime: killing of innocent people, purges, and assassinations—the entire ideology of Soviet Fascism. Do you remember the special operations by *the Organs?* You can find them activated in Iran by Ahmadinejad. The victims and targets of his regime are the same: the youth and the West. The youth should be indoctrinated to be loyal to the new leaders of the Soviet molding to fight the West. Look at Ahmadinejad's policy of targeting students and his obvious participation in the Kremlin's conspiracy of oil terror, which is the real "accomplishment" of Soviet Fascism in the Middle East. All Ahmadinejad's activities and words spoken prove my analysis—he is far-left on the political spectrum, called Soviet Fascism. This movement should be called a Cult as it was under Stalin.

If you read the entire piece you will find other elements of Soviet Fascism in Iran. For example, the second Ayatollah Khamenei ordered to set up different neo-Islamic fundamentalist groups to defeat outgoing President Khatami's faction after the parliamentary elections in February 2000. I have already told you about Soviet political games with different Islamic factions. The conclusion is that those factions had been created decades before and used when the world situation has required changes in Iranian politics or maybe to prepare Ahmadinejad for the presidency. He was used in 1979, but after that he was taken out of the world's eye to be returned in 2000, by the design of a new Ayatollah. It is obvious to me that the headquarters of the games located in Moscow conducted the special operation, which is familiar to me. Please, keep in mind the major point of the Iranian predicament—the KGB is working on two fronts legally and illegally, covering up a criminal secret design of oil conspiracy. The Russian technical staff is there to speed up all the high-tech Iranian development—keep in mind that Putin is a former agent of the Soviet counterintelligence! Dealing with Iran, remember the active KGB long-range design working against the West.

Another dirty trick will also confirm the Soviet design. When you read the entire article mentioned above, you will find an interesting detail. When in 1979, the plan to seize the United States embassy had been at work, Ahmadinejad had offered to seize the Soviet embassy simultaneously. What a typical Soviet trick to divert attention from the Soviet's full participation in the ordeal! You have to know all their methods, tricks, and deceptive maneuvering to read correctly all the world events. I am a messenger to deliver them. I see my duty as giving the information in hopes that the younger generation will continue my research. Ahmadinejad is the next War Criminal to be tried! He benefits the Soviet mafia by betraying the Iranian people. By the way, I heard Senator McCain say that Iran is training Al-Qaeda. He was right on the money and Senator Lieberman erroneously corrected him—Iranians do train Al-Qaeda to kill Americans and Iraqis, fighting insurgency! I suspect the training camps in Iran run by the Russians with their usual agenda—to train snipers, assassins, bank robbers, and other thugs-gangsters.

To grasp the entire predicament in Iran, I have to explain the difference between some of the terms. The first term is the SERVICE. It means completely different actions and activities in the American society than in the countries with Stalinist's regimes. For example, under Soviet Socialism service (sluzba) means a job as a duty for the government, to follow a cause given by the Party or the government. It is "SLUZBA" within intelligence agencies, providing security to the entire country or in the armed forces defending the country. Remember, the Soviet concept of security—Bezopasnost, means ATTACK to CONTROL. The Russian word service has a long history; it is derived from the Cheka's time and the activity of its secret cadres. The KGB, MVD, and others with analogous functions would be called today the special services—the Para-Military establishment or *the Organs* carrying on the concept of service— "sluzba." In America, the word "service" means the opposite actions which are really servicing other people in different capacities and activities every day—the customer services in our society are known to every American. Soviet Socialism did not serve anyone; it exploited the entire population of the world. The sense of real service for people does not exist in the Russian vocabulary; the word "sluzba" is associated with the Organs, military, or the special operations. In America, the word "service" is associated with consumer satisfaction—this is the crux of the differences between Russia and civilized America— the cultural differences in the meaning of the same word!

Returning to the Iranians—they share the same meaning of the term service with their handlers, the Soviets. I would argue that Iran has Soviet-style military, Intelligence services, and security forces. We often use the term Islamic Revolutionary Guards as a unit sponsoring terrorism. And it is a true terrorist one. Yet it is only a part of a more complex subdivision in the Islamic Republic of Iran's military. IRG subordinated to the Army of the Guardians of the Islamic Revolution—AGIR. And AGIR is only one branch in the Iranian military. Listen to how this branch has been equipped: AGIR has its own ground forces, navy, air force, intelligence, and Special Forces. "The force's main role is in national security, responsible for internal and border security, as well as law enforcement. It is also responsible for Iran's missile forces. The operations of the AGIR are geared towards asymmetric warfare and less traditional." Wikipedia. In this quotation I recognized a typical Soviet structure; camouflage by Iranian titles!

Don't you think that the AGIR set up in 1979 was copying the Soviet Intelligence Agencies? It also geared towards asymmetric warfare in its narcotic crusade across the world. Besides, both entities subordinated to one man, Commander-in-chief—the AGIR to Ayatollah, the KGB to Andropov in 1979. I am writing this page after the Iranian provocation in the Persian Gulf and fourteen British sailors were taken hostage by the Iranian Revolutionary Guards. Provocations are the usual Soviet ways of igniting the crisis. Igniting the crisis is the Kremlin's modus operandi to act in the murky waters. Therefore, I am warning you that we can expect in the future all the familiar tactics and techniques of Soviet Fascism displayed by Iran: provocations, disinformation, fraud, hoaxes, and a constant threatening of America and Israel. Please, read my characterization of Putin's character, the mentality where the prevailing thoughts are carrying revenge, threat, and defiance, *The Russian Factor*, pp. 215-217. To grasp the events in Iran, you should know the main Kremlin's concept of revenge, which is the driving force of the *International Soviet Mafia*. To sum up my analysis, several patterns can characterize and identify Soviet Fascism in Iran—fraud and money laundering, brutality, torture, and killings. Watch Iran, you perhaps do not know what is going on there, but in time you will find all of the above characteristics in Iran.

Talking about Iran, I can give you another similarity in crime—very often crashes of planes resulted in dead leaders of the opposition or journalists. In January 2006, a plane crash killed the head of Iran's Revolutionary Guards ground forces Ahmed Kazemi and another ten to twelve people. Among those killed, included a number of top commanders including an intelligence chief. Another military plane crashed in Teheran killing 128 people. The plane hit a ten-story apartment building. Read *The Russian Factor*—the dirty tricks, using plane crashes, to kill political adversaries started in Moscow in 1964 and has been going on since, especially by Moscow's students. I believe that Ahmadinejad and Ayatollah are Moscow's students! Just watch their relationship with Putin—they belong to the same mafia. Also pay attention to another extremely important fact of sabotage; the terrorists have studied not only how to hit buildings, but also how to damage planes on the ground to cause the crashes. Pay attention to the planes that crashed a few minutes after taking off. I have read lately that a strange plane crash occurred soon after a new government was elected in Argentina. Pay attention to Argentina...!

The behavior of two other obvious Soviet henchmen, Hugo Chavez and Evo Morales do not need any analysis—they are loud and arrogantly display their loyalty to the Kremlin and ignorance in fighting for Socialism, which they do not know. Any comments are unnecessary—you have heard their speeches and seen their deeds. They are first trashing Bush and America like other far-left Kremlin henchmen. Their domestic policy is identical. Just watch suppressed media, attacks against the opposition, and propaganda Soviet-style. Compare these events with what is going on in Russia—you will find a lot of similarity—they are all Moscow's students. The march of Soviet Fascism is going on now along Latin America as well. Yet the target is the same—Western civilization. I have no doubt that all the world affairs directed against the West and especially, against America, have been designed and thought over in Moscow. It was fifteen years ago when I wrote in *Baltic Winds*: "The Stalinist system is responsible for the enormous suffering of millions, for 'killing fields' in Russia, Ukraine, China, Tibet, Vietnam, Cambodia, Afghanistan, Kurdistan, and many other places. Stalinism is the global tragedy of humanity. As with the Nuremberg trials, an international tribunal under the auspices of the United Nations should be set up to render judgment in cases of the Stalinist criminals of the past, present, and future. It must be a trial in Moscow, a real Show Trial condemning Stalinism globally. That tribunal should halt the spread of Stalinism—unpunished crime breeds repetition,." p. 539, *Baltic Winds*.

I gave you a small part of my lecture at the Mensa, on April 27, 1992, titled "From Stalin to Saddam Hussein." Even then in 1992 I knew that principal War Criminals were situated in Russia. It is no coincidence that I am describing thoroughly the activities of Yevgeny Primakov in both my books—primary menace had emanated from him. And I am not alone thinking so:

"'"Seven years ago, the man who tried hardest to shield Saddam Hussein from the coming Desert Storm was Russia's Yevgeny Primakov. He was then a KGB biggie and is now Russian foreign minister... And if that weren't enough, Yevgeny, this week is carrying water for another unindicted war criminal, Serbia's Slobodan Milosevic. It was vintage Primakov who said coolly after Serb police massacred men, women, and children in Yugoslavia's Kosovo province last week: 'It is quite obvious that in these conditions we must not concentrate entirely on punishing Belgrade. As a result of his obstructionism in the United Nations' contact group with Serbia, it came up with only mild punishment for the latest Serbian bestiality." "Fire Primakov," *The Wall Street Journal*, March 12, 1998.

I have chosen the quotation for a reason—it confirms two my points: First, in addition to my writing, it gives you more information about Primakov. Second, it identifies the typical behavior of the Soviet Mafia within the legitimate world's organization— obstructionism. Pay attention to the word obstructionism! It is a substitute for the war against the West—the only possible form of resistance within the legitimate organization, acting openly before the world's eyes. When Chekists can't kill, they obstruct. You will meet this behavior many times in the future, in the different locations of the world. It will help you to recognize Soviet Fascism...

I can tell you even more. Now in 2007, and knowing Russia's design for oil terror and looking back to Primakov relationship with Saddam, a strange idea came to my mind. Russia was the country interested in the elimination of the two other world's oil resources in Iraq and Iran—to usurp oil power and dictate the oil prices and policy to the West. And perhaps it was Primakov advice to Saddam to start the war with Iran in 1979. Watching today Ahmadinejad's ascend to power, there is another point to confirm this suggestion—he is the leader of the Soviet molding to recruit youth for the war, giving him the leading role in the entire ordeal. Do you know that Ahmadinejad was a Commissar? Read the data about him and your eyes will open wider. Also, please, remember all the crimes committed by the Soviet Cheka and the Commissars.

I would add to that the timing factor that provides support for the assertions made before. Going back to the Iranian Revolution, we can find interesting events, confirming my main idea of the Soviet's oil terror conspiracy. So, living in France, Ayatollah Khomeini was preparing the revolution in Iran and after strikes and demonstrations in 1979, he returned to Iran in February 1979. On April 1, 1979, Iran officially became the Islamic Republic. After Shah fled, Ayatollah Khomeini had been pronounced its Supreme Leader in December 1979. In this respect, I have to discuss with you the Iranian Revolution. I would argue that it was a unique historical adventure, produced by outside forces; I believed by the Soviets.

Let's do what one Iranian scholar suggested putting it this way: "clear an occurrence that had to be explained." The revolution surprised the entire world, because it lacked many of the historical causes of the revolutions that occurred before. I agree with Wikipedia, which has listed some of them: "...defeat at war, a financial crisis, peasant rebellion, or disgruntled military produced profound change at great speed, overthrew a regime thought to be heavily protected by lavishly financed army and Intelligence apparatus..." The Islamic Revolution in Iran has created an unprecedented outcome—it had replaced an ancient monarchy with a theocracy based on the Guardianship of the Islamic Jurists. As a result, the Islamic Republic of Iran found itself "under the guidance of an eighty-year-old exiled religious scholar from Qom."

You perhaps already know my idea about the Islamic Revolution of 1979, that it was prepared, instigated, and brought to live by the Soviets. I suspected that all of Islam was infiltrated by Moscow's students, including the Khomeini's entourage in Iran and in France, where it was initiated. I have already dedicated many pages to the issue of the Soviet infiltration of different religions, the Orthodox Russian Church, the Catholic Church and Islam (Read *The Russian Factor*). To confirm my main idea, I will give you the explanation of other occurrences, confirming one circle of long-range strategy that unites all the events of 1979.

The Islamic Revolution of 1979 was not the only surprise of the year, another two events followed it. On July 16, 1979 Saddam Hussein—a close friend of Mr. Primakov had become President of Iraq. And this was not the last surprise of 1979. At the end of December 1979, the Soviets had undertaken a bloody overthrow of the government in Afghanistan. I do not need to comment on Soviet criminal action, Communist Vladimir Zhirinovsky, a mega-horn of the KGB, has done it so vividly that my analysis is unnecessary. He said: "I want to clean my boots in the

Indian Ocean." Though his knowledge of geography is left to be desired, nevertheless, the motive was obvious—to go further, closer to Iran, to its oil.

The thought process of all Communists is so identical, that hundreds of miles from Moscow, my Communist husband, Garrik, a Secretary in the Communist Party of the Bar Association, told me the same story only with different words and expressions. The conversation between us took place in front of the television on the evening of the Soviet invasion in Afghanistan, December 29, 1979, *Baltic Winds*, pp. 252-253.

"Garrik, what is going on in Afghanistan?" I asked.

"A lot of people have been killed, but we have control over the situation."

"I mean very simply that in two or three months, the north of the country will be ours; then we will move further, and in two or three years, we'll have a gate to the Indian Ocean."

"...You believe that fighting in Afghanistan to gain access to the Indian Ocean is the right thing to do?" He thought for a moment and responded:

"I really don't know whether now is the right time. But I believe that our leaders certainly know when and how to fight. By the way, have you heard about the new theory developed by the Academy of Science?"

"About what?"

"About the oil resources. The Academy of Science is convinced that, within a decade or two, the world's oil supply will be exhausted. That means that whoever possesses the oil at that time, those people will be able to conquer the world without firing a shot. Our leaders are not fools; they have forecasted long-term objectives. Afghanistan is just the beginning of the road to the oil. As soon as we are in the Indian Ocean, we'll close the gate to the Persian Gulf, period! Don't you understand that oil is our weapon against the West?" That was said almost thirty years ago!

In conclusion: The Iranian Revolutionary Guards—a terrorist organization—is the political base and security of Ahmadinejad like the KGB was a political base and security of all Soviet leaders. They are alike. *The Russian Factor* describes how those agencies acted combining legal and illegal actions. We have found a lot of weaponry in Iraq that was allegedly produced in Iran. I suspect that weaponry had been produced in Russia with a fraudulent label *made in Iran*. I purposely dedicated some pages to the Iranian Islamic Revolution—the next hostility or maybe a war will take place there or by Iran. Remember the Russian factor. I would relay to the young researchers to continue my analysis and prove that I was right. A small note: Some in the media are confused—it is The Iranian Revolutionary Guard, not The Republican Guard. Nice try by Moscow's students to associate the Republicans with the criminals…!

It is happened that being interested in the history of the Iranian Islamic Revolution, remembering China and suspecting Kremlin's influence to it, I went back to the time of the Soviet infiltration across the world in the 1920s, looking for the word communists in Iran. What I found completely satisfied me—I was right looking for the Soviets in Iran. They were there. Aren't you surprised that talking about the Islamic Revolution in Iran, you have never heard about the communists? Don't be surprised—they were there under another name—a typical Soviet disguise! And what I found proved my theory of a long-range Soviet strategy for world domination and the role that Islam and oil had played in the agenda.

Somewhere in the beginning of the 1950s, my father often mentioned the name of the Iranian Prime Minister Mossadegh. Remembering that, I went through the internet to find out about his activities and found much more than I had expected. Being close to Russia, Northern Iran became the center of underground Marxist and social democrat political activity. Do you remember the Chekist Jacob Blumkin? He was there. The Communist Party of Iran was founded in the province of Gilan in June 1920. As a matter of fact, it was only the beginning of the communist's activities—the Soviet Republic of Gilan was established with the assistance of the Red Army. With help from the British, the central government of Iran had defeated the newly formed Soviet Republic of Gilan. The Communist Party had been prosecuted and banned—communists and social democrats once again went underground.

The Allies Invasion of 1941-1942 resulted in the end of Shah's reign. Many political prisoners were subsequently released and under this new atmosphere, nationalist and socialist groups once again flourished. On September 29, 1941 the Tudeh Party[82] (the People's party) was officially founded. It was WWII where the Soviet Union was an ally and some Soviet military forces were staying in Teheran. The Tudeh Party actively participated in the 14th Majlis election and eight of its candidates were elected in 1944. From that time on the Tudeh Party grew immensely and became a major force in Iranian political life. Do not forget that the Tudeh Party consisted of the nationalists, communists, and social Democrats. Please, take into account that the Soviet Army was an occupational force in Iran at the time and consider the Soviet two-fold infiltration—legal and illegal to cover up the Soviet ideological molding of the Iranian leaders and penetration to Iranian institutions and organizations.

Certain actions and behaviors of the Tudeh Party had disclosed its essence—an attempt to assassinate Shah Muhammad Reza Pahlavi in 1944 had confirmed the communist's modus operandi. The party was banned again; however, it continued functioning underground for a time before being able to operate in the open beginning in the1950s. In 1951, Shah appointed Muhammad Mossadegh as Prime Minister of Iran. It was Mossadegh who established a close relationship with the Tudeh Party, nationalists, and the National Front of Iran. And it was Mossadegh who introduced many socialist reforms including nationalization of the oil industry taking it away from Anglo-Iranian Oil Company. In this familiar political environment of oil and the Soviet- communist influence, I have to admit that it was Iran that was probably the first step to the Soviet long-range strategy of the oil conspiracy. Perhaps recruitment of Arafat in 1957, which I called before the first step in the oil conspiracy, was the next step after Iran. Forgive me—while writing I am learning as well. But the term of modern Islamism, which is a symbiosis of religion and politics, has definitely been born in Iran.

It was during the Cold War, the Americans and British were afraid that Iran might be establishing closer ties with the Soviet Union, and Mossadegh was ousted by a coup d'etat. Most political groups, including Mossadegh's National Front and the Tudeh Party, have been banned and continue to function underground. In the beginning of the 1970s in northern Iran, which bordered the Soviet Union, the Iranian guerrilla movement had begun. "The 1970s also witnessed the birth of widespread worker's strikes and demonstrations and university campuses became a hotbed of revolutionary activity. The Tudeh Party drastically increased its activities, recruiting many youth and organizing regional committees. The Tudeh Party from this point on becomes established as one of the strongest underground movements and helps to pave the way for the forthcoming Iranian Revolution of 1978." Do you grasp now the political game in Iran run by Russia? The Tudeh Party is the Communist Party of Iran! When did you hear about the guerrilla movement, strikes, demonstrations, and other revolutionary activities inside the universities? Please, do not be fooled.

To sum up the Iranian case, I believe that the seeds of Stalinism were blended with Islam and inculcated into the Muslim soil and psyche of its youth, producing a movement we call Jihad today. The exact time could be the 1920s or the 1940s. Experts should determine it. That movement also gave birth to the notion of Islamism—spreading of Islam throughout the globe. In this respect it is worth comparing two concepts presented by me in the book—Sovietization and Islamization. You will be surprised at how identical the two are by modus operandi and objectives. Go back to the first chapters and you will see that Stalin used violence as the main method to obtain power and world domination. Jihad has the same agenda—to achieve world domination through brutal violence. The next most vivid similarity is the recruitment and use of young people. The communists have always used youth to obtain power. Jihad does the same—Fascism is always Fascism. This means that Israel is on a threshold of repeating a brave act of saving the West the second time around. It was nuclear reactor in Saddam's Iraq in 1981, now it will be Ahmadinejad's Iran. The West and Israel have allies in several Muslim countries with no Jihad: Dubai, Jordan, Turkey, and other—they are free from both Sovietization and Islamization, they can help to fight Soviet Fascism!

There is another Islamic country to watch closely—Pakistan. For several decades thousands of Pakistani youth have studied in the Soviet Union under the supervision of the KGB. The Soviets, like Stalin decades ago, were busy creating a loyal leadership among foreign young people studying on Soviet territory. Do you remember the *People's Friendship University of Russia?* For your information, thousands of Pakistani youth had been studying there and as usual were recruited by the KGB. Returning to Pakistan many of them went to serve in Pakistan's intelligence. As you can see, the situation in Pakistan is a very unstable one and we can expect another attempt to assassinate General Musharaff. Pakistan, which borders Afghanistan, is also a Soviet target—revenge is still in their mind. We can conclude now that the infiltration of the Soviets in China to build a communist state in the 1920s is going on throughout the world still. Considering the time passed, maybe methods and techniques have changed a bit, but the scale of infiltration and penetration has grown substantially. It really covers a lot of territory—from China to the Middle East, and therefore to Jihad and in between!

Talking about Afghanistan I would like to remind you that my opinion on the war with the Taliban and Al-Qaeda has not changed since 2003—Russia is behind them and arming both. After the defeat of Afghan's Communists, more than one million Afghans fled to the former Soviet Central Asian Republics, where they were used later by Russia. I have predicted then that the Taliban and Al- Qaeda would regroup with Afghans, Uzbeks, and Tajiks coming from the former USSR to continue fighting our forces. I was right. Now I want to give you an interesting fact of geography that can prove my opinion. On the Northern part of both Afghanistan and Pakistan lays the long range of Hindu Kush Mountains, which are the westernmost extension of the Pamirs Mountains. The latter presents a territory of the former Soviet Republics in Central Asia: Turkmenistan, Uzbekistan, Kyrgyzstan, and Tajikistan. You can find there a Peak of Stalin and a Peak of Lenin. The terrain is the most intriguing one in Asia: it is a knot, a juncture of several borders, an oil-rich cultural quilt including Uzbekistan, Tajikistan, Afghanistan, Pakistan, and China. And the oil-rich area is predominantly in China. Watch it! Pay attention to Kazakhstan, as well, Russia's security forces are very influential and strong there! I have two points to discuss. First, the KGB is behind Al Qaeda and the Taliban. Second, Bin Laden can be in one of the former Soviet Republics and not at Torah Borah. Five years ago, I presented all my analysis on Al-Qaeda and the KGB that established and organized all its activities in the beginning of the 1990s, *The Russian Factor*, chapter 11, *Perestroika* and *Bin Laden*. Today I can give you even more. Have you heard about the Merchant of Death? This nickname was given to Victor Bout, a former KGB man, who has supplied arms to the Taliban and Al-Qaeda by following the assignment received from his masters in the KGB apparatus. He was illegally supplying arms in Africa, Europe, and Asia. He also provided weapons to Columbian guerrillas fighting against the American influence! Do you remember my story of the word Willis? Don't you see, the circle of the KGB's activities around the globe is exposed? Hence, my first point is proved to be true. Bout's nationality has also played a role—Victor Bout is a Tajik speaking the language of the Hindu Kush Mountains and easily blending in with the locals..... I do not know which way the Merchant of Death illegally transported the arms to the Taliban and Al-Qaeda, but researching the terrain of the Hindu Kush Mountains where only Muslims reside, I got the idea.

The Northern part of Afghanistan and Pakistan has a long border with all three former Soviet Republics. Look at the map: Turkmenistan has a border with Iran and Afghanistan. Uzbekistan borders Afghanistan, Tajikistan borders both Afghanistan and Pakistan. There are two ways to bring illegal arms to Afghanistan and to Pakistan. One is by way of the Amu Darya River, which is rising in the Hindu Kush Mountains in Afghanistan and flows between Turkmenistan and Uzbekistan. Another path could be the Hindu Kush Mountains with its caves and tunnels. Keep in mind that digging bunkers and using tunnels is and was the Soviet military Doctrine. The Soviets once had drilled a tunnel in the Hindu Kush Mountains. "The Salang tunnel at 3, 363 m and the extensive network of galleries on the approach roads were constructed with Soviet financial and technical assistance and involved drilling 7 miles through the heart of the Hindu Kush." Wikipedia. That is why my idea about the intriguing terrain of the Hindu Kush can be used by both Bout and Bin Laden. Please, put together my current observations with those of 2003 and, perhaps, you will agree with me on the issue just discussed.

I can give you another vivid example and statistics of Mr. Bout's activities throughout the world. The KGB not only molded and created the Soviet-style leaders especially in many African countries, but also supplied them with weapons and arms, thanks to their officer Victor Bout and others. As a result, for your information, 45,000 people are killed by the gangs every year in the so-called Democratic Republic of Congo. The situation in Mozambique is horrifying—the war for independence that started in the '60s has destroyed the country. Life expectancy in that beautiful country is forty years! Africa has become a killing field, a continent of human disaster due to the Kremlin's anti-colonial aggressive policy during the last several decades. We gave a ton of money to the African countries, yet we do not know who is who in running them. The best example is Robert Mugabe—a Moscow student and a criminal of the twenty-first century.

No less disastrous events occurred in the South American continent—the Moscow henchman, Hugo Chavez is trying to overthrow a legitimate Columbian Government, funding and arming the quarreler's forces. Of course he is doing that with the Kremlin's help, arming the guerrillas with weaponry. Do you remember Columbia's guerrillas? Now their army has grown into the army of FARC—Former Revolutionary Armed Forces of Columbia. They are a formidable force flooding America with drugs, arms, and saboteurs. In Columbia they are fighting lawful government, killing civilians, and kidnapping hundreds of hostages. Doesn't it remind you of the Stalinist, European scenario of the 1950s-1960s? Watch also the Russian weaponry and arms sold in billions to Venezuela lately. I am afraid that the Soviet mafia wants to establish a kind of oil syndicate with Venezuela and Iran to keep our dependency of oil or establish the gas syndicate with the same agenda—a march for world domination is going on. One syndicate of the criminal gangs on the land rich with oil has already been established in Mexico, next to us. Keep in mind that the hunt for natural resources started in the 1950s-60s when the Soviets invaded Africa. Go to Zimbabwe to see how the Soviet henchmen demolished Rhodesia, a dreadful result to grasp the magnitude of Africa's tragedy. Mexico is on the way to disaster— the government is unable to stop criminal drug-trafficking gangs dealing on our borders. The subject of criminal gangs within our land under the KGB's supervision I have already discussed in the *Russian Factor*. Remember geography—the Mexican tragedy started in the 1980s, when the Democrats blocked help to Nicaragua's Contras. Keep in mind that organized crime is the main component of the Soviet Mafia "working" in Mexico. President of Columbia Uribe succeeded in fighting the Soviet henchmen in his country and the drug-trafficking clan moved to Mexico, which provides oil to the U.S.

In connection with the subject of oil, let me remind you of historic facts that shed some light on the contemporary situation in the world. I have already discussed the partnership between Hitler and Stalin in the beginning of the book—Stalin openly supported Hitler in his expansion in Europe. The rivers of oil and grains had flowed to Germany from Russia. I just want to add some historic facts that prove it. In February 1939, Moscow suddenly stopped providing all foreign companies with oil. The German and Italian companies were the exception—they continued receiving oil. In August 1939, Stalin and Hitler signed the Soviet-German Pact that made them allies and partners. September 1, 1939, WWII began. It is interesting to know how Mussolini reacted to the events described above: "Bolshevism is dead; instead we have a kind of Slavic Fascism." To a certain degree Mussolini was right—I have identified the

Russian regime as Soviet Fascism, giving it a political platform based on Stalinist ideology. Be very careful dealing with Russia—those who did not learn from the past are doomed to make the same mistakes.

Returning to the issue of the war criminals, I would suggest that you continue my analysis mentioned above for this issue as well. For all of the reasons, plus the duration of the crime, and the Kremlin's leading role in the oil conspiracy, I consider Yevgeny Primakov War Criminal No.1 in the long list of other world criminals who must be tried. Look at the photo of two comrade- criminals, *The New York Times*, 3, 31, 1999. The picture confirms completely my conclusion. Alas, under current circumstances and the situation in Russia it is impossible to bring it about today. I will continue to discuss the events in Russia in the next chapters. In summing up, I would say that by illegal activities described in this chapter, the Kremlin had created not only *The Red Menace: From China to Jihad, but the Evil Empire of Global Terrorism* on our planet.

CHAPTER 10

Face to Face with Soviet Fascism

Have you noticed lately the constant use of the term "Fascism" in the arena of world politics? I have. That is why I decided to discuss with you the term and variety of its forms. As a rule the word "fascist" is identified with Nazis. And that is true, considering their brutality and crimes committed against humanity. But "fascist" party came to life much earlier, adopting the Roman fasces (wooden rods), symbol of strength and unity as its emblem. Fascism exemplifies an ideology of a totalitarian state. People use the word in its narrow sense, as soon as brutalities and atrocities occur, and they are missing the wider meaning of the term. Fascism is an ideological system of a government—a merger, an amalgamation of the one ruling party, militarized security forces, and economy.

In this context, I read interesting information in the Columbia Encyclopedia: "Mussolini in 1922... presented himself as the strong-armed savior of Italy... He had taken over from Russian Communism a system of party organization based on a hierarchy and cells; this became typical of fascism everywhere." p. 658. That way the first of Europe's Fascist dictator Mussolini came to power in 1922. The tactics and strategy to hold power has been characterized by one capacious sentence: "The emphasis on youth and struggle became paramount." p.658.

In light of this statement, I recalled a conversation with my friend Vlad before my immigration to the United States in 1980. He told me that both Hitler and Stalin came from the radical left and transformed their labor parties respectively, Hitler into the National Socialist Party, and Stalin into the Communist Party, creating similar one-party militarized police states. Both men had been seething with madness. Acting identically and using scapegoats, they placed all blame on others—Hitler on the Jews, Stalin on the West and conservatives. They played expertly on national sentiments, deceiving and promising along the way. Uneducated psychopaths, but excellent actors, they hypnotized people, following the same motto: The bigger the lie, the more believable it is.

After the collapse of the Soviet Union, however, I have found crucial differences between Germany and the Soviet Union. Germany was militarily defeated, all its leaders together with their fascist ideology discredited. Unlike Germany, after the collapse of the Soviet Union nothing similar has occurred. On the contrary, the old *Formula for Power*, designed by Stalin was saved and used by the heirs of the Soviet Union, belonging to the same clan. Soon after Yeltsin's relatively young democracy, the KGB and its Soviet mafia came to power. And that is the crux of the matter in the comparison of Fascist Germany and Stalinist Russia. Wherever the Soviet mafia resides it immediately instills its modus operandi and the ideology of Soviet Fascism. I am an American citizen and for a clear reason, my concern for American national security keeps me writing and warning America about an upcoming danger.

And though I have already presented all the arguments concerning Soviet Fascism in *The Russian Factor*, I ought to expose again the sources and remind you of the identification of the Soviet mafia and its ideology of Soviet Fascism in our days. To conceive that you should be better informed of what is going on today in Russia to grasp the actual Soviet Fascism in action… there is no doubt that Russia of 2007 has changed the main composition of the Soviet mafia, but it was done intentionally to deceive and fool you, and of course to fool and deceive the Russian people as well.

Somewhere in the beginning of the book, I had warned you not to be confused by the numerous abbreviations of the former KGB. Constant changing the names of the security and intelligence agencies had been routine behavior of the Communist/Soviet government to cover up all the crimes committed by those agencies. What we see in Russia today is a complete repetition of the past maneuvers—today it is not experimenting only with the agencies, but with the parties as well. The intent is obvious: the crimes committed by the Communist Party must be covered up! And the best way to do it is to create a new name for the party—to divert attention from the criminals. That way the party of *United Russia*[85] organized by the KGB came to life. What is currently going on in Russia today can be identified as an amalgamation of the ruling party with the business—the major element of fascism.

Keep in mind that all former members of the KGB, the founders of United Russia had been Communists, which means they were also the Soviets. So the party of United Russia was constituted by the same three components that the Soviet mafia had been concocted with. Hence the substance of the new party has not changed, the agenda remains—only the name has changed. The familiar maneuver of the past was successfully executed, bringing to life again a *vertical of power for one party system, a totalitarian one.* Moreover, like Stalinist law in the 1930s, the current Russian law serves again the *vertical of power*, the one party system. The Russian people missed or swallowed that creation of *vertical of power* with ease. That was the first successful manipulation by the KGB that brought United Russia to power—the Soviet mafia had become the Russian government.

Definitely, Putin has played a major role in that transformation and if you want to know my opinion of him, please read *The Russian Factor.* I have described in detail my attitude toward him there. Knowing the Soviet mentality, and Putin's growing personality cult, I had predicted all of that in the book five years ago. What I did not show then, was a striking similarity with another famous personality, who had created his new party ninety years ago. Please, listen to the history of that other party described by the Columbia Encyclopedia. "National Socialism, political and social ideology of the National Socialist German Workers' party... in Germany after the First World War. It became the program of the totalitarian dictatorship (1933-1945) of Adolf Hitler. The term Nazi was derisive abbreviation of National Socialism. The nucleus of the party was the small German Worker's party, which Hitler joined..." p.1361. Don't you see some similarity in creation of the new party between the National Socialist Party in Germany and United Russia in the Post-Soviet territory of Russia? Both parties derived from the far-Left political spectrum to establish a totalitarian regime. Do you agree with me? Maybe the next quotation can help you.

Now I would like to give you the identification of the totalitarian system by the Columbia Encyclopedia: "Totalitarian government is most easily conceived as implying an absolute rejection of the concepts of personal and economic liberty... The unifying and directing force in the state is the official party, headed by the dictator, the object of propagandistic glorification assuming the status of a cult. The dictator to survive must improvise a program design to allay or suppress domestic discontent. ...Totalitarianism breeds the police state... Variants of totalitarianism were established as Fascism in Italy and National Socialism in Germany..." p.1996.

Writing *The Russian Factor*, I did not use the Encyclopedia, relying only on my personal knowledge in identifying Soviet Fascism. I have titled chapter 9, *The Mysterious Aggressor: Soviet Fascism*. Now, five years later, I am surprised of how right I had been then. Listen to how the Columbia Encyclopedia describes National Socialism in general and the German's one in particular: "In its program of action National Socialism was not entirely based on racial theory. Its success depended less on the truth of its ideological premises than their propaganda appeal. (In fact, serious modern scientists have totally rejected the concepts of racial inequality and racial purity.) National Socialists were hostile to democratic equalitarianism not only because it conflicted with their racial doctrine, but also because it appeared to them as an invention to bolster the weak and the mediocre and to inhibit the strong and the dynamic. Moreover, they regarded democracy as inefficient tool for national aggrandizement." p.1361.

The next quotation is no less important: "In *Mein Kampf*, Hitler outlined his program with cynical frankness and detail. The first step—to seize power in Germany—was to be accomplished by a 'legal revolution,' i.e. by using parliamentary methods to end parliamentarianism. The next step was the creation of a totalitarian state, entirely control by Hitler through his party. Next, taking advantage of the weakness of the 'decadent' Western democracies, Germany was to break one by one the clauses of the Treaty of Versailles. United and once more in possession of a strong war machine, Germany then could—either by intimidation or actual aggression—reunite all German speaking peoples (see Pan-Germanism) and embark on its venture for world hegemony... Not only labor, but also youth, schools, and the press were 'coordinated' under party control. A 'German Christian Church' was set up by Hitler with the purpose of gaining control over the Protestant Churches, and Pastor Martin Niemoeller, who led the Protestant opposition, was arrested." The Columbia Encyclopedia, p. 1361.

Hitler united all stratums of the German society under the ideology of National Socialism while propaganda as a major tool had served Hitler pretty well giving him time to build a strong German state. It is no accident that history remembers the name of his Minister of Propaganda Josef Goebbels. He had it right, "Just tell people big lies often enough and they will believe them." Hitler called him "minister of popular enlightenment." As a matter of fact, Goebbels had a tremendous propaganda apparatus—his propaganda machine had included his wife Magda Goebbels, too. Her "achievements" were no less significant; she organized and inculcated German women in the tenets of the Nazis' ideology. Her radio show attracted millions of German women and she was given the opportunity to appear on the first TV show in 1936. The Nazis' propaganda machine had employed all modern facilities for spreading untruth, "exploiting mob emotions to the maximum."

I gave you some pieces of history to compare the social and political development in two countries: Germany in the 1930s and Russia in the end of the twentieth century and the beginning of the twenty-first century. Despite the difference in time, the political environment in both countries is absolutely similar; modus operandi and philosophy are identical. For example there was cooperation between the Gestapo and NKVD. You know what it means. Both regimes consider and manipulate their own people, especially youth, as a biological substance. Further analysis will testify for that. However, the predicament in contemporary Russia is much more dangerous for many reasons and particularly because of the leadership in Russia: Hitler had never been an agent of Gestapo, recruiting foreigners; Putin had been exactly that man. As the officer of the Soviet counterintelligence and the Chairman of the KGB, Putin followed all the Chekist's rules. And this is the crux of the matter. Considering the nature and modus operandi of the agency, and knowing its objective of world domination, we can now see implementation of those rules throughout the world.

I would like to submit to you another staggering similarity in a malignant evil modus operandi of the Nazis and the Soviet KGB. Nazis had an apparatus for mass killing—gas chambers. To achieve the maximum number of dead people, they used hydrogen cyanide and carbon dioxide in the gas chambers—both are lethal agents. Today we call these agents WMD—Weapons of Mass Distraction. In this connection, let me remind you a couple of tragic episodes connected to contemporary usage of WMD by the Soviet mafia. Do you remember the Gulf War illnesses in the 1990s? As I described it in *The Russian Factor*, Saddam had mixed poisoning agents and filled them into the weaponry used against Americans. The same criminal poisoning under Putin's leadership took place in the tragedy of the *Moscow Theater* where 300 people had been murdered in 2002. The President of Ukraine had been poisoned by dioxin in 2004. Both cases are similar because the basic motivation for murder had been revenge—the KGB's motto. There are even more dangerous signs I have already elucidated.

In the last several years, I have noticed the strange disappearance of the top people working on research of preventive vaccines against bio-weaponry, especially the famous microbiologists around the world. All had different causes of death, but none died of natural causes. One jumped from a bridge, another committed suicide, and several just disappeared under very strange circumstances. I have interpreted the situation as preparation of our enemy for a bio war—germ warfare Soviet-style. To my knowledge the Soviets and later Russians had been involved in genetic engineering and had never stopped. For example, further development of different strengths of nerve gas, regardless of signing the documents prohibiting the activity. My thought is that Putin's motivation and preparation to use some of the prohibited agents is clear. He can provide any subordinated groups in the strategic part of the world with the bio-agent in the time beneficial to Russia. The same way he can use a nuclear material as well—the task is the same to kill as many people as possible, to destroy as much land as possible. Don't you recall Hitler's solution for the world…?

I have already researched Putin's ascendance to power in *The Russian Factor*, especially emphasizing the events in St. Petersburg when he was the deputy of a real democratic mayor who suddenly died. Then in 2004, I was not aware of some of Putin's activities while he worked as the deputy of St. Petersburg's mayor. Lately, I have heard from the opposition in Russia that Putin has been connected to the business mafia of St. Petersburg at that time. Now, I am not surprised, watching how he has developed the same political climate in Moscow, the capital of Russia, where the former KGB members are the owners of all serious Russian industries and simultaneously the members of the new party—United Russia. Reportedly there are 600,000 of them. This is a virtual amalgamation of economy with politics—the task and agenda of Soviet Fascism. Putin has achieved it in Moscow— the next step is world domination. Hitler had the same objectives. Don't you fear those similarities? I do...

In the beginning of this book I warned you about an upcoming election to Duma[88] (the Russian Parliament); because I knew that Putin would do everything possible to bring victory to United Russia. He could not afford to lose the parliamentary election for personal reasons—too many skeletons in the closet and the upcoming presidential election. Losing the election for his party in Duma could have put him in danger later on. I am writing this chapter in December 2007, after the election to Duma. It should be noted that December 2007 was a month with extremely rich and important events in Russia, where United Russia and Putin played a major role in all of them.

Talking about the party you should know that President Putin does not belong to any party, but you also know who has created United Russia. One of the first violations and abuses of power had taken place three months before the election, when President Putin, using his personal popularity, became a spokesman of United Russia agitating its victory throughout eleven time zones. There were no debates at all in Russia—Putin did not participate in any. Yet all print, TV, and radio called it a referendum on our national leader, the party's slogan—vote for our national leader. At the same time the voters were unable to see or hear the leaders of the opposition—the national Russian media had closed its doors for them. Putin has constantly appeared on all national TV channels, the media printed his portraits, and radio stations constantly praised him. The overall picture has reminded me of my youth and the election under Stalin's time.

Perhaps, you are still unable to perceive how Russian people see Putin's leadership. It is not an easy matter for you living in democracy to comprehend what is going on in Russia. It is also hard for me to explain it. I will try. First, you should take into account and imagine the suffering, anguish, torment, and deprivation the Russian people have gone through for the last ninety years. As a result of constant crisis and fear, Russia's national psyche has been transformed and the standards of morality changed with it. You can learn from my books how people lived under Stalinism. After the collapse of the Soviet Union in 1991, the Russian people lost all their money, in the Russian national banks. The scale of alcoholism is directly related to the male life expectancy, which is fifty-seven years. All of that can give you the big picture of current

Russian society. Putin has definitely brought some kind of stability (in my opinion an illusory one), but the price of that stability is too high—it gives time and help for Putin and the Soviet mafia to build a strong totalitarian state. The rising prices of oil are helping them. The methods used in the election to Duma are the best examples of how the totalitarian state has been functioning.

I am using the word totalitarian and totalitarianism for a reason—it is an embodiment of CONTROL and POWER, the major characteristic of the Russian, KGB's government. To call the election in the Duma *the dirty election* would be an understatement. It was an attempt to turn or convert a current power of legislature to the permanent one, by consolidating success and securing the victory of United Russia. To achieve that Putin's administration had used all the KGB's methods of special operations: blackmail, bribes, fraud, intimidation, infiltration, and some force—the government's money was poured by the millions into one party—United Russia. The American media has reported about many violations during the election to Duma in Russia. Nevertheless, I would like to give you an example of the violation that will shock you.

Have you heard the term *carousel* (roundabout) used in the election to Duma? Do you know what it means? Hearing this word in Russian, I did not understand its application at first. The events that followed had given me the meaning of the word. The United Russia party together with the Kremlin's administration had organized the youth movement's groups providing them with a caravan of buses. The vast majority of youngsters were called NASHISTS. I watched them on Russian TV. Young people, wearing shirts with Putin's portrait, singing with enthusiasm bordering on euphoria, occupied the buses and moved along the streets to the voting precincts one after another. The voting ballots were waiting for them and they all voted for United Russia. Then they left for other voting places where they voted again and again for United Russia. Reportedly, in several cities printing houses reported that 109 percent voted for United Russia. Do not be surprised. Welcome to the country of Soviet Fascism run by the Soviet mafia!

I will give you another example so you can fully comprehend what is going on in Russia. A couple of months before the election the Kremlin had issued an order to all enterprises and offices throughout eleven time zones. The order had requested all the workers of the above mentioned plans and offices, students and teachers to take the absentee ballots from their places of residence and vote in their place of work or study. The heads of all offices were told to watch how people were voting and provide United Russia with the victory. Moreover, the policy of infiltration from the past became clear to present Russia. Do you remember Chekist Blumkin, a member of the SR's Party? Look at Alexei Arbatov who is a member of Yabloko! For those who know the man, the strategy is clear—infiltration to destroy Yabloko from within! Do you get the big picture of the parliamentary election in Russia on December 2, 2007?

Foreign watches from the European Union issued a statement: "Our main concern about the Russian election was the merging of the state and political party, in this case United Russia. We considered this an abuse of power and a clear violation of the Copenhagen commitments, which, in paragraph 5.4 say that 'a clear separation between the state and political party, in particular, political parties will not be merged with the state.'…The once promising democratic transition has come to a stop in Russia. Perhaps it has even taken a step backward." The OSCE and the Council of Europe's assessment of the parliamentary election in Russia.

I would use stronger words than the European assessment did. The agenda to deceive the West has produced an imitation in form, fraud, and substance—the Soviet-style election. And I would argue that the step backward Russia made many years ago, when the world had ignored or appeased the Kremlin was Soviet- style. In this connection, the time has come for us to return to the process of Hitler's appeasement in the past and his program of building Fascism in Germany. Do you remember Hitler's steps in that direction? I will remind you.

"The first step—to seize power in Germany—was to be accomplished by a 'legal revolution,' i.e. by using parliamentary methods to end parliamentary." Look at Putin's ascendance to power. He used Yeltsin's legal revolution, deceived him and his group of real democrats, and with the help of Old Guards—the *Organs* legally came to power. The next step is the similarity with Hitler's program to use parliamentary methods to end parliamentarianism. The parliamentary election on December 2, 2007 in Russia testified to that. On the banner of Putin's personality, he and hundreds of members of United Russia were elected to the Duma. And after that, Putin and others members of United Russia, had turned their mandates to the members of United Russia who did not participate in the election at all. That step not only criminalized the democratic process, but in fact, ended with parliamentarianism as the governmental system. That environment had given Putin even more—it created an obedient Duma for the presidential election. Look at what is being presented; thousands of enthusiastic NASHISTS showing their choice—Putin.

You can ask me how it was possible to create a cult of Putin supporters for only a couple of years. The answer is simple—the *Department of Agitation and Propaganda*. Stalin's creation is alive and well as his Organs, both working in unison. Do you remember how these two created the cult of Stalin's personality? The same exact way they have created the Putin's personality cult seventy years later. Let me remind you of the principal function of the mentioned department—it is choreography of image making! The task is twofold: creating a cult of personality for the Communist leaders, or destructive images of their adversaries. Goebbels by his propaganda machine, with tenets of Nazism, helped to create a cult of personality for the Hitler-Furor, which lasted twelve years. *The Department of Agitation and Propaganda* has never been eliminated—with the experiences of the past seventy years its "sophistication" has quadrupled. You are the witnesses of the result—Putin's cult of personality. Recall the pictures of a sea of German youth, all saluting Hitler. Compare those to the brainwashed NASHISTS voting for Putin in 2008. The Department also concocted negative images of the political opponents they were trying to defeat, with great success. The Russian people had abbreviated the department's name, calling it—Agitprop.

Returning to Germany, in Hitler's program, "the next step was the creation of a totalitarian state, entirely controlled by Hitler through his party." That exact environment had been "achieved" by Putin after the December 2007 election to Duma. The entire force of the legal opposition had been eradicated from political life in Russia. Only so-called controlled opposition was allowed to exist. That environment of totalitarianism in Russia will progress to the long-term's task more easily than in Germany—Russian background of Stalinism propelling the order. The Kremlin's agenda is the next similarity, the most threatening one.

In the Hitler program, after creation of the totalitarian state, the next step was "...taking advantage of the weakness of the 'decadent' Western democracies, Germany... united and once more in possession of a strong war machine,... then could—either by intimidation or actual aggression—reunite all German speaking people... and embark on its venture for world hegemony." It should be noted that the world community had untied Hitler's hands and he was free to develop his agenda. After WWI, people in the destroyed areas of Europe and particularly Germany were easily deceived and fooled by Hitler's promises. At the time, America was hit with a Great Depression and there was great suffering and work to merely survive—Hitler's hands were untied.

The situation in Russia at the beginning of Putin's reign was analogous to that of the Weimar Republic in the beginning of the '30s. However, the world community has presented a completely different picture, which is more reminiscent to the appeasement of the Nazis' Germany at the end of the '30s. As a result of that appeasement we had millions of deaths in WWII and again, Europe was destroyed. For those who know Soviet Fascism, the development in Russia was clear—the building of the totalitarian state under leadership of the former KGB Chairman Putin. The big picture of the World today is similar to that of 1938-1939. We did not learn our lesson from WWII; we are again appeasing the aggressor!

The next comparison is absolutely identical. "Not only labor, but also youth, schools, and press was coordinated under party control. A German Christian Church was set up by Hitler with the purpose of gaining control over the Protestant Church..." Do you remember how in the beginning of the book, I warned you about infiltration into the Russian Orthodox Church and the youth movement NASHI established by the Kremlin? You saw the pictures of enthusiastic youth whose choice was Putin in the election of the Russian Parliament, Duma. By the way, he is the President, head of the executive branch, not a legislative one. But in the totalitarian state anything is possible. The scenario described by the steps Hitler had taken is a carbon copy of Russia 2007. If you remember, the Russian Orthodox Church had been infiltrated early on by Stalin. There is a joke in Russia that two former KGB's agents came to power; one runs the country, the other the Russian Orthodox Church.

I hope that now you have the real picture of what is going on in Putin's Russia and the world—the similarity with the German way of building a strong Fascist state are striking. And again the West is swallowing the Kremlin's spectacle. But even Hitler did not come up with the idea of connecting the youth movement with the Church—to bring to the movement some flavor of spirituality. Reportedly, after such a "successful" parliamentary election, Putin gave an assignment to Vasily

Yakemenko (NASHIST's founder) to establish a connection with the Orthodox Russian Church and establish a movement of the Orthodox youth based on the experiences of NASHISTS in the parliamentarian election in December. Do you remember that NASHI had been formed as a "paramilitary force to attack Putin's harshest critics" and as a banner of anti-Americanism? You have to see and listen to them to grasp their endless hatred of America. My conclusion is that Putin has been preparing the loyal forces for the Russian presidential election in March. Please, remember Putin's background—he called himself a Chekist. It is worth reminding you that Nazis had dozens of military officers attempting Hitler's assassination— there was none to assassinate Stalin! He was the Chekist's real leader!

It would be an incomplete picture of Russia if I evaded the main attribute of the Soviet mafia's activities—corruption. Putin virtually distributed all Russian wealth between a few oligarchs closest to him—banks, industry, and natural resources. It is worth showing the special assignments of those few people closest to Putin. An Oligarch is a person of tremendous wealth who directly influences the policy of the government promoting a monopoly of political power. In this case a group of Oligarchs is the Russian KGB's government. The arrangement contains another similarity between the Russian KGB's government and Nazi Germany. The Nuremberg Trials' documents identify the status of the "war criminals." Among the defenders you find not only military officers, but other participants in crime. Next to Herman Goering you can see President of the Reichsbank Walter Funk, Reich Youth Leader, Baldur von Schirach, and Editor of the newspaper Der Sturmer, Julius Streicher, as well as the industrialists who financially sustained Hitler. Doesn't it remind you of the contemporary Russian KGB government? Just add the Soviet *Department of Agitation and Propaganda* to the picture and you will have the same predicament.

The prosecutors at the Nuremberg Trials had charged the defendants with conspiring and launching aggressive war and committing war crimes and crimes against humanity. The statement of an American Judge presiding at the Nuremberg war crimes trial gave an objective verdict: "The crimes which we seek to condemn and punish have been so calculated, so malignant and so devastating, that civilization cannot tolerate their being ignored, because it cannot survive their being repeated" (Associate United States Supreme Court Justice Robert Jackson). Sixty years later I have found a stunning similarity with the events preceding WWII, described by the Nuremberg Trials Justice and the predicament in Russia that cannot be ignored by the civilized world. The Kremlin's activities described in this book can be qualified as calculated, malignant, and devastating to the civilized world. Moreover, the scale of the Kremlin's corruption has surpassed all human imagination—institutionalized corruption is one of the tools of Soviet Fascism. A virus of bribes permeated society from top to bottom. The notion of accountability, integrity or shame does not exist in the Soviet mafia—Mafia is a mafia whenever it runs the country.

There was one oligarch in the 1990s in Russia under Yeltsin's government. Putin's KGB government had "nourished" seventy- eight oligarchs with tremendous wealth in the billions of dollars. They are obsessed with money and buying Real Estate throughout the world, especially in Europe. It is not a coincidence that the amount of money flowing to the Kremlin is so staggering. On his birthday, Putin got a present from drunk with money oligarch Abramowich, a yacht—approximate value: $59 million. But secretly, Putin reimbursed him with billions—Siberneft (Siberian Oil), stolen from *Ucos*. Yet, it is important to grasp not only the amount of money going through the Kremlin's gates, but the number of Russian institutions that are completely corrupt. The Russian National Bank is run by the Kremlin—all private banks are run by the Kremlin's friends. Those corrupt institutions and the oligarch's obsessed and drunk with money attitude constitute the Soviet mafia, the heart of which is located in the Kremlin. Therefore, the Kremlin virtually runs the entire Russian financial system and contemporary industry. Enormous bureaucracy, consolidating money and power is robbing the population. Like in the Stalinist movement a lot of Jews participate in Putin's Oligarchy of Soviet Fascism with quadruple imperial syndrome.

To perceive that political swamp and culture of corruption within the Soviet mafia, you should know that the seats in the Russian Duma are for sale; you can buy them for big money. Remember, Duma is equal to our House of Representatives. A total lawlessness reigns along eleven time zones. Let me give you some other examples of enormous corruption in Russia. Several years ago I was invited as a consultant to an American business firm. The firm was dealing with the Russian Hermitage—the pearl of the world's best museums. After several meetings with people from Russia, I gathered the American team and told them that we were dealing with people from the KGB, and that I would not recommend continuing business with them. The American team was shocked, but continued doing business with them. A couple of years later, I found out that 200 exhibits had been stolen or replaced with fraudulent articles in the Hermitage. An investigation was launched, but I am not sure of its result. This is another example:

In your mind, the police are the most trusted individuals in America, yet in Russia, the police are the least trusted individuals. Drivers in Russia always have money in their pockets because if stopped, a bribe is the only way to be free. Yet the corruption within the entire law enforcement institution is more detrimental than just bribes. Real Estate in Moscow is the most expensive in the world and the most desirable as well. Due to the Russian housing system, the policemen would know where all the old people lived in the good and big governmental apartments. Several years ago, there was an epidemic in Moscow of old people dying suddenly. Their apartments were sold or given to the high-ranking people from the government. A few policemen had been charged with murder, but only a few. The murder of citizens by policemen is a regular event throughout Russia—the MVD runs the police. Do you remember the agency called the MVD? The mechanism of corruption in Russia has turned to different forms of crimes where the Soviet mafia is catching fish and money in murky waters. To become the head of a security agency costs $100 thousand to $1 million. This is a reality of life in Putin's Russia—the staggering amount of money flowing through the Kremlin's gates. Corruption is not an element of Soviet Fascism, it is its essence.

To grasp the activities of the Russian KGB's government and to have a real picture of the enormous corruption within the Kremlin and the Russian business, I would recommend reading three chapters of the study by Boris Nemtsov and Vladimir Milov, assessing Putin's reign. They are careful, but I would evaluate their work as a highly professional, and factual. To be honest, I was stunned by their bravery and incredible knowledge of the subject matter. While reading the study of Boris Nemtsov and Vladimir Milov, a strange idea flew through my mind—these two Russian specialists are the real political leaders of the future Russia. I personally knew one of them—Boris Nemtsov. Sometime toward the end of the 1980s, at the time of perestroika, as a expert on the Soviet Union, I received an invitation for a private meeting in the Upper East Side apartment, the subject of the meeting—the future of Russia. There were five to six people and among them two from Moscow.

I was pleasantly surprised by one of them—a young, energetic man from Russia, Boris Nemtsov. Nature gave him all the attributes of a leader: good looks, brains, tenacity, and confidence in the right direction for Russia. Today, twenty years later I can conclude that had the political situation in Russia been changed, the country would have a chance for a politically literate, constructive, and peaceful leadership toward the world... Alas, it is only a dream. In reality, Russia desperately needs systemic and structural political reforms, the first is having valid election.

It is imperative for the Western world to understand who we are dealing with in Russia today. During the last nine decades the Russian political landscape has experienced a selection of the sort—a biological, political selection—annihilation of the Russian aristocracy, intelligencia, the genetic fund of Russia. Since the time the Cheka had begun the slaughter of the political dissent, the annihilation of the people in opposition never stopped in Russia. The Civil War took away the cream of the crop of the Russian military—the most active, valorous, and honest people sacrificed their lives fighting against the Bolsheviks for a better future for Russia. Stalin's policy of collectivization and industrialization cost Russia tens of millions of victims and economic calamity. The crimes committed by the Cheka and the *Organs* drastically devalue LIFE itself and show a principal policy of vicious and ferocious violence against any dissent to implement Stalinist's Socialism in Russia and then to achieve world domination.

Though I have already discussed the crimes committed by the Cheka in the preceding chapters, Russia continues to suffer the effects of those enormous crimes today. The best human resources of people, the smartest and most intelligent, the most honest and conscious had been systematically liquidated. After the collapse of the Soviet Union under Yeltsin it was a span of time where there was rest for the nation. With Putin as the Chairman of the KGB everything came back—the substance of crimes remains the same, but perhaps the methods have changed. It is now the murder- contracts or poisoning, prevailing in political revenge against the opposition in the twenty-first century. And we are dealing with a corrupted dictatorship, with the former Chekists whose agenda remains the same—destruction of the Western civilization and world domination.

In all preceding chapters and especially in *The Russian Factor*, I tried to show the transformation that occurred within the Russian culture. As a matter of fact, during those nine decades the Soviet counterculture has waged a war against traditional Russian culture. The vast corruption and violence is only a part of the result. The entire traditional Russian culture has experienced a fundamental transformation being defeated by the Soviet counterculture. It is for that reason I am constantly reminding you about the *Department of Agitation and Propaganda*—the major device or mechanism in the war against traditional Russian Culture. Do you remember the KGB's infiltration into the Russian Orthodox Church? It was the beginning of the war against religion—implementation of one of the most important devices or vehicles against a traditional culture. The incremental war has infiltrated the Russian Orthodox Church and defeated traditional Russian culture—that way Soviet Fascism had proceeded and won.

A fuel of the counterculture had always been its ideology spread by the *Department of Agitation and Propaganda*. The above mentioned department is alive and well today—agitation influences people's mind and consciousness—propaganda enrages their emotions. And the image of the "enemy" is concocted, like in the 1930s. The department is a universal one and continues concocting both images—the image of an enemy and the image of a leader by shaping a cult of personality. Do you remember Stalin's cult personality? You could see the repetition in the last election—Putin's power has no barrier, he can do whatever he wants using his *Department of Agitation and Propaganda*—today it is the ideological department of the party called United Russia, but the ideology itself is the same.

A return to the Stalinist past illustrates another change of Yeltsin's policy. Do you remember Yeltsin's order to withdraw old History textbooks from the Russian educational system? It has been done and the new textbooks reflecting the real events in the country were published. Putin has reversed this policy— the Russian youth will now study History by "new" textbooks portraying Stalin as a Great Manager and a Leader of the country. Like in Stalin's time, when movies and songs glorified him, today Putin's portraits hang in every classroom and children sing old songs glorifying Stalin. By Stalinist traditions, youth must be ready to continue the Party's line. Today, the name of the Party has changed from the Communist Party to United Russia, but the policy's substance remains the same—to promote the same objectives of world domination. This example can help you see more clearly the future of the Russian youth movement vis-à- vis the Western world, especially the group called NASHISTS. Please, remember this name, you'll hear it in the future.

At this point, I would like to introduce another historian, Valeria Novodvorskay. It is not only her incredible knowledge of Russian history that attracted me—her comparative approach to world history has no match. Most valuable to me is her analysis of the Russian and American histories; their similarities and deep differences. There are some similarities between Russia and America: a variety of different ethnic groups and different religions in both countries could predict an analogous historical development. Alas, it does not for the reason of deep contrasting social and political distinctions. The United States was formed voluntarily by the Thirteen Colonies to obtain independence from the British in 1775.

On July 4, 1776 the Second Continental Congress declared the independence of "the United States of America" in the Declaration of Independence. "The new nation was dedicated to principles of *republicanism*, which emphasized civic duty and a fear of corruption and hereditary aristocracy." The historical development of the Russian state has a completely different manner and shape of social and political formation. A Grand Duchy of Moscow located in W. central Russia was first mentioned in the twelfth century. It gradually began expansion of the Slavic neighbor's territory in cahoots with the Mongols in the thirteenth century. That way the Russian Empire of eleven time zones had been build later. I hope you see the fundamental differences between the two countries. To understand Russian behavior in the twenty-first century, please, remember the Russian historical DNA, its genetic code—expansion, which is used by the Communists and their KGB heirs in the quest for world domination.

I can't help but give you another example analyzed by historian Novodvorskay,[90] where she compares the societal level of civic development and people's responsibility in both countries. Both Russia and America had the Revolutionary and Civil Wars; however, she presents crucial differences in their societal responses. In America, everyone from farmer to shoemaker took a rifle, left their home and went to defend the country. They all carried on a sense of responsibility for their country. The citizens of the United States have saved the country first from King and then from division—their consciousness drove them to do that. It was a completely different picture in Russia—the passive population was lacking a sense of responsibility for their own country.

When revolution and civil war started the farmers and shoemakers were busy salting cabbage and pickles, soldiers threw out their arms and returned home from the front to do the same. They did not feel it was their responsibility to save the country from the Bolsheviks—they virtually helped them take over and have the power. The policy of Military Communism confiscated all their goods and nationalized their property. Later, The Red Terror did not leave a chance for them to resist—it was too late. Speedy, aggressive actions had provided the Bolsheviks with total control over the population. Dealing with Russia in the twenty- first century we must remember these two major characteristics of the Russian people and the Power that runs them, presented by a most knowledgeable and trusted historian in Russia—Valeria Novodvorskay. She has given a crucial lesson to the entire world. I would add to that a small comment: Russians are still living within total lawlessness like centuries ago—America has been a law abiding country since its inception. Pushkin characterized Russians as lazy and apathetic people…

…The world had not yet gotten over the Russian parliamentary "election" as Mr. Putin shocked us again—another act on the Kremlin's stage. Four leaders of the controlled opposition have come to the Kremlin to offer Putin the name of Dmitriy Medvedev[91] as his heir and the next President of Russia. The following day, when Putin offered this plan to Medvedev, the letter answered that he would accept it only under the condition that Putin would move to the prime minister's office. "If our people will trust Mr. Medvedev and elect him the new president of the Russian Federation, I will be prepared to continue our joint work—in this case in the position of premier of the government," said Putin. What a happy ending at the Kremlin's Theater, where the Soviet mafia runs all political affairs! What an unprecedented political arrangement, openly made before the world! And the West had swallowed it like it did the Munich Pact sixty years ago. The similarity is striking and the roots of Russian history make it even more perilous. Do you remember what Ivan the Terrible wrote to the Queen of England? He had written that he as the Russian Czar was the only one who could judge or pardon his people. Please, remember: Putin is forever. It is a typical game of the Soviet mafia to fool the Russians and the West.

The events that are going on openly before our eyes in Russia would enrage any ethical government. Not the Russian leaders— they have perpetrated enormous fraud and there is no shame on their part—

condescendence and arrogance is the major attitude— Stalin has injected superiority in every cell of their bodies forever. There are other features in place as well from Russian history. For those who want to know the real Russian History, I would recommend reading Mrs. Novodvorkay's essays.

The Western media very calmly reacted to the events in Russia. I see the arrangement as a continuation and escalation of the long-term agenda—oil conspiracy against the West, let alone many other steps and maneuvers to undermine America. The first would be the choice of an individual like Mr. Medvedev, a yes-man and loyal comrade since both Putin and Medvedev had worked together in Leningrad. Medvedev is the first deputy prime minister and chairman of Gazprom, which means—oil and gas industry. There is no need to translate the word gas, prom is promyshlennost-industry. Gazprom is a combination of these two words, a sort of abbreviation, but a real monopoly in the world. I had asked you to remember the word Gazprom in 2002, in *The Russian Factor*, because I had known then about the oil conspiracy against the West. Putin has a paranoid idea of power and world domination—the oil conspiracy is the major tool in accomplishing the objectives.

Do not believe one word coming out of his mouth. In 1999, becoming President of the Russian Federation, Putin had promised to continue building democracy and civil society, to undertake economic reforms and to strengthen the rule of law. He also promised cooperation with the West. When in fact, he had done nothing like that. On the contrary, Putin had dismantled all of Yeltsin's achievements—freedom of the press and freedom of the assembly—the historic and unique accomplishments of Yeltsin. The appointment of Dmitry Medvedev is one link in a chain going backwards, to follow the main agenda—the oil conspiracy and world hegemony.

If you haven't read my two books, you would have no idea of the oil conspiracy, because secrecy is a must within the Kremlin. The evil plot against the West had been initiated by the Kremlin in the '50s. Recruitment of Yassir Arafat was the first step to activating the conspiracy, which has never ended since. Do you remember Mao's words about the guerrilla warfare in Kashmir having a connection to the Muslims of the Middle East? Nothing has changed since—the oil-terror conspiracy continues.

Besides, Medvedev is the Chairman of Gazprom, the oil and gas industry, he is a participant of the oil conspiracy and will go along with all of Putin's orders. To observe the constitution, Putin had two choices of his heirs, Dmitry Medvedev or Sergey Ivanov. I am not discussing the normal choice of free election—it was Putin's choice. Medvedev was chosen for many reasons; including one that only a former Soviet citizen can grasp and comprehend. Medvedev's mother is a Jew, his wife also a Jew. In case of trouble in the Russian economy and in a completely destroyed infrastructure, it will be he; Medvedev proclaimed guilty of any of that. For your information, several Russian cities suffered from cold this year, when the heating system was completely broken during winter. Can you imagine the panic and hate towards the government? It is enough only to hint that Medvedev, a Jew lover, is guilty of that. To understand that Soviet tendency you need to know the Russian culture and the Soviet mentality.

The other point for choosing Medvedev is a very simple one— he is the man who cooperated with Putin in the beginning of his new career in Leningrad in the late 1980s and early 1990s. Before that Putin had been a member of the KGB's counterintelligence in Europe for fifteen years. Together they joined a business and there is information that it was a mafia business. In *The Russian Factor*, I have already discussed the story of the Leningrad's democratic Mayor Sobchak, who suddenly died. Putin was his deputy. Putin and Medvedev belonged to the same Soviet mafia in Leningrad. After Putin's endorsement, Medvedev's rating rose to 70 percent. And that is despite the 20 percent inflation, stagnation in industry, ruined agriculture, systematic killing of journalists and others in dissent, overwhelming brutality of various crimes, across eleven time zones. There are no elected officials in Russia any longer— they are all more or less appointed by Putin in a country that is unable to secure and maintain its nuclear arsenal and is torn apart by wars and terrorist acts. Add to that vast alcoholism and use of drugs, especially among youth, and the picture of the country becomes more real. Yet nobody cares about the country—Moscow's Kremlin is busy—sustaining and developing a permanent *vertical of power*.

You can say that Medvedev was practically appointed by Putin and after the fact the Russian voters got the opportunity to elect him President of the Russian Federation. You are right. That exact proceeding or transaction had taken place. However, I can predict today that Putin will appoint himself as a Chairman of the party United Russia to continue being a boss. That inside dealing and distribution of the posts has been a regular business within the Soviet hierarchy as well. *The Organs* run Russia and its people.... Dealing with Russia, please, always takes into account the Russian nature and the structural peculiarity of the Russian government—the Soviet mafia, like any other mafia has unlimited and infinite power. The same situation has happened in other Soviet mafia countries—North Korea, Libya, and Syria in the past and Cuba currently. Fidel Castro is sick and he appointed his brother Raul Castro as president of Cuba in 2006. Just wait, there will be the same spectacle later on—the Soviet mafia has an identical script for all its henchmen in all activities. Please, keep in mind that Raul Castro is a man who under Soviet supervision has inundated America with drugs since the 1960s. This is also a confirmation that Soviet Fascism worked the same way in the countries that adhered to its ideology. Moreover, the people of those countries are treated the same way and as a result they behave accordingly—intimidated and silent, they listen to the words of their leaders. Always remember the "creativity" of Soviet Fascism to produce a cult of personality on the one hand and the evil image of the enemy on the other—the Stalinist's *Department of Agitation and Propaganda* is alive and well.

Have you ever heard from the people of Cuba, Syria or North Korea about their misfortunes? No you have not. Intimidated people in the countries of Soviet Fascism do not have their own judgment. I could have explained why they are silent, but a famous Academician Ivan Pavlov has done it much better characterizing people of Stalin's era in the 1930s. Sorry, it will be my translation from Russian: "I must express my sad opinion on a Russian man— he has such a weak brain system that he is unable to perceive reality the way it is. Only words exist for him. His conditional reflexes are not coordinated with actions but with words." I believe that Academician Pavlov's expertise gives us a correct diagnosis of the people under Stalin's reign. This quotation was unknown to me before. I took it from the article of a contemporary and respected Russian scientist, political writer, and analyst Andrey Piontkovsky. The article was published in America, the *Jewish World*, December 20-27, 2007.

Moreover, the author explains Stalin's trick with words: "Even Stalin could not call openly for destruction of the Russian peasantry and even his shameless propagandists could not dare sing the praises of the program. The word 'peasant' was substituted by the pejorative nickname 'kulak' and the best representative of the Soviet intelligencia from Gorky to Sholohov had welcomed merciless destruction of millions kulaks." Please, go back to my description of the *Department of Agitation and Propaganda* in this book and you will find a similar explanation of Stalinist tricks. That was only one of the methods Stalin used in building the Soviet system and its ideology. In general the Stalinist system was built on the corpses of the dead and on abuses of those who had survived. Now do you understand the reason for people in the countries of Soviet Fascism to be silent? I believe Mr. Piontkovsky agrees with me in an extricable juncture of the past with our present tied by the agency with three letters—the KGB.

I cannot tell you how I feel when I read the article—the author was discussing another tragic event that I had narrated twenty years ago in *Baltic Winds*, chapter 17, *Beyond Three Dimensions: Soviet Fascism*. The author of the article titled it "I Have Treated a Paranoiac lately." It is a story of another distinguished and famous Russian scientist and psychiatrist Professor Vladimir Behterev, who had examined Stalin and diagnosed paranoia. A couple of days after the article came out, Professor Behterev was poisoned and died. But the most intriguing thing is that the article was written on the occasion of Putin's speech in the Luzniki stadium and the result of the election to the Duma. Mr. Piontkovsky called Putin a National Spiritual Leader, whose speech was endlessly broadcasted by radio and all government TV channels. Unlike him, nobody heard or saw the opposition leaders and activists of human rights including Sergey Kovalev on TV.

Criticizing Putin's speech for its arrogance in mentioning the Jackals, traitors, and enemies of the people, Mr. Piontkovsky wrote that 96 percent of people voted for Putin's "Luzniki's Sermon." The author of the article is calling those people the *aggressively- obedient crowd* and comparing our time with Stalin's era, writing that, "We all together saw one paranoiac lately and we all liked him." The essence of the article is as significant and profound as consequential—the author made a collective diagnosis of the people that participated in the election of Duma and those who listened to Putin in the stadium and praised the speech. Moreover, Mr. Piontkovsky agrees with me on another critical point as well. He wrote that "for the masters of Putin's nomenclature, 1937 is in our backyard." Do you remember the first chapter of this book?

Returning to Putin's appointment of Mr. Medvedev, there are many reasons that Sergey Ivanov had been passed by. The most critical one is that Ivanov has an extremely important job (sluzba), which Putin cannot hand over to anybody else—he is waging the asymmetrical war for our destruction. Just recall my description of the KGB and its brother GRU—military intelligence. Ivanov is the ruler of GRU, and he works to execute WWIII. I have already mentioned GRU, recently I got additional information from the former member of GRU: "...compared to the U.S. Defense Intelligence Agency, the GRU's activities encompass those performed by nearly all joint U.S. military intelligence agencies as well as other national U.S. organizations... GRU and KGB SIGINT network employed about 350, 000 specialists. ...GRU is 'one of the primary instructors of terrorists worldwide." Stanislaw Lunev, the highest GRU defector. Besides that, the *Department of Agitation and Propaganda* is also under Ivanov's supervision. Do you see how "busy" Sergey Ivanov is? He is irreplaceable!

I hope now you understand that the Russian KGB's government is working simultaneously in two directions to destroy us: 1) by the oil conspiracy to suffocate our economy and 2) by the military intelligence to infiltrate our institutions, organizations, and businesses. I do not want to repeat my description of Sergey Ivanov: I did it in *The Russian Factor.* Returning to Medvedev, I can guarantee today, in December 2007 that Mr. Medvedev will be elected as President of Russia by approximately 65-70 percent of the Russian population—nobody can criticize or contradict the "National Spiritual Leader," as Mr. Piontkovsky called Vladimir Putin. I am calling him the Godfather of the Soviet mafia—Don Corleone; Soviet-style. However, looking at Putin's character from a historic and theological perspective it would fit another name as well—Antichrist...!

December of 2007 has really presented a lot of news concerning Russia vis-à-vis the world. On December 21, I expected some articles about Stalin—it was his birthday. Can you imagine how surprised I was to see a picture of Putin in all newsstands around! It was a day when *Time Magazine* announced its *Person of the Year.* And though the official date of the *Time* was December 31, 2007, the magazine had been available on December 21, 2007, when I bought it. The articles about Putin in *Time* made me both disappointed and gratified. I do not agree with some descriptions of the characteristics of Putin. Yet, I am thankful for some observations of the Russian social, economic, and political paradigm skillfully, professionally, and memorably portrayed by the author who traveled across the country. His narrations of the Russian countryside and the Russian Orthodox Churches he visited, have told me a sad, but true story reflected by the country's history. One note: the author uses information about the best developed part of Russia—the area between Moscow and St. Petersburg. Go to my first chapter, and keep in mind—this is the land where the first Russian railroad had been built in the nineteenth century, the area mostly developed by the Tsars.

Let me give you some descriptions of the Russian countryside by Nathan Thornburgh from his road trip through the Russian heartland: "Beyond Moscow is a country where the average man doesn't live to see 60. ...A hundred miles outside Moscow, the main federal highway melts into another century... There are no children here, and the school down the road is closing... With a low birth rate and lack of opportunities, villages are few and far between, separated by miles of forest and fallow fields. ... While the countryside is economically stagnant, it is undergoing a spiritual renaissance." I would not use the word renaissance in relation to the Russian Orthodox Church; therefore, the subtitle *Russia, Born Again* is not the real reflection on the past, a lot of misreading in-between.

Reading about the current countryside's grave predicament, I found complete unison with the events I have chronicled and illustrated in my books. Furthermore, giving the historical observation of the severe and urgent situation in the countryside, the author reminds us of the Soviet era destruction, which means Stalinism and all the consequences we just discussed a couple of paragraphs above. Yet I don't discuss the Russian Orthodox Church described by the author—he did not read my books and had no idea of the close cooperation between the KGB and the Russian Orthodox Church. And without that particular awareness even a beautifully written overview observation sounds superficial and shallow. It is not *Russia, Born Again*; it is the return of Stalinism with the powerful Ckeka ready to deceive the worn out people of Russia.

I have already told you that I do not agree with the *Time's* portrayal and characteristics of Putin. And again a lack of historical reality and knowledge of the past had swayed the *Time* to get Mikhail Gorbachev to give his view on Putin. The title of Gorbachev's piece "Russia Needs Putin" exposes his short-sightedness or maybe it is fear for his life. Listen to this: "Putin's mission is not to win over the West. It is to restore to

Russians a sense of their nation's greatness, something they have not known for years." My entire writings for the last twenty-five years were to prove to the readers the opposite point of view, the aggressiveness and treachery of the ruling elite. I hope that finally the world will read my books and grasp the threat coming from Russia's KGB government. Perhaps, Garry Kasparov, the World Chess Champion has been closer to reality by warning the world saying: "Putin's system is more like Mafia than democracy." He knows the truth, but he has not read my books yet to deliberate his opinion.

A group of the *Time's* correspondents had interviewed Putin at the presidential dacha for three and half hours. The interview disappointed me greatly—the journalists had not been prepared for the conversation with Putin. He was elitist, arrogant, condescending, and rude, yet the correspondents swallowed his ill behavior and sheer deceit. For example, Putin said, "Russia has no intention of joining military political blocs because that would be tantamount to restricting its sovereignty." What a mere combination of hypocrisy and deceit! But none of the journalists reminded him of the issues discussed in the preceding chapters of this book or Putin's plan to relocate the Russian fleet from Ukraine to Syria and build a military navy base in Venezuela. They also could've asked about the psychiatric abuses against the human rights activists like Eugenia Albats. They did not. Do you remember I told you about psychiatric abuses under Stalin? They have returned in the Russian psychiatric practices under Putin.

The journalists were not well prepared, they did not know Putin's character—he hates all journalists, especially the American ones and successfully deceived them all. Perhaps, the journalists did not remember that Stalin had injected all Chekists with the venom of superiority to others—Putin is one of the Chekists. He is not familiar with the words—a "humble servant." The Chekists are not serving people—they are giving orders to be executed. The Chekist-murderer of Alexander Litvinenko in London, who used Polonium-210, is another one, he was elected to the Russian Parliament lately—clearly the Russian system lacks morality!

But the next article had shocked me completely. Henry Kissinger[94] surpassed the ill-informed journalists in their incompetence. Listen to his characteristics of Putin: "Putin is not Stalin who feels obliged to destroy anyone who might potentially at some future point disagree with him. ...Therefore we do not observe a general assault on civil liberties."

Unbelievable! That is exactly what we have observed since Putin has come to power! Moreover, his view on the future of Putin's Russia vis-à-vis America is threatening: "Putin... will try to balance us—not deprive us of where we are but keep us from going further. At the same time in Putin's geostrategic conception, America would be the logical partner of Russia. ...We can collaborate on global security." Unfortunately, we did cooperate with our foremost enemy and you can see the result! We are losing one government after another to Soviet Fascism: Iran, Venezuela, Bolivia, and Ecuador in recent years. The same way we had lost Syria, Iraq, Libya, and Lebanon decades earlier. In my opinion, Mr. Kissinger surpassed the appeasement policy of Mr. Chamberlain and we are paying a dear price for that in our lives and finances in the twenty- first century. I am going to discuss the severe consequences of the appeasement policy in the twenty-first century in the next chapter, yet I would now call Mr. Kissinger—Henry Chamberlain! His comparison of Putin to the Russian reformer Peter the Great is clear blasphemy— "Peter the Great had brought to Russia brutality of modernization, Putin—brutality of degradation." Valeria Novodvorskay, a historian, dissident, and a real democratic politician. I agree.

A small but significant note: I have found very interesting information in the Time's material that enforces my own observations. Describing Putin's ascent to power the author narrated a factual story.

"He was a career KGB man. Yet just as 9/11 helped define President Bush, so did external challenges allow Putin to grow into a leader. His first steps on the world stage were tentative. His global coming-out had occurred in Auckland at a 1999 meeting of heads of APEC (Asia-Pacific Economic Cooperation) nations. Sestanovich, who was traveling with President Clinton, remembers meeting Putin at Clinton's hotel suite. "He was new on the job then," says Sestanovich, "not at all sure of himself... But Clinton was willing to work with him. Putin tells us how, at an APEC dinner at which he was feeling somewhat lost, Clinton crossed the room past other world leaders and leaned down to talk to him. 'Volodya,' Clinton said, using the familiar form of the name Vladimir, 'I suggest we walk out together from this room.' Putin rose to his feet, and the two men strolled out together. Everyone applauded, 'I will remember that forever,' Putin recalls.

It was Putin's only sign of softness during the 3 and half hours we spoke." It is interesting to know what Clinton and Putin had discussed in a separate room. I have an idea…

I would like to remind you that Putin is a very well trained liar—it is his profession to project a false impression. The entire story brings to mind a completely different explanation why Clinton and Putin needed a separate room to talk. Why couldn't they continue conversation at the presence of other world leaders? What secret forced them to go to a separate room? I did not know about that story when I wrote the first chapters of this book. Yet please, read again my conversation with Michael in the first chapter, and you will find my suspicions concerning Clinton and therefore a complete logical trend of Clinton's behavior meeting Putin in separate room. By the way, it was not the first meeting between Putin and Clinton—the first one (if the first) took place in St. Petersburg in 1996. Twelve years later you can see better the consequences of their friendship…

December 2007 ended with tragedy—Benazir Bhutto was assassinated in Pakistan! Several months before the assassination she stated: "I am what the terrorists most fear." And she was right! She was America's best hope in the region. Maybe it is true or maybe not. But the stability of the region was definitely our hope. Now it is gone and nobody can predict the future in such an important Muslim region close to Afghanistan and Iraq. I do not know who killed Bhutto, but her assassination has benefited only the dark forces of Soviet Fascism! Again we are face to face with Soviet Fascism—destabilized Pakistan can negatively impact our war against terrorism worldwide. Moreover, the tragic event will raise the price of oil and that will definitely benefit Putin's Russia. Let me refresh your memory about the real face of Soviet Fascism. Fifteen years ago, completing *Baltic Winds*, I purposely narrated a tragic story of the *Katyn Massacre*. I did it to expose the character of the Soviet government and its modus operandi. So, in short, the chronicle of events was as follows. In 1943, during WWII, the Nazis announced to the world that they had unearthed the mass grave of thousands of Polish military men in the Katyn forests. They said the Poles had killed by the Soviet NKVD. Moscow was outraged and called the announcement a lie, accusing the Nazis of murdering the Poles. Several international committees observed the mass grave and concluded that the Nazis had killed 10-20,000 officers, the cream of the Polish Army's crop. The only member of the committee who had doubts and suspected the Soviets had been Mr. Harriman's daughter.

Several years later, in 1952, the 82nd Congress of the United States had issued a House Final Report No. 2505. To be accurate, let me give you the description from the Final Report of the American Congress: "...The Katyn massacre involved some 4,243 of the 15,400 Polish Army officers and intellectual leaders who were captured by the Soviets when Russia invaded Poland in September 1939. These officers were interned in three Soviet prison camps... They were permitted to correspond with their families in Poland until May 10, 1940. ...their whereabouts was unknown until several mass graves containing remains of Polish bodies were discovered in the Katyn Forest, USSR, by the German troops in April 1943. The Katyn massacre was one of the most barbarous international crimes in world history.

"On July 2, 1952, this committee filed with the House of Representatives an interim report (H. Rept. 2430) in which it fixed the guilt for the Katyn massacre on the Soviet NKVD. ...there does not exist a scintilla of prove or even any remote circumstantial evidence that this mass murder took place no later than the spring of 1940. The Poles were then prisoners of the Soviets and the Katyn Forest area was still under Soviet occupation. In the interim report this committee recommended the Soviets be tried before the International World Court of Justice for committing a crime at Katyn which was in *violation of the general principles of law recognized by civilized nations.* The United Nations Charter presently carries provisions for the legal action recommended by the committee." (H.Rept. 2430).

The record of evidence presents a frightening picture of what was going on with the imprisoned Poles. Every night the members of the NKVD interrogated them to gain collaboration. Do you remember the constant interrogations of innocent people by the Cheka in the beginning of the Socialist Revolution in Russia? As a rule, all interrogations by the Cheka took place at nights. The same methods had been applied to the imprisoned innocent Poles to force them to collaborate with the NKVD. The documents spoke louder than words—only six traitors had been recruited by the NKVD. The rest were murdered by the Chekas, execution style. This Report had identified the first phase of Soviet Fascism.

I salute the brave and knowledgeable members of the U.S. Congress who, sixty years ago in 1952, had a sober evaluation of the events and open eyes for the future dreadful developments. "Furthermore, this committee called attention to the striking similarity between the Katyn massacre and events taking place in Korea today. For 2 years the Soviets disavowed any knowledge of the vanished Polish officers and deceived the Polish Government in its search for these men. Today the Communists are similarly prolonging the Korean peace talks because they cannot account for the 8,000 American soldiers reported by General Ridgeway 'killed as war crimes victims.' There are many indications that Katyn was a blueprint for Korea." How right the committee was!

The witnesses and documents had drafted a big picture of the Soviet design; I am trying to deliver in all my writings. *"It appears from the record that the Katyn massacre...was a means to an end. The Soviets had plotted to take over Poland as early as 1939. Their massacre of these Polish officers was designed to eliminate the intellectual leadership which subsequently would have attempted to block Russia's ultimate design for complete communization of Poland. This was but a step of the Soviets toward the complete communization of Europe and eventually the entire world, including the United States."* What a brilliant but scary prediction made almost sixty years ago by the real patriots of America warning the population of the upcoming threat.

What I read next in the report under the title *Misjudging Russia,* made my blood boil "...the cover-up of the facts of the Katyn massacre and withholding them from the American people was but a part of the desire on the part of the Democrat administration to cover their basic and colossal error in their foreign policy judgment." The words of the report written sixty years ago sound exactly like the voicing of our problems today. Just watch Russia's connection with Iran—that "friendship" is preparing a "very spicy meal" for the Western world. I recommend those who want to know the truth about Russia to read the Report No. 2505, because the investigation by the committee explains many other events that were not clear to the world and especially to Americans since then—the Kremlin's patterns of behavior. I would call the finding of this Report a *Precedent of War Crimes Against Humanity.* This Precedent should be known and considered in all future dealings with Russia.

I am writing this page in the beginning of the year 2008 of the twenty-first century. We know a lot of how Russia provides its henchmen with ideological foundations and arms to secure the criminal regimes. And what I found today will make you extremely angry. I found out that in 1940, the entire Katyn massacre of the captured Poles had been filmed by the NKVD and that film was sent to North Korea as the instruction in dealing with POWs. I wonder who else has received the film. Maybe watching events in the Middle East we may have the answer? Please remember that whatever the name is: the NKVD, KGB, or FSB—that institution represents the bloody force of Stalinism, the executioners, and terrorists. The written confirmation of that can be obtained from the essay "The Kremlin's Killing Ways, a subtitle"—"A Long Tradition Continues," by the highest-ranking Soviet Bloc intelligence officer and defector Mihai Pacepa, National Review Online, November 28, 2006.

Do not be surprised by the application of Polonium-210, or a deadly poison of other names used. Do not be surprised by cruelty, brutality in Iraq, and the savage assassination of Ms. Bhutto. She was assassinated to destabilize the region and country that cooperated with America, to undermine a friend of Israel, President Musharaff[95]—Pakistan is a long-term Russian target. Some suspected rogue elements in the ISI; I would check the rogue elements in the CIA as well. I have already told you where Mr. Khan had gotten a blueprint for the atomic design and he used it to create a destabilizing predicament in the Muslim country vis-à-vis India. Remember Mr. Primakov and his area of activities—South Asia. The master plan consisted of pitting Pakistan against India and vice-versa—to destabilize the entire region of East South Asia. Several years ago I wrote the following: "Today is November 7, 2002, two days after the congressional election. It is also the day of the October Socialist Revolution in 1917—a day the globe became divided into the Western civilization of the free world and its enemies. Our election reflects that division, as those events are inextricably connected, where bin Laden and perestroika demonstrate the embodiment of that division—a lethal combination of brutal force and sophistication in deception attacking the free world." Six years later I would like to widen my statement and identify it with additional precision. In the 1920s, our globe had become divided physically and psychologically, when the *Stalinist Organs* had become embarked in hostility against the West, waging an ideological expansion to obtain world domination—the dawn of terrorism began. Absence of our enemy's clear identification confuses and reverses the reality. Ironically, *the Organs'* war against Western civilization, today we call our War on Terror.

Returning to the "achievements" of the Soviet mafia and knowing its desire to ruin capitalism, my thought process is going further. There were two attacks on the financial capitals of the world in New York and London. South Asia is in my mind now, where three other financial centers are—Hong Kong, Bombay, and Bangkok. The government of India, the largest democracy in the world, has thc audacity to be friendly to the U.S.—a sign of danger in the contemporary world. Hence, similar attacks are going to be perpetuated in South Asia. Instability in Kashmir would be a pretext, but you know the ideology of Soviet Fascism is beyond Kashmir and that the *guerilla war* of the Muslims in Pakistan against Hindu in India was plotted and planned in the 1950s. It is a typical scenario of Moscow to pit one religion against the other, which benefits only the Kremlin. Just look at the murder of Israeli athletes by Arafat's terrorists in the Munich Olympic village in 1972 and recall who trained them. Remember also that diplomats of Libya and GDR plus the German Stasi participated in the plot to murder the Israeli athletes. Everything mentioned above comes from the institutions described by me in this book—the Russian KGB's government comprises them all. The second phase of Soviet Fascism came to life with Putin in 1999—*The Organs* now run Russia and are fighting for world domination.

Russia's Internal Security System has not been changed by the Collapse of the Soviet Union in 1991 and it is intact today. To learn it, please read my article: The Soviet Internal Passport System, The International Lawyer, Vol. 19, No. 3, Summer 1985.

CHAPTER 11

All the Planet's Blood and Treasure

When a medical doctor treats a patient, he or she fights against a disease and its causes. As a rule, after finding the causes a doctor deals with the disease. That way the patient is cured, his body is healed. These physicians are knowledgeable professionals with experiences to make a right diagnosis. However, unlike the latter specialists, the medical profession has another type of doctors— they treat the symptoms of the diseases. In this case the patient will never be cured and the treatment will never bring healing. This is similar to politicians at the world stage—the leaders of the Western civilization. At the time of war, while we are fighting terrorists, knowledge and the ability to arrive at the right diagnosis, it is only in identifying the enemy that we have the assurance of success and victory in the War on Terror.

History of America's presidents knows leaders who based on their knowledge and ability to correctly assess the world predicament have united all citizens to rebuff the enemy. Under leadership of such leaders the country eventually had been winning the war and healed. Immigrating to the United States in 1981, I have been watching one great leader. There are no words to express my love for him, because he saved not only America, but the entire planet. His vision of the world, his knowledge of the enemy, and guts to deliver the truth made him the greatest leader of the twentieth century. President Ronald Reagan unified all Americans; Democrats and Republicans, white, black, Latino, and Asian, by telling the truth in identifying the Soviet Union as the Evil Empire! He was right in all accounts, though many people did not know a lot of information then. It became known later. Yet, trusting the

President, the country joined his motto *Peace Through Strength* and the great leader of the twentieth century had been born!

You know the rest of the story—the Evil Empire collapsed. And the irony of our time is striking—we have the same predicament in the world and the same enemy in the twenty-first century. The only difference is that unfortunately we have no President Reagan with us. None of our presidents after President Reagan had followed his policy of *Peace Through Strength* and this is the crux of the matter which is explaining the enormously troublesome situation we are currently facing in the world. Neither President Bush-Papa, nor President Clinton adhered to Reagan's policy. There are different reasons why not, but none of them continued Reagan's policy of exposing the adversary and telling the truth to the American public. The current President, George W. Bush, like his predecessors, regrettably does not tell the truth either.

Have you ever thought about all of President Bush's impressive plans which have never been realized? He planned to change the tax code with the tax reforms, he promised to reform our social security to save and preserve it for the new generation, he was talking about improving our educational system, and many other promises. He has done nothing! And I can tell you why and when the disaster started. President George W. Bush, like an incompetent medical doctor, treated the symptoms of the disease and not the disease itself. As a result, nothing of his good intention to improve the state of affairs in our country he was able to realize. The failure started early and very imperceptibly.

When President Bush met Putin for the first time, his view of Putin determined the outcome for the following years. "I looked the man in the eye and I found him to be very straightforward and trustworthy… I was able to get a sense of his soul." It was a historic blunder! Mr. Putin has no soul; instead it is a dark hole of emptiness, where evil reigns. If you have already read this book and my previous one, you have an idea of the man he is, which had escaped our president. All the countries which have been discussed are identical, the symptoms—they are infiltrated and penetrated by the forces of Soviet Fascism, and they are under the auspices of Putin's KGB. They are the symptoms—Russia's KGB government and its activities is the *DISEASE—the CENTRAL CHALLENGE*. I suspect that Henry Chamberlain or Ms. Rice consulted President Bush in foreign policy, while neither of them is familiar with the concept of Soviet Fascism.

As a result, President Bush has lost eight years—he did not fight the disease, he fought the symptoms and he did not tell the truth, let alone communicate with the American people on the subject. At the same time he legitimized criminals worldwide and kept the American public in the dark. Hence, America does not know its foremost enemy and can make a wrong choice in the upcoming election of 2008. It is an American saying "time is money." Due to the absence of Reagan's policy *Peace Through Strength* and the unnecessary deaths of thousands because of that, I have changed the saying "time is money" to "time is blood and money." Considering all the years I've watched Soviet Fascism, I concluded and wrote in *The Russian Factor* that we are at war, and have been in WWIII for many decades now. We have been systematically targeted on different fronts and locations. Alas, my beloved America has not recognized it yet. I am surprised by Dick Cheney's silence in this respect. That war cost us an enormous amount of money and lives during those several decades, but neither Henry Chamberlain, nor Ms. Rice informed the president. Moreover, 70 percent of Americans believe that we are on the wrong track. They are right—the Bush administration did not acknowledge the real enemy of ours keeping Americans in the dark—this is the crux of the matter for future defeats!

Let me give you an example of time, money, blood, and presidential blunders. I have already discussed with you Russia, its henchmen throughout the world and their conspiracy of oil terror. In this war, however, Russia has two primary targets—America and Israel. The latter because of its geographical location in the Middle East, the former as a principal adversary of totalitarianism. As you now know, the strategy for oil terror had been widening at the meeting between Stalin and Mao in 1950. Remember, it was Mao who openly spoke about both—*guerrilla movement* and the intent to infiltrate the Middle East! The Kremlin had fifty years to prepare the "environment" in the Middle East. It did. And it had done the maximum in accordance with the oil terror conspiracy's design. Look at the Middle East today and you will see Israel surrounded by the *symptoms*: Hamas in Gaza, Hezbollah in Lebanon, Syria and Iran as the states of Soviet Fascism—their common objective to wipe Israel off the world map. If you add to them North Korea, Burma, Iran, and sixty countries infiltrated by Al-Qaeda, you will see the *Global Evil Empire of Terrorism*. The absence of the *Peace Through Strength* policy, after Reagan's presidency, wasting of time, legitimization of the Soviet mafia, and other mistakes in foreign policy have tripled the cost of our blood and money.

Pay attention to the time, the leaders of the countries surrounding Israel, and their relationship with Russia—they are the *symptoms of the disease.* Moscow provides all of them with arms, new technology, and political support in the world arena. I can identify something even more substantial and frightening then that—a political development within the human resources at the listed locations. The twentieth century had given to the world Hitler-Jugend which had become a Great German Youth Movement, the Nazi Party's official organization, which was comprised of children thirteen to seventeen years old. If you remember the Pioneers and Octobrists in the Soviet Union, they consisted of children between six and twelve years of age. They were the youngest political formations before the membership in the Komsomol (Young Communist League. Some authors mentioned the term Stalin-Jugend lately.) The twenty-first century had introduced to us a phenomenon of the Middle East where indoctrination of the children to kill the adversary started at the age of toddlers—three to four years old! Judge the "progress" in the twenty-first century! Please, keep in mind "time is blood and money."

I gave you the last example with the toddlers in Gaza to show you Bush's failure in his peace diplomacy in the Middle East. The area is comprised of the *symptoms of the Disease*—Russia's henchmen of oil terror conspiracy. There will be no peace in the Middle East while the price of oil stays high. And maybe this is the mutual failure of both the U.S. and Israeli's governments. In the beginning of the book, I discussed two Israeli prime ministers who allowed President Clinton to twist their arms and by doing so to compromise with Arafat. I am afraid that current situation is similar to that, let alone the Prime Minister Olmert, a popular bumper sticker says: *Olmert, You Disgust Me.* I am stunned watching the degradation in Israeli's spirit and strength—the consequences of Clinton's policy of twisting arms in the 1990s. The Israeli's political environment has worsened since—the country has been demoralized by the cronies at the top of the government. I suspect infiltration of the Soviet mafia into the top echelon of Israel.

Besides that, it is the lack of knowledge of the real and foremost enemy of America and Israel, which has caused the failure of both administrations. Hence Bush's *road-map policy* is doomed to fail. The Middle East has become the embodiment of the motto "time is blood and money." Bush's inability to diagnose the major global DISEASE and keeping Americans uninformed in terms of Russia's involvement also caused lack of confidence in the Republican Party. Moreover, his acquiescence with the Russian KGB's government giving legitimacy to criminals had emboldened all terrorists' gangs. The entire terrorist world built by the Organs was thrilled and in euphoria celebrated triumph over "A Great Satan." President Bush had not grasped it. He decided to play a chess game with the professional thugs and terrorists. The result is obvious—America, the Republican Party, and the world had lost. I am writing this chapter with my blood and tears, because I love and respect President Bush. Yet the truth must be told.

I hope now you comprehend the significance of knowledge of both the Soviet mafia and its ideology of Soviet Fascism as well as the enormous detriment and destruction they had brought to America and to our planet to achieve world domination. I can predict that a lot of troubles are still ahead of us—I know the iron determination and hate Putin is carrying in his revenge! *The Organs* had been on the march to destroy America and the Republican Party since the 1950s, the agenda is not accomplished yet…! Watch also Moscow's henchmen emboldened by the situation—the world will hear about them soon.

In his mistakes Bush had "help" from a former President. I have already written about Clinton's deeds in the beginning of the book. When I became familiar with his current activities my hair stood up. The former president had established the *Clinton Global Initiative* to deal with the third world countries, predominantly in the continent of Africa. He collected millions of dollars, but I am afraid that he will help Moscow's students to continue destroying their own countries and destabilize the neighbors who are on the right track. I had been writing a lot about Africa as the prime casualty of the Soviet mafia. President Mugabe of Zimbabwe represents a dreadful past and future for Africa—inflation in his country is 2 million percent. It did not stop the Clinton Global Initiative to fool the donors who contribute to the rogue states and the activities towards further destruction. Clinton had received $100 million for his trip to Kazakhstan and millions from Dubai and other foreign countries. I want Americans to know about all his alliances and the money involved to make an intelligent decision in an upcoming election. I personally want to know Clinton's connection with the Muslim's world and Russia. I also want to know why he pardoned Mark Rich, terrorist of FALM, other criminals and destroyed Haiti. All of that has the same roots. I know those roots. Doesn't Aristide remind you of Mugabe?

Only now can we return to the war in Iraq—one of Bush's right foreign policy decisions. America should be grateful—he kept us safe. Considering what is written above, I would argue that Iraq was chosen correctly to respond to the permanent aggression of Soviet Fascism—national dignity and self-respect are spiritual virtues of the American Republic. Iraq was not a mistake; we were saved because of the war in Iraq! It is another issue that our administration was not prepared for a war—it did not know the enemy and had not identified the regimes of permanent terrorism. And this is the crux of the matter! I did everything to inform the administration about the enemy and handed over the chapter *Evildoer: The Formula for Power* to a representative of the Pentagon on June 9, 2002. Perhaps it did not reach the addressee or was left without attention. Moreover, in *Baltic Winds*, ten years ago, I also warned America of a formidable aggressive force fighting us in different fronts around the globe. I have repeated the warning in my second book. Nobody heard it. The result was obvious—we were losing. This was written in 2004, *The Russian Factor*: *From Cold War to Global Terrorism*, page 303:

"Though Iraq was the right country to begin a war, nobody within the administration anticipated a dreadful aftermath of the postwar guerrilla activities. Had some of them read *Baltic Winds*, pp. 540-550, they would've avoided putting our army between two fascist states, Syria and Iran, who are providing men and arms to fight us. Knowing the predicament, we should've gone ahead to Syria immediately after Iraq (the assault on our embassy in Damascus equals to a declaration of war) to establish two new governments of native dissident as soon as possible. By doing that, we would've prevented war in two fronts and consequently the entire harmful situation created by the global terrorist force coming in to Iraq from a contaminated world." Do you remember that time is our blood and money?

I also criticized the Bush administration of making several mistakes, and a general one was the lack of knowledge of Soviet Fascism. A few components of those mistakes constituted a chain of erroneous actions I described in *The Russian Factor*: "We had won the war militarily in May 2003; we are now fighting tentacles of Soviet Fascism with a modus operandi familiar to you: assassinations, kidnapping, explosions, and so on. To preserve the integrity of Iraq an ethnic, cultural, and religion arrangement with local authorities should be built in the future with awareness of Soviet Fascism. There will be challenges, because the latter one will try to exploit ethnic and sectarian hostility and rivalry to instigate a civil war and derail the democratic process." I was right—look at Al-Qaeda, it is doing just that!

So, I insist that considering everything written above and to secure the future development of Western economies that needed the engine of our freedom—the oil reserve; the war in Iraq was a necessary step. It was done to stop the march of Soviet Fascism across the world, to suffocate us, to cripple and bankrupt our economy and national security. I can add to this new information I got lately. The long friendship of Saddam with Russia had a result. Besides earning training for Saddam's security and intelligence apparatus and the sale of a tremendous amount of arms, Russia has earned half a billion dollars for lobbying on behalf of Saddam before the United Nations.

It was money earned for our blood. I warned America then in 2003 by my introduction to *The Russian Factor*, writing that Putin's Russia is not only "the world's most virulent kleptocracy," but an underreported ticking time bomb. That Russian Intelligence acts as the central nervous system, coordinating different terrorist groups in the global war. Five years later, I am again warning you by writing this book—time is blood and money, knowledge of the real enemy is a must. General Garner's plan to appoint a group of Iraqi Generals to run the country was a smart, needed one, and the right way to manage the country after Saddam. Instead, the Iraqi Army that was more benign than security apparatus trained by the KGB, had been discharged. And that has untied the hands of the security apparatus—the nucleus of the Iraqi insurgency. Pay attention to their criminal activities and you will find the analogous modus operandi going on throughout the world—blowing up police stations, kidnappings, and explosions in crowded places to kill as many civilians as possible, and so on. Watch Afghanistan, it will come there too. Never forget the Katyn Massacre—Stalin's 1937 crime is marching across the globe.

Besides that, the henchmen of the Soviet mafia in Iran are also fighting us in Iraq—Al Sadr, Moscow's henchman is a criminal and his place is in a prison. Instead we gave him time to establish and regroup a criminal army. Please, remember the insurgency in Iraq and Afghanistan has the same modus operandi and source of coordination. I am also concerned about Tony Blair's withdrawal of British forces from Basra—a strategic area with oil reserves. I am afraid that the Soviet mafia is plotting something to undermine our Iraqi agenda.

It is for a reason I am trying to show you the big picture of the world outside America, and the march of infiltration in the countries of the world. For your information, that march was even more intense with digging the soil of our country with infiltration and penetration into our government, institutions, and organizations, which has also started in 1920s. The long-term strategy for world domination has included infiltration into the United States as well. When I read *History of Soviet and Russian Espionage in the United States*, my hair stood up. The list of Americans that cooperated with the Soviets was long and frightening. If you read this list your hair will also stand up—*History of Soviet and Russian Espionage in the United States* gives you a list of the American traitors.

To widen this list you can go to the website of Whittaker Chambers. This man should stay in our memory as a hero who was the first to expose the methods and tactics the Soviets used in recruitments during the 1930s-1950s. To see an even greater list of traitors you can go to *Venona Intercepts*, which will give you the latest list of American traitors in the Venona Project of the 1950s. The document is the best evidence of the Kremlin's aggressive behavior and its motivation. Moreover, the Venona papers corroborate all the ideas expressed by me in my writings. The scale of the Kremlin's infiltration in the United States should frighten every decent citizen of our country. The recruitments and infiltration into the American government, institutions, and organizations that started in the 1920s has never ended, only progressed.

The Internet can acquaint you with the history of the Soviet infiltration. I see it as my duty to give you my personal opinion based on my professional experience in Russia and life in the United States during the last twenty-five years. I am writing these pages in the beginning of 2008—America is at war and all the institutions of media and print are blaming the Bush Administration saying that the desire of having oil prompted America to war. If you read my books or even this one, you know that is not true, and the authentic knowledge has escaped our media. I do not want to repeat what I have already written many times, I intend to give you my vision of the events going on in America today. And this is an immense concern of mine.

In all my writings, I have intentionally introduced a variety of patterns which constitute Soviet Fascism. I want you to know Soviet Fascism and its Soviet mafia. My intention to do that has started many years ago. For example, I titled the last chapter of *Baltic Winds*; "The Soviet Mafia is Coming," in 1992. I did it for a reason—the Soviet mafia has always instilled its ideology of Soviet Fascism throughout the occupied land. You can be offended by my words because America is not occupied by the Soviet mafia. You are right. But the Soviet mafia is in the process of doing so. I have already written about WWIII against America; however, that multifactorial war has many nuances yet unknown. For example, a law allowing the FSB, (a former KGB) to operate all over the world was enacted by Duma in September 2006. I was unable to get a copy of the law. I believe it has a classified stamp. You can try to investigate the matter. Good luck! Meanwhile I will continue my observations.

Do you remember the Russian politician Vladimir Zhirinovsky? He is a member of the Russian Duma, the man who dreamed "to wash his boots in the Indian Ocean." Under the roof of Duma, this man is using his fists against the members of opposition quite often. He is also very close to Putin's government than is apparent on the surface. Being drunk on the party of his adherents, he proposed a toast for President Bush, saying something to this effect: "Poor George, do you know that 10,000 of our boys are 'working' on your soil?" Knowing Vladimir Zhirinovsky and his closeness to the Kremlin, made his words threatening. I believe in his statement, presented by the people in his encirclement. Besides, I have already written in *The Russian Factor* about those people on our soil, the only thing I did not know was the number of them. Now I know the number and that is not only threatening me but also forcing me to return to those people and describe their activities again—they are the saboteurs fighting America on our soil, to be precise, they are also fighting the Republican Party of America—the old Soviet design.

You will also share my fear and concern reading again how the term *guerrilla* war came to life in the chapter "Stalin and Mao— Friendship Forever." In Russian, especially in the Soviet time, it was called the *Partisan's War*—the war against the enemy. At the time of WWII, the Soviets massively organized and implemented the army of the Partisans throughout the European part of the Soviet Union occupied by the German Army. Their everyday activities were well known: ambushes of the Germans, using assault rifles and grenades, sabotage in many different forms, blowing up of bridges, derailment of trains, arsons, explosions, and so on. All the partisan's activities had been supervised and coordinated by the Soviet intelligence and security apparatus. The most important operations under the military intelligence were that of gathering information for the Soviet army and intensive propaganda campaign. Knowing the *Department of Agitation and Propaganda* now you can recall all the methods of their operations— "the enemy must be destroyed..."

I remind you of that information for a reason—America and its Republican Party is now enemy No. 1 with all the negative consequences for America. That is why the numbers of saboteurs "working" on our soil is critically important—the attempt is to destroy us from within.

Please, listen to what I wrote in *The Russian Factor* in 2002: "It was President Carter who started the destruction of our security forces, and President Clinton completed it. They left us blind under attacks of vicious and merciless force, the former by his incompetence, the latter for political reasons. As a result, our Intelligence agencies cannot identify agents and operatives of foreign power that harm Americans every day in a variety of unpredictable ways: plane crashes, train derailments, arsons explosions, and many other criminal acts. ...Fifty years ago an American patriot, Whittaker Chambers, had defined both culprits, the Communist Party and the KGB: 'I became convinced that it was evil and a threat to Western civilization.' ...The Evil Empire may be dead, but not the evil that drove it—the Soviet mafia. Until this evil is exposed, there won't be stability on our planet." *The Russian Factor*, p. 149.

I agree with every word written above, but now I would add more and that is the reason I am continuing to expose the Soviet mafia. Whittaker Chambers himself had been a subject of recruitment and later on exposed the predators of 1930s-1950s. At the time the Kremlin predominantly infiltrated the governmental structure of America. Fifty years later, Vladimir Zhirinovsky talks about enormous numbers of people infiltrated into all areas of American society. The process of the Kremlin's penetration has widened since then—the targets multiplied as well. I do not want to repeat again what I have already written during 1998-2004.

However, the situation within our country has drastically worsened since then. And in light of the information about "10,000 of our boys are working" in America, I have to return to the issue of sabotage, infiltration, and penetration.

People in the Soviet Union could not travel freely abroad. Only sportsmen and musicians were allowed to do so. The permission to travel abroad resided in the hands of the KGB. Some people getting permission received an assignment from the KGB. All Soviet people knew the routine of those days—only those who got the KGB's assignment could travel abroad. After the collapse of the Soviet Union and especially with the KGB's government coming to power in 1999, the scale of travelers abroad increased dramatically and with it the opportunity for infiltration and sabotage on the soil of the adversaries. Listen to a former KGB officer Stanislav Levchenko in his article *The KGB*: "I was in Tokyo when… the so-called 'detente' was signed… I read a top- secret cable singed by general Kruchkov. This cable ordered every KGB officer stationed in every country in the world immediately to double recruitment efforts against Americans and citizens of other NATO countries." Levchenko also described in his article another angle of the agency's foreign involvement:

"During its 70 years of existence, the KGB has developed a highly professional external intelligence service that is also the world's largest. The KGB and the GRU are extremely aggressive and cynical intelligence services. They use any relaxation of the climate…to enhance their recruitment efforts…" *The KGB, New Counterpoint7*, No. 2, Winter 1992. The former KGB officer confirmed my every word concerning that criminal agency. The KGB's recruitment efforts we can see in both anti-war and anti-nuclear protests in America trying to paralyze our ability to function successfully. As usual it was done by recruiting and training organizers and leaders of both movements to protest America's policy, to undermine, erode, and sabotage our way of life. Remember Stalin's—the masses must be organized…

Don't you see a precise correlation and coordination between the Kremlin's oil conspiracy against the West and anti-energy activities of the anti-nuclear and environmental protests? Both movements are increasingly dangerous—they are preventing America from building nuclear powers plants and drilling in ANWR or other location with oil. Had the American public been well informed and acquainted with the Kremlin's criminal design—the tentacles of Soviet Fascism waging the energy warfare; it would promptly mobilize people and urge change in the psychology of energy consumption. Because no government's law is able to change public attitude toward our energy problems—only the truth can do that. Unfortunately, the Russian criminal long-term oil-conspiracy is not known to the American public. And whoever the Republican presidential nominee will be, he or she should educate the public in the truth about the Russian by showing radical changes within the environmental movement. Thirty years ago the conservatives were fighting for a clean environment, today the radical took over. Don't you see the Russian connection?

Another former officer, Anatoliy Golitsyn,[98] the KGB's "think tank" analyst who defected to the United States predicted further development in Russia along the long-range aggressive strategy of world domination—secretive military buildup, recruitments, and infiltration into the institutions of the free world. He outlined the Kremlin's two-fold strategy and objective: "(a) an active increase in its own capacity to expand its own potentials; (b) a simultaneous reduction of the adversary's capacity." *The Perestroika Deception*, Edward Harle Limited, 1995. "To reduce" the capacity of the Western world the Soviet intelligence services used many different methods, devices, tools, and techniques. The oil-conspiracy against the West is one of the methods "to reduce our capacity." *Sabotage* is another one. It is the most devastating method, directed against the civilians, terrorizing their psyche with extremely violent special operations.

I am writing this book to acquaint you with the methods, tools, and techniques used by the KGB "to reduce" the capacity of the Western civilization, American national security, and our capitalist economic system. *Sabotage* has produced the climate of terror and undermined people's respect for the government's ability to run the country. *Sabotage* is the most effective method to achieve "the reduction" of human capacity to sustain. And as the agenda of the Soviet *Partisans* in WWII, the agenda of the saboteurs of our days remains the same—to inflict as much damage to the adversary as possible: To create one crisis after another, and an atmosphere of fear and panic within the adversary's society—to demoralize the population and destabilize the normal rhythm of the country's life. Our radio and TV constantly talk about bank robberies, kidnapping of children and young girls, unprovoked murders, and so on. In many such crimes, I recognized the handwriting of the Soviet mafia.

To continue our discussion about activities of the Partisans and saboteurs and the similarity between them, let me remind you of a tragic event in the Olympic village of Munich in 1972. The Israeli athletes had been brutally murdered there. I can write a long story of that inhumane deed, but I will not. Instead, I will tell you a story of one place in the Crimea peninsula. The Soviets organized a terrorist camp in Crimea, where so-called Palestinians were trained. The crux of the matter is that some of their teachers and instructors were former Soviet Partisans. Those trained Palestinians had committed the crime in the Munich Olympic village in 1972. Don't you hear all the news full of unknown crimes and other tragic events lately? Living in America, I would answer, yes. When I came to America in 1981, in some states people did not lock their doors. Twenty-seven years later it sounds laughable. There were rare bank robberies, murders, rape, and other violent crimes. I would argue that life in America has drastically changed. Let me give you some official statistics: "United States Crime Rate 1960-2006. The United States Crime Index Rate per 100, 000 Inhabitance went from 1,887, in 1960 to 5,897 in 1991. Crime in the United States accounts for more death, injuries, and loss of property than all Natural Disasters combined. The Disaster Center is pleased to be able to provide you with access to the statistics of crime compiled by the Federal Bureau of Investigation."

If you want to check the statistics you can do it, but I believe that a substantial part of the crimes have been committed by the saboteurs foreign and domestic. Let me give my thoughts in light of the crimes committed. In the election of 1998, in New York State Senator Al Domado, a Republican, lost to a new Senator Schumer, a Democrat. The election was determined by one shot of a sniper. The assassination of a physician from the abortion clinic was a decisive factor in the election. The FBI found the sniper and he was convicted by the court. The sniper was a traveler; his passport indicated he had traveled to fifteen different countries...

Reading about him, I knew that he was trained by the Soviet mafia and traveled around carrying out special assignments. The FBI did not publish any conclusions. I do not know why, and I don't know why the FBI didn't identify his country of origin. Can you imagine living in a country where security agencies are clueless? Completing *The Russian Factor* in 2003, I wrote: "Wake up America, we are in grave danger; listen to the voice of reality! Our children are under attack! We are dealing with thugs, gangsters, and implacable murderers! A specter is haunting the world—the specter of Soviet Fascism..."

Today I would argue that all Conservative Republicans are the party of most formidable enemies of Soviet Fascism and they should be prepared for revenge. The threat should be known to all Conservatives in the world especially in the U.K. I believe that Sonny Bono was assassinated—he used to bring too much money to the coffer of the Republican Party. Pay attention to snipers. I also suspect that Rev. Jerry Falwell was assassinated as well. He was a determined leader of the Conservative movement, bringing victory to the Republican Party. The FBI didn't know where to look for the criminals, or did not want to look there. Alas, the British security is also uninformed in terms of the vindictive methods of the Soviet mafia. Just recently, a Jewish spy "Angel" was thrown out of a balcony in the center of London. He helped Israel in the 1973 war, providing crucial information. Just apply logic and you will know who the "Angel's' enemies are. I have another suspicion as well. The catastrophe of the Space Shuttle in 2003 was not accidental. A member of the team, Ilan Ramon, from Israel was researching the way to change the climate—the subject of the Soviet's monopoly. Read how the Russians tried to change the climate and about Pluton in *The Russian Factor*, pp. 306-308. For decades the FBI failed to expose Soviet Fascism.

Talking about the FBI, I want to tell about other examples of its incompetence. 1. The shooting of our children will continue because the Columbine case was not fully investigated and the real predators were not convicted. The shooting will continue in other places, too. 2. Another example, also connected to the war against the Republican Party was Jack Abramoff's case. He is one of the henchmen of the Soviet mafia with an assignment to infiltrate our Congress and corrupt its members, predominantly naive and ill- informed Conservative Republicans to discredit them later on. I believe that Rep. Cunningham was one of them. As in the first example the FBI missed the opportunity to expose the Soviet mafia, "working" on our land. The FBI had no idea that the KGB targeted the recruitment of people with Jewish and Slavic last names. 3. At the time of the Katrina tragedy, the Democratic government of New Orleans and a Director of FEMA had a few moles working within, operating in cahoots with organized crime to discredit and undermine all the effort of the Bush administration—millions had been stolen. 4. The Oklahoma case and the Chandra Levi murder case had been screwed up by the FBI, though the latter one was easy to solve, knowing the Democrat's ties to organized crime. The FBI did not know where to look for the criminals or did not want to go there, maybe because the Democrats had been involved there, too…?

For your information, the KGB's moles have already infiltrated the three states' top administrations in America. Moreover, "the fixer" in the party called Democratic, had fixed some results in the election of 2006. I do not know how many "fixers" the Democrats have, but I know one, he is a member of the House Intelligence Committee. In cahoots with the Governor, he had fixed the results in several precincts of the state. Something is very, very wrong in America. And nobody, including the FBI and our law enforcement, even knows about the crime committed, let alone the information about "10,000 boys working on our soil." I have the impression that the FBI has failed to properly investigate many other cases concerning the Democrat's activities, because it was lacking real experts and competent specialists. Hence be attentive to the enemies within our intelligence and security agencies.

We are at war in WWIII, and have been for many decades. Talking about the war against our country besides, arsons, sabotage, or orchestrated car and plane crashes, I have indicated three main targets of the Kremlin: the traditional American culture, the American capitalist economic system, and our intelligence, security, and law-enforcement agencies, *The Russian Factor*, pp.167-205. Discussing again the main targets of the Kremlin, I would like, however, to start with our security and intelligence agencies, as I have just discussed the failure of the FBI above. In 2002, I relied on my experiences and knowledge of the KGB and accused our intelligence of sabotaging our national security. Besides, the ban on access to my books is one of the forms of sabotage. You have not heard and read my two books because they have been sabotaged by our intelligence. In 2002, I did not know the inside story of the American intelligence and security agencies. Six year later the situation has changed—I got the inside story and it confirms the veracity of my accusations. Can you imagine my feelings when I read the chronicle of the CIA's sabotage of our national security?

In the middle of 2007, I heard about a new book titled *Sabotage: America's Enemies Within the CIA*, Regnery Publishing, Inc., 2007. At the time, I was busy writing my third book and had no time for reading. I was wrong disregarding that incredible book, missing the opportunity to arrange my third book differently. As a matter of fact, in *The Russian Factor* I have mentioned the CIA's sabotage many times. It was my personal opinion based on my knowledge of the KGB and its global infiltration with proclivity to penetrate the adversary's intelligence, security, and law enforcement agencies. When I finally read *Sabotage*, I got confirmation of all my allegations against the CIA. The author of the book, Rowan Scarborough, covers national security for the *Washington Examiner*. A Navy veteran, he has covered the Pentagon for the *Washington Times* for two decades.

According to Rowan Scarborough, significant elements within the CIA were undermining both the president and national security through leaks, false allegations, and outright sabotage. The author paints a disturbing picture of partisan politics endangering the success of our campaigns abroad and the very lives of our soldiers and agents. The author also calls the CIA *A Rogue Agency*. He directly accuses the CIA in leaking details about classified intelligence programs with the intent of ending them and damaging the president. "The Agency's headquarters in the Tony Langley neighborhood in North Virginia, run for more than ten years by Bill Clinton's choices, includes holdover George Tenet... Though incompetence, leaks, and false allegations within the CIA, an agency charged with a lead role in the War on Terror, the CIA has become one of President Bush's most damaging political enemies."

The author, revealing the accusations expressed by Mr. Hoekstra, the Chairman of the House Intelligence Committee that some within the analytical and operations branches had sabotaged the President and the War on Terror. "There has been much public and private speculation about the politicization of the agency. ...I have been long convinced that a strong and well-positioned group within the agency intentionally undermined the administration and its policies. ...In time of war, Bush faced an unprecedented challenge. An agency he relied on to fight terrorists was actually working against him." The author describes some of the methods the CIA employs to undermine the Bush administration.

Intentional leaks played a role in an attempt to discredit President Bush and his administration—a tool used by the Soviet mafia. Reading the book, I found a familiar combination of several methods used together to achieve the planned objectives in the Clinton's administration in the 1990s. The story of two knowledgeable and valor officials narrated the criminal intent of some in the CIA to get rid of them. One of them was Michael Maloof. He helped to expose the Clinton administration involved in dubious deals between some of America's largest weapons makers and Communist China. "This embarrassed the administration, because several of these companies had previously flooded the Democrat Party with campaign cash. Maloof had also helped Congress's Cox Commission in its investigations, which revealed an extensive Chinese spying network, defense industry collusion, and apparent lack of interest in such espionage and arms sales by the Clinton administration. Clinton's political appointees labeled Maloof a leaker to the press. Maloof was ostracized and exiled." A smart, professional man, a hero who exposed our enemies was thrown out to be replaced by Clinton's mediocrity, let alone a more serious motivation.

When I heard about the Chinese espionage in the 1990s, I had known then that Clinton was dealing with the Soviet mafia. I just did not know the name of the hero who exposed the deal, but I had reacted immediately then. Chapter 5 of *The Russian Factor* reflects my concerns. "It is not an accident that today, in 1999, the war in Yugoslavia coincides with the news of the Chinese espionage. Both issues also directly connected to Elia Kazan's past and the debates about his Oscar, a lifetime achievement award. All three events have one common answer—Russia, its criminal past and murky future. ...Has anybody noticed that the last three Russian prime ministers came from the KGB? It is an ominous sign for the future. Has anybody ever heard about the Soviet mafia? Perhaps only Elia Kazan had grasped that threatening notion forty years ago. We, Russian immigrants, found out the new term by reading Arkady Vaksberg's book *The Soviet Mafia*, St. Martin's Press, 1991." Then, in 1999, I have the chapter *The Soviet Mafia and Its Formula for Power.*

As you can see, in the 1990s the CIA was fighting those who exposed the enemies. Later on, when the Bush administration came to power, the CIA was fighting the Bush administration by leaking intentionally classified information. Rowan Scarborough tells us that "White House aides complained among themselves that they were fighting three enemies: Al-Qaeda, the Democrats, and the CIA. ...While CIA bureaucrats have anonymously attacked Bush administration figures through leaks to the press, the CIA was docile during the Clinton years, and even, according to one inside source, punished conservative analysts." The other example of the CIA's prosecution of the smart professional officer was regarding the ouster of President Aristide of Haiti.

I am giving this example from *Sabotage* for a reason. As a matter of fact, many years ago I was writing about that exact event in *The Russian*

Factor. At the time, I did not know anything about the events within the CIA, but was very close to reality, because I had known the Soviet mafia. So the next victim of the CIA was the officer named Brian Latrell. A national intelligence officer for Latin America, he briefed the Senate Foreign Relations Committee in 1993 on ousted Haitian leader Jean-Bertrand Aristide's mental state. "Republican Senator Jesse Helms used Latrell's testimony to bash Clinton who wanted to restore Aristide to power. Latrell found himself transferred to the Center for the Study of intelligence, from where he retired." Later on the former analyst said, "Many of my colleagues lay low or took foreign assignments in 1993 and 1994 to escape the crackdown on conservatives in the agency." I see the behavior of some within the CIA as a direct deprivation of the experienced professionals to effectively serve our interests in the world. I would call the CIA actions in this regard sabotage, too.

Though the political systems of the United States and the Soviet Union were different, the events in the CIA during Clinton's administration had some similarity. The crackdown on the conservatives within the CIA, described by Rowan Scarborough, has reminded me of the cleansing in the Soviet intelligence and security agencies during the Stalinist reign. Though the scale and methods are different—the objectives are in the same direction— power. I have described Stalinists methods in the preceding chapters. The other similarity is the infiltration to the adversary's agencies by the KGB. Listen to Rowan Scarborough talking about officer Latrell and other conservatives; he describes the same substance of infiltration with the agenda of subversion, but does it by using different words:

"The irony to Latrell, and other conservatives, is that liberals, longtime foes of CIA operatives in the Cold War and Vietnam, have embraced the Agency as the internal opposition organ to Bush." The author had no idea of the name the *Organs*, the word Soviet people had invented in the 1930s, yet his usage of the terms *the internal opposition organ* to Bush illustrates the universal significance of human feeling towards oppression. And in this case, the CIA has acted as an oppressive organ against the Bush policy. Please, recall all my attempts to give you a big picture of the KGB's activities around the world. It will help you to grasp and understand what goes on in America, and particularly within the CIA.

Another honest and knowledgeable officer of the CIA, Michael Maloof, who completed the terror-linkage report in December 2001, suddenly found himself under attack from known and unknown adversaries. "The known was... Michael Hayden, who then ran the National Security Agency and would later become CIA Director, Hayden accused Maloof of leaking classified material to the press and wanted his security clearance pulled—a death blow to a defense analyst." Though Maloof denied the allegations and passed a polygraph test, the newspaper articles suddenly began appearing about his case. "Discouraged, Maloof subsequently retired after more than twenty years of tracking arms proliferation between Western countries and the bad guys. The intelligence community had bagged Maloof. ...Other targets awaited..."

Michael's superior in defense of Maloof wrote: "Michael Maloof is a member of the Policy staff reporting to me directly I want the Security Appeal Board to know of my confidence in Michael, rooted in his many contributions to national security, his patriotism and sense of duty and his commitment to security.

...I am proud to have Michael on our team and strongly urge the Security Appeals Board to reinstate all of his clearances to permit him to continue his important work to contribute to our national security." Douglas J. Feith, Under Secretary of Defense for Policy. It is interesting to know why the attacks on the knowledgeable professionals within the CIA had taken place during Clinton's administration. The Maloof case can help us to grasp the situation within Clinton's CIA and after him. As I found out from *Sabotage*, Maloof had the audacity to believe that the Lebanese Hezbollah, an arm of Iran, had played a role in the 9/11 attack. If you read *The Russian Factor*, you should remember that I have the same opinion, viewing all terrorist factions as Moscow's students. Yet some CIA higher-ups had found Maloof wrong-headed. Maloof recalled of his October 2001 trip to Langley: "When I drove out to the CIA, I thought we would be a team. As I tell people now, Rome was burning and the Barbarians were at the gate. By October, it was open warfare. They began leaking and making accusations and accusing us of setting up an operation to bypass the agency.

They went after me for political reason. And they won..." And again, I agree with Michael Maloof's opinion.

Reading *Sabotage*, I also found out about the anti-Bush activity by some senior analyst at the CIA. The author accuses the current and former CIA officers of fueling conspiracy theories that President Bush orchestrated the 9/11 attacks on America. If you read *The Russian Factor*, you know my view on the sinister attack on 9/11. Maybe those who accused President Bush on being a part of the "inside job" orchestrating the 9/11 attack, are trying to cover-up the real criminals? This is the subject for further investigation. However, one story narrated by *Sabotage*, does not require further investigation for me—I fully believe in it. If you read *Baltic Winds*, you should remember that I predicted a gang coming from Mexico in the 1980s. I did it after our Senate voted for Ballen amendment against arming the Nicaragua's Contras. It had happened in the 1980s and I had known then that our policy in Latin America was wrong. *Sabotage* has explained it in detail.

The story of John Bolton is more than only the disgusting activities within the CIA against him; it is also the explanation of our failure in Latin America... Fulton Armstrong had been the Clinton administration's Latin American expert on the National Security Council. He, like many other liberals, wanted to normalize relations with Fidel Castro. John Bolton, like most of the Bush administration did not want it to happen. Like Bolton, another man in the administration, a conservative Otto Reich did not want it to occur. Cuban by birth, Reich had helped carry out Ronald Reagan's anti-Communist policies and later served as ambassador to Venezuela. In the 1980s, "...The Washington liberal establishment was concerned: he opposed Fidel and, during the Reagan administration, had argued for supporting the anti- Communist Contras in Nicaragua."

In my opinion, both Mr. Bolton and Mr. Reich were right. Had Senate helped the anti-Communist Contras in Nicaragua in the 1980s, we would have not faced the anti-Americanism of Latin America today. The Soviet henchman Ortega has been again elected as the President of Nicaragua in 2007. That means, we can expect a lot of troubles at the border with Mexico—arms, drugs, provocations, saboteurs, and other criminals flooding our country. Mexico had been targeted by the Kremlin since the 1930s. Watch Mexico...!

...Unfortunately, the CIA and NIC held another opinion. Fulton Armstrong, the top Latin American analyst on the National Intelligence Council in cahoots with powerful Senator Dodd and his staff had begun a real war against both John Bolton and Otto Reich. You have to read the methods and tactics they had employed to damage the reputation and credentials of John Bolton and Otto Reich. I got the impression that the Senator, some members of his staff, and Fulton Armstrong had not been acting in the interests of our country. And some information in the ordeal made me very suspicious. During his narration of the story, Mr. Scarborough had touched another event, giving us the information about Ms. Ana Belen Montes. She had been the Defense Intelligence Agency's senior analyst on Cuba. Ms. Montes was also a spy for Fidel, feeding the Communist Cuba reams of U.S. secrets.

The author of *Sabotage* calls her "one of the worst spies in U.S. history." Yet when the idea was raised to go back over all the intelligence community's products that contained input from Ms. Montes to provide clues to what she gave Castro, Mr. Armstrong had vehemently opposed that. He said that he had worked on the same assessments as Ms. Montes and was sure she did not distort them. A Pentagon official told the author, "I think she was there not so much as an agent of influence but as a genuine spy, collecting information and probably recruiting others who I'll bet you anything are still there."

Mr. Scarborough has drawn a very unpleasant even repulsive picture of some Democrat Senators fighting the Bush administration by dirty methods and constant investigations of the president's cabinet. There was no surprise when I read a story of how a CIA analyst worked together with Democrats to sabotage the nomination of John Bolton to the UN. The story was disgusting and damaging for our national security and the dirty methods had been used again. You have to read *Sabotage* to know about unethical behavior of some Democrat Senators to conceive their very questionable activities working with Armstrong to tarnish Bolton's credibility. "…if a Bush official questioned the work of a CIA analyst, he or she risked a Democrat-inspired investigation." And though Armstrong's accusations of Bolton had not been proved, "Armstrong's allegations became part of the Democrats' case to deny him the ambassadorship" in the UN.

Considering everything I had written about the KGB before, I really want to know the motivation of the Democrat Senators and Mr. Armstrong in their war against John Bolton. I also want to know who personally had decided Armstrong's next position. "Armstrong left his senior post at the NIC. The CIA sent him abroad as an analyst in the clandestine service. The Agency declined to make him available for an interview." Can you imagine his behavior in the clandestine service? We can only guess, knowing the opinion of his friends, Democrat Senators.

"During one Senate Committee hearing, Senator Dodd even scolded Secretary of State Condoleezza Rice for criticizing Hugo Chavez, the virulent anti-American leader of Venezuela who is not only a Castro ally, but who has also pledged his support to Iranian president Mahmoud Ahmadinejad. Chavez used a speech at the United Nations to refer to President Bush as Satan." My only reaction to that is to refer you again to my description of the KGB, Moscow's students, and its activities throughout the world.

It so happened that a couple of days ago I read a small article in *The New York Times*, describing an interesting episode which occurred in Latin America. That small article had confirmed the truthfulness of all my analyses concerning the Soviet mafia and the situation in Latin America: "A Miami man who brought $800.000 in a suitcase into Argentina this summer was trying to deliver a campaign contribution from the Venezuelan government to an Argentine presidential candidate, Cristina Fernandez de Kirchner, American prosecutors said Wednesday. ...Five men were charged with acting and conspiring to act as agents of the Venezuelan government within the United State...in a scheme that prosecutors said involved the highest levels of President Hugo Chavez's government. ...This could be the smoking gun that Chavez has been actively financing campaigns in Latin America..." *The New York Times*, "U.S. Links Smuggled Cash to Venezuela," December, 13, 2007.

There is another ominous sign of Soviet Fascism in Latin America—flood of drugs. Do you remember an inundation of drugs in Columbia organized by the KGB? You could read about that brilliant research in *Red Cocaine*, by Joseph Douglas. Since then the drugs have been spread to other Latin American countries: Argentina, Brazil, Bolivia, and Peru. The article in *The New York Times* confirms that: "Cocaine seizures and major drug raids in Argentina and Brazil have surged in the past two years. The influx of raw cocaine paste used to make crack, from both Bolivia and Peru have been particularly acute. In Brazil, such seizures by the federal police nearly quadrupled from 2006 to 2007... Cocaine is no longer the drug only of the elite, the irresponsible spread of paco, and a highly addictive, smokable cocaine residue that had destroyed thousands of lives in Argentina and caused a cycle of drug-induced street violence never seen before in this country." Of course you want to know how it has occurred, and the article has answered it. Do you remember the list of the war criminals, I discussed earlier? Listen to the explanation in the article:

"The scourge underscores a significant shift in both Argentina and its larger neighbor, Brazil. Brazil now ranks as the second largest consumer of cocaine in the world after the United States, the State Department says. …The Surge in drug use has been fueled by porous borders and more recently the rolling back of restrictions on coco growing since President Evo Morales took office in 2006 in neighboring Bolivia. The result has been the democratization of cocaine in this part of South America, which has become the dumping ground for cheaper, lower-quality cocaine" *The New York Times*, "Cheap Cocaine Devouring Lives in Argentina Slum," February 23, 2008. The drugs distribution is one of the patterns of Soviet Fascism; the other is a murder of the adversaries by orchestrating or manufacturing the plane crashes. In all my writing I have warned you about the plane crashes—an action to damage the flying machine on the ground to cause a crash. The same article told us about interesting events that are going on in Venezuela under another war criminal Hugo Chavez. Especially suspicious is the last plane crash, with forty-three passengers and three crew members. It had slammed against a mountain shortly after taking off.

"The crash of the Santa Barbara Airlines plane is the latest of several airline accidents that have raised worries in recent weeks about the safety of air travel in Venezuela. In January, a small twin- engine plane carrying 14 people, including 8 Italian citizens, went down at sea on a flight from Caracas… 'There has been a string of accidents in the last two months that stand out,' said Antonio Rivero, the national civil defense chief, in comments broadcast on Union Radio. Mr. Rivero cited five separate incidents involving aircrafts of different sizes." Now after the events of our days we can return to *Sabotage*, which is giving us a big picture of the events within the CIA. Those who know the Kremlin's tricks and techniques never have doubts in the activities of its henchmen—Moscow's students. Rowan Scarborough's *Sabotage* has definitely helped us to appreciate the causes of our failures…

The culmination of the *Sabotage* is the chapter "The Clinton Disaster." Its description of the factual events and analysis are the real crux of the matter. It confirms all my suspicions that I have raised in my books for the last fifteen years. The author of *Sabotage* has no suspicions.

Based on his professional experiences and analysis of the actual events within the CIA, he is calling a spade a spade:

"Much of the blame for the decrepit state of the CIA's operations and its faulty analysis can be traced to the Clinton administration and its eight years of eroding the Agency. Searching for a post— Cold War peace dividend, Clinton did more than slash the military. He targeted the intelligence community. He shrank the CIA's analytical and operation branches by at least 30 percent. Stations in Latin America and Asia closed or downsized. In Indonesia, the world's largest Muslim country had only three CIA officers by the mid-1990s."

The author is giving us a scary picture of Clinton's America, our country is ready to capitulate in the face of global terrorism. To bring you to the present time and explain the difficulties we are experiencing in the Middle East, I am purposely choosing the words of James Woolsey, Clinton's first CIA director. He had resigned in protest over President Clinton's apparent lack of interest in the CIA. I would not characterize Clinton's directions in the case as a lack of interest in the CIA. In fact, it was a direct action to undermine our intelligence capacities. And again it had been done with the initiative of a Democrat Senator.

We are talking about the so-called "Torricelli Principle," that dealt with the new rules for recruiting agents. The CIA officer could no longer recruit a potential agent if he or she were absolutely pure and clean. Testifying before the Congress in discussing that exact "Torricelli Principle" James Woolsey said: "These rules make absolutely no sense with respect to terrorist groups because the only people who are in terrorist groups are people who want to be terrorists. That means they have a background in violence and human rights violations." Mr. Woolsey also gives an example of the situation in the Middle East, a very important one. "If you make difficult for a CIA case officer in, say, Beirut, to recruit spies with this sort of background, he'll be able to do a dandy job for you, telling you what's going inside, for example, the churches and the chambers of commerce of Beirut, but we don't really care what's going on there. He'll have no idea, however, what's going on inside Hezbollah." This is a verdict against Clinton's CIA, considering the war we are in with the Middle East today!

Sabotage is rendering a guilty verdict to Clinton's CIA by its two former directors—a Republican and a Democrat. In the spring of 2007, Defense Secretary Gates, a former CIA director, characterized the Clinton years this way: "By the mid-1990s, recruitment of new case officers at CIAhad hit a historic low, and the agency's funding was a prime target for budget-cutters, …within three years of my retirement in 1993, CIA's clandestine service had been cut by 30 percent—just when Osama bin Laden was gearing up his war on the United States." A devastating criticism also came from Clinton's own CIA director, George Tenet: "The fact is that by the mid-to-late 1990s American intelligence was in Chapter 11, and neither Congress nor the executive branch did much about it." The author of *Sabotage* is rendering the last words in the guilty verdict personally to Bill Clinton. It was President Clinton, who "had let the CIA and NSA degrade to a dangerous level."

"In *Sabotage*, Rowan Scarborough exposes the CIA bureaucracy as a petty, vindictive lot bent on destroying a president because it did not agree with his policies. Various bipartisan commissions have documented the CIA's failures before September 11, 2001. Scarborough reveals its anti-administration tactics after the attack. The CIA could not find bin Laden. But, as Scarborough shows, it still found time to try to bring down Bush." Bill Sammon, bestselling author of *Fighting Back and Strategy.*

Do you grasp now the critical predicament worldwide we are in at the year 2008? Don't you think that the CIA had castrated itself by firing the real experts, knowledgeable and competent conservatives and by doing that degraded our national security? There is no need for me to add anything else to the verdict, but directing you again to my report on the KGB, its proclivity to infiltrate our society, government, institutions, business, and other organizations. In my writings, I called our intelligence and security agencies incompetent and clueless, and therefore unable to withstand the enemy's attacks. After the information filling the pages of *Sabotage*, an even more tragic idea came to my mind— the idea of a deep *diabolic ideological expansion*. I leave the conclusion to you.

The book had given me another interesting angle for my discussions of Soviet Fascism. In *Sabotage's* Appendix, Rowan Scarborough had placed enormously powerful material— Unpublished Article by Colonel David Harvey written in 2005. It is a list of recommendations to the Joint Chiefs of Staff concerning the war in Iraq. As a matter of fact, General David Petraeus, then commander of the U.S. Combined Arms Center, read Harvey's article and told him not to publish it because it was too damming. There are no doubts that the article presents brilliant collections of the new rules in the war. One of the points among others caught my eyes by the similarity of the subject, I am trying to acquaint you with and describe in all my writings. "...for continuous comprehensive analysis over time requires the following ingredients currently missing: 1. Investigative work similar to police dealing with gangs/mafia." A brilliant suggestion and assessment—a clear indicator—the man has knowledge of the Soviet mafia.

You can argue that David Harvey is writing about Iraq, the recommendations have been addressed to our military. Yes, you are right. But before him I wrote in 2004 that we have already won the war militarily and now we are fighting the tentacles of Soviet Fascism. As a matter of fact, I have focused all my writings in this particular direction—gangs/mafia, the main components of the Soviet Mafia and therefore Soviet Fascism. It does not matter if it is Iraq or any other country in the world where the Soviet mafia is fighting a legitimate government. You will find similar criminal actions there—explosions, arsons, unprovoked killings, plane crashes, and so on.

In Iraq, the Soviet mafia is fighting for oil it used to share with Saddam. After his defeat, another member of Iran's mafia with the oil resources has taken his place, but the tools, devices, and methods are the same whether in Iraq, Iran, Madrid, London, or New York City. We are dealing with the *international terrorist network*. I do not trust Nouri al-Maliki, a head of the Iraqi government. He is Shiite, who will find a common language with Iran. That means the pathway for Russia to Iraqi oil. The circle will be closed— the policy of the West's suffocation by the *international terrorist network* continues.

That *international terrorist network* has definite political trend and supervision. It was Madrid, three days before the election, when the terrorists had struck to sink the Conservative government to help elect a Socialist government in Spain. Like in Spain the same situation of ideological violence occurred in Greece's election of 2007. To topple Greece's Conservative New Democracy Party the *international terrorist network* and particular *November 17* political gang has spread the enormous fire throughout Greece. The method however was changed. If killing civilians is the usual way of violence, in Greece it was arson—Greece was in flames, an overwhelming fire. Fortunately, the crimes in Greece did not help the Socialist to win.

All preceding chapters of this book are conveying just that simple idea that only knowledge of the enemy is the solution for the world. The term *The Soviet Mafia*, I took from a book by the Soviet lawyer and journalist Arkady Vaksberg. Introducing his book, I tried to show the inextricable connection between a political party and organized crime—*the international terrorist network*, which has been a subject of my writings during the last twenty years. Yet don't take only my words. I would suggest that all Americans read The Soviet Mafia to learn the intimate association of political leadership and organized crime and subordination of ethnic mafias to a political one. By the way, the author also indicates this connection by the sub-title of the book—*A Shocking Exposure of Organized Crime in the USSR*. The book gives us an understanding and picture of what happened in Soviet territory and what is going on now in America. How different gangs, including drug-trafficking gangs and street gangs, are working in coordination with the political mafia, growing on our soil since the 1950s.

The year 2007 had brought an enormous destruction of our forests. The forests fire and wild fires had been spread across the United States. I saw a report of one firefighter who said that he "Hadn't seen or remembered such a dreadful extent of fire in his entire thirty years of experience as a firefighter." Thousands of acres of our land had been burned; the real estate damages had amounted to billions. I cannot tell you that all the fires were from arson. No. But some of them, in substantial numbers, had been. I know that because I know the modus operandi of Soviet Fascism— arson is one that is usually used. And again like in Waco, the clueless FBI and CIA had no idea of where to look for the criminals, the same way they had screwed up the Columbine massacre of our children—the shooting and other crimes will continue.

Please, remember the agenda of the Soviet mafia to "reduce our capacity" by instilling fear or many other forms of terror—to terrorize us. I would like to remind you of an episode that almost destroyed our planet in Russia's desire to terrorize the world. On October 30, 1961 by the Khrushchev order, Russia tested a hydrogen Tsar-Bomb the most powerful ever exploded on Earth. The hydrogen wave had been running around the globe three times. As a result the world's surface of oceans and seas was covered with white dust and millions of dead sea-gulls. Can you imagine harm to humans? Please, remember this story when you see green or anti-nuclear movement preventing us from building secure nuclear power plants in America. President Bush could have reminded us of the story to show the real ugly face of his friends in Moscow. Unfortunately, he did not and the attempt "to reduce our capacity" is going on.

Do you remember "10,000 boys working on our soil?" You can add to them thousands of gangs across America. Most of them created and subordinated to the Soviet mafia and connected to the political party. You can recognize that connection in the example presented by me about the aftermath of the Katrina tragedy— shooting, killing, looting, and robbery. It was humanitarian disaster—coordinated criminal activities. And do not forget all the patterns of Stalinist Socialism including science and pseudo- science, which are both serving Soviet Fascism in its war against us. In America we called it a junk-science—a fraud serving a political party. Remember also the components of Soviet Fascism—infiltration into foreign governments and institutions. For your information, the Kremlin's moles have already infiltrated the top of our administrations in three states. Katrina was a preparation for the election of 2006. You know the end of the tragic story.

It did not surprise me that the real fraud with its worse forms had become an everyday occurrence in America. As a matter of fact, fraud cannot be transmitted by air or winds—corrupt people have perpetrated all forms of fraud. Do you know that every three seconds one American is losing his or her personal identity? I will remind you that fraud is the integral part of Soviet Fascism. I investigated the subject of fraud in many details in *The Russian Factor* and warned you about the infiltration into our cyber system ten years ago, p.103. One of the first hackers who cracked security of the City Bank in New York was a man from St. Petersburg, Russia. There are many other criminal developments from the same source that have happened since then.

There is another troubling sign you cannot miss. Don't you notice an enormous increase in brutal crime against our children, boys and girls kidnapped, young women raped and murdered; and extremely violent scenes of brutality which have entered our everyday life? What happened to the kind, compassionate, and fun loving people of America? It is not the America I witnessed twenty-seven years ago and it is definitely not the America of fifty years ago. And like fraud that incredible violence is perpetrated by people—the criminals. Don't you think that this is the job of some from the "10,000 boys working on our soil?" I am sure of that, based on my experiences and knowledge of Soviet Fascism. It is for that reason I have introduced in the beginning of the book the essence of Stalinism and its principle method—violence in many different forms.

Besides, please read again the House Report No. 2505. The conclusion has been based on the unspeakable violence against the Poles in the Katyn Massacre by the Soviets: "...*This was but a step by the Soviets toward the complete communization of Europe and eventually the entire world, including the United States*." The fifty years that have passed have brought some difference in the identification of the Soviets—the Report called it communization, I called it Sovietization of Europe in the twentieth century and eventually the entire world and America in the twenty-first century. In principle, the Report No. 2050 of the American Congress had agreed with my view completely and should be seen as a Precedent in all future dealings with the Russian KGB's government, because the process of Sovietizaton continues around the world.

Many years ago while talking to my friend Michael; I was frustrated by his unawareness of the term Sovietization. Now I have the answer—only people who have experienced Sovietization, the system of rules and arrangement to enslave the populace can feel and grasp it instantly at any territory. If violence in life and its reflection on TV is visual enough to scare the public in America, other methods of Sovietization and its ideology of Soviet Fascism are not so apparent. They are hidden, concealed, and aimed at the destruction of the American traditional culture—to destroy us from within. And that is the crux of the matter because culture is the face of the nation and its cornerstone—sine qua non. Don't you see how drastically that face has changed lately in America? I was scared by the speed of those changes and dedicated dozens of pages in analyzing all the patterns of the Kremlin's hidden aggression "to reduce our capacity" in 2002, chapter 9, "The Mysterious Aggressor: Soviet Fascism," pp. 167-205, *The Russian Factor*. Unfortunately, you were prevented from reading it and seeing the devastating consequences that cost us blood and treasure, a lot of blood and treasure.

I blame President Bush and his administration. It is inconceivable to me that the people in the State Department, the CIA, FBI, and the Bush Administration do not know what had been written by me during the last twenty-five years, or maybe somebody from the government blocking the information: My computer is monitored and my telephone is wiretapped. If they are not familiar with the issue of the Russian treachery—they are displaying unforgivable ignorance. If they are well-informed, but uneasy to reveal the crime committed by the Soviet mafia—they are giving a layer of legitimacy to criminals, prolonging bloodshed and more disasters around the world. I have no answer. I have my conclusion—Soviet Fascism has stolen our planet's future. Yet the summary of all my thoughts brilliantly and diplomatically expressed a great man of our time the former President of Czechoslovakia and the first President of the Czech Republic Vaclav Havel in his speech at NATO Summit in Bucharest in April 2008:

"The system of... one party rule familiar to us from Communist times is being revived. The secret police is once more becoming all-powerful. The nation's enormous wealth is passing into the hands of the powerful or their friends... everything that is free and had any major influence is destroyed in subtle ways. Important international humanitarian organizations made to leave the country. The best journalists are leaving the media. Troublesome people disappear mysteriously or are murdered. Political murders and even major terrorist operations are never properly investigated. The judiciary is becoming an offshoot of the executive. An enormous nation inhabiting an enormous territory is lapsing into apathy and adopting the status quo. It is accepting the propaganda- fed cult of the leader that is even sometimes reminiscent to the cult of Stalin. Those who have read the book about Litvinenko's death or *The Russian Diary* by murdered Anna Politkovskaya will know what I'm talking about."

Reading my third book, you now know what President Havel is talking about. He also agrees with my perspective on our future in dealing with Russia. "I believe none of us has the right to remain silent and pretend—maybe for energy-saving reasons—that we can't see these things. Politeness and falsehoods have never yet preserved the peace." I would add to President Havel's incredible historic axiom only two sentences. The statute of limitation has no application to those who committed war crimes against humanity! For the sake of the children and grandchildren of the world, we must speak the truth...!

CHAPTER 12

WWIII on America's Soil or The Russian Connection

There is a wonderful English saying—you know it when you see it. I hope you trust my knowledge of the Soviet mafia. I have seen it in Russia. And I am seeing it again, this time in America. No need to repeat what I have already written about in regards to the destruction of the traditional culture in Russia. Alas, the replication—déjà vu of that I see in America. President Adams was right saying that our constitution was made for moral and truly religious people. We are united by our values and principals and that makes morals and religion the targets of the Soviet mafia. Six years has passed since my last observations of the attacks on the American traditional culture, described in *The Russian Factor.* The attacks continue and I have to add some very unpleasant developments, I am constantly observing lately in America.

We all exist in a context of culture—culture made us all. It shapes our character and taste, the food we prefer to eat, the music and sport we adore. I love America with all my heart. Yet if you see me watching a soccer game, you will be sure—the European elements of culture has made me, but I have assimilated completely with the fundamentals within the culture I live in. I love classical music, American jazz, and blues. The recent Black rap-music with its vulgar, filth, and violent messages makes me angry—I reject it. It is subverting the traditional American culture from the Black gospel music and blues I like—a virtual change in the Black community as well. These elements of culture are a barometer and compass of any society, identifying and reflecting the changes of its real life.

Walking along the streets of the city, watching people, their faces, and behavior you will feel the culture of the location, its temperature and pulls. We are the product of culture and to change it you have to change people's mental outlook, the state of their consciousness, their taste, spirit, and the people's behavior and character will follow in changing accordingly. Like in Stalinist Russia, where counterculture had defeated the Russian traditional culture, a *diabolic ideological expansion* in America targets not only elements but the fundamental social fabric of our traditional culture—family, morality, and religion to tear them all down.

Family is the first basic cell of a huge body that constitutes our society. That is why the institution of family is under attack—to redefine the concept of the family and marriage. Homosexuality is not a human rights issue like some present it. Homosexuality is a private matter of choice, making it public is divisive and immediately affects the entire society negatively—it targets our traditional culture in a variety of ways. I knew a few homosexual Republicans, they kept their sexuality private. Ten year ago, I warned you to watch the infiltrated homosexual community and of course I was thinking about the usual suspect. Don't you recognize a familiar modus operandi—to infiltrate and destroy from within? Today the situation has worsened. Distressed, I was watching enormous numbers of sex scandals within the Catholic Church, I knew who orchestrated them. Infiltration into the Church continues to undermine it. Now homosexuals are fighting constantly for changes in the definition of the concept of marriage led by very questionable leadership.

Look at our society where this questionable leadership has incited the sex war. Our boys have become feminized and the movement has become more aggressively arrogant and politicized in 2008. Look also at our militant women who are obsessed in fighting for abortions. Both cases are disproportionally foreign to our traditional culture—the signs of a counterculture attacking our values system. The groups assaulting our culture are mushrooming in America, look at the huge number of new groups tearing apart our morality. I can remind you about a governor of New Jersey to show how homosexuality and corruption intertwined to destroy our traditional values system—religion, morality, and traditional concept of marriage.

At the time I lived in New Jersey, the wonderful Garden State... with corrupt governor McGreevie. As a gay man, he had ignored 700 victims from our state killed on 9/11 and appointed his sex partner, an incompetent foreigner, as the homeland security man of New Jersey. Disgusting! A few years later he publicly introduced himself as "I am gay American." I saw that press conference. Surprisingly no journalists reacted to his description of himself as "gay American." I did immediately, because it was a very unusual statement. Have you ever heard a similar introduction by a gay person in another country— "I am gay French or I am gay German?" I have not. It was a deliberate attack on a traditional culture on the part of the former governor to make a private matter public! His behavior reminds me of a disgusting scene on our national TV, when Bill Clinton discussed boxers and briefs. That was also an attempt to undermine our morals! You know the rest of the story and the result of that on our youth. McGreevy left to the next New Jersey's administration more than sixty cases of corrupted public officials! These two Democrats deserve each other in their negative influence on our youth and a country as a whole.

In respect of morality and religion, equally attacked by the Soviet mafia, we need to discuss it in more detail and precision. For most Americans a Judeo-Christian philosophy is a source of divine inspiration, moral guidance, and the foundation of Western civilization. We are a Judeo-Christian nation—religion is a basis of our country and the defining issue of our culture. Our value system flows from Judeo-Christian philosophy and ethics. Moreover, we are a cultural, ethnic, and religious melting pot, which comprises all the denominations of Christianity, Judaism, Islam, and others into a faithful society of goodness. And that exact unity of the houses of faith is the primary target of the Soviet mafia. The war against America's traditional culture and our values system is waged by a counterculture. I called that war a Sovietization of America for a reason—the war is aimed at the basic institutions embodying our nation and its traditional culture—the Judeo-Christian philosophy. Aren't you surprised by the recent quarrels between different denominations within Christianity and even a division within some churches? Who is provoking such disputes to destabilize the unity of the Christian Church, and who is the benefit of that? Who benefits from the confrontations between

Christianity and Islam or Christianity and other religions? The answer can be found in the preceding chapters—a totalitarian adversary—the Soviet mafia. I can even offer a scenario of how it had been done.

The war against all religions had started on the second day after the October Socialist Revolution in Russia in 1917—the clergy had become the main target of the Soviet Government. Most houses of worship had been destroyed or turned into stables and storages. Hundreds of thousands of clergymen had been killed, deported, or had simply vanished throughout eleven time zones. Infiltrated by the KGB, only congregations subordinate to the agency could function. Besides, a few cults and sects were artificially created under auspices of the KGB to indoctrinate people to follow the Socialist precepts. It took several decades and the Russian Orthodox Church had become an appendage of the Socialist government. The same policy was implemented in the territory occupied by the Soviets. Just ask the Poles or Czechs, they still remember a *diabolic mental expansion*. As a result, a former KGB agent is the head of the Russian Orthodox Church in twenty-first century Russia. The KGB did not change its methods of infiltration into different religions throughout the world—it just widened the recruitments of priests, pastors, and imams, or other heads of the houses of worship to brainwash and indoctrinate the faithful.

Only the priests that cooperated with the KGB in Russia could serve the faithful within the Russian Orthodox Church. And this is the crux of the matter—the same exact scenario was implemented across the globe. The recruitments of the clergy around the world had started decades ago, at the time when WWIII began. You can see it in the example of the war against the Catholic Church. I have no doubts that the two attempts to assassinate Pope John Paul II were organized and carried out by the KGB's henchmen—the first attempt through the Bulgarian henchmen in May 1981, the second in Portugal two years later. I had always admired Pope John Paul II for his global fight against Soviet Socialism and therefore he became the No. 1 target of Soviet Fascism. He also constantly battled against Liberation Theology—the Soviet creation to fight, discredit, and undermine the Catholic Church from within, a link in a chain of endless wars against the church and its moral leader, Pope John Paul II.

This multifaceted sinister war against religion had started somewhere in the 1960s in America as well. I have already discussed the subject in *The Russian Factor*, but I have to remind you of some occurrences of a cynical and *diabolic ideological expansion* against religion in America. First, the Soviets infiltrated the Christian Church in South America with their pseudo- scientific theory of Liberation Theology as a banner of fighting the oppressors. Like Scientology Liberation Theology was a tool to destroy the Christian Church from within. The Liberation Theology was reinforced by the Communist Sandinista government of Nicaragua, Central America. From there it was spread to North America and contaminated both the Catholic Church and the Black Churches. As a matter of fact, the Black Church was one of America's strongest institutions of the traditional conservative culture and therefore—a target of infiltration by the Soviet mafia. It was a simultaneous two-fold Soviet special operation: 1.

Masses of black people were converted to Islam, changing their English names into Muslim. 2. The tenets of Liberation Theology were injected into the Black Church of America to indoctrinate blacks and to confront whites. I called that a cynical design because it was a divisive way aimed at the unity of the churches within American society—to pit black against white—the constant Soviet objectives and the way of destroying our traditional culture to "reducing our capacity."

As a rule, the recruitment among the black population has helped to achieve the goal. It was time when Farrakhan started organizing his Nation of Islam and the Black Panthers become known for their violence and torture. It was also the time when a great American leader, Martin Luther King Jr., a register Republican, who preached love for the enemy, a man of non- violent protest had been assassinated. His place was occupied by a militant front-man propagating the Black Liberation Theology—Rev. Jesse Jackson, a Democrat. The Black community had received an injection of the Stalinist ideology, implementing the propaganda of the "white oppressors," pitting Blacks against the other races. The ideology of Black Liberation Theology has been confronting civilized America since then.

You can see the dreadful result of that within the Black community—an *ideological expansionism* had created a fraudulent sect within the party called Democratic. Like insurgency in Iraq fighting the American military forces, the same way the insurgency of Black Liberation Theology is fighting the "white oppressors" on American soil. The similarities of their targets are striking— police, civilian population, and the American military. The term "white oppressors" is not accidental—it means the

Western civilization. Pay attention to the leaders of Black Liberation Theology, Rev. Jesse Jackson and Louis Farrakhan, the Supreme Minister of the Nation of Islam. They are representatives of a Black African Culture, as they do not profess American culture. Watch their behavior, the words and methods of propaganda they use, and you will grasp the meaning of the Soviet *diabolic ideological expansion* on American soil, infiltrated by the cadres of the Soviet mafia. "To reduce" morality of our culture, the Kremlin had targeted the Black community acting through it for decades. You can see the result! Look around America—the standards of our morals are the lowest as ever! We lost our way! We are in the midst of spiritual crisis!

Meanwhile, the war against the Catholic Church continues. The decades of divisive activities has brought negative multifaceted results. One of them we have experienced lately. The strange wave of sexual abuses in the Catholic Church of America is one of the methods to discredit the Catholic Church. Though humans can make mistakes, this method has an awful smell of infiltration— the patterns of abuses to undermine credibility of the Catholic Church from within are obvious. Our male population has become feminized—"to reduce our capacity." Unfortunately, none of our security agencies had checked the Catholic priests coming from Colombia for example, where the KGB was "working" since the 1960s. Do you remember how Cuban and Soviet agencies organized the drug-trafficking operations into America? We are still fighting the drug-war started by the Soviets then. All of that has pertained to "reduce the adversary's capacity." The Soviet arsenal of different forms of sabotage and subversive activities has no limits to undermine our traditional culture, economy, and our national security.

You can justly ask me how I know about the Soviet's activities in America in the 1960s. Of course, I hadn't been in America in the 1960s. However, I know a long-term, constant Soviet agenda of world domination and the entire modus operandi to achieve the goal. I also know that no KGB Chairman can change the agenda; on the contrary, like any other Soviet blueprint it has a successive nature and each head of the KGB must follow all preceding activities of the agency. Let me give you an example. In 1957, when Arafat was recruited by the Soviets, Yuri Andropov served in the Soviet embassy in Hungary and perhaps did not know Arafat personally. But as soon as he became a Chairman of the

KGB he was successfully enforcing the agenda. Listen to what Ion Mihai Pacepa, a former highest ranking officer of the KGB defected to US said:

"KGB chairman Yuri Andropov in February 1972 laughed to me about the Yankee gullibility for celebrities. We'd outgrown Stalinist cults of personality, but those crazy Americans were still naïve enough to revere national leaders. We would make Arafat into just such a figurehead and gradually move the PLO closer to power and statehood. Andropov thought that Vietnam weary Americans would snatch at the smallest sign of conciliation to promote Arafat from terrorist to statesman in their hopes for peace." "The KGB's Man," *The Wall Street Journal*, September 22, 2003. Please, pay attention to the KGB's opinion about Americans— "they are naïve, gullible, and crazy." You can also see that venom of the KGB's superiority is alive and well—from the first Chekist, Felix Dzerzhinsky to Yuri Andropov and Vladimir Putin. Just look at the Soviet henchmen around the world—they all were well- trained and inherited an audacity of arrogance and superiority in their behaviors from the Stalinist Chekists…

This conversation also confirms several of my points, yet the major one is that we must assess all the enemies' activities through the prism of their objectives and prior knowledge of their operations around the world. Please, remember—youth is the prime target in WWIII. Therefore, the American educational system is the next target to undermine our traditional culture. I have already discussed the issue in *The Russian Factor* in 2002, warning you. However, I could not imagine the speed of the traditional culture's destruction then. Today, six years later, the word "God" is practically removed from our public schools— violence and crimes have entered them instead. The students bring loaded guns to schools and no metal detectors can solve the violent predicament. Two hundred years ago a great American, Benjamin Franklin, said that if people can be so bad with religion, how bad they would be without it. America the Beautiful experiences that awful predicament today.

To fully evaluate the predicament in our public schools, let me give you some numbers. "An average student entering kindergarten today will have more than $100,000 spent on his or her behalf by taxpayers before finishing high school. We believe that families should have greater control over this investment; specifically, the power to choose a safe and effective school for their child." *American Education is in a State of Crisis*, The Heritage Foundation Report, 2008. I agree with every word of this report. The mess in our public schools is obvious. The statistics on the U.S. High School Dropout Rate will frighten you. *The Christian Science Monitor* presents the following numbers of the graduation rate among fifty largest U.S. school districts: Detroit—21, 7%, City of Baltimore, Md.—38, 5%, New York City—38, 9%. This widespread failure is only one miscarriage of the public schools— the absence of needed discipline is even more frightening and imperils our national and economic security. Our children are not ready for a global competition ahead of them—they are not taught the goodness of America, but indoctrinated with anti-Americanism instead. They are casualties of the violent ideology. You can see it in the fallen scholastic tests as well—morality is inextricably connected to any achievements!

Benjamin Franklin was right 200 years ago and he is right today—we are witnessing how bad people could be without religion. The scale of violence in New York City's schools is rising tremendously—the stabbings are leaving some students paralyzed or severely injured, let alone shooting with unpredictable consequences. Moreover, now violence becomes directed against teachers as well—several teachers have been injured by the students! The public schools have become a hotbed of violence, along with the lowered standards of morality among the students. Once I heard a teacher speaking over the radio that girls at eleven can abort their fetuses without parental consent and 25 percent of female students have sexually transmitted diseases. It is not a coincidence that promiscuity and teenage pregnancy has mushroomed. In addition to that, violence among girls has escalated immensely and adults just follow the violent behavior. Teachers in the public schools sexually abuse our children—both girls and boys. What a grim moral picture our public schools present! And this is a direct result of a godless education.

Schooling is more than English and math—morality is the cornerstone of any education, especially in dealing with children. Our public schools rejected teaching religions and, therefore, teaching the difference between right and wrong. The Public schools do not teach our children to think and learn—you witness the results every day. I would say that our educational system has also ignored the law—the responsibility of adults and minors are differentiated. Adults are responsible for minors, and the first precept is teaching and educating the minors in elementary literacy of behavior, which is completely absent in the public schools. Our children do not respect the elderly, their parents, and teachers— they are brought up to live in a climate of total indulgence, behaving accordingly with no awareness of any personal responsibility. And though we spent billions if not trillions, no money or classroom's size will change the predicament in our public schools. We are wasting money and losing a generation. Young people are not familiar with cultural and social literacy—nobody taught them a major subject in life: the American traditional value system— morals, decency, civility, and self-reliance.

The situation in the black community is even worse; thanks to the self-appointed black leaders, like Jessie Jackson, a Democrat, who is blaming the white majority for everything, inciting confrontation, and at the same time playing the victim. Meanwhile, in fact, Black on Black crime is growing making our prisons overcrowded with disproportionate number of blacks. Do you remember the graduation rate in Detroit? Teenage pregnancy drives crime in the public schools, yet the single mother status within the community had become normal, thanks to the leadership of the Democrats. They do not care about morals, they are fighting for power! Look attentively at how the black leaders like Jackson are using the minority issue as a trump card to pit one ethnic group against the other—the Soviet-style divisive policy. Jackson's son is the same ilk. Bringing the race card into politics, the Democrats are manipulating and keeping the Black minority in dependency, depriving them of incredible economic opportunities in America. The Democrats need that dependency in the voting booths and have never given real freedom to the black community. As a result of that, uneducated black youth and fatherless children are on display forty years later in America.

Look at the situation today—none of the Democrats take responsibility for political wrongdoing such as exploiting the black population. Do you remember the Democrat leader like Jackson and his activities? They are fighting the "white oppressors" and brought the fight not only to the school but to the entire Black community. In this respect, I would like to give you my vision of Jesse Jackson and the radical transformation within the Black community. It started with the assassination of the real Black leader Martin Luther King Jr., a registered Republican and deeply religious man. I heard him say that we must eradiate hate. What a prophet! He preached and practiced non-violence with the civil rights movement and those peaceful activities are what caused his death. You know that the KGB wants violence. I believe that King's group was infiltrated and those drastic changes in the Black community after his death testifies to that.

One of the new leaders who transformed King's non-violent policy was Jesse Jackson. Watching him for the last three decades and witnessing other events has reinforced my suspicions about him, especially his constant struggles against police and the attention to America's schools, the youth as a whole—one of the KGB's targets. And again you can see the familiar method of infiltration "to reduce the moral capacity" of the American society. I hope that time and diligent research will prove my opinion. Meanwhile, our schools are under constant assaults—WWIII is going on in America. The first brigade fighting against Western civilization is Black Liberation Theology. I hope you grasp the main idea of the war.

In respect to our schools, my conclusion is: control over the public schools under the unaccountable and failed leadership of the Democrats should be transferred to the local communities with the establishment of alternative, private schools and vouchers so parents can choose. The absolute absence of accountability of the Democratic leadership working in cahoots with the Teacher's Union has destroyed our public schools. Indoctrination and anti- Americanism has many different forms. You are now familiar with some of them and you will be the judges. Please, also remember that our children are the casualties of the left-wing clique running and failing our children's education, shaping an army of mediocre followers to build the Democrat's majority. Look at our teens; they are obsessed with cell phones wasting hours on mindless chats instead of studying real American History. We are losing responsible citizens and creating inept ones.

To be fair, I have to admit that like Black leaders, the white Democratic leaders are guilty as well. And no one was held accountable yet! Let me give you other leaders and their unethical impact on our traditional culture.

For your information, there are 129 cases of corrupt public officials under another Democrat governor; Corzine of New Jersey. I did not like Corzine from the beginning when I found out that he came from Goldman Sacks. For several reasons I have suspected the firm is involved in some shenanigans. Corzine's morals are also questionable. In addition to that, New Jersey has the largest deficit in the country. You can't even imagine the level of corruption, abuse of power, and nepotism in the state of Illinois, especially in Chicago run by the Democrats. Infiltration and recruitment had started in the 1960s in Illinois and if you read this book attentively, you can figure out how I know about all that is going on in Illinois. To see a real face of the Democratic leadership look also at other leaders and their deeds. Governor Spitszer of New York had his sex scandal and was involved in the unlawful troop's activities to get rid of a Republican leader. Senator Edwards is talking about "two Americas" and at the same time dealing with a very questionable Hedge Fund. He also covers-up his child out of wedlock—an incredible hypocrisy! Meanwhile, the Democrats continue undermining our culture. Look at the corrupt mayor of Detroit and several corrupt mayors of Newark, N.J. Some Democrats offered sex education for kindergarten. Don't you see the central elements of the Soviet mafia within the Democrat's party run by DLC? Disgusting! Are they confronting Soviet Fascism or they are helping our enemies? This is a judgment you must make. Yet, you won't argue that our standards of morality are quickly and constantly degenerating. There is no more talk of "don't lie, don't steal, and don't kill"—the code words of Western civilization—Sovietization of America is on a march.

There is another warning sign for me in connection with the crooked politicians with Unions and organized crime, usual practices of the Kremlin—it runs both. Some years ago I watched a criminal case against several Union leaders in New York accused of briberies, racketeering, and connection with organized crime. For me the District Attorney had the obvious evidence to expose at least two of the criminals and his criminal connections. Using a pay phone, I even called and talked to her assistant pointing out that organized crime was a part of the Soviet mafia. The conversation did not last long. The man had no idea of the connection—an absolute lack of knowledge in terms of the Soviet mafia on the part of honest but deceived Democrats. The criminals were acquitted. Distressed, I watched the result of ignorance and victory of the Soviet mafia that had encroached political correctness into American society. Ignorance and the war against religion have the same source. Just watch the war against Christmas at the end of the year and you will see it clearly—Modern Liberals hate Christmas, that Judeo-Christian sparkle of hope for humanity. They are using the word separation of Church and State as an argument in some perverted way. In fact, they are separating individuals from God—infringing on a personal relationship between an individual and God, depriving an individual of learning morals, ethics, and personal responsibility. If you haven't seen the result yet, you will see it very soon.

Political correctness used by the Democrats and destroying our America has many different forms. The attack at the institutions of our Higher Education is the next one. Recent statistics show that 90 percent of the academia in the field of social studies and science are Liberal-Leftists, who know neither Stalinism, or the Soviet mafia, or Soviet Fascism. They are unable to teach the subject, they have no knowledge or expertise. As a result, we are left blind and mute attacked by the Soviet mafia. Our morality has been at the lowest level since the '30s-40s. Do not be surprised by an escalation of cheating and troubles of different kinds within our campuses: youth copy adults.

This is a result of systematic assault aimed at undermining our traditional culture. It is easier to deal with deceived, corrupted, and perverted people than with decent, knowledgeable, and ethical ones. It is also obvious that fraud, deceit, double-dealings, and cheating cannot be transmitted by wind or air: corrupted Modern- Liberals are the nucleus of the force sabotaging our culture in academia. Moreover, I also see the ideological expansion in their activities—teaching anti-Americanism, they are molding up the next generation of Modern-Liberals! And there is no accountability; nobody dares to accuse the Democrats of a moral crime they had committed. Do you remember the Soviet's cadres teaching our youth in the 1950s? Nothing has changed. I was kicked out of the academia because I was telling the truth about Russia. Then, the Soviet's cadres continued destroying our youth, our culture, and our country.

Just watch how our culture is rapidly eroding, shifting away from traditional values, the adversary's ideas infiltrating and inculcating the mentality of our youth. The army of the loyalist to the party called Democratic is building by the Modern-Liberal professors in our colleges and universities. I have an impression that the *diabolic ideological expansion* of collectivism has come to our soil—it runs our colleges and universities. Just take the textbooks, written by these professors, they have distorted real American history, revising it by bashing America and stating that democracy is an economic equality. Wow! They instill radicalism and intentionally mislead the students by not giving them the full explanation of Jihad—the same agenda. The recent statistics reveal: 100 Liberal celebrities gave the commencement speeches to graduates, and only 6 conservatives. Moreover, the major aspects of our Founding

Fathers' legacy: freedom of religion, protection from the government, and individual liberty are under attack. The preservation of their legacy is the only solution for our survival. It is the crux of the matter for our High Educational System. The understanding and knowledge of the Soviet mafia assaulting the nucleus of our existence is a must…!

In the beginning of the book, I told you the story of my departure from the teaching position in *the New School for Social Research*, in New York City. Then, in 1993, I did not know the cause, and figured it out a couple of years later. It was 1992; America was campaigning for a new president. My dislike of Clinton had overwhelmed me to a degree that I could not remain silent. And despite my poor English, I dared to call Rush Limbaugh. He was the only person I could trust—his awareness of Clinton's danger coincided with mine. So talking to him I went straight ahead and warned him and his listeners about the Soviet infiltration and other negative features of Soviet Socialism. *Baltic Winds*, pp. 570-573. The trouble started shortly after Clinton became president. My course, *Russia in Transition*, was cancelled. The truth about Russia made some politicians uncomfortable. The Democrat Party had their Modern Liberals to brainwash our youth—I lost my position, the truth about Russia left academia with me.

The result is now obvious—the vast majority of Americans, especially our youth, is kept in the dark and cannot objectively evaluate a contemporary situation in our country, let alone the outside world. That vast majority had no idea about my books tirelessly warning them. America has been deceived and has no idea of our foremost enemy that is constantly attacking us. Moreover, absence of the truth allowed youth to be deceived and seduced. If you remember the Russian youth movement NASHI, pay attention to a new youth movement in America. They are internationalists and globalists who hate capitalism and intending to spend America's money for the poor of the world. Do you grasp the picture and know who is behind the movement in America? Perhaps the last chapter will make you aware of that. There is no end to my despair. Where are you, the real leaders with integrity in America…?

The next Soviet target to "reduce our capacity" is our economic system of capitalism. As a matter of fact, the Soviet Socialist system was full of the underground economy and the speculators who managed it during the Soviet era. Legitimacy of the Russian KGB's Government, a destabilizing force in the world, had opened a Pandora's Box—saboteurs, hackers, charlatans, speculators, money counterfeiters, swindlers, provocateurs, and other scoundrels and rascals, flooded our country and the world. I have already described in *The Russian Factor* the mechanism of penetration into our economic system by the Soviet speculators and recruited domestic crooks, whether it concerns oil or other commodities, it is identical—henchmen-speculators are well- trained in all the diversity of economic crimes. Yet several very suspicious cases were not fully investigated by the FBI in 1999- 2003 after the bubbles in the stock market. I would like to remind you of several names involved. One of them, Terry McAuliffe, had appeared in two cases.

"In 1999, the U.S. Department of Labor sued Jack Moore, pension fund manager for the International Brotherhood of Electrical Workers, on the bases of several deals made with McAuliffe. In one deal, McAuliffe and the pension fund partnered to buy commercial property in Florida, with McAuliffe investing $100 while the pension fund put up $39 million. McAuliffe received a 50% interest in the partnership and emerged with $2.45 million from his original $100 investment." Wikipedia. To make a long story short I can report to you that McAuliffe was not charged with any wrongdoing and continued his activities, being a Chairman of the Democratic National Committee under the Clinton presidency. The second case had brought him even more money. In 1997, McAuliffe purchased a pre-IPO $100,000 stake in Global Crossing. A year before the troubles in the stock market when the bubble blew up in 2000, McAuliffe sold his investment, which was then valued at $18 million. The company went bankrupt in 2002 in the middle of what *The New York Times* called "many of the same accusations that have Enron into one of the largest corporate scandals in history."

I completely agree with the opinion. And again, he was not accused of any wrongdoing. I believe it was another scheme "to reduce our capacity." Our economic system is based on trust; making money is our way of life, but it should be done within the parameters of the law. I do not believe Mr. McAuliffe followed those precepts, though the Chairman of the Democratic National Committee was supposed to act more ethically. Don't you see a striking similarity in corruption and behavior of the Kremlin's bosses, described in the preceding chapters and the bosses in the Democrat Party? Pay attention to the senators who help destroy the CIA, they can be "very helpful" in undermining our economic capitalist system as well. Don't you see a kind of a shadow government that is fighting the Bush administration? Do you remember how the Kremlin runs the entire Russian economy…?

I gave you these ideas for a reason. The Kremlin, especially after the beginning of Putin's era, has constantly studied the possibility of infiltrating our economy, especially aiming at our financial private institutions. One Russian writer, telling the story of the Great Depression in America, had described the failure of the banks as a major factor bringing down the market in America during 1930. The author did not exclude that exact failure of the private banks and other financial institutions to occur in the future. He was right—it took place in America in 2007. The private banks lent mortgages to people with no credible financial history and ability to make mortgage payments, which has created a housing bubble and enormous economic anxiety in America. The scheme started in one California's community and spread across America. I am afraid the crisis can spill over to Europe and to the world to "reduce capacity" of the world financial system. My heart goes to the people losing their homes, yet I would notice that the Bush administration has not learned the lesson of the previous bubbles created by the domestic crooks in cahoots with the *International Mafia* and as a result got the next one. I am not sure there won't be other bubbles in the future and the taxpayers will again pay for the crimes committed—our economy is under assault by a very determined enemy.

We live in an open society; the infiltration into our institutions and organizations is quite an easy one. Our stock market is an open window to the world and those who want to harm us are using this window by deceiving and corrupting people in our institutions. Do we know how many Russian cronies are officially involved and corrupting our Banking system? In my opinion the mortgage crisis like preceding bubbles was created for a certain reason— "to reduce our economic capacity" to bring anxiety and dissatisfaction of Americans with the Republicans and the Bush administration. I suspect some Democrats in the House and Senate were "working" with the banking institutions. We now see the result.

Do you remember chapter 7, WWIII? I mentioned the bubbles of Enron there. I saw the scheme as a warning sign—a harbinger for the future. Unfortunately, the Bush administration had not learned the lesson then and was doomed to have the same troubles again— our enemies are very determined to destroy us! The Kremlin attempts to establish criminal capitalism with oligarchs in America by infiltrating management of the targeted institutions, banks, and businesses. The Kremlin has a special proclivity to infiltrate businesses carrying the name "International" or "Global." The agenda is to create a global economic calamity through America's demise. Reading this book you have learned that. Pay attention to our icons JM and JE—they are targeted, America's big business and big banks, too. Besides, do you remember the changes in the banking system made by the Clinton administration in the 1990s? Clinton practically induced the bubbles.

I believe that the scam in California is a continuation and the consequence of a calculated design to discredit free market capitalism by destroying our private banking system. Those changes will affect other financial institutions to do "the job" of "reducing our capacity" and influence the public against the Republican Party in the upcoming 2008 election. It also can be a combination of the foreign gangsters acting in cahoots with our domestic crooks—a subject of thorough criminal investigation by the FBI or Attorney General to end the assault on our economy. Time will tell us the result—the next bubbles or absence of them would be the answer.

From this I am reminded of some old information from the 1980s. I have read that the Soviets were researching a design to "demolish the American Government." During Reagan's time it sounded unthinkable. However, today that scenario can be inserted into a big picture of a master plan to achieve world domination. Knowing the Department of financial intelligence, Putin consumed with envy and considering his determination to destroy America by all means possible, plus the incompetence of FBI and CIA, I suspect that a lot of crises "to reduce our capacity" are ahead of us. As a matter of fact, the Kremlin knows well how to create crisis. It ran the country through crisis the entire seventy years of the Soviet Union—it solved none. On the contrary, exaggerating the crisis and prolonging it, and creating panic, the Kremlin was screwing up the population and economy even more at the same time.

There is another similarity—the criminal scams of Pyramids. After the collapse of the Soviet Union and relative freedom in the Soviet economy, the different types of criminal Pyramids have flooded the country. The naïve Soviet people were defrauded and burned for millions by the Soviet charlatans and rascals. The scheme that started in California reminds me of the Pyramid schemes in the Soviet Union. Both organized by criminals against ordinary people. What has happened in America has had specific timing—one year before the election. It is not an "irrational exuberance," it is a long range strategy well thought over and practiced for decades. By targeting the world economy in the era of globalization to achieve world domination, Putin and his henchmen are aimed at "reducing capacity" of global economy through demise and calamity of America's private banks and free market capitalism.

As you know there are several other happenings to agitate people against Bush. He is blamed for the deaths of our soldiers, killed by the Iranians in Iraq, though the Democrats do not want to fight Iranians-henchmen. He is blamed for America losing prestige and image around the world, which is in fact a result of the constant attacks and smear of America's image and prestige around the world by the henchmen of the *Department of Agitation and Propaganda* for the last ninety years. Look at the political theater going on in our Congress. The Democrats pronounced that the war in Iraq was lost. Disgusting! That statement not only helped our enemies, but it also demoralized part of the American public at a time of global war. Can you tell me the motivation of some Democrats for doing that? Don't they understand that our national security suffers because of their actions and statements? Why had they invested in our defeat? What side are they on…?

Living in America for twenty-six years, I noticed some kind of pattern—a year before the election or during the year of the election a tragic event or economic crisis occurred to blame the Republican Party. In 1987, it was black Friday in the stock market to blame the Reagan administration. In 1995, before the election of 1996, it was Oklahoma after the Republicans won both houses in 1994. At the time Clinton blamed the Conservatives' talk show for inciting the tragedy in Oklahoma—the Soviet-style of false- accusation. In 2000, before the election, it was the bubbles in the stock market to incite the public against the Republican Party. Somebody has been "working" hard against the Republican Party for a long time. I suspect Gorge Soros is one of them—a currency speculator No.1, who had once bankrupted the English pound. Yet nobody investigates him and his very questionable Hedge Fund. Perhaps he had help from a small clique of Democrats: watch now for our $$. The dynamics of the contests between the parties are revealing the sharp division—Republicans fighting for national security, individual rights of the citizens, and capitalist economy; Democrats for Socialist economy, redistribution of wealth, and collectivism. Just research the Democratic governments of New York State and New Jersey—you will find money wasted, sex, and corruption on a monumental scale! And again, I see the same similarity between the Kremlin and the Democrat Party.

I know that you have doubts in my theory of infiltration into our institutions and organizations by the Soviet mafia and subversive activities of "10,000 boys-saboteurs." So, God was with me to convince you in the truthfulness of my theory. John Huddy, a former *Miami Herald* columnist and critic, a network producer, whose print and broadcast subjects have included Charles Manson, has written a book *Storming Las Vegas*, Ballantine Books—New York, 2008. It is an incredible documentary of the Soviet's criminal activities against Western civilization—a chronicle of the Soviet modus operandi described by me in all my writings and especially in the pages of this book. It is a book which is presenting "How a Cuban-Born, Soviet-Trained Commando Took Down the Strip to the Tune of Five World-Class Hotels, Three Armed Cars, and Millions of Dollars." This is a story of Cuban-born Jose Vigoa, a Lieutenant of the Soviet Army, trained in Afghanistan and Angola and finally exported to America by the Cuban Soviet mafia.

If you remember the Mariel boat lift from Cuba, Vigoa gives interesting details in the book about the boat. It was the Cuban operation "to reduce our capacity" by exporting to America "a significant number of criminals and mental patients, released from jails and asylums and men from the Cuban intelligence: 'As the boat filled up, I began to notice other young men about my age climbing aboard… I counted about twenty-three of these men. I knew they were military like me. I could tell by their physical condition and bearing. Some were from intelligence" This is a description of what had happened in 1980. Can you imagine the number of military men from the foreign intelligence twenty-eight years later? Perhaps, Vladimir Zhirinovsky had given us the right numbers—"10,000 of our boys working on American soil." The last page of the book confirms those numbers.

Let me give you the conclusion of the book, which is confirming all my fears expressed in this book. "Jose Vigoa as an example of the criminal to be most feared in the future." Sheriff Bill Young said, "We in American local law enforcement know exactly how to deal with the homegrown street thug but are way behind the curve with the foreign born and trained who are smart and not committing crimes because they are addicted or need money for drugs. We're seeing more and more of these types in Vegas, particularly from the Middle East, Israel, the Baltic States, and South America. Their values are far different from ours, and the ruthless side they display leaves many American cops stunned. Many of these guys have military background and are sophisticated and well read. It's going to take a concerted effort on our part to effectively deal with the Jose Vigoas of the world." This is a stunning confirmation of all my writings and predictions—it is a sad story of our time. I was narrating this story and warning you this past twenty-five years. But you are unaware of that—you were kept in the dark by the CIA.

So I could have completed this book on a high note of approval, but I can't: you heard only my voice and that is not enough—I want you to hear the voice of a young man who came to America "to reduce our capacity." I want you to hear Jose Vigoa, the lieutenant's antagonist that cooperated fully with the authority. "My name is Jose Vigoa. So, you want to know what I am doing in Las Vegas, Nevada. You want to know why. Why the shootings, the robberies, the raids on the famous American hotels? And *where*. Where did I get my guns, my AK-47s and Chinese copies, the hand grenades, the explosives, sniper rifle, and all of those things? Where did I come from? Where would I strike next? Where did I get my intelligence about the truck and its wonderful money? You want to know my secrets, do you not? And you want to know who I really am?" And he continued presenting himself:

"I am a former Marxist who was trained by the communists. I am a killer, more than police know, more than federals know.... My story is not about one man, and it is about the world and the times we live in. You should know me well and understand who I am, because there are others like me, and they will be coming soon to visit, of this I am certain. Some will be Cuban, Or Russian, Or Israeli, Or Chinese, and Or Arabs. We are children not only revolutions and violence but of history you have made yourself. It is true; I organized, trained, and led the gang that robbed many hotels, and many cash-filled armored trucks serving the rich casinos and the wealthy suburbs. I take from the homo-faced rich people... I have so much cash I buy a hotel on the beach if they let me. Or maybe I buy a whole town..."

Now you know why I was so driven to write my books. And now that you are acquainted with the criminals acting on our soil, let me tell you more. We know that a robber produced by Soviet Fascism is only a drop in the crime within the big picture of worldwide terrorism. There are many other actors-gangsters on our soil. They were trained to orchestrate accidents with trucks transporting hazardous cargo, to blow up industrial buildings producing chemicals, and to inflict anxiety upon the civilian population— fear is a powerful weapon. I have to remind you again that Soviet Fascism has a multifaceted body with numerous tentacles aimed at the civilized world to terrorized and demoralized people. And I believe that Soviet Fascism has achieved a partial victory. Look at what is going on in the world—hundreds of people are killed every day in the quest for power, cities and villages destroyed, and America portrayed as a guilty party of all of that. Don't you think that *the Department of Agitation and Propaganda* "working" so diligently for several decades can celebrate a victory? Moreover, to my surprise, some Americans believe in their guilt! And that makes my blood boil. I put my life on line to tell you the truth about real criminals and all my effort is in vain.

I am especially frustrated watching the Jews—they greatly disappoint me. For many years I have been a member of JCC in New Jersey—a wonderful complex for recreation. We have a Women's Club there, embracing women of different nationalities, but predominantly Jewish women. Naturally I have some friends there. When my first book was published we discussed it on a usual gathering in a big hall. There were a lot of questions and I tried to answer all of them. It was a very joyful time for me—the book I had been writing for a decade was finally published! My presentation was met very warmly by the audience. I was very happy. The meeting lasted more than two hours. To my surprise the next day some Jewish women stopped talking to me. They did not like the truth conveyed in my book. They also did not perceive how a Jew could be a Republican. I was shocked. My friends calmed me down saying that the Jews in New York City had the same way of thinking—they hated the Republicans. Life proved their words. Today I am shocked even more by the behavior of some Jews—they are helping Soviet Fascism to create the Second Holocaust. Just watch a raising wave of anti-Semitism in America and the world!

Yes, you are not mistaken; I am talking about the Second Holocaust for a reason. The environment in the world is quite similar to that of the 1930s, when National Socialism had been emerging in Germany and Russia—two governments had helped each other. Unfortunately, in establishment of Stalinism in Russia, the Jews constituted a substantial part of the Stalinist movement— of twenty-two first Commissars half of them were Jewish. Most of them were liquidated later on among other millions. The Russian people remember The Great Purges perpetrated by *the Organs* seventy years ago. In Germany of the 1930s Hitler also cherished the idea of avenging the Jews; he waited for the "proper" time. That time had come in 1938, after The Great Purges in Russia of 1937. Hitler needed the occasion and it came. The Crystal Night of killing Jews and destruction of their property had started in the night of 9-10 November 1938 in all German cities big and small— Fascism has always been very well organized in quickly spreading deceit, fraud, and corruption implemented by militant brutality!

The Gulag in Russia was also exceptionally organized. The Father of the earliest sites of the Gulag was Chekist Naftaly Frenkel. Just read about Stalin's assignment to build the White Sea Canal managed by Frenkel and you will see they were well organized and it was the first major project of the slave-labor institution, killing millions and, Russian writers used deceit, fraud, and corruption to cover up the crime. Please, remember that Fascism has identical strategies and tactics regardless of ethnicity. Look at the different reaction of the Jews in two countries with the ideology of Soviet Fascism. Today, in Russia, you will find a lot of Jews cooperating with the Kremlin in its economic policy of criminal capitalism. Some Jews of Venezuela are leaving the country—they recognized the first sign of the upcoming troubles. Do you remember what happened in Germany in 1938? My books are testifying to similar events under Stalinism. With great sadness I have to admit today that the West ignored those identical features of Fascism many times for many years.

I am not alone warning you, I am in good company with Elie Wiesel:

> *Why Remember? Why remember, why remember at all?*
> "We must remember, not only because of the dead; it is too late for them. Not only because of the survivors; may it even be late for them. Our remembering is an act of generosity, aimed at saving men and women from apathy to evil, if not from evil itself. The tale must be told in its totality, before it is too late, before the last witness leaves the stage and takes his testimony back to the dead."
>
> –Elie Wiesel.

I am the last witness and am responsible for giving you those two tragic events of history—with witnesses gone the truth is substituted with myths. This is the reason for writing all three of my books. Like under the Stalinist movement and under Putin's Soviet mafia, the Jews again blindly follow the path of the Democratic Party in America. You might be angry for the comparison. Hold your horses. The Jews are not the only people who are blind followers. There are others too. I believe that the Soviet mafia had infiltrated America decades ago and produced a tragic evidence of its presence. Some years ago, I watched a TV Documentary *Jonestown*. Sitting frozen, I couldn't believe my eyes. It was a miniature picture of the Stalinist slave-labor camp with overwhelming fear, secrecy, physical abuse, lies, and indoctrination of the Socialist ideas. At the same time the words like dignity and economic equality for the proletariat were used to mesmerize and seduce the audience—a wonderful socialist utopia. Those words were so familiar to me that the similarity had stunned me. The tragic end in *Jonestown* with hundreds of dead bodies on the ground and 300 dead children made me sick and angry.

Who could perpetrate such a horrible crime against civilian Americans, poisoning all of them with cyanide? Researching the story of the *Jonestown* tragedy I have found interesting facts. A leader of the movement, who perpetrated the crime, Rev. Jim Jones was a pastor who established the Peoples Temple—a cult. Eloquent and smart, operating with false but appealing terms, he attracted a substantial group of Blacks and Whites who had believed in his propaganda and followed him to Guyana. He had help from several organizers, as well. It was there in Guyana, pretty far from the American authorities where the unspeakable crime took place. I see the *Jonestown* tragedy as a disaster orchestrated by *the Organs*—the test of the "naïve and gullible" Americans. Do you remember how the KGB's Chairman Andropov characterized the people of America? Analyzing all aspects of the Jonestown events, you will find all the elements of the Stalinist cult of personality, schooling indoctrination and training, a typical attempt of mind control.

Can you imagine my feeling when I heard a *Jonestown's* survivor's story? He told that the people of Jonestown had to study the Russian language and he, the survivor had an assignment: Rev. Jim Jones asked him to bring a suitcase with money to the Russian Embassy in Guyana. That is why he survived. After that story a wild thought flashed through my mind—maybe killer-Mason had the same assignment to commit unspeakable murders, too? Do you perceive now the Russian connection? Please, think about the depth of our problems. To help you, I would ask you a question to think about. What's does the fate of Princess Diana and a political scandal *Iran-Contra Affair* have in common? If you answer this question you will conceive the depth of our problems and the essence of the Russian connection.

Meanwhile, the catastrophic fire is burning our forests and hundreds of our homes; numerous violent storms and tornados and flooding are devastating millions of acres of our land, killing Americans. The number of plane crashes is mounting; the price of oil is swelling, and the cost of life tremendously increasing. And that is not all. Unknown before natural disasters came down upon our American land with unprecedented numbers of heavy rains, historic flooding, storms, tornados, and so on. For example, in 2005 there were 234 tornados, in 2008—more than 700 up to April. I warn you again: we can expect in addition to that—the volcanoes' eruptions, earthquakes, record level of rains, arsons, and other disasters on our land and across the world. Don't you see a coordinated effort to destroy America? Please, remember the 2008 is the year of a presidential election in America—Soviet Fascism will be very active in many different fronts to "reduce the adversary's capacity," to create anxiety around the world. To grasp my ideas, please read the last chapter of *The Russian Factor*, I warned you then, in the 2004 presidential election about Soviet's experiments with weather. And keep in mind that the Island of Cuba where the Soviet nuclear missiles were once aimed at us is still ninety miles off our shore.

To make a better explanation of the Soviet's experimentation with nature, I can give you several examples. The Soviets had been experimenting with nature, especially manipulating weather to change climate for decades. They were working within the atmosphere, creating clouds to produce rain. They were also dispersing clouds by using high energy when it was needed. At the time, the Soviet's obsession with victory over nature and climate had created a slogan even among children: "We Must Conquer Nature!" Billions were spent and as a result there was destruction of land and water. The Soviets used science in different manners: for destruction and sometimes for good reasons. I found out lately that during the Olympic Games in Moscow in 1980 the sky was quite clouded and the Soviet scientists had applied high energy to disperse the clouds. They cleaned Moscow's sky for the time of the Olympic

Games. However, the main application of the scientific developments had been used against the adversaries.

There are data about a new weapon of destruction called Pluton, invented by the scientists of the Russian intelligence. Pluton—a device like a mole or water snake programmed to deliver one or more bombs or warheads and able to move in different directions. I narrated the information on p. 307, *The Russian Factor.* Somewhere in the beginning of the 1990s, at the time of Perestroika, I read an article about the KGB's ability to orchestrate earthquakes using a new device—perhaps it was Pluton. Please, read the last chapter of *The Russian Factor.* A note: *the Organs* will use every new technology in WWIII against Western Civilization. Be ready!

The story of Pluton and the Soviet's development of the device to orchestrate earthquakes I wrote four years ago. This year, watching TV, I became acquainted with the American effort in researching the bottom of the ocean seeking for oil. I was shocked.

The device searching for oil was a carbon copy of Pluton! I could not believe my eyes. It was the same technology to move the device. The only difference was the motivation—the Americans were looking for oil, the Soviets had equipped the device with several bombs to orchestrate an earthquake or do other damage. If the West is looking to develop a technology—the Kremlin is seeking a weapon of destruction, a spectacular one with a lot of casualties. Now I believe that the original device had been stolen by the Soviets from the appropriate owner and modified by them to be a military weapon of destruction. If four years ago I suspected that some earthquakes were orchestrated by the Soviets, now I think they have already used their creation several times around the globe including in our land. You can consider the earthquakes in Indonesia with involvement of a volcano, a lethal earthquake in China in the year of the Olympic Games, and Katrina—a man- made disaster using a force of nature.

Let me give you another tragic story to show the consequences of the Soviet's deeds on their own territory, using water as WMD— Weapon of Mass Destruction. Have you heard about the Aral Sea in the Soviet Union? The sea was full of sea flora and different fish: sturgeon, carp, perch, and others. In the trouble years of famine and war, the Aral Sea had provided thousands of people with fish, helping them to survive. The experimentation with building canals for irrigation from the Aral Sea was started under Stalin's order somewhere in the 1930s and resumed after WWII. By the 1970s the result was stunning—the Aral Sea had ceased to exist, the land along thousands of acres contaminated, ecological balance destroyed, people had to leave their homes to survive. Perhaps you have never heard about the Aral Sea's ecological catastrophe and about the suffering people there. It is another example of how the Soviets used nature as WMD.

Though I have no scientific expertise, I know the mind-set of our enemy; and that is the source of my suspicions about all recent tragedies on our land. That is also the reason I do not believe in the *Global Warming* theory—it is another KGB hoax "to reduce the capacity" of the capitalist's world, to attack Western civilization, threatening its people and covering up a real motivation by bringing a fake motor of the *Green Environment* and *Change.* Isn't it suspicious that constant propaganda of *Global Warming* coincides with numerous arsons, and enormous harm to property? Please, also recall the anti-war and anti-nuclear movements, incited and run by our enemies. A big picture brings even more. Do you remember the Stalinist pseudo-science and historians serving the ideology? All of that has the same source and agenda to demoralize people, to stop America's free market economic achievements, growth, and profitability. It is ideological weaponry against capitalism, now serving and promoted by the Democrats.

In all my writings, I am trying to focus your attention on the root causes of worldwide instability, which is the aggressor's attempt to CONTROL and RULE the world. Forgive the repetition of these two words. I am intentionally delineating and repeating for you the basic, motivation, ideology, and the manner of its formation from Stalin to Putin—two phases of Soviet Fascism, assaulting the West and organizing defeat from within during the last ninety years. Do not expect the Russian KGB's government to retreat—the multifaceted body with its venomous tentacles is growing up! Like advanced Soviet Fascism the number of Modern Liberal Democrats have been gearing up since President Wilson who refused to sponsor a fight against the Russian criminal regime in its inception, in 1918, *The Russian Factor*, pp. 219-220.

My fellow Americans look around! Do you recognize your "America the Beautiful?" I do not! Watch how the small clique of Democrats is destroying our country! Do you remember that the notion of accountability, integrity, and shame did not exist in the Kremlin's paradigm? I am afraid that the same notions are absent within the Democrat Party. Using political expediency the clique creates crisis, fear, and anxiety for political advantages, the same way Stalin had built his Soviet Socialism; Soviet Fascism.

Moreover, in some states the Soviet mafia has infiltrated the entire top of the administration with enormous corruption, like in Illinois. They are destroying the moral fabrics of our society—the cornerstone of the American Democratic Republic—dear to us legacy of our founding Fathers! Don't you see it and conceive now the Russian Connection? Don't you understand now who created the *Global Evil Empire of Terrorism*, while blaming America and calling Cheney a war criminal? You know those charges are false. What you perhaps forget is that this a quintessential Stalinist's principle and method against political opponents—putting blame on the opposite side. The time has come to openly call a spade a spade otherwise Soviet Fascism will celebrate a total victory. My fellow Americans! You are the last stand for the Truth! Stop the march of the enemy along our land! Let's roll the truth out…!

CHAPTER 13

A Final Phase of Diabolic Ideological Expansion

Yes, look around and you will not recognize our America. It is the reason I have introduced to you WWIII and its components to show the dreadful result of the war. Infiltration or penetration was one of its components. We have already discussed different kinds of infiltration and various Soviet targets like foreign governments, institutions, businesses, and other organizations. The mental infiltration is the most pervasive and effective one having a long duration and longevity. Of course you have already learned about the *Department of Agitation and Propaganda*; but there is more. I am going to give you some additional examples of mental expansion, naming some people and their actions. Given the ideological division in our country into liberals and conservatives, I promised to discuss the subject. And this is the time for me to carry out my promises.

In the beginning of the book I promised to answer an extremely important question of our day and identify two terms: "Classic Liberals," and "Modern Liberals." Who are the "Classic Liberals" today? They are people with strong principles and beliefs, embracing various types of individual freedom, such as religious liberty, political liberty, freedom of speech, right of self-defense, strong national security, and the like. They are for all the liberties plus they are the patriots of their country, pursuing national security matters along the path of the truth. They love their flag, country, and their religion. Who are the "Classical Liberals" in the twenty-first century? What is their name or designation? For me they are the Conservatives! They have survived all the attacks Soviet Fascism undertook against them. They are Conservatives in America and France, Germany and Italy, the nucleus of their respective nations—the embodiment of self-reliance, individual freedom, wisdom, decency, civility, and pride. They are the custodians of national security and therefore the enemies of Soviet Fascism and its quest for world domination.

Unfortunately, the term Conservative is used very loosely and often wrongly to deceive or cover up a real intention. The Mullah's Government of Iran is not a Conservative one—it instills Soviet Fascism. Remember Stalinist infiltration into the Churches and charlatans using religion: you have it in Iran. The name Conservative had become a political symbol, an antidote to Soviet Fascism. The title "conservative clerics in Iran" is an oxymoron—conservatives are the targets and victims of Soviet Fascism in a permanent war. The answer to the second part of the question is a more complicated matter. So, who are the "Modern Liberals?" First of all, they had usurped the name of liberty that has nothing in common with their activities and agenda. They are predominantly the top leaders in the Democrat party, lacking a grasp of reality. They were actually soft on Soviet Socialism and now soft on Soviet Fascism. Michael Savage, a conservative radio- show host called them "the subversive force corrupting America." He is right. I called them Leftists—far-left radicals fighting the traditional American culture and by doing that corrupting America and its people. That exact group of leaders is propagating Socialism and imposing the idea on the rest. I have already given you the examples of their dreadful activities that are changing America.

The vast majority of the rest are the decent people, the followers. As a rule they are ill-informed, misguided, and therefore easily indoctrinated, duped, victimized, and defrauded. They are the followers of the false labels and slogans—the casualty of the socialist propaganda similar to the victims of *the Soviet Department of Agitation and Propaganda* in Stalin's Russia. I had been brainwashed for many years and know the subject. The dissidents- psychologists called one unit of that department—*the KGB's mind controlled unit.* My heart is bleeding when I am watching familiar indoctrination of Americans. Maybe *the Department of Agitation and Propaganda* has already come to our land? Do you remember who invented it? My heart especially bleeds when I see an indoctrinated community of American Jews—fooled and duped, they lost their memory of the Holocaust, supporting the Democrats and becoming the casualties of Soviet propaganda!

They still hate President Nixon and are unaware of the fact that he and they are the victims of the same enemy.

Who are the small group of Democrats that propagandize, brainwash, and misguide our people, corrupting America? And life again gave me the answer. As a matter of fact, I am a political junky, but being busy with this book, and trying to complete it as soon as possible, I had no time to watch TV. One evening, preparing dinner in the kitchen, I turned the TV on in the living room. A man's voice talked about the election, I did not care at the time—too early. Suddenly the voice, the manner of delivery, and the substance of news changed. The yelling voice was bringing a completely different subject to the air—it was familiar Soviet propaganda full of accusation while slamming and trashing America. I ran to the living room. At first, I was shocked—in front of me stood Vladimir Zhirinovsky, with his well known gesticulation a-la El Duche-Mussolini and theatrical manners of speech, so familiar to all Russian émigrés. He was yelling about the white Americans who invented the HIV virus and injected it into the Blacks. The subject was also familiar to me. I myself heard many times regular Soviet propaganda about a military laboratory in Maryland that invented the HIV virus to genocide the Black population.

Confused, I stood in front of the TV. Vladimir Zhirinovsky was dressed very strange—his shirt was not a regular one with a tie, but he behaved as usual with habitual routine and temperament accusing America. Then I noticed that his English was almost perfect. When I heard him some years ago, his English left much to be desired. I was still confused, as he continued bashing America with such high emotions that the mesmerized audience became inflamed by his oratory skills. And that Black audience returned me to reality—it was not Vladimir Zhirinovsky, it was not Russia. It was America! I was stunned. I could not believe my eyes and ears. It was typical Soviet-style agitation and propaganda—first to deliver false information and influence the mind of the audience and then to incite and enrage the people's emotions. Who is the man repeating those Soviet-style slanderous accusations? Where had he learned the Soviet propaganda, so familiar to all Russians?

The smell of burning food forced me to run back to the kitchen. It was there in the kitchen that I heard the name of the man spewing the Soviet propaganda—Reverend Jeremiah Wright,[102] of Trinity United Church in Chicago.

The situation has so frightened me that since then I have not missed any events of the primary and spend more time watching TV. My antennas went up—America's future was at stake. As a matter of fact, I mentioned Chicago as a "special location for foreign agents" four years ago, The *Russian Factor*, p. 296. Then in 2004, I could not speak freely in terms of the KGB's infiltration—you were not ready at the time. Now at the end of my third book, I can. I had noticed the KGB's operatives in Chicago many years ago and wrote then, in 2004: "A nation cannot survive treason from within" Cicero. I realized the danger by watching patterns in events happening in Chicago. Listening about the events in Chicago again, in 2008 has definitely captivated my attention—political management of religion like in Russia scared me. Religion plays a major role in my country—the American people grew up around their houses of worship.

Rev. Wright was spreading false information, and I was aware of that. The HIV virus was researched and produced by the Soviets in Africa, during the 1960s. I have already written about it and if you ask former Soviet Foreign Minister Edward Shevardnadze,[103] he can confirm the fact, as some research of the virus took place in the monkey nursery in Sukhumi, Abkhazia,[104] Georgia. By the way, the current, constant, aggressive action by Russia against Georgia can be the reason of that—Russian passports are spread by the thousands to Abkhazians to get back the territory. For your information the so-called Russian "peacekeepers" have been stationed on the Georgian territory by the international mandate for many years. The title of any Russian military force as "peacekeepers" is an oxymoron. Please, remember Budapest, Chechnya, Prague, Afghanistan, and other places to predict the real intentions of the Soviet Mafia. That is why Georgia and the accusations of Rev. Wright are very important signs. The past is determining our future and I want you to be totally informed and aware of that.

The monkey's Research Center is still in Georgia, where the Russian "peacekeepers" are and the people who might have known more than Russia wanted to become public are there, too. Isn't it a strange fact that a Black Reverend in America is blaming us for the crimes committed by the Soviets? Plus the manner of his speech is identical to that of the Soviet *Department of Agitation and Propaganda*. He is combining a lot of lies with a seed of factual truth to be believable, inculcating the audience with deception. His self-confidence, indignation, and tone of voice demonstrate all elements and desire to brainwash and intimidate the audience. Now you can understand why listening to Reverend Wright my antennas went up—too much similarity!

I knew that Chicago was the location where the KGB placed it's headquarter—I did not know exactly where. The Rev. Wright has indicated a possible location; however, one example was not enough for me to make a definite conclusion. I started watching Barack Obama, who called Rev. Wright his "spiritual mentor." I found that like in Stalin's Russia, faith and politics have become intertwined in America—Christianity and Islam intertwined under the umbrella of Black Liberation Theology,[105] serving the Democrat Party. There were several indications of Obama's far- left vision for America. Yet I continued watching for a special sign of fraud to make a final decision. I really did not know what I was waiting for, but when I saw Obama walking up the stairs to the podium, his bended arms freely moving accordingly—the lightening of memory went through my mind—I have already seen that gait before.

Living in the Soviet Union, I did not know anything about the American Presidents, except for one—John F. Kennedy. He was the only one often shown on the Soviet TV. I loved him and I saw him on the Soviet TV numerous times. He had that incredible and specific light gait with arms freely moving while he is going up the stairs or down the stairs. Once I saw Obama imitating that exact light gait of JFK—my pulse rose. I got what I was waiting for— the Soviet training. Now the picture of the Chicago location has become clearer—it was not only the Soviet-style of propaganda, it was also a result of the Soviet's training. These several signs indicated the Soviet's presence—the patterns of infiltration. I was sure of that, as the Democrats have always yearned for another John Kennedy. They have found and trained one! In addition to that, the wife of Obama, Michelle, was imitating Jacqueline's personality, dressing in her style. Yet, unlike charming Mrs. Kennedy, angry Michelle does not appreciate America.

And God helped me again by giving another example. I have already discussed with you the Soviet infiltration into the Catholic Church to discredit it from within. Can you imagine my feeling when I saw Rev. Michael Pfleger, another one of Obama's "spiritual advisors" for many years, performing a sermon in the Trinity United Church in

May? What a performance it was! The familiar theatrical manners, style, and gesticulations had electrified the audience of Trinity United Church! People were applauding, cheering, and loudly supporting Rev. Pfleger. The racists and sexist divisive substance of the sermon against Hillary created an enormous emotional outburst within the audience...

Like the sermons of Rev. Wright, Rev. Pfleger's sermon had nothing to do with God—it was clear political propaganda, a performance on behalf of Obama. The cynical and obvious circle of the KGB's presence has been closed—the familiar signs of its visibility did not leave any doubt in my mind. My heart bled, I did not know what to do—the future of America is at stake—the Soviet mafia had infiltrated the American houses of faiths...! Can you compare these priests with Dr. Martin Luther King Jr.? Do you understand now why Dr. King, who preached non-violence, was assassinated and who did it...? I hope you do... I am speechless! I went to the internet to find out information about Rev. Pfleger.

A German-American from Chicago, he was ordained a priest for the Archdiocese of Chicago on May 14, 1975. Since 1981, he has had his own Catholic St. Sabina Church in Chicago, where he has been a senior Pastor for many years. Can you imagine the Catholics-parishioners and their worldview under the auspices of Rev. Pfleger? A close friendship between the Reverends Wright and Pfleger might have answered the question. "Pfleger's social activism has brought him attention throughout Chicago and beyond. He has often collaborated and associated with African American religious, political and social activists such as Jeremiah Wright, Jesse Jackson, Cornel West, and Louis Farrakhan." Wikipedia.

This group of people presents a real political force that catapulted Obama to the top, creating his cult of personality on an empty place. When I found out that Rev. Pfleger was a close political friend of Louis Farrakhan, the big picture of the Chicago political machine became even more dangerous. It was a familiar pattern, a connection to the Soviet-style infiltration into the houses of worship for political propaganda.

Yes, political propaganda. You heard it. I have already written about it describing its use during Stalin's time. I know the smell and I want you to know it, too. The Soviet's invention was used in Chicago—agitation to influence people's mind and consciousness with lie, deceit, distortions, fabrications, and fraud. After that, propaganda enraged people's emotions making them the followers of the political agenda. Just recall the speeches of Farrakhan, Wright, and Pfleger—they are identical in form, substance, and objective. Yet those agitators are not alone. There is another one— more sophisticated than others.

Many journalists had been amazed by Bill Clinton's actions. Do not be surprised by his strange behavior. He will do everything in his power to make Obama the Democrats' presidential nominee, up to torpedoing Hillary's presidential aspirations. He has already undermined her campaign by planting three stooges that helped to betray Hillary. He has always accomplished all the assignments received—read again the second chapter of this book. Can you imagine—I had sympathy for Hillary Clinton. The Democrats treated her very unfairly! Whatever our political disagreements, Hillary is a very talented and smart woman with a bright future if she could untie herself from the scoundrel who continues betraying her.

Barack Obama had grown up politically in the predicament of the Democrat Party—it was a dirty swamp of Chicago's political machine, full of mafia activities increasingly resembling the operations within the Soviet mafia. Obama's title of a *community organizer* adds to the predicament typical socialist vocabulary and agenda—the essence of Obama's activities. *A community organizer* is a code word—euphemism for the socialist political agitator—symbol of a class warfare. The term was imported to Chicago from the old Soviet Socialist vocabulary, perhaps twenty years ago…

The term is foreign to the American culture and unknown to the rest of the country. I have found an interesting peculiarity in Obama's environment—the Christian-Islamic connection—a typical Soviet technique—political management of the religions in fighting for power. Moreover, I also found the connection between the anti-American brand of Black Liberation Theology and the Arab American Action Network, a supporter of Yasser Arafat—the KGB's man. Considering all the preceding chapters, I got additional information to identify Obama's ties with all the enemies of America infiltrating and undermining our country.

It is for a reason I gave you the history of Soviet activities against Western civilization in chapter 7: "WWIII." I identified the specific details of how the process was going on using infiltration. Do you remember how the Chinese communism had been built by organizing people into groups and injecting them with the Soviet ideological tenets, influencing them with the new social and cultural conducts? (The masses must be organized). It was a typical Soviet way of indoctrinating millions of Chinese. If you recall the scene in the Trinity Church during Rev. Wright's and Rev. Pfleger's sermons, you will see the result of Obama's communal activities—the audience's overwhelming enthusiasm, enraged emotions, and approval of the hateful anti-Americanism displayed within the Trinity United Church. Obama's activities can be judged by another result—an overwhelming, terrifying, and bloody crime within the community in his district. In this combat zone more people were killed than in a real war in Iraq during this year.

The similarity with the Trinity Church and Obama's personality and character continues—in 143 days as U.S. Senator, he demonstrated a very rare arrogance in lecturing us, by inciting our emotions like his "spiritual mentors" did. So Obama possesses some oratorical skills, but he presented no original substance. Pay attention to his boastful tone and manner of delivery—he is not just speaking, he is prophesizing as playing the oracle, mesmerizing the audience, building the cult of personality. *The Audacity of Hope* was a ploy to fool us pretending he was a trustful man. In real life it is his audacity of arrogance, in his old Soviet-style rhetoric—a decoy, an empty suit stuffed with old slogans and symbols with no substance, he is promising us a great future in "all fifty-seven states" of America.

The landmark of Soviet behavior is arrogance. Insulting, smearing, and intimidating an adversary and playing the victim is also the embodiment of the Soviet Socialist style as a substitute for civility, knowledge, and vision. I see it in Obama's speeches and his conduct during the last months. Do you remember the elements of the *Department of Agitation and Propaganda* in the Rev. Wright's sermons? Obama has exhibited all of them. And Obama admitted that he felt like a spy behind enemy lines. What a revelation!

He is very well-trained by his "spiritual advisors" and others, who shaped his personality, character, behavior, and worldview for twenty years. Experienced agitators, they taught Obama how to use the words people would like to hear: change, revival, unity, renewal, and the FUTURE to fool, seduce, and deceive you and our youth. Meanwhile, his current team consists of Bill Clinton's machine which is manifesting the past, not the future. Pay attention to the close ties between the two teams. I would say it is one team fighting the Conservatives in the Republican Party. We can expect a massive amount of manipulations, fraud, and deceptions—remember Clinton's triangulation of the past; you will see it again in

2008. You will see a copy of Clinton's campaign strategy and methods. Watch Clinton's yes-men, like Bill Richardson and Rahm Emanuel; they will serve Obama the way they obediently served Clinton.

I'd like to submit to you an interesting fact I found out recently. Mr. Primakov was not the only architect of the Oslo Agreement that undermined Israel; Rahm Emanuel helped him a great deal working with Arafat! Do you remember who Arafat and Primakov were? If you do, you have before your eyes a real Russian Connection! Under the leadership of another one of Clinton's yes- men, Richardson—stealing of several of our nuclear secrets took place in the Department of Energy. Maybe those stealing had been organized from within? What do you think?

The last information is bringing us from the past to a very murky present and a dangerous future with Obama. Trust is the key issue and Obama lacks that trust. By familiar ideology, the next step requires building of the cult of Obama personality. His entire campaign will be packaged and marketed around his personality making him a leader of the civil rights movement, a hero of the American people, and compared to Martin Luther King Jr. At the same time, the campaign will not cover Obama's Socialist ideology and his obscure past. The fake image will cover up the reality. They will fool us all! The yes-men from Clinton's machine will work to repair Obama's image, after he insulted small-town Pennsylvanian people "get bitter, they cling to guns or religion or antipathy to people who aren't like them..." Disgusting! Old Soviet Socialist orthodoxy that the working class is distracted by religion. Just watch how he repeatedly changes his views—a political expediency in action on Obama's team! What an arrogance and audacity of a man serving only 143 days in the U.S. Senate! I do not believe a word coming out from his mouth, the same way I do not believe Bill Clinton or Vladimir Putin.

Watch Obama when he answers questions, he speaks slowly as if looking for the appropriate words, even though English is his native language. I have the impression that he is looking for the words to cover up his real thoughts. He reads pretty fast the text prepared for him on the teleprompter. I have read interesting information about Obama's printed piece of work about the "Soviet Nuclear Disarmaments" in the 1980s. What? Disarmaments? The Soviets had never disarmed or honored any international agreements—they fooled and deceived the entire world!

Because of that data, I also suspect that Obama is subjected to the hypno-therapy or Para-psychology treatments—the KGB's regular techniques.

I believe that Obama's campaign will also use psychiatric power and Para-psychology in preparation of his speeches and debates. Watch it! To seduce and deceive the voters Obama's campaign will use a smoke-screen of subliminal messages to confuse the psyche of the American public—old Soviet tricks. There is another psychology; Soviet-style will be used as well. Obama will mention the names of the Republican leaders to make reference to the adversary, to cling himself to them—an old Soviet trick to associate even phonetically with the adversary to benefit the Soviets at the appropriate time. You will often hear the name of Ronald Reagan to seduce the Republicans and evangelicals. Just watch a distortion of history Soviet-style—Obama will be compared to Abraham Lincoln. Watch how for political seduction the image of Lincoln or other conservatives is blended with Obama to create his cult of personality. Disgusting! The Chicago, Illinois mob-school had prepared Obama for fighting the Republicans, making them the ENEMY. He is a byproduct of the Chicago political machine, the Soviet-style mob-school, embracing distortions, deceit, fraud, and other machinations including "false flag operations" to win by hook or by crook. Like in Moscow, the graduates of mob-schools have always implemented mob-rules.

In terms of upcoming presidential debates, let me tell you a story that happened many years ago, yet it is a trick that can be repeated by the KGB again. The world chess champion Victor Korchnoi defected from the USSR in 1976. In the next world championship he played against the Soviet chess-master Anatoly Karpov. It was "one of the most bitterly contested matches in WCC history, filled with high political drama, tension, and accusation. Korchnoi continuously complained that he was being stared at by a member of Karpov's team during play, a parapsychologist supposedly with hypnotic power." *History of the World Chess Championship.* Korchnoi lost the world chess champion title. Knowing the tricks and techniques the Soviets used, I believe that Korchnoi's accusations had been true in reality. He was doomed for defection and revenge by the Soviet Intelligence. I gave you that example to be aware that in upcoming debate between McCain and Obama the old technique can be used again. Just watch the debates and remember the story of Victor Korchnoi.

It is for a reason I mentioned Para-psychology and hypno-therapy. Both are the major elements of the Soviet *Department of Agitation and Propaganda*, which is now used for different tasks on the American soil. Creation and building the cult of personality is the other task. The word "advertisement" you are aware of, was well known to the Russian people as well—it existed to market and promote a leader of the Communist Party and the party itself by seducing, deceiving, and tricking the Russian people—the major activity of the *Department of Agitation and Propaganda*. I see the activity of the Obama's campaign very similar to the Department. Obama's campaign is carefully crafting a cult of his personality, manipulating and abusing people's minds. The same way the cult of Putin's personality in Russia had been built.

Besides that, just watch different organizations and institutions using a tremendous amount of money to advertise a two-year Senator and promote him by using unprecedented tools, devices, and tricks, Soviet-style. Also watch attacks against the Republican leadership, politics of personal destruction out of the Stalinist play book. The perverted psyche will make McCain a terrorist not Ayers. I remind you that agitation was to influence people's mind and conscience with distortions, fraud, and intimidation and after that, propaganda enraged to inflame their emotions to make them the followers of the agenda. Just watch Obama and his friends in America and the world and you will see all of that, performed by *the International Soviet mafia.*

You want to know who Obama is. What his values and worldviews are? The Russian saying answers those questions: "Tell me who is your friend and I will tell you who you are." Our friends have always exhibited our real face in life. It is definitely true in the case of Barack Obama—the company you keep reflects your worldview. And I would say that Obama's company is quite a questionable one. Researching the activity of each of his friends will make the picture clearer. His first friend and "spiritual mentor" Jeremiah Wright taught him anti-Americanism and all the methods of agitation and propaganda for more than twenty years. The result you see today. His second friend, William Ayers was a fugitive for many years with his wife, fellow radical Bernadine Dohrn. Both were members of the Weather Underground, a radical terrorist group that was responsible for a series of bombings including explosions at the Pentagon, U.S. Capitol, and other locations. Both expressed their hate of the American capitalist economic system. Ayers admitted bombing of the Pentagon, but… as usual due to the FBI's failure and prosecutorial misconduct the charges against them were dropped.

Today, an unrepentant terrorist is a professor teaching our youth at the University of Chicago (do you remember how the Liberals are indoctrinating our youth?) and a member of Chicago's intellectual establishment. Ayers hosted a meeting-the-candidate session for Obama at his house, when Obama first ran for office. Their friendship was confirmed by the Obama's campaign manager in 2007. But I found a more concrete cooperation between the two—they have been friends since the 1980s. Ayers was not only a neighbor as Obama presented him—Ayers and Obama were partners. In the 1990s Ayers, a professor-terrorist had proposed a project to reform the schools in Chicago, infusing radical activism. Knowing Ayers' negative attitude toward our capitalist system, the school project was used to instill and indoctrinate our youth in the radical tenets of Soviet Socialism.

For your information, as a head of the project, Obama positively commented on it and gave a grant of $50 million to Ayers to indoctrinate the American youth—a sign partnership sharing the same ideology. And the same methods and tactics on education were shared with another terrorist—Hugo Chavez. As a matter of fact, the professor-terrorist Ayers had presented his ideas in the conference for education in Venezuela. Chavez had applauded him—they shared the ideas. And there is more than ideas only. I have read that Ayers' wife, also a terrorist, was Michelle Obama's girlfriend for decades. For your information, Michelle's thesis from Princeton is not available until November 5, 2008. I suspect militants and radicalism there. I have already warned you about Michelle and her family's relation with Jesse Jackson—the virus of ideology is coming from the connection to him. Hence we have a partnership plus the friendship of the two families which means common worldviews—an identical political orientation!

This political orientation brings together patterns of the past and present. On the last day of his presidency, Clinton pardoned two members of the Weather Underground—an ideological political orientation had been transferred to the twenty-first century. There are four main radical ideas of the past by a professor-terrorist that should alarm everyone. 1) Ayers' attempt to over throw the government of America, bombing the Pentagon and the police station directly correlates with Bin-Laden's action of destroying Twin Towers in 2001! 2) Ayers had assigned people to recruit students and create revolutionary cells across America. Do you remember the Communist cells in China? 3) Bombing the apartment of the judge who tried the Black Panthers' case. Black Panthers were the creation of the Black Liberation Theology.

4) The Ayers' terrorist group used nail-bombs to inflict as much damage to the civilians as possible—Bin Laden did the same. My four points constitute and represent the patterns of KGB strategy, tactics, and agenda during the twentieth and twenty-first centuries. By the way, like in 1960-1970 the anti-war movement that protested against the Vietnam War, is the same movement fighting against the war in Iraq. Now you know who is behind both… If not go figure.

Another friend, who has helped raise campaign money for Obama, is a businessman Anton Rezko. He is currently charged with twenty-four counts, involving mail fraud, wire fraud, money laundering, and aiding and abetting bribery. This man has ties to Obama in other ways as well. Rezko and his family donated money to Obama and advised him on the purchase of a new Chicago home—a very intricate and puzzling deal. What does Obama have in common with a crony? Another of Obama's friends is Rashid Halide; who is also a scholar and teaches at the University of Chicago. He and his wife Mona hosted a political fundraiser for Obama. While Obama served on the board of the Woods Fund, the charity gave money to the Arab-American Action Network. That friendship generated internet headlines such as— "Meet Obama's Terrorist Friend." There are some of Obama's friends/ criminals on his team you do not know about. I do. Obama's friends, in my opinion, comprise all the attributes of the Soviet mafia—anti-American agitation and propaganda, terror-violence, drugs, corruption, and raising a lot of money legally and illegally. Unfortunately, the FBI has no idea where to look.

Obama indeed has a lot of "friends" in Europe as well. A state Senator, yet his *Audacity* was published in France, Italy, Germany, Spain, Denmark, and Greece. He definitely has a lot of "friends." I have an impression that a solid international force is behind Obama spinning his new image to promote his presidential candidacy in the world. This force reminds me of the activities of *The International Soviet Mafia* building the cult of Putin's personality. Something similar to that is going on in the building of Obama's cult of personality. As a matter of fact, I have been dealing with the publishing business for twenty years—very unsuccessfully. A solid force is definitely "working" behind the scene making Obama President of the United States. The question is the reason, the benefits, and the consequences of that for America.

Who is Barack Obama, a Muslim or a Christian? The answer is neither one. He is pro-partial-birth abortion and said: "I do not want my daughters punished with a baby." It is not a coincidence that Obama deliberately distorts the Bible. Obama is not a religious man—he is a secular ideologue of the Soviet style, a good-looking Black man, who used drugs in his youth. I would suggest you go back and remember the Soviet drug-warfare against America and subversion of our youth researched by Joseph D. Douglass, Jr., in his *Red Cocaine.* Please, read also the Soviet's opinion of the American people, expressed by the Chairman of the KGB, Uri Andropov: "They are naïve, gullible, and crazy." Remember that Uri Andropov is Putin's "spiritual mentor!" they are "superior to the ordinary people" based on Stalin's teachings. Consider the Soviets' criminal intent plus similarity in Obama's activities pointed before, and the big picture of the Soviet mafia with all its tentacles and ideology would appear before you in America! Knowledge is the only SOLUTION for our survival. Do you remember *Putin? Who's he? Ahmadinejad? Who's he?* Today I can add to those names "Obama? Who's he?" All three are identical, in the beginning with—they suddenly appeared; all three were cooked up behind the scene. The Chinese writers have given me an idea and a name for Obama—a Trojan horse.

To add the last critical link to a big picture of the events during the last several decades in Chicago, I would pay attention to Jesse Jackson and Louis Farrakhan, the carriers of Black Liberation Theology and reverse racism, fighting for power against the "white oppressor" in America. Both men are strong anti-Semites and the major figures of the Chicago political environment. As a matter of fact, I would start digging deeper into the backgrounds of the two radical Black nationalists. I did it in *The Russian Factor,* pp. 193, 203-204, and 273. Please, read them and the big picture of those who shaped Obama's background will reveal a great deal of his inextricable connection to the two propagandists of Black Liberation Theology—Jesse Jackson and Louis Farrakhan. Also, please take into account a close relation between the families of Jesse Jackson and Michelle Obama lasting for decades. Knowing Jackson's past, I believe that two elitists, and activist Michelle, and a *community organizer* Barack will cook "very spicy meals." I took this expression from the Russian Socialist history—it fits Obama's agenda.

A connection to Hamas is also logical—the same tentacles of the hydra are identical in their structure and agenda everywhere. This negative picture will scare you, as it presents the result of the Soviet mafia scheme on American soil, propagating Socialism, inciting racism, and Balkanizing our traditional culture "to reduce our capacity." If you remember how Putin organized the presidential election in Russia, you can see its repetition in America. We can expect a lot of fabrications, imitations, hoaxes, false, sleazy, and slanderous gossips and rumors from Obama's campaign—knowledge of the Soviet mafia is a must in order to perceive what is going on within the Democrat Party in the year 2008 of the presidential election.

The Russian style corruption, bribes, and voter-fraud in Obama's team are stunning. I took some information from Michelle Malkin's website: ACORN —Association of Community Organization for Reform Now is Obama's one of the major sponsors. In fact, the organization "promotes the welfare state and undermines capitalism and self-reliance... had been implicated in perpetual illegal immigration and encouraging voter-fraud"—all elements of Socialism. For decades ACORN takes its revenues from American taxpayers and has leveraged nearly four decades of government subsidies to fund its affiliates. "ACORN's activities grew substantially under Bill Clinton—Obama just continued activating its development. Chicago-based ACORN has commingled public tax dollars with political projects." A community organizer and legal representative of ACORN, Obama trained its Chicago members in leadership seminars for several years—sitting on the boards of foundations which poured money into ACORN's coffers. Members of ACORN were activating their "work" during the election time in America. For me it is a fraudulent entity run by the KGB's henchmen to "reduce our moral capacity." We will see ACORN "working" in cahoots with the Black Panthers—two of many other long hands of the Black Liberation Theology.

The Wall Street editorial described it this way: "In Ohio in 2004, a worker for one affiliate was given crack cocaine in exchange for fraudulent registrations that included underage voters, dead voters... During a congressional hearing in Ohio in the aftermath of the 2004 election, officials from several counties in the state explained ACORN's practice of dumping thousands of registration forms in their lap on the submission deadline, even though the forms had been collected months earlier." I expect that fraud we learned in the Russian election will be repeated in America—senior citizens and homeless could be bussing like NASHI in Russia. Even more, do you remember Obama's friend and businessman Anton Rezko and their dealings Obama's new house? There is a tie with ACORN again—housing and money. The ACORN Housing Corp. has received millions from HUD and... worked to obtain mortgages for illegal aliens in partnership with Citibank! An undocumented income of illegal aliens provides money paid "under the table"—a typical Russian system of bribery. As you can see, Obama's environment presents the major components of the *International Soviet Mafia*—fraud, money, corruption, and propaganda. I see ACORN as a copy of the Soviet unit lead by the KGB—the units from *the Department of Agitation and Propaganda*. Keep in mind Shakespeare—poisoning can go through ears too. Pay attention to many other forms of voter-fraud and simple vote stealing. Also remember America's infiltrated cyber-system.

I am afraid that Senator McCain has no idea of what is ahead of him—the harbinger of the defeat. Besides an incredible corruption, I really expect that the adversary's campaign will try to downgrade Senator's military record and his bravery by redefining the term "patriotism" the same way they try to redefine the institution of marriage. Just watch an incredible meanness, Soviet-style from Clinton's and Obama's combined teams. It will mock Senator McCain and viciously smear his pick for VP, whoever he is. You will see the audacity of arrogance in action. Do not forget— we are dealing with a determined adversary whose objective is "reducing our capacity" to obtain world domination. It will be also an attempt to infiltrate the McCain campaign to destroy it from within. Only a grasp of modus operandi of Soviet Fascism can bring an adequate comprehension. Senator McCain should read this book. Yet, taking into account the forces suppressing all my books, I do not know when my writings will have the opportunity to be known to America. And that brings a historical similarity with another tragic past event....

When I wrote chapter 9, I did it to show you the similarity between German Fascism and Soviet Fascism. It has another similarity with nowadays—German's and the world intellectuals did misread the predicament and... Nazism destroyed Europe in WWII. The situation in the world has repeated itself today—Soviet Fascism has spread its tentacles across the world, acting almost freely in America, and intellectuals are misreading the predicament in the world for the second time around. The objectives of Soviet Fascism now should be clear to you after reading this book—a destruction of American capitalism. The entire twentieth century and the Cold War illustrates the competition between Socialism and Capitalism. We won and that is the crux of the matter. The war continues now as an asymmetrical one on our soil illustrating the nature of Soviet Fascism's ideology—revenge and determination for world domination. Obama can help Soviet Fascism to achieve both—the ultimate goal of a global world government. I believe the special operation has been started by *the Organs* many decades ago. It is now in its final phase. To me Obama is a robot constructed and supervised by somebody else—a charismatic robot that often malfunctions.

People have short memories and many were born after the Cold War. I am not sure that the American voters are fully informed and can answer all the questions left unasked by the media. Do they know that Obama's parents met in a Russian language class? They had studied the Russian language together in the '60s. Wow! Aren't there a startling number of Russian connections? Moreover, do people know for example who really paid for Obama's expensive high school in Honolulu? He described his mother as a single one, abandoned by her husband and living on foot stamps. Maybe somebody else outside the family helped to get Obama education? He was not taught religion—his mother "touted herself as an atheist," close friend Maxine Box has stated. And that adds to my opinion that Obama is also very far from being a religious man—it is a simple camouflage on his part. Besides, he gave his daughter a Russian name—Sasha. In the midst of Chicago the Russian connection sounds quite strange.

I also want to know who paid for Obama's education at Colombia University and at Harvard Law School—both are very expensive for an average person. And there is no paper trail from either, though we know that Obama used drugs there at Colombia. A very strange absence of real facts from Obama's past. Like somebody had covered up it—there is no information. Moreover, Obama's fraudulent statement about his father confirms my view on him. Obama's description of his father as a "freedom fighter" is an utter lie! His father was a member of the most corrupt and bloody government of Kenya connected to the Soviet communists. Please, remember: Most African governments are run by Moscow's students—read about President Mugabe, the leader of the liberation movement. Aren't there too many coincidental connections to Russia…?

I came from the past and I can predict your future! My life experiences provided me with basic knowledge and survival instinct. My dislike of Obama emanates from my inside and a chain of the "coincidences." His radical Muslim Father and atheist Mother met studying Russian language in 1960s America! They married and their son Barack, a *community organizer* adhered to their ideology and tried to implement Socialism and its main postulate in America—redistribution of wealth. His long-term association with the real terrorists illustrates his acceptance of violence—a definite sign of anti-American behavior on his part. And last but not least is the suspicious, premature death of both of his parents.

His Muslim father was killed in a car accident (?), his mother had cancer…. In this respect, many people have questioned to Barack Obama, but his campaign made him untouchable—any criticism or even questioning him is not tolerated and seen as racist. It is for a reason I compare Obama with Putin. Nobody can criticize Putin. Don't you remember Putin and the election in Russia? Just compare it with the activities of Obama's campaign! And also watch our media. Doesn't it remind you of the *Department of Agitation and Propaganda* rooting for Obama and promoting his cult of personality?

Obama's love for "big government" and a state planned economy is a very troubled sign—doesn't he know that Hitler, Stalin, and Mussolini were building a big and strong state at the expense of the individuals? Instead of promoting private enterprise, his friendship with the infiltrated Unions, is also a sign of Soviet-style Socialism—Soviet Fascism. I remember pretty well the Soviet slogan: *Unions are the School of Communism!* The Unions will vote for Obama—they are deeply infiltrated by Moscow's students to undermine our economy.

I also suspect the presence of the KGB in his deliberate strategy of blaming Republican McCain even before he criticized Obama. I described in all my writings in details the strategy of being an aggressor but playing a victim and being offensive—patterns of the Soviet's behavior and trickery. It is my knowledge of special operations, molding the Soviet-style leaders and their ideology that intensifies the previous view of Obama. By the way, the notion of *Molding the Soviet Style Leaders* is not my invention; it belongs to a Russian Journalist, described on p. 235, *The Russian Factor.*

Just recall the leaders molded by the KGB in the occupied Europe.

Predicament in today's America is analogous. Obama set up his campaign in all fifty states—a total control of the process with more than a million volunteers. We can expect a massive voter- fraud in the 2008 election by the Soviet-style Democratic mob- machine that has several fixers to do that! I see a lot of activities that remind me of machinations within the apparatus of "the Soviet." I have planned to write an article to Wikipedia to identify properly the structure and the task of "the Soviets"—it has not been done correctly since its inception. This is a subject of vital importance for the West's future to see the similarities! Due to them in some events; I suspect that Rahm Emanuel in cahoots with the Governor had fixed the election in Pennsylvania in 2006. The similarities with the election in Russia are striking. Do you remember the Nashist's youth movement in Russia? Obama will follow the strategy using the American youth by infiltrating the youth organizations in all fifty states. It will be a massive attempt to brainwash, dupe the army of youth, and exploit them in Obama's propaganda campaign. The liberal professors had already started the process of indoctrination in colleges and universities. Obama's campaign will continue using the youth's enthusiasm in many different activities, including the illegal ones. You will be the witnesses of the cause and effect! Knowing the Soviet-style politics, I suspect that Obama may seduce a lot of naïve Americans, Black and White—ill-informed people have no idea who they are dealing with.

Talking about the Soviet-style Democratic machine brings Indonesia to mind—a country Obama grew and spent many years in. It is not his fault, but a fact of life. And that is another coincidence in his mother's life—her second husband came from Indonesia. I have already listed my suspicions concerning Obama's parents. This is another one—Indonesia. I remember well the connections of the Democrats with Chinese and Russian businessmen in Clinton's reelection campaign in 1996 with a lot of money going to Clinton's coffer. The media called all of them—"the cash-loaded crooks." There were several close friends of Bill Clinton, one attracted my attention—Mochtar Ready, a businessman from Indonesia. His unprecedented access to the White House and a lot of money he donated amazed me—what kind of relationship can there be between President Clinton and the Indonesian businessman? He was accompanied by the Russian and Chinese crooks and that has brought to my mind Indonesia again and the activities of the Soviet mafia and its special operations in the twenty-first century—the stunning similarities....

Unfortunately, the same special operations are going on unreported around the globe. Considering the information I have already narrated to you—we are at war waged on us by Soviet Fascism. Therefore, my thinking process works accordingly and knowing the Soviet mafia's proclivity to mold the Soviet- style foreign leaders or to recruit them and infiltrate the foreign governments; I want to at least observe their activity. You can judge how to name the characters participating in those activities— they are all the adversaries of America. Why do they preach and propagate Socialism defrauding the majority of their own people? What do we know about those leaders who are against America's policy and act accordingly in their respective countries? What is the base of their close friendship with Putin? I have already discussed some of them in *The Russian Factor* and time along with additional evidence of my suspicions proved to me they were correct.

For example, I did suspect Chancellor of Germany Mr. Schroeder and now you see his open friendship with Putin and dreadful consequences of that for Germany. Can you imagine the scale of infiltration into the German security apparatus under this Chancellor? I have no doubts that the German intelligence and security agencies are infiltrated by Putin's KGB. Please, remember that the 9/11 attack was originated in the German city of Hamburg...

To plant democracy in Afghanistan is laughable—it is impossible to build democracy in caves of the Stone Age— people are not ready there. Analyze creation of the Karzai presidency under German supervision and you will know the future of Afghanistan. Read *Baltic Winds* for the explanation. Remember also that 1.5 million Afghans fled to the former Soviet Republics of Center Asia after the Soviet departure and collapse of the Communist government of Nadjibullah. Those people can be trained and returned back to fight us. Unfortunately, I have no staff to research all the nitty gritty politics of Afghanistan. I am only one woman. I hope for the young people, especially in Germany, to continue my work.

Another example is President of France Jack Schiraque[109]—a real opponent of the American policy in the world. I would suggest to the young researchers in France to evaluate his friendship with Putin and the negative consequences of Schiraque's presidency for the world. The

Arab's invasion has practically destroyed his country's social fabrics and traditional culture. It had occurred under Schiraque's presidency. My hope for France lies in the presidency of Mr. Sarkozy. Both he and President of Italy, Berlusconi, will be targeted by the KGB.

The most critical consequences to consider had occurred in Great Brittan under Tony Blair, the first friend of Putin and Bill Clinton. His reign of power, like in France, had brought tremendous numbers of Arabs to the country and we do not know how many Moscow's students among them had invaded Great Britain. The building of Mosques mushroomed, let alone the terrorist activity in England. You know today the result of Mr. Blair's policy— the book *Londonistan* has presented it in details. Another result is even more harmful. "...nearly a quota of British teens... think Winston Churchill is no more real than Spider-Man. Meanwhile 58 percent thought Sherlock Holmes was real." Doesn't it remind you of the failure in our educational system? Do you remember the old BBC? I do. It was my preferred foreign station with the incredibly brilliant Maxim Goldberg—a star voice of a free Europe thirty years ago. The station is unrecognizable today—the word "terrorist" is forbidden there—the cause and effect are obvious.

Blair's British economy is in a free-fold together with health care—both had become socialist ones! Blair's decision to take out the British force from Basra in Iraq in the critical moment of our effort to win over the insurgency in April 2008, made me very angry. His friendship with Putin has added to those suspicions. He is now a master of the Middle East—nothing good to expect from there. In this connection, I would like to give you a similar story. I saw an intriguing article about another PM of England on the internet titled "Who was plotting an Army Coup to Get Rid of Harold Wilson?" By Paul Routledge, 3/16/2006. I will just give you some quotations from this article. "It was an announcement that shocked the nation. Thirty years ago today, Harold Wilson told Britain that he was stepping down as a Prime Minister with three years still left to run. No adequate reason was given for his decision and speculation and rumor spread like wildfire. In the view of hard-right MI5 mavericks like 'Spycatcher' Peter Wright... Socialists were the same as Communists—intent on delivering the UK to the Kremlin..."

After reading this book you can imagine how pleasantly surprising his assessment was to me. Hard-right maverick Peter Wright made his statement forty years ago and his opinion had confirmed all my writings.

There was other information interesting to me: "It was also claimed that Wilson had taken bribes and supplied classified information to Soviet 'moles.' A Soviet defector fingered the Prime Minister as a KGB agent, and claimed there was a Communist cell on Downing Street." Please, think about both statements given forty years ago and please, interpret correctly the environment in the world we are all facing today.

Forty years ago it was the Kremlin's policy of Sovietization, today we can acknowledge that Sovictization now is going on hand and glove with Islamization! Pay attention to a common feature in all three European examples—the process of Islamization is changing demography and the future of the three largest European countries. Do not forget it was Stalin who started using Muslims in his war against the West. I am not discussing Romano Prody of Italy—his connection with the KGB is known to many. I also do not talk about Mr. Sabatier of Spain—the analogous case. Watch the parliament of Canada! Some members of it have already been recruited by the KGB. Do you see now the big picture of the world's future? I do. And that image is making me increasingly nervous. And if you add to the picture the European Union's Representative for Foreign and Security Policy, Javier Solano diligently carrying out Putin's assignments, the big picture of the world has become lethal for the entire globe. You know now the Big Brother-Predator.

The situation in America is equally bad. People call our current Congress "Do Nothing Congress." It is not correct. I would argue that the energy warfare continues and there is no legitimacy for not building the nuclear power plants. The Chernobyl tragedy cannot be a reason and excuse—the Russian design did not have a contained building. In terms of oil, let's analyze our trouble. For the last twenty years, we did nothing to prevent the catastrophe. President Reagan was the last one who solved the consequences of the oil conspiracy of the 1970s—he with the help of Saudis had provided free market with an abundance of oil, and... the crisis was over, the price dropped to $9 a barrel. Bush-Papa did not deal with energy matters—the Evil Empire was collapsing and that occupied his entire presidency. Pay close attention to the next President—Clinton did everything to worsen the situation. He vetoed a Republican bill of drilling oil in the ANWR's reserve, let alone his policy to prevent dealing with coal. President W. Bush had 9/11 and that directed his entire presidency to the field of national security.

Just analyze the energy policy of the Democrats who came to power in 2006. I would not call them "*Do Nothing Congress*," because they did everything possible to tie our hands not to resolve the energy crisis, the same way Clinton had done before. The clan of obstructionist Democrats even refused to vote for the Republican energy bill. We are paying $4 for gasoline as a result of that and it hurts us all in 2008. Meanwhile, the Kremlin's henchmen are laughing at us around the world and especially in Moscow. Don't you see the Stalinist policy of oil conspiracy is working with the help of the Democrats? Their presidential candidate to cover up his real agenda uses the Soviet-style symbols, labels, and false promises in his quest for power.

Watch him, he will blame everyone and especially the oil companies and never allow drilling oil in America. He will go for gimmicks of ethanol or other alternative sources that in fact produce only 3 percent of energy now. Obama will continue Clinton's policy to cripple our economy and national security. He wants Russia to hold us hostages of the oil conspiracy—his policy against the war in Iraq, beginning with withdraw of our forces from Iraq, now confirms Obama's real agenda. Do you think Obama cares about our national security? Like Obama, Congress invested in our defeat in Iraq. Incredible! Soviet Fascism is marching along America. The Democratic Congress of 2008 is not the "Do Nothing Congress!" It is much worse—the American people have become its hostages and casualties…

CHAPTER 14

The Russians are Coming!

Three things cannot be hidden: the Sun,
the Moon, and the Truth

The Buddha

Many years ago, I suspected that the Democrat Party was infiltrated by Moscow's henchmen and expressed my suspicions in *Baltic Winds.* I also was surprised by the movie *The Russians are Coming!* What a wrong image of the Russia's character and nature it promoted! Four years ago I repeated the same suspicions in *The Russian Factor.* It was not only my intuition, but the knowledge of the subject and a long research of the issue. Barack Obama has brought my suspicions into a conclusion that I am on the right path to the reality of the lethal truth. The triangle of Kenya, Hawaii, and Chicago gave me a big picture of the skeleton in his closet. I called Obama a decoy for a reason—he is not the person he and his team are marketing him to be; as a man who loves America and Americans.

I felt just the opposite and his connection with Kenya was one of the answers. I have written pages about Africa, devastated by the Soviet infiltration and the molded Soviet-style leaders, building Socialism there. One of them was Obama's Father. His extensive cooperation with Islam's radical politics and the meeting of Obama's atheist-mother in a Russian language class made my adrenalin rise! The blowing up of the American Embassy in Nairobi came to my mind immediately. Knowing the Soviet modus operandi and Clinton's sex scandal had tied both together. *The*

Russian Factor, pp. 106, 232. The bombing in Kenya occurred two or three days after the FBI asked Clinton for his DNA—the blue dress cost a lot of innocent lives.

Obama's activity in Chicago perhaps would be clear to everyone knowing the Chicago Black community's machine and the leaders like Jesse Jackson and Louis Farrakhan. They had demonstrated their anti-Semitism and anti-Americanism numerous times. Obama is their complete byproduct with a more decent appearance and ideological exposure. I have to admit that the additional evidence of Obama's anti-capital ideological tendency I took from the book *The Obama Nation* that helped me enormously. To tell you the truth, I would have completed this book earlier, but I did not have enough evidence of Obama's political background—I have diagnosed only the result comparing the events with my experiences. *The Obama Nation*, by Jerome R. Corsi[110], Simon & Schuster, 2008, provided me with the additional information to my observations. The book in researching Obama's background and his political activity in Hawaii, Chicago, identifying his communist-mentors by their names—they are radical revolutionaries. To me they are the Soviet communist-indoctrinators—the handlers of a *diabolic ideological expansion*.

Moreover, the book has some interesting data that corresponds to my book, and confirms my idea that the KGB is using Islam and other religions in its war against the West by infiltrating all of them. Obama's father's connection with Islam and Barack's association with the Trinity Church both testified and exposed the Soviet modus operandi—political management of religion, the *diabolic ideological expansion.* A red flag was raised when I read about Frantz Fanon and his influence on Obama. Fanon was a psychiatrist, philosopher, revolutionary, and author from Martinique. He is known as a pre-eminent thinker of the twentieth century on the issue of decolonization and the psychopathology of colonization. His works have inspired anti-colonial liberation movements for more than four decades. Do you remember who formulated the idea of anti-colonial liberation movement and spread it through the world? I have dedicated pages to the issue. The Soviets introduced the concept in the 1950s and infiltrated their emissaries armed with the ideology throughout the world. That way the anti-colonial war run by them had inflamed and destabilized the world and especially the African continent. You know the result.

Corsi wrote "…Fanon's writings defined much of the anticolonial movement that swept across Europe and Africa in the 1950s and 1960s. During the Algerian revolution in 1954, Fanon went to Algeria and joined the Front de Liberation National, the radical socialist party then fighting for independence from France. In his classic study of the Algerian revolution, A Savage War of Peace, historian Alistair Horne wrote that Fanon 'became one of the revolution's most articulate and extreme ideologues, and a violent exponent of anti-colonialism in any shape.'" And again I want to remind you of Stalin's and Mao's meeting in Moscow in the 1950s. Do you remember when the term the National Liberation War was born? Yes, it was born then and there in Moscow. We did not participate in the meeting; however, Mao had brought the term to the surface of the public domain later on. We also know the Soviet's anticolonial propaganda.

I have reminded you of the term National Liberation for a reason. Do you know how many wars were started under this name of National Liberation throughout the world? Those wars were inspired by the Soviet henchmen to fight Western civilization and achieve world domination. And Africa is the best example of that. Though I have already written a lot about infiltration of Africa, nevertheless, I want to return to Africa because of Obama's father who as a politician fought for power there. Corsi connected him and Fanon as the similar ideologues for independence. "Fanon achieved world fame with Black Skin, White Masks in 1952 and the book was almost certainly known to Obama Senior, especially given the role Obama Senior planned to play in the Kenyatta government following independence. The revolution in Algeria against the France set the stage for Jomo Kenyatta and Tom Mboya's anticolonial revolution against the British in Kenya." I would add to that Mboya was the author of the *Principles of African Socialism* and the anticolonial propaganda was the Soviets' slogan brought to Africa.

Corsi continues: "We do not know if Obama Senior shared Fanon's writings with his son, but much of the expression of black resentment Obama offered in *Dreams from my Father* appears strongly influenced by Fanon's pages. Many ideas appear similar enough that Obama could easily have internalized Fanon's arguments into his own thoughts." I agree that Fanon and his ideology deeply affected Obama's worldview. An interesting detail I found in Fanon's bio; when seriously ill with leukemia, he went to the Soviet Union for treatment, at the time most people of the world were struggling to get treatment in the U.S. The level of the Soviet medicine was dismal at the time and only ideological unity could prompt Fanon to ask for help in Moscow—he was not cured. Finally he went to the U.S. for treatment. I am sure that Fanon's ideology definitely deeply affected Obama's worldview. A story about Obama's third trip as a U.S. senator to Kenya in 2006 revealed real worldview of Obama. You should know the mindset of contemporary Kenya—people there are poisoning lions to prevent attacks on cattle…!?

Several times in my writings I have described Africa as a casualty of Soviet Fascism, which infiltrated the continent and its tribal system with the Soviet molding tribe leaders. Do you remember the *Patrice Lumumba University* in Moscow which has changed its name to the *People's Friendship University of Russia*? If you do, you know what had happened in Africa. And Kenya was the best example of the dreadful consequences. To grasp the issue completely and see the big picture, you should know that Kenya borders Somalia, Ethiopia, and Sudan. The Soviets waged the war against a country of Haile Selassie for thirty years, like the Italian Fascists before them did—the country had been destroyed. If you recall our U.S. Rangers were killed in Somalia by the people of General Aidid's Russian trained military. I believe that the forces of General Aidid and his henchmen are alive and well. They have built a new force against Western civilization, especially organizing Somalia's Islamic youth. Do you remember a so-called Institute of Social Science in Moscow that trained terrorists from Africa?

Somalia is identified lately as a country of modern-day pirates attacking ships in international waters. The pirate's gang is a criminal syndicate managed by Somalia's Islamic youth on the land. They use an Old Russian trailer as the Mother-ship and attack international ships big and small by speedy small vessels.

Doesn't it remind you the act of kidnapping people on the land or hijacking them in the air? As the mentioned crimes, the pirates are also demanding ransoms in millions, let alone a huge damage to the global free trade. Don't you see the tentacles of Al-Qaeda and modus operandi of Soviet Fascism in destabilizing the world economy? They are just the other terrorist's branch of the Kremlin's henchmen "to reduce" the capitalist trade. If we don't stop the pirates in Somalia now, the world trade will suffer more— unpunished crime breeds repetition… I remind you that the WWIII was coordinated by the Moscow recruitment of the communists, see the Table on p.248 of The Russian Factor. That way *the Global Evil Empire of Terrorism* has been built!

That is not the end of tragedy in Somalia. If you recently read about the events in Mogadishu the capital of Somalia, you would know about the starvation of people and brutal violence going on there. I am not describing what is going on in Sudan, another friend of Kenya. You know that. How do you like the area? Those are the neighbors of Kenya, Balkanized by the Soviets…

There was a tribal war in Kenya as well, incited by the Kremlin and executed by the Moscow henchmen. One of them was Raila Odinga, a radical leftist politician of Kenya, educated in the Communist East Germany in all aspects of Soviet Socialism. Do not be surprised—Odinga participated in the tribal political battles, "pushing Islam" and Shariah Law in Kenya. As a matter of fact Kenya is a Christian country—85 percent Christians, about thirty million and minority Muslims, about only ten million. It is a strange phenomenon that Raila Odinga a brought up and baptized Christian was advocating Islamization of Kenya. His father Odinga commonly known as "Double-O," a Communist with allegiance to the Soviet Union, a partner of a socialist Mboya in the 1960s. Now we can understand why Raila Odinga was sent to the East Germany to be educated there. Perhaps, in the East Germany he stopped being a Christian. By the way, "the Luo tribe, of which Obama and Odinga are members of, is Kenya's second- largest tribe."

This is only the beginning of the story. Can you imagine what happened to me when I read that in his third trip to Kenya in 2006, U.S. senator Obama had publicly supported Raila Odinga against Kenya's President Kibaki? "Obama visited Kenya while President Kibaki was locked in a presidential election contest against Raila Odinga. During his visit, the Kibaki administration objected that Odinga was using Obama's visit to win votes. Obama's repeated public appearances with Odinga and his almost daily criticism of the Kibaki government added to the Kibaki administration's dismay at how the U.S. senator conducted himself in their country….Obama's support for Raila Odinga is understandable, not just because his father and grandfather, like Odinga, were from the Luo tribe, but also because Obama's roots include an intellectual connection for decades of anticolonial political philosophy in U.S. African-American radical political writings that he had studied since his teenage years at the elite preparatory Punahou School in Hawaii."

Wow! Now you can have a conclusion—Obama had become an influence in Kenyan politics today, supporting socialists. Please, remember the Kremlin's anti-colonial policy, recruitments in Africa, and molding the Soviet style tribal leaders there...

Don't you see Fanon's legacy in Obama's behavior? I believe that the preceding quotation has explained completely Obama's worldview: He is a typical byproduct of the anti-Americanism created and exporting by the Kremlin's henchmen throughout the world for decades. And there is more. A solid Corsi's research of Saul Alinsky has ultimately unmasked the entire mechanism of subversive activities by the radical Left, showing again where Obama came from. Alinsky, a son of Russian Jewish immigrants, championed new ways to organize the poor to create a backyard revolution in cities across America. In his *Reveille for Radicals* in 1971, he made "change" his credo. "Change" for Alinsky, invoked radical socialism and meant the redistribution of wealth. Alinsky advocated creating change through a set of carefully calculated power-politics tactics, where the end always justified the means." Doesn't it remind you Soviet style Socialism reiterating in America? And Corsi went further:

"In *Rules for Radicals*, Alinsky sought to articulate his methodology of 'community organization' for future generations of leftists....Alinsky goal was to set in motion a peaceful revolution, using the ballot box, not bombs or bullets, to wrench power from the hands of capitalist elites and business leaders currently in charge. ...Denying the truth or plain lying were both acceptable tactics as long as the cause was advanced. 'Change' was always Alinsky's code word for creating a socialist revolution. ... Alinsky taught organizers to hide their true intentions in the words they spoke." Do you remember how I identified a title of a community organizer? It was a code word—euphemism for socialist political agitator. Was I right?

Reading about Alinsky, I found his other motto— "think globally, act locally." Sounds familiar? The translation is clear to me—to achieve world domination you should infiltrate locally. Obama does just that. Look at his emotional refrain of "Change." Wrapping up his personality into promising ephemeral words, giving no specifics, he reminds me discussed above Dictator Mussolini and Putin. In fact, Obama is hiding his true intention and fooling the entire American population. His real intention coincides with Putin's one—world domination. By the way, Bolsheviks had won the October Socialist Revolution of 1917 by promising "*Change*" to the Russian people. You know the result. By the false promises of "*Change*," with his Teflon-synthetic smile, Obama is exploiting people's despair and hope for the future.

Obama has practiced that exact Alinsky's method of hiding the true intentions for years... And as soon as being exposed, he is finding excuses and inadequate explanations. Just recall his excuses when he was caught in a friendship with Rev. Wright. When the new undisputable facts came to the surface, he found other excuses and apologized again. If ignoring war on terror during Clinton's presidency helped to produce 9/11, Obama's will quadruple the damage and tragedy. A diligent Alinsky's disciple, Obama is hiding his main agenda—distraction of our America the Beautiful. If elected, Obama will complete a total infiltration of our government and institutions by *the Organs.*

Alinsky taught him how to do that, presenting a mechanism of infiltration the Churches and act through them. You have witnessed in reality the sermons of the Obama's "spiritual mentors" in the Trinity United Church, served by Rev. Wright and Rev. Pfleger. A small note: Rev. Pfleger came to America from the Communist East Germany—Odinga studied there and then returned to Kenya. Don't you see and feel that a well-organized sinister force is behind all of them? I have identified this force for you in the preceding chapters.

Corsi's book has confirmed a lot of ideas expressed in my writings. However there was a missing link in his solid research, a void—Obama's connection with the Kremlin and the Russian KGB's government in Moscow, Ideology is the crux of the matter and Russia is behind all our troubles, including Obama. I believe that my books are filling that void and you can see clearly the war against Western civilization. Do you know now who real Obama is? I do. Look attentively at Obama and you will find that his personality synthesizes and reflects the patterns of the backgrounds and worldviews of his mentors, associates, and friends—they all adhered to the same ideology of anti-Americanism. I hope you recognize the ideology and know its origin. The ideology was very successful and spread throughout the world in the twentieth century—reading the Italian communist and anarchist Andrea Granchi will help you to grasp the extend of the spread.

Now to prove Obama's connections, his politics and behavior, let me analyze his latest positions in the presidential campaign.

1. Barack Obama was against the war in Iraq from the beginning with. If you read only this book, you know that defeat of Saddam Hussein and liberation of Iraq was a necessity to stop the Soviet's oil conspiracy and strive for world domination. Obama voted against the bill providing our troops with needed ammunition. He was against the surge in 2007, because he hoped that the war was lost. Disgusting! After the surge's incredible success in 2008, he refused to admit his error. Now he insists on our withdrawal from Iraq regardless of the condition on the ground and possible devastating consequences for America and the world. He is either an incompetent Senator or he is intentionally acting against America's interests in the world and against the well-being of all Americans.

2. Barack Obama's suggestion of bombing Pakistan and taking troops from Iraq and bringing more combat troops to Afghanistan is a trap—a border to the former Soviet Republics gives Putin an advantage to kill more of our soldiers. Do not be surprised by the Taliban's military sophistication. Nevertheless, Afghanistan has no military solution—read about the partisan in WWII. The country lives under the Stone Age rules—a huge expense of land with tough terrain. We should set a very low bar dealing with Afghanistan. For several centuries Afghanistan was targeted in attempt to conquer it by Arabs, Turks, British, and Russians—they all failed. Iraq is the central front against the terrorists—oil is there and we are winning. This is the reason the terrorists moved to Afghanistan. Knowing the history of Afghanistan and its proximity to Pakistan we should be very careful and act only within the NATO command. To destabilize the predicament within the friendly to us Pakistan has always been the Kremlin's agenda. Remember Putin's desire—to return to Afghanistan on a white horse, defeating Americans. Remember also who sponsored the Taliban and consider the KGB's plan to pit India against Pakistan and vise verso to destabilize South Asia. We should act very delicately and wisely—Afghanistan is a gate to Pakistan, a country with nuclear arms, the long-term Russian target...

3. First, I remind you of the Russian Connection. A Democratic President Clinton made several steps to increase our energy dependency—we feel it today, ten years later. Obama continues the policy—he is the sole sponsor of legislation to block geological research to locate offshore oil. This is a restriction to our energy field a la Clinton and coal. He offered to release a strategic petroleum reserve—a trap in the case of a world conflict or natural disaster. Disgusting! His energy plan has no immediate drilling offshore oil or building of the nuclear power plants—a death sentence to America's capitalist economy. He and the Democratic Party's bosses have always been against drilling in our national reserves, collaborating with the environmental movement, anti-nuclear crowd, MoveOn.org, and George Soros, a currency speculator No.1 in the world. The situation in our country is critical today— oil affects us all, our industry, transportation, business, the price of food and other goods, the wellbeing of all Americans. The Republicans proposal to drill and drill now is the best immediate solution. We need fossil fuel now to continue growing our economy and to help all Americans to meet their ends. Obama's rejection of drilling and his arguments for the alternative fuel is also a trap. The ethanol example Obama championed has already proved its inefficiency and negative consequences for our economy. A technological research for any alternative sources of fuel takes time and it is not there yet. Hence the Republican proposal of drilling now and any renewal alternative fuel our technology may introduce later, presents the only right policy under the current circumstances America has experiencing. We do have oil to drill today, especially in ANWR. We do not have a sufficient alternative source of energy to replace fossil fuel today. Drill today is the only responsible answer. We must drill for another reason as well—the Kremlin's oil conspiracy is intact today and tomorrow. We need a domestic supply of energy for our independence!

4. Obama's policy of redistribution of the wealth is a typical anti-capital Soviet Socialist policy—a design for destruction of our capitalist economy. A practitioner of the Soviet-style politics,

> Obama introduces class warfare in America by pitting one group of citizens against the other. Obama's promises to raise our taxes are dreadful to the free market and our economy at a time of distress. His radical plan to fund a global poverty redistribution program ties to the Kremlin. Soviet Fascism is the vicious predator that has been destroying the globe for the last ninety years. Yet Obama plans to pay for the Kremlin's crimes with the money of America's taxpayers. UN pervaded with its Russian operatives will help him "to reduce our capacity."

Considering all the information conveyed in this book I believe Obama is a real danger for America and the world. The way Putin deceived Bush; the same way Obama and his wife are deceiving and fooling the American public, especially the youth and the faithful… A mediocre man well trained and programmed by the Kremlin's-mentors, Obama lacks elementary knowledge, right judgment, and a grasp on both foreign policy and the economy. I hope the preceding chapters prove my points and are enough to give you a big picture of Obama's activities in the past, present, and the dreadful picture of our future in case of his presidency. It will be the end of our America the Beautiful. Socialism, Soviet-style will destroy our America! The Kremlin has tried to infiltrate the democratic process of America's election for decades. Knowing the KGB, I am afraid that 2008 can be their success. Putin and the Organs will run and destroy our country from within! A monumental level of corruption, fraud, and waste will dismantle our economy. Our political sovereignty will be obliterated. Our money will go to the packets of the Obama's friends. Embolden Left will Balkanize America even further. You can imagine our future…!

In connection to my conclusion, I have a recommendation to our Congress. Considering all the suspicious events described in the book I believe that the situation in our country resembles the predicament we experienced in the 1930s, when the Special Committee on Un-American Activities, HUAC, was established. The House Committee on Un-American Activities authorized to investigate Nazi propaganda and other propaganda activities in America. HUAC became a permanent committee in 1945 investigated suspected threat of communist subversion and propaganda that attacked "the form of government guaranteed by our Constitution."

That exact HUAC our Congress needs today—it is an emergency call to save America from the Soviet mafia and its terrorist activities. Besides we need a new definition of the notion of TREASON. We cannot wait until it is too late. The presidential campaign of 2008 revealed the depth and size of the foreign operatives' entrenched into all strata of our society "to reduce our capacity." The only differences with the past are the names. I hope you remember that the change of the names means nothing—the substance of the agenda aimed at acquiring means to achieve the goal. I have purposely delineated all the changes in the names of the Kremlin's intelligence in the beginning of this book. You know the Organs! Act accordingly!

Coming to completion in my journey of writing this, my third book, a massive picture of the Kremlin's onslaught of subversive activities including illegal money has appeared before me with all its frightening details and designs to destabilize our globe and through America's deterioration to obtain world domination. The Obama's story is a carbon copy of others molded Soviet- style leaders known to me. The story of the Arafat's recruitment confirms its identity even in methods and tricks. I have heard that Obama's birth certificate is not valid—it was forged. You know the real story in this respect of Arafat's birth certificate the KGB had forged. The fact was documented in the memoirs of the KGB's General Ion Mihai Pacepa in the 1980s. And the answer to the question why the information about my books was blocked came easily to me—it was done for the exact reason—to cover up the main issue of the election in 2008—the candidate's real, dreadful past. I rely on you to find the culprits who kept you in the dark by suppressing information about my books to make Obama a presidential candidate.

In the meantime, I continue living in the iron cage. My computer is monitored and my e-mails are going with the warning stamp or seal "suspect." My telephone is wiretapped, I cannot talk freely and my mail is arrested the way it used to be in the Soviet Union. Some defaming information has been spread about me and a few of my "friends" stopped communication with me. I can't call any radio show—my phone will be disconnected immediately. Moreover, this manuscript is read by Obama's campaign—he is changing his behavior in accordance with his exposure by me. This means that the Kremlin read it also and is changing its politics accordingly. I do not know how many days are left for me. Yes I am in despair, but I will never commit suicide. I have not flown since the

1990s—I do not want to die in a plane crash. I remind you again that car accidents and plane crashes are the Organ's devices to get rid of political opponents. I am one of them. I hope now you have an idea of who is suppressing information about all my books and why. This book is ready to go to you, but my hands are tied—I am in the iron cage waiting for help to open the door.

I also warn you about Obama's energy policy. I suspect that he will continue Clinton's policy to prolong America's energy dependence. Do you remember how Clinton dealt with coal? I have described it in the second chapter. Obama promises in unison with Clinton "to bankrupt a coal industry:" he will do the same to help the Kremlin to suffocate our economy, "to reduce our capacity"— energy is a life blood of any industry. You have to remember how the Organs, the Soviet Gestapo operate. I purposely described it in the beginning of the book and in chapter 7; WWIII. The Bible in the Book of Revelation predicts that the Antichrist acting together with the False Prophet will bring Armageddon to our Earth. Please, remember that…!

If you love your country, and I believe you do, you have to remember my words as I am warning you now: If Obama is elected you will experience the same WWIII—the Organs are ubiquitous they have no ethnicity, religion, or nationality—they destroy everything on their way to obtain power…! Though publicly there will be a game of bipartisan unity in Obama's administration, yet underground, in secrecy the second and third echelons of power, the Organs will do the "job" of "reducing our capacity." I expect a kind of a shadow government to damage our system. The war against the terrorists will slow down if not end. What I can also predict is that of the repetition of the scenario played in the Clinton administration—stealing our nuclear secrets, our space developments and alike. They will do it from within our security apparatus and the important businesses to undermine our national security, economy, and defense capacity. Watch the new army of inept yes-men emerging to help Obama to destroy America the Beautiful…!

One picture is worth a thousand words. I have already provided you with many thousands words identifying the Soviet mafia and its ideology of Soviet Fascism. Let me add to them the picture that confirms all my words and also show the contemporary crimes committed by the International Soviet mafia—the correlation between the country of DISEASE, Russia; and the country of symptoms Sudan. In the first chapters of this book I mentioned HOLODOMOR—a starvation in Ukraine perpetrated by Stalin and his henchmen from the Organs in 1930s.

Look at the picture of a Ukrainian child and you will be surprised by resembles of the picture in the 1930s to the children of Darfur, Sudan in 2007. The difference is in the numbers of the civilians killed: Ukraine—7 million, Darfur—2.5 million, Ukraine under Stalin's Russia, Darfur—under Moscow's student—al- Bashir of Sudan. The pictures of dying children are identical. The International Soviet Mafia is killing people of all colors, races, and ethnicities, the forces of The International Soviet mafia is devastating the lands in all inhabited continents of our globe, fighting against Western civilization for CONTROL and POWER of Soviet Fascism.

Knowing what is coming, I am in agony and many other people feel the same way. I know Soviet Fascism and my desire for you is that of knowing our foremost enemy as well. Moreover, I have to admit that I am currently adamantly anti-Democrat Party leadership and philosophy as I am of the Soviet Mafia's. These people are the traitors, collaborating with our enemy to "reduce our capacity." Collaborating with our enemy in many different ways, they are destroying America. In general, the oil issue is a matter of supply and demand—the Democrats refusal for decades to drill oil on our Federal land has exposed them as the accomplices of the Soviet's oil terror-conspiracy, which is succeeding in America today.

We are at a real energy crisis and every missed day of drilling our American oil resources, brings victory to Soviet Fascism. Now you know who Modern Liberals are! Cicero was right: "A nation cannot survive treason from within." A radical Left is equally dangerous for our country—it is lethal for the entire democratic system to the American Republic! The radical Left destroys our country from within…!

My fellow Americans! The Soviet mafia has invaded our country to destroy America from within. You know who Balkanized America and the world—the Kremlin is behind all the troubles, including Obama. Sleep no more! Now you know all the tentacles of the evil Organs. Fight them to rescue and liberate our America the Beautiful! Look around closely and you will recognize corrupt Americans working in cahoots with our enemies. Do not allow evil to triumph! Stop today the Plagues of Soviet Fascism! People of the world are looking up at you with hope and pray: O Lord, Safe America from Soviet Fascism, help America to survive for all who dwell on earth! O Lord…! Bless America…! O Lord, Hear my voice, please, open blind eyes…!

If justice should ever happen it needs to happen to all victims of Soviet Fascism alive and dead! This is the reason I should speak my mind. This is my life's purpose…

RECOMMENDATIONS

To the governments of the United States, Great Britain, France, Germany, Italy, India, Japan, Turkey, Israel, Poland, Georgia, Ukraine, Lithuania, Estonia, and Czech Republic.

1. Establishment of an independent investigative body to research all the war crimes against humanity, committed by the Russian Government, indicated in my three books. There is no statute of limitation for the war crimes against humanity.
2. Establishment of an independent War Crimes Tribunal to render the cases against the Russian Government, responsible for the crimes committed during the last ninety years.
3. Establishment of the Legal Council, a group of qualified lawyers to bring the class action suits against the Russian Government in behalf of people of the world: killed, injured, suffered, and those who lost property and savings as a result of the Russian Government's criminal activities.
4. Secure the publication of the ongoing investigations and the work of the War Crimes Tribunal by the media of the listed countries at the time appropriate for that.
5. All schools, colleges, and universities, especially law schools should study the ideology of Soviet Fascism by analyzing events presented in my books....

The first West German Chancellor Konrad Adenauer had recognized the obligation of the German government in 1950s to compensate Israel as a representative of all Jewish people. Since then billions has been paid to the victims of Holocaust, their heirs, and other Jewish victims.

Currently the Conference on Jewish Material Claims Against Germany, Inc. continues paying compensations to the Jews and other victims around the world.

The End

July, 2008

P.S. Today is August 8, 2008, the Russian tanks, army, and security forces have invaded Georgia—WWIII has entered its final stage. The fifty-eighth Russian Army has entered the Rocky Tunnel at night—the territory of Georgia. The Russian special operation, Soviet style is an attempt to overthrow democratically elected Georgian Government, to liquidate President Michael Saakashvili, and to establish a puppet government—he is "guilty" because he destroyed the old Soviet Criminal Georgia! He tried to build a new, democratic Georgia...

The preceding two months showed constant provocations from Ossetia, where the Russian peacekeepers are located. The term "Russian peacekeeper" is an oxymoron—Russia and peace are incompatible. The military operation was planned years in advance and came to life at the time beneficial for Russia during the Olympic Games—the time when the West was occupied by a global friendship. It is a historic repetition of Hitler's invasion of the Sudetenland, the area of Czechoslovakia in 1938, and Stalin's invasion of Finland in 1939—Fascism has a common strategy and implements identical tactics, regardless of ethnicity.

The world at war and Europe should participate in it equally by helping America. That has not happened. Some members of the U.E. could have prevented the Russian aggression to Georgia by promising membership in NATO to Georgia and Ukraine in April 2008. They had not done that. Now you are witnessing the result of appeasement I warned you about in all my writings! Embolden by some European leaders, Soviet Fascism is on the march. Watch events in Ukraine—Russia wants access to the Black Sea and will never agree with the Ukrainian Crimea! Like in South Ossetia the process of providing population with the Russian passports is going on there! Watch also the escalation of terrorism across the globe! The end of 2008 and the next year will not be quiet. Watch all Moscow's henchmen around the world—they will never surrender until exposed and defeated!

WWIII will be combined with all the tentacles known to you and possible military actions in strategic areas involved. Besides Middle East, Iran, South America and South Asia are those strategic areas, which could be used against the U.S. I have no crystal ball to predict the details. Yet I know that the war is the last chance for Russia to survive, because it is also a beginning of the Russian Federation's End. The Russian government will lie, trying to deceive the world again, yet the mask that served it well for the last decades has been taken away exposing the ugly face of Soviet Fascism.

Just remember, Russia is a HOUSE of CARDS—its major force is the rest of the world: recruited leaders of other countries and infiltrated moles. I can predict that the patience of the fooled and living in misery people in Russia has already dried up and a gloomy economy would incite vigorous public protests and civil unrests. As the Cold War, caused the collapse of the Soviet Union; WWIII will expedite dissolution of the Russian Federation.

Of course, the process will take time and the price of oil will determine it, however, the first step to that direction has been taken. I hope the world understands now what it is doing in dealing with the Russian KGB's Government. All countries, I addressed my recommendations, should learn the ideology of Soviet Fascism and act together accordingly to save Western civilization. Remember the ruined Soviet agriculture—Russia is unable to feed her own people in the 21st century. Yet the end of the Russian Federation can be prevented by the decent people, who remember the real freedom granted to them by Yeltsin. Fortunately, Russia has smart and talented leaders to change the predicament in the country. One of them is Boris Nemtsov; I have already introduced him to you. The West should hope, help, and pray for him…

The speed of the Russian Federation's destruction also depends on the events in America—Obama's victory will prolong Russia's existence. The world can face a set of harmful events: military conflicts, killings of the opposition leaders, arsons, plane crashes, mysterious car accidents, and "false flag operations." You know all of that; you have already read how Soviet Fascism operates and know its ultimate goal—destabilization, destruction, and demoralization of the democracies in the world (3 Ds). Israel will see Obama's real ugly face. Watch an increase in our casualties in Afghanistan. Be prepared for unexpected mysterious events harming people and property in America, too, unexpected shootings for example— "10,000 boys" are still employed and "working" on America's soil sometimes in cahoots with crony- Democrats and home-grown terror-gangs of Jihad.

Please, remember the KGB's motto—revenge. Putin sees the collapse of the Soviet Union as his personal and national tragedy. Maybe he made Obama an instrument of his revenge? America, be ready for revenge! Let your conscious be your guide. Remember the policy of infiltration and penetration! Watch the triumph of Black Liberation Theology, its obsession with race, and burial of America's pride. I am afraid that to prolong Russia's regime, Putin in the audacity of arrogance, using Obama and relying on the moles inside America, will start military actions somewhere in the world. Using Moscow's henchmen to help Obama's Democrats to win the 2010 and 2012 elections, I don't exclude a repetition of the lethal strike on America's soil, by the Kremlin's henchmen. Remember who you are dealing with!

Meanwhile, Obama's victory in 2008 is also a death to America the Beautiful—an incredible harm will be done to our country. Just watch political intimidation of the opposition, the class and psychological warfare, our economy with "reduce capacity," our schools with new textbooks and our Higher Educational system run by Modern Liberals. Indoctrination of our youth will proceed with incredible speed! Watch criminal gangs acting under the KGB's supervision, unexpected shootings a-la Columbine massacre, arsons, and so on. Remember also the Tsunami in Indonesia as the aftermath of a volcano's eruption in 2004, and be prepared for the earthquakes in any other locations of the globe. You will see an open season on the Republicans and Conservatives making them "the enemy of the people." Watch the destruction of our military, intelligence and security agencies from within and other harmful developments. The fight against terrorists around the world will end. Some of them will be welcome to our soil. Moral and psychological degradation of America will stun you!

Thousands of voices and souls of the people killed and tortured by Soviet Fascism are reaching me and knocking on my heart with anger demanding actions. I have done everything possible to inform you and stop Obama by writing this book and sending hundreds of messages. The rest is beyond my power. Whatever it will be, my conscience is clear—I completed my civic duty. I did the right thing. Now it is your turn—the torch is yours.

S. P.

EPILOGUE

Four years have passed since my warning about the Obama presidency. During these years we have witnessed gradual downfall of our country. In this book I have given you solid reasons to believe there is one evil menace causing most of it: Soviet Fascism and its advent of World War III. By reading my book you have been introduced to a basic knowledge of Soviet Fascism and how it has recently changed its tactics in a new spiral of war on the world, waged from the heart of the Kremlin. As a result, Americans—be they Democrats, Republicans or Independents— are being basically deceived and misled.

If you have any doubts about my fingering Soviet Fascism as the cause of World War III, go no further than the first person to confirm the identity of both—the Chairman of the KGB from 1967-1982, Yuri Andropov. No less authority than Lt. General Ion Mihai Pacepa, the highest-ranking KGB officer ever to defect to the U.S, tells us of a meeting he had with Yuri Andropov:

"In 1972, the Kremlin decided to turn the whole Islamic world against Israel and the U.S. As KGB Chairman, Yuri Andropov told me that a billion adversaries could inflict far greater damage on America than could a few millions. We needed to instill a Nazi- style hatred for Jews throughout the Islamic world, and to turn this weapon of the enflamed emotions into a terrorist bloodbath against Israel and its main supporter, the United States. No one within the American/Zionist sphere of influence should any longer feel safe." ("Russian Footprints," by Ion Mihai Pacepa, *National Review Online*, August 24, 2008.)

General Pacepa wrote in the same article: "According to Andropov... the Muslims had a taste for nationalism, jingoism, and victimology. Their illiterate, oppressed mobs could be whipped up to a fever pitch. Terrorism and violence against Israel and her master, American Zionism, would flow naturally from the Muslims' religious fervor, Andropov sermonized."

What can better confirm both of my terms "Soviet Fascism" and "WW III" than those words? They summarize my entire book. I remind you that under Andropov the infiltration by terrorists into Western civilization had tripled. Under his watch occurred the bloodiest terrorists' attacks in the world, from the Munich murder of Israelis in the Olympic Village to the James Jones cult massacre in Guyana. As a matter of fact, the current Russian President Vladimir Putin, a former Chairman of the KGB is a devoted disciple of Yuri Andropov…

Throughout this book you have seen the genesis, the growth and now the results of what I call Soviet Fascism and "a new spiral into WW III. The world is going up in flames, with hot spots all over the globe. Actually, this has been going on for a long while but since 9/11 we Americans are more aware of it since the war has been brought to our own soil. Let us begin to connect the dots:

1. During the last several decades the Kremlin has taken advantage of erroneous American foreign policy. Instead of fighting the enemy, we Americans were now attempting to reshape the enemy and were reluctant to expose our foremost adversary, Russia. The "Arab Spring" was orchestrated through a series of well coordinated actions to bring so-called new leadership in the Middle East and Islamic world—the Muslim Brotherhood and Radical Islamists. The Stalinist postulate *cadres decide everything* now had prevailed once again in the twenty-first century. The old dictators and criminals I called the Kremlin henchmen have exposed themselves in the era of the internet—the Kremlin sought and found new cadres. Mullah Omar replace the liquidated Osama bin-Laden in Afghanistan—the Stalinist policy of liquidation is alive and well and going on around the world.

2. As you might know, Egypt's President Mubarak graduated from the Soviet Air Defense Academy and became the Vice President of that country. I believe that the assassination of President Sadat took place for one specific reason: to make Mubarak President of Egypt in 1981. But over time Mubarak had become

too independent and made peace with Israel. Moscow does not like the "enlightened" independence of its students—you then saw the result, a shameful humiliation in a-la Stalinist Show Trial in Egypt.

3. At the same time, Assad of Syria, an obedient henchman of the Russians, continues killing his own people in a desperate attempt to hold on to power. There is an interesting connection between the present and the past in the Mubarak case. Al- Zawahiri, who joined the Muslim Brotherhood at fourteen, participated in Sadat's assassination. He is a top leader of al- Qaeda today. This illustrates that when we know the acting characters and history of Soviet Fascism, we can see how the circle closes.

4. The orchestrated and well-planned "Arab Spring" did not succeed in Libya during the first few months, and there were rumors that al-Qaeda had infiltrated the rebel forces in Libya. As a piece of useful background information, Gaddafi had refused to pay for an enormous quantity of arms provided by Russia. The Kremlin became worried. Extra measures were needed to secure the plot of "Arab Spring" in Libya. And the Kremlin found the help—Europe, dependent on Libyan oil, suddenly became interested in military involvement and. President Obama hesitated for weeks before finally confirming America's military participation. That was a double victory for the Kremlin. It finally achieved its long-planned strategy to infiltrate NATO and use it to force completion of the "Arab Spring" in Libya.

The demise of Gaddafi came in a most shocking manner. In October, 2011, we witnessed the new "Islamic Democracy" in action in Libya—a badly wounded dictator was shot in the head in point blank, execution style— a-la the murders by the Cheka. Decent people around the world were disgusted. I would prefer to have had a lawful trial by a Military Tribunal like in Iraq, which had given us the first *war criminal* of Soviet Fascism, Saddam Hussein. Instead we were witnessing the first action of Libya's so called "Islamic Democracy"—a mob lynching, so to speak. The scene gave us a first glance into the future of the Middle East and North Africa. The European reaction to the event stunned me.

Europe tolerated a *war crime,* disregarding and retreating from civilized postulates of *due process.*

5. We also saw a logical result in the first country of the "Arab Spring"—Tunisia has become an Islamic Republic and is imposing Shariah Law under the leadership of the Muslim Brotherhood. Now in Egypt, a number of elections and disputed results are leading to the inevitable "Islamisation" of the country, as predicted by Andropov and planted by the Soviet Fascism in the Middle East during 1950-1990s.

6. The plot to assassinate Saudi's ambassador to the United States is in the same vein. Saudi Arabia, a holder of huge resources of oil, has been the target of Soviet Fascism for the last several decades. There were at least fourteen Saudis who perpetrated the attack on the World Trade Center on 9/11 in 2001. Guess who was behind the crime, and why! The simple truth is that a new spiral of WW III is marching across our planet.

7. Remember also the Russian-Iranian connection (and the Obama policy cooperating with Russia—a sponsor of international terrorism). I refer you to the patterns of Soviet Fascism: Russian cooperation on nuclear matters with North Korea decades ago. The same happened with Iran—Russia has already secretly provided Iran with nuclear equipment, technicians and top scientists. The crucial factor is that Russia has provided Iran with vital information in creating its nuclear program.

I was greatly disturbed by two events that took place in October, 2011: the interview Fareed Zacharia (CNN) held with President Ahmadinejad of Iran, and Obama's decision to pull out all our troops from Iraq, when everyone knew that Iran is waiting in the wings. Look at Ahmadinejad's appearance while being interviewed by Zacharia. Like bin-Laden's fake pictures (more on that later), you see a total transformation in Ahmadinejad's appearance. He is wearing glasses and a tie, speaks quietly but arrogantly with condescending confidence, and pulls over lying without blinking. You were watching the Kremlin stooge lecturing an American student—a Stalinist political technique brought forward into the twenty-first century and used to perfection by the President of Iran. Analyzing the common factors in each of these events bring us to the conclusion that there is an active legitimization of Soviet Fascism and an insidious and united front against Western civilization in the world.

8. I believe there is also a connection between NATO in Libya and the presidential election in France in 2012.

9. If you analyze the actions of the Occupy Wall Street movement, you will discover a conglomerate of ill-informed, duped, confused and frustrated young people, energized by leftist provocateurs to enlarge the army of voters for Democrats. The movement is global in nature, a continuation of "Arab Spring" and financed by the forces identified in this book. Therefore, you can expect fraud, drugs, crimes and anti-Semitic behavior from the crowd of Wall Street Occupiers. Watch as well the influence of ACORN and Unions behind the scene, "helping" and organizing so-called "youth movements" to create social chaos and perpetuate revolution. These events can also help you to grasp the real identity and purpose of George Soros, Imam Feisal Abdul Rauf and Michael Moore... Be ready for racial riots, sudden street violence and shootings and ultimate anarchy—remembering the *modus operandi* of Soviet Fascism.

10. Besides creating chaos, the current mission of Soviet Fascism is to impose Gun Control on America. This militant ideology pushes to disarm you of your guns, while exploiting everything to this end. The seemingly senseless shooting in Colorado will be used to this exact end by the united leftist forces of the Democrats. They had been trying to ban guns in the hands of citizens for the past forty years, despite the simple fact that it is the crime of the person who shoots the gun and not the fault of the gun itself. The simple fact is that there are evil and mentally ill people in our midst and they continue to be a threat to our society. There is the third and very real prospect—that evil people are using the mentally sick ones for their own purposes. Consider this as a very strong possibility whenever you hear about a public shooting. Moreover, the Colorado tragedy was

preceded by a murderous terrorist attack on Israeli tourists in Bulgaria. Did you know that the terrorist in the Bulgarian case spoke Russian? All of that is going on, and perhaps is intended to provoke public outcry, while the United Nations discussing the Small Arms Treaty. It is not out of the realm of possibility that these unprovoked shootings will continue until our government used them to impose Gun Control on America, thus violating our Second Amendment and destroying our traditional culture.

11. The operation *Fast and Furious* falls under this heading. It is a part of the message that I convey in this book. My suggestion to investigators is for them to go back to the Clinton's administration to the cruel attack by the ATF (Alcohol Tobacco Firearms Agency) on the Branch Davidians in Waco to find the perpetrators and the roots of the crime. The operation *Fast and Furious* was preceded by a long and bloody history of using ATF as a main force in the presidency of Bill Clinton. Like the recent leaks of classified vital information from the White House and the Obama "kill list," the operation Fast and Furious is but one link in the chain of assaults on our national security for the past several decades. All three events are integral parts of a long-term and ongoing war against Western civilization that I call World War III and was spelled out in this book...

Considering the facts already known to us, I would suggest the investigation of Fast and Furious to proceed in two main directions. The first part should consist of the search for the history of a special connection between ATF and Eric Holder in both the Clinton and Obama presidencies. Eric Holder was one of the first appointees of the Clinton Administration, which named him the U.S. Attorney for Washington D.C. The subject of guns definitely connected him with another branch of the government dealing with the guns—ATF. The second part of the investigation would be to apply the information about the Concept and Doctrine of WW III. My belief that the Democrat Party has been infiltrated by the Soviet Mafia is still intact. Just follow the activities of both Democrat Presidents Clinton and Obama to see how that is found in their domestic policies as well.

12. Do you remember the fraudulent activities of the organization called ACORN? Based on ACORN's activities, there appears to be an ideological and financial connection between Obama and Clinton, for the purpose of increasing votes for the Democratic Party. ACORN is a typical entity of National Socialist Movement, which grew substantially under President Clinton during the 1990s. As a legal representative of ACORN, Obama developed it further—the policy of both presidents is seen to be identical and very consequential for our country. I see this policy as being aimed at undermining our national security and our capitalist economic system while creating financial crises.

At this juncture, we can draw some dismaying and sinister conclusions. While American were preoccupied with going about their daily life, raising families and working in their careers, seemingly while nobody was looking, the American economy began a catastrophic descent. The early stages of the real estate cries started taking shape and by 2008, the true scope of the devastation became crystal clear. (The Aftershock Survival Summit Transcription Broadcast of Newsmax Media, October 11, 2011.) Had awareness of the forces of what I call Soviet Fascism existed in the public domain, we could have reacted promptly against the manipulations of our banking system, the beginning of outsourcing to China and the surrendering of our technology by the Clinton administration during the 1990s. Tragically, we did not.

Today, in 2012, we are paying a price for the reluctance to call a spade a spade. Furthermore, we are not reacting adequately to the recent recording of the personal conversation between Obama and the President of Russia. In that brief peek behind the curtain, we understood that they both adhered to the same ideology. Obama's promise of "flexibility" means his intention to work towards the ultimate destruction of America. He has been called *The Great Destroyer* by David Limbaugh and he is right. America has not paid enough attention to the very unusual cooperation of our two Democrat Presidents with Russia.

My idea of "cooperation" between the two Presidents and Russia can be magnified by *The True Story of the Bilderberg Group*, by Daniel Estulin, TrineDay LLC, 2009, p. 52. In this book we learn that on June 9, 1991, two-and-a half months before announcing his candidacy for the U.S. Presidency, Bill Clinton flew to Moscow. *The Arkansas Democrat* ran the story under the headline "Clinton Has Powerful Buddy in the U.S.S.R.—New Head of KGB." Do not be surprised as Clinton helps Obama to win the second term and was called upon to introduce him at the Democratic Convention—they are adhered to the same ideology and have the same agenda.

Four years ago I called the Democrats the obstructionist party. I call them obstructionists today. The Republican House submitted fifteen bills to the Senate controlled by Harry Reid and the Democrats. The bills were aimed at healing our economic condition and increasing employment. The Democrats in the Senate blocked all fifteen bills and called the Republicans the obstructionists. This is a typical, Stalinist political trick which blames the adversary for the actions they, in this case the Democrats, themselves had been committing. I believe the Democrats continue reading my manuscripts and attacking my arguments and the Republicans as well to pervert the reality and divert attention from the real truth. The bare facts prove that the Democrats show constancy in an obstructive policy. Take for example the blocking of access to sources of energy on a federal land, the delay in the granting of off shore leases for oil exploration, and the halting of the Keystone Pipeline…these are all examples of their policy of obstruction. As a result, the American people are still being held hostage by the Democrats in 2012.

The Russian lawyer and journalist Arkady Vaksberg had introduced the notion of the Soviet Mafia to the world. I have extended the notion and call it the *International Soviet Mafia*, a movement which is fighting for power and money in the world. Money is a powerful instrument in winning an election. After what we called "the fall of Communism" we know that the Kremlin came into control of extraordinary amounts of money and allowed out- of- control corruption, and developed what we now call Crony Capitalism. In our country, just watch how the financial markets are manipulated to discredit American capitalism and American businesses, and even the Republican Party. Observe how the White House gives money to the Obama's donors and friends, including the Russians. Watch the manipulation of public opinion with the fraudulent "Green Energy" initiatives, a hoax eating up billions of dollars. The Obama's campaign 2012 even employs Republican words and phrases to confuse and fool you—LIES and FRAUD are the universal devices of the *International Soviet Mafia*. We are witnessing the new low standards of the Obama's campaign 2012: the same devises will be used to divers your attention from the Obama's murky past.

Soviet Fascism is not a gray area any longer. In a recent article, *Unprecedented Obama*, by Michael Obernford, RPA, Sunday, July 21, 2011. The author openly identifies the Democrat Party as a neo-fascist party. The article was reprinted by *Canada Free* Press with the added line: "From a Strong American Who Sees the Picture Exactly as It Is. Worth the read!" I wholeheartedly agree with this view.

I am convinced that The Kremlin continues reading my writing. In anticipation of the upcoming publication of this book and exposure of Soviet Fascism, the Kremlin suddenly changed its tone, threatening NATO and the United States with activating the Russian missiles system. This is a typical Stalinist trick—to go to offense to divert attention from the exposure, using as a pretext the NATO countries' missile defense system in Europe. Reading this book, you will know the tricks and the KGB's general *modus operandi.* This is the systematic, global Stalinist ideology with lies, fraud, treachery, deceit, and distortions and it is very active in the twenty-first century.

Watch events play out in Syria. Russia will defend a killer- regime by all means possible in the world arena and at the United Nations. Basher Assad, much like his father, also a Moscow henchman, will kill his own people to their last drop of blood to stay in power. Russia has many of its own interests in this strategic region: it acquired access to the Mediterranean Sea with its Navy base in a Syrian port. Russian arms are flooding the Middle East through the regime, which is destabilizing its neighbors like Lebanon, the Palestinian enclave, Iraq and Egypt and through them, Israel itself. But the most dangerous issue is that of weapons of mass destruction, or WMD. We will see how Russia had provided Iraq, under Saddam Hussein, with weapons of mass destruction. At the time of Saddam's defeat, to cover up its crime, the Russian Security Forces transferred those WMD to Syria. The Russian WMD are still in Syria and Russia will do everything possible to cover up the existence of these weapons to prevent an international scandal exposing the evil face of the Russian KGB's Government. Soon you will have the opportunity to watch its duplicity and *modus operandi* described in this book.

Our national security is a key issue in the 2012 election. Fifty years ago the FBI Director, J. Edgar Hoover warned John and Robert Kennedy about the dangers of Communism. You know the tragic end of both Kennedys. For the last twenty-five years I have been warning my readers about these dangers in hopes of being heard. Up to now only the Tea Party people are awakened and acting accordingly. Clint Eastwood had brought the issue of our national security to the forefront in the nationwide discussion in his film *J. Edgar*, where the process of an ongoing WWIII is eloquently revealed.

I love my adopted country, America.
I know she is in danger.

This nation will remain the land of the free only so long as it is the home of the brave. ~Elmer Davis

August 2012

NOTES

Chapter 1: 1937—A Year of Infamy

1. *Propiska* - a residential permit, an official seal in the internal passport of every citizen. Passport was the major document of identity in the Soviet Union and is still a major document of identity in contemporary Russia. A seal of *Propiska* is also a must in current Russian law,
2. *Kerocenka* - an oil or paraffin stove with one burner. In our kitchen all *kerocinkas* worked on kerosene.
3. *David Oystuhk* - a violinist. Later he became a worldwide known violinist,
4. *NKVD* - People's Commissariat for Internal Affairs; an apparatus of all security forces of the USSR in the 1930-1940s. The NKVD had comprised of security and intelligence agencies—a precursor of the KGB. It should be noted that Commissariat for Internal Affairs has nothing in common with the American Department of Interior.
5. *Solomon Mikhoels* - a Jewish actor, director of the State Jewish Theatre in Moscow. Mihkoels also served as the Chairman of the Jewish Anti-Fascist Committee during WWII.
6. *MVD* - Ministry of Internal Affairs. In 1946, the NKVD was divided into the MVD and MGB. The People's Commissariat (NK) was designated as Ministry (M). The MVD has nothing in common with the English word interior. To grasp the significance of the MVD, just go to internet and learn the equipment's the MVD uses.
7. *MGB* - Ministry of State Security, *a* precursor of the KGB.
8. Victor Abakumov-Minister of the State Security, MGB 1946-1951.
9. *Gennadiy Kostyrchenko* - a historian and writer, the author of "How Mikhoels Had Been Killed" and a researcher of Stalin's policy of anti- Semitism.
10. *Perez Markish*, a well-known Jewish poet.
11. *The Organs* - a collective term for all security and intelligence agencies in Russia.

12. *Holodomor* - a man-made famine, starvation in Ukraine orchestrated by Stalin and other leaders of the Communist Part in the 1930s.
13. *Chechnya*-a small Muslim republic with in Russia. It is located on the Northern part of the Caucuses Mountains. People of the republic had experienced a tragic deportation by the Stalinist regime to Central Asia and Siberia in 1944.

Chapter 2: My Hopes and Disappointments in America

14. *Komsomol* - Communist Youth League—a major reservoir of human resources for the Communist Party and the KGB.
15. *Zhirinovsky Vladimir* - Chairman of the Liberal Democratic Party LDP in Duma. He is a mega-phone of the KGB and the current Russian Government. I described in detail his ascent into Russian politics in my book *Baltic Winds: Testimony of A Soviet Attorney*, Xlibris, 2002. You can read about the man in *The New York Times Magazine*, "Why Russia Loves This Man," June 19, 1994.
16. *Primakov Eugeniy* - a journalist, who, in the beginning of his career was frequently sent by the KGB on intelligence missions to the Middle East and the United States under a code name MAXIM. His political career is tightly connected to the KGB's activities. He served as Director of the Institute of Oriental Studies under the Soviet Academy of Science. He served also as First Deputy Chairman of the Soviet Peace Committee, a KGB foreign propaganda front organization. The KGB continues its infiltration into a new government of Russia after the failed August 1991 putsch, and Primakov was appointed First Deputy Chairman of the KGB. After the formation of the Russian Federation, Primakov was appointed Director of the Foreign Intelligence Service SVR, 1991-1996. Despite Yeltsin's resistance, he was forced by Duma to appoint Primakov as a Prime Minister of the Russian Federation. 1998- 1999. Primakov is Putin's ally and his adviser.
17. *Arafat Yasser* - a Chairman of the terrorist organization PLO—Palestinian Liberation Organization for several decades. Arafat was recruited by the KGB in 1957.

Chapter 3: A Lesson to Learn and Remember

18. *The Cheka* - the first Soviet Intelligence agency of Russia after the October Socialist Revolution in 1917. Literary it means an abbreviation of the words the Extraordinary Commission. From its founding the Cheka was

an important military and security arms of the Bolshevik, communist government—a brutal and vicious lawless organization, whose traditions are alive in the 21st century. A member of the Cheka is called a Chekist.

19. *GPU* - the State Political Directorate or Management, the next Intelligence agency formed from the Cheka.
20. *OGPU* - All-Union State Political Directorate, formed after GPU. The OGPU—a secret police organization was responsible for the creation of the GULAG, a system of murders and repression of millions of innocent people. The system of forced labor camps was established in 1929-1930, several years prior to 1933, when Hitler came to power and learned about the concentration camps from the Soviets. To grasp the success of the OGPU in intelligence operations, read about the *Trust Operation* of 1924- 1925.
21. *Beria Lavrentiy* - a Chief of the Soviet security and secret police apparatus—NKVD, 1930-1950s. He served as a de facto Marshal of the Soviet Union in command of the NKVD different field units, killing innocent people of different ethnic groups, race, and religion. Just remember two events where he played a major role: Beria was primarily responsible for the Katyn Massacre. Second, he played the decisive role in coordinating the Soviet Partisans, FSB-Federal Intelligence agency, a contemporary apparatus of repression that replaced the KGB and all its precursors. Vladimir Putin is a former Chairman of the FSB.
22. *GRU* - Main Intelligence Directorate of the General Staff of the Arm Forces. Military Intelligence is the largest Foreign Intelligence and counterintelligence apparatus of current Russia,
23. *Yeltsin Boris* - the first President of the Russian Federation after the collapse of the Soviet Union in 1991. Boris Yeltsin, an honest person, who had attempted to bring real freedom to Russia. We do not know the circumstances that forced Yeltsin to appoint Putin to the top posts in government. We also have no information about the last years of Yeltsin's life. I do not exclude that he was killed—he knew too much. History will reveal the circumstances of his life and death,
24. *Litvinenko Alexander* - a former KGB and FSB agent, who escaped to London and became a strong critic of the KGB and FSB. He wrote two books: *Blowing Up Russia: Terror From Within and Lubyanka Criminal Group*. The first book was written in collaboration with Yuri Felshtinsky. Litvinenko was poisoned by Polonium-210 by another KGB agent in 2006. I see it as an act of nuclear terrorism by Russia,
25. Politkovskaya Anna-Russian journalist, a brave woman, who openly criticized Putin's war in Chechnya. She was assassinated in 2007,

26. *Militia* - a police force run by the NKVD and currently by the MVD. In 2011, Russian President Medvedev in his policy of modernization has renamed Militia as a Police force. Please, recall the Soviet history of changing names within the security forces to cover up the crimes committed,
27. *NASHI* - a youth movement similar to Hitler's Jugent in Germany, established and financed by the KGB government. Vladimir Putin is their hero and mentor. HASHI have a motor—to safe Motherland from colonization by the United States.
28. *Yabloko* - a political party with the Right tendency,

Chapter 4: And Evil is Alive and Well

29. *Yurovsky Yakov* - the chief executioner of the Russian Royal Family in 1918. I had described the event in *The Russian Factor: From Cold War to Global Terrorism.*
30. *Dzerzhinsky Felix* - the first Chairman of the Cheka and GPU.
31. *Gulags* - The Chief Administration of the Labor Camps and Colonies. The term can be used in plural form.
32. *Article 58 of Criminal Code* - Counterrevolutionary agitation and propaganda,
33. *Psyhushka* - slang for psychiatric institutions.
34. *Octobrists* - an ideological establishment or unity for children at all schools dedicated to the October Socialist Revolution. Octobrists are the children 6 to 8 years of age,
35. *Pioneers* - an ideological foundation for children of 8 to 12 years old at all schools.
36. *Morozov Pavlik* - a hero of the Soviet children who informed the Cheka about grains in the possession of his parents, I described the story in my book *Baltic Winds: Testimony of a Soviet Attorney*, Xlibris, 2002.
37. *Oprichnina* - a Medieval, brutal, and vicious secret police established by Tsar Ivan the Terrible. We can call it a parent of the Cheka.
38. *Lysenko Trofim* - Russian Academician in the field of agriculture 1930-1970. Lysenko was fighting genetics all his life. A pseudo-scientist, he had helped Stalin destroy the entire Russian agricultural system,
39. *Academician Vavilov* - Nikolai Vavilov a prominent Russian and Soviet botanist and geneticist. He was arrested for his work and for being a geneticist. He is a definite casualty of the ideology and pseudo-scientist Comrade Lysenko,
40. *Kun Miklos* - a Hungarian historian, writer, and researcher of Stalin's life.

41. *Winston Churchill* - several terms as prime minister of Great Britain. Churchill was right saying: "Russia's greatest misfortune was Lenin's birth. Russia's second greatest misfortune was his death,"

Chapter 5: Tell Me Something I Don't Know

42. *Jacque Duclo, Marcel Kashen, and Morris Torres* all three were the First Secretaries of the French Communist Party in the 20th century,
43. *Mao Tse-Tung* - First Secretary of the Chinese Communist Party,
44. *Chiang-Kai-Sheik* - military and political leader of China at the beginning of the 20th century. He also was a leader of the Nationalist Party 1927- 1949,
45. *Sun-Yat-sen* - the first provisional President Republic of China after the collapse of the Empire in 1912, a pioneer of Nationalist China. Sun-Yat-sen saw Moscow as a friendly partner and his real intensions are obscured. He died in 1925.
46. *Jacob Blumkin* - a Chekist who assassinated the German ambassador in 1918. It was probably the assignment he had received from his superior. In 1920, he organized a Persian Soviet Socialist Republic in Iran, the Soviet Republic of Gilan. Pay attention to this story—the similar activities of the Cheka are going on today around the globe.
47. *Chou-En-lai* - a leader of the Communist Party of China, a very capable man who collaborated with Moscow in the beginning of his career. His death is very suspicious to me.

Chapter 6: Stalin and Mao—Friendship Forever

48. *Lenin Vladimir* - a Father of the October Socialist Revolution in Russia in 1917...
49. *Averill Harriman* - politician and diplomat, an American Ambassador to the Soviet Union 1943-1946,
50. *George Marshall* - General Marshall was a Secretary of State and an adviser of President Truman on China,
51. *Molotov Vycheslav* - the Soviet Prime Minister and Soviet Foreign Minister; 1930-1950s.
52. *A.Q. Khan* - Abdul Qadeer Khan, a Pakistani scientist. I suspect he collaborated with the KGB and carried out its assignments,
53. *The Soviet Partisans* - guerrilla or insurgency forces fighting on the occupied territory,
54. *Raoul Wallenberg* - a Swedish hero, who was kidnapped by the Soviets and disappeared in 1945,

55. *Aldo Morro* - the Italian Prime Minister for two terms. He was kidnapped by the Red Brigades and assassinated in 1978,
56. *Che Guevara* - a terrorist from Argentina, the Soviets' and Castro's friend,
57. *Dang Xioping* - a founder of the free market capitalism in China,

Chapter 7: WWIII: Recruitments and Drugs, Infiltration, and Assassinations

58. *LSD* - the psychedelic drugs used by the Soviets to brainwash soldiers and citizens. Perhaps today in 2011, we can call this drug WMD.
59. *Stanislaus Mikolayczik* - the Polish Prime Minister in exile at London during WWII,
60. *Jan Masaryk* - a Foreign Minister of Czechoslovakia in 1940s.
61. *Lt. General Ion Mihai Pacepa* - the highest ranking defector from the Soviet KGB,
62. *The Estonian Korpus* - a military unit within the Soviet Arm Forces during WWII.
63. *James Forestall* - American Secretary of the Navy and Secretary of Defense between 1947-1949,
64. *Walter Krivitsky* - a head of the Soviet military intelligence in France, who defected in 1937. His biography can tell you about tragic events of people within the NKVD,
65. *Patrice Lumumba University* - the Soviets' educational establishment for training students in the tenets of Socialism and Communism,
66. *Senator McCarthy* - a Senator who had warned America about Soviets' infiltration since 1940-50s,
67. *Nouri Maliki* - Prime Minister of Iraq. I was right not trusting Maliki then in 2007, and the evidence is obvious in 2011—Russia got access to Iraqi's oil.

Chapter 8: The Red Menace: From China to Jihad

68. Carlos the Jackal- a terrorist who massacred the members of OPEC in 1975, I had described the story in detail in *The Russian Factor: From Cold War to Global Terrorism*, Xlibris, 2006.
69. *The Muslim Brotherhood* - one of the largest Islamist parties and political organizations in many Arab countries. Established in 1928, it cooperated with German Nazis and after WWII with the Soviets. The Muslim Brotherhood's agenda is that of creating a Muslim Caliphate and uniting the world against Western civilization,

70. *Al-Zawahiri* - a terrorist trained by the Soviets. In a group of Egyptian military, he assassinated Egypt President Anwar Sadat in 1981. He is currently a head of al-Qaeda after Bin-Laden's official death.
71. *Arkadiy Vaksberg* - Russian lawyer and journalist, the author of many books including *The* Soviet Mafia, St Martin Press, 1991. Vaksberg gave us a new definition of old political forces previously known as the Soviets, the Communists, and the KGB. He introduced a notion of The Soviet Mafia; a collective identity for the old three terms.
72. *Saddam Hussein* - President of Iraq 1979-2003, a Soviet henchman and terrorist,
73. *The International Soviet Mafia* - a global ideological force of Soviet Fascism acting under the umbrella of the Russia KGB government,
74. *Hamas* - Muslim military and political force, build by the Soviets to fight Israel.
75. *Hezbollah* - Muslim military and political force like Hamas, build in the Middle East by the Soviets to fight Israel and Western civilization,
76. *Gamal Abdel Nasser* - President of Egypt and a Soviets' friend 1956- 1970,
77. *Khrushchev Nikita* - First Secretary of the Communist Party of the USSR 1955-1964.
78. *Soviet Fascism* - the ideology of different political groups, an amalgamation or partnership of Marxists, Communists, Socialists, Anarchists, radical Islamists, and other left-wing groups around the globe, united under Kremlin's umbrella to fight Western civilization,

Chapter 9: The Evil Empire of Global Terrorism

79. *Mahmoud Ahmadinejad* - a President of Iran, a Soviet henchman and terrorist,
80. *Hugo Chavez* - a President of Venezuela, a Soviet henchman and terrorist,
81. *Ayatollah Khomeini* - a religious leader of the Iranian Revolution in 1979,
82. *OSU* - the organization that administers unity between the University students and the students of Theological Seminaries. I gave you the description of the OSU for a reason. You can see in Iran patterns of Soviet Fascism in its activities and direct involvement of Ahmadinejad. Just recall the Stalinist political management of religion in the S.U. You will find the same activities in Iran. There is another pattern in Iran: 40 per cent of Iranian economy is managed by the Revolutionary Guard, like in Russia by the KGB,

83. *The Tudeh Party of Iran* - in reality it is a Communist Party of Iran: a usual Soviet trick changing the name to cover up the substance, p.180. Just read *Brief History of the Tudeh Party of Iran* by M/.Omidvar, March1993.
84. *Mohammed Mossadegh* - a prime minister of Iran. Mossadegh had a friendly relationship with the Soviets. He nationalized all Iranian resources of oil in 1953.

Chapter 10: Face to face With Soviet Fascism

85. *Benito Mussolini* - the fascist dictator of Italy.1924-1943,
86. *Adolf Hitler* - a Chancellor of Germany democratically elected in 1933,
87. *United Russia* - a ruling political party in contemporary Russia, like the Communist Party used to rule the Soviet Union,
88. *Joseph Goebbels* - a Reich Minister of Propaganda in Nazi Germany,
89. *The Gestapo* - Secret Police under the administration of SS in the Nazi Germany,
90. *Duma* - the Russian Parliament. The name was taken from the time of Tsarist Russia.
91. *Oligarch in Russia* - a person possesses an enormous wealth. This wealth is not earned by the Oligarch: It was created by the party bosses' machinations and given to an Oligarch for obedience in serving the ruling party, Just watch a current case of oligarchs Abramowich and former oligarch Boris Berezovsky in London in 2011. You will learn a lot about "business" in Russia.
92. *Valeria Novodvorskay* - Russian historian, journalist, writer, and human rights advocate. She is the voice of the Truth from Russia. You can rely on her judgment.
93. *Dmitriy Medvedev* - a Current President of Russia.
94. *Andrey Piontkovsky* - Russian scientist, writer, and political analyst,
95. *Sergey Ivanov* - a Minister of Defense in Putin's government 2001-2997. He was appointed Chief of Staff Presidential Administration of Russia in 2011. He is still a ruler of the GRU,
96. *Henry Kissinger* - a former US Secretary of State, I called H. Kissinger Henry Chamberlain, shocked by his opinion on Russia. Later I read the book, that I would recommend for you to grasp the activities of Henry Chamberlain and Bill Clinton. The title of the book: *The True Story of the Bilderberg Group*, TrineDay LLC, 2009.
97. *General Musharaff* - President of Pakistan 2001-2008, he was a friend of America.

Chapter 11: All the Planet's Blood and Treasure

98. *Whittaker Chamber* - an American patriot, who warned about the Soviet threat and infiltration in the 1940s.
99. *Venona Project* - official information about the Soviet espionage apparatus in America,
100. *Anatoliy Golitsyn* - a former KGB officer, who started warning America about the Soviet design of war in the 1960s, p. 240. He is the author of *New Lies For Old* and *The Perestroika Deception.* He also predicted the Second October Revolution in the world.
101. *Senator Schumer* - a Senator-Democrat, Just read how Jack Schumer had become a Senator. *The Russian Factor: From Cold War to Global Terrorism*, Xlibris, 2006.
102. *Jerry Falwell* - a leader of the conservative movement in America, a founder of the Liberty University. I suspect that he was assassinated.

Chapter 12: WWIII on America's Soil or The Russian Connection

103. *Andropov Yuri* - Chairman of the KGB 1967-1982, the First Secretary of the Communist Party of the USSR 1982-1984. Andropov was a smart and vicious man, he perfected the KGB to the highest rank of the intelligence agency—infiltration into the West had tripled. He died in 1984,

Chapter 13: A Final Phase of Diabolic Ideological Expansion

104. *Reverend Jeremiah Wright* - Obama's spiritual adviser.
105. *Edward Shevardnadze* - the USSR Minister of Foreign Affairs 1985-1991. He is a Georgian by nationality.
106. *Abkhazia* - a part of the ancient Georgia, the area located on the shore of the Black Sea, currently occupied by the Russian forces, p. 300.
107. *Reverend Michael Pfleger* - a man from the GDR, the Soviet sector of the divided Germany.
108. *Louis Farrakhan* - a leader of the Nation of Islam in America, a friend of Libya's Dictator Gaddafi, I have described both in *The Russian Factor: From Cold War to Global Terrorism*, Xlibris, 2006.
109. *Black Liberation Theology* - a relatively new theological perspective found in some Black Churches in the U.S. They emphasize blackness and freedom from the oppressor.

110. *ACORN* - Association of Community Organization for Reform Now, ACORN is a typical National Socialist Movement, growing substantially under President Clinton in the 1990s.
111. Jack Chirac-President of France 1995-2007. I recognize the Soviet stooges by their deeds. Can you imagine how much harm Chirac had brought to France and to the world during twelve years of his presidency? He is currently stands trial on corruption charges,

Chapter 14: The Russians are Coming!

112. *Jerome R. Corsi* - a political commentator, conspiracy theorist, writer and researcher. He is well known for several bestsellers: *The Obama Nation, Unfit for Command*, and *Where's the Birth Certificate*
113. *Soul Alinsky* - The founder of modern community organizing and the author of the book *Rules for Radicals*, 330.

A Note of Sources

The main source of this book is my personal and professional experiences as a Soviet defense attorney for twenty-five years. Yet, I would have not been able to complete the book without works of other authors, who have researched the same subject. Their individual revelations have widened my horizon and brought unique additional information, their passionate voices organically intertwined into the conversation I have with a reader.

1. *How Mikhoels Had Been Killed*, by Gennadiy Kostyrchenko, War, Holocaust, and Stalinism.

A documented study of the Jewish Anti-Fascist Committee in the USSR.

2. *A Tale for Our Times*, by Gavin Gatenby, Deep Geopolitics, November 30, 2004.
3. The Columbia Encyclopedia, Second Edition.
4. "Don't Mess With Russia," *Economist*, December 16, 2006.
5. *Baltic Winds: Testimony of a Soviet Attorney*, by Simona Pipko, Xlibris, 2002.

6. *The Russian Factor: From Cold War to Global Terrorism*, by Simona Pipko, Xlibris, 2006.
7. *Mao: The Unknown Story*, by Jung Chang and Jon Holliday, Random House, 2005.
8. *Red Cocaine; The Drugging of America*, by Joseph D. Douglass Jr., Clarion House, 1990.
9. *The Kremlin's Killing Ways—A long Tradition Continues*, by Ion Mihai Pacepa, National Review Online, November 28, 2006.
10. *Ahmadinejad? Who's He?*—Iran's New President Has Mired in Controversy, Iran Focus Special Wire news, Tehran, June 25, 2005.
11. "Fire Primakov," *The Wall Street Journal*, March 12, 1998.
12. *Time's* Interview with Vladimir Putin, December, 2007.
13. The House of Representative Report—H. Rept.No.2430 on Katyn Massacre A Final Report of the 82d Congress of the United States No.2505, July 1952.
14. *The KGB*, by Stanislav Levchenko, The KGB's New Counterpoint7, No.2, Winter 1992.
15. *The Perestroika Deception*, by Anatoliy Golitsyn, Edward Harle Limited, 1995.
16. *Sabotage: America's Enemies Within the CIA*, by Roman Scarborough, Regnery Publishing Inc., 2007.
17. "The KGB's Man", by Ion Mihai Pacepa, *The Wall Street Journal*, September 22, 2003.
18. *Storming Las Vegas* by Jose Vigoa, Ballantine Books—New York, 2008.
19. *The Obama Nation*, by Gerome R. Corsi, PhD, Simon & Shuster, 2008.
20. *Russian Footprints*, by Ion Mihai Pacepa, National Review Online, August 24, 2008.
21. *Unprecedented Obama*, by Michael Obernford, RPA. Sunday, July 31, 2011.
22. *Soviet Socialism in the 21st Century* Part 1-XIX by Vera Berg,

GLOSSARY OF SOVIET/ RUSSIAN TERMS AND ACTIVITIES

1. *Propiska—a stamp in an internal passport, identifying a certain dwelling of the individual— city, street, the building number and the apartment number.*

2. *Soviet Passport—The implementation of the passport system was based on the law About the Issue of Passports to the USSR Citizens in the territory of the USSR of April 22, 1933. The document declared that all citizens at least sixteen years old residing in the cities, towns, as well as residing within one hundred kilometers of Moscow and Leningrad, within fifty kilometers of Kharkov, Kiev, Minsk, Rostov-on-Don and Vladivostok and within the hundred-kilometer zone along the Western border of the USSR were required to have a passport with propiska. Within these territories passports were the only valid personal identification document. It took several years to establish a nationwide database, but by 1937 all passports had a photo headshot of its owner.*

As you can see, Passports were introduced for urban residents only. It should be noted that according to the 1926 Soviet Census 82% of population in the Soviet Union was rural. Kolkhozniks—members of kolkhozes and individual peasants did not have passports and could not move into towns. It was a very shrewd law under Stalin's supervision. Though there were not any statutes forbidding freedom of movement in the Soviet Union, the combination of passport and propiska created the exact prevention of free movement in the country. The rural population was practically enslaved to work in highly unpopular Kolkhozes. The law had also created a conducive police-state environment to fight any dissident movements. Doesn't the brutality of Stalin's law against his own people remind you of Nazi Fascism

3. *Blat – "connections with reciprocal favors" – specifically, knowing someone who had access to goods. The word is a typical creation of the Soviet vocabulary, which is inextricably connected to the bad economic condition in the country. The constant shortages of food and the desire of people to feed their families formed and shaped a new social agreement or deal within the society. The condition has changed the moral environment in Russia, where a BRIBE has become a legitimate way of life. Blat has corrupted the entire ruling political elite, as well. Seventy Soviet years created this universal corruption from bottom to top and instituted lawlessness into Russian society.*

Bribes and a lawless behavior in connection with the Stalinist security apparatus constituted the Soviet Mafia, identified by Arkady Vaksberg. The current KGB government is a typical product of the Soviet Mafia, practicing the Stalinist ideology of Soviet Fascism.

4. *Stalinist Model - Dealing with the population in executing his power in the 1920s, Stalin designed a formula a model for substituting the result with the process. During his entire reign of power Stalin used two key concepts: promises and an indefinite time span to fulfill the promises. Using time, while promising "a bright future," private property was confiscated and nationalized throughout all eleven time zones. Stalin mesmerized and fooled a vast majority of the Soviet people by the process of promising. Impressed, they trusted him totally and never got a promised result. The formula was a significant part of Stalin's fraud and was easily transformed to political correctness in the 1930s. Look closely at the Obama administration, you will find a lot of similarity with the Stalinist model and political correctness.*

5. *Political Correctness - a permanent deceit, the game of words, a continuation of Stalinist Model or Formula and another fraud implemented by Stalin in the 1930s: Political Correctness is a*

Stalinist policy driven by the political agenda, a skillfully crafted design of essentially a system of lies and a long-term strategy of war against Western civilization and the creation of a One World Socialist Government. It was political correctness that forced the citizens of the Socialist countries to live Inside A Gigantic Network of Falsehood.

"In the early-to-mid 20th century, contemporary uses of the phrase "Politically Correct" were associated with the dogmatic application of Stalinist doctrine, debated between formal Communists (members of the Communist Party) and Socialists. The phrase was a colloquialism referring to the Communist party line, which provided for "correct" positions on many matters of politics." According to American educator Herbert Kohl writing about debates in New York in the late 1940s and early 1950s. I completely agree with this American educator.

Today, decades later, you can see how political correctness works in connection with Russia's geopolitical-chess game with the terror attacks in Paris, Beirut, and Mali. Watch Russian behavior. Russia is not interested in fighting ISIS, it is a Russian creation. The French President is a socialist, a person unaware of Soviet Fascism, so he is trying to involve Putin in the fight against ISIS. Putin will not effectively help, he wants and needs only to save Assad and infiltrate the Western coalition. A misperception will rise in the world, with an absence of political clarity, which will (as usual) allow Russia to use that unawareness to fish in the murky waters of world confusion, created by political correctness.

6. *Soviet Fascism - the ideology of Soviet Socialism invented and shaped by Stalin spread throughout the globe for the last 7-8 decades. Soviet Fascism is incorporated into the ideologies of different political groups, an amalgamation of Marxists, Communists, Socialists, Anarchists, Radical Islamists, and other left-wing groups around the globe, united under the Kremlin's umbrella to fight Western civilization.*

7. *Extremist Muslim Jihad - a violent mix of Soviet Fascism and Muslim Jihad, initiated and established by Stalin at the end of WWII. The end of WWII brought a notorious Muslim Brotherhood member from Berlin to Moscow. This was the time when Stalin's*

old idea of infiltrating Islam came true. As we know today "the Soviet Union hastened to set up points of liaison in the East; and in so doing, Stalin, just before his death, invited Amin al-Husseini (d. 1973), the Mufti of Jerusalem and friend of Hitler, to Moscow."[2] Adding the description of the Muslim Brotherhood Part 1: The Genesis of Euro-Islamic Racism by Hans-Peter Raddatz

Since than Islam has been infiltrated, politicized, and equipped with the Soviet long-term strategy of a war against Western civilization. The Muslim Brotherhood was established as an Islamic Politburo, it was the beginning of Extreme Muslim Jihad. Arafat was the first leader molded in the Soviet Union; you know the result. The logical chain in space and time is bringing you to other terrorist groups: Hamas, Hezbollah, Al-Qaeda, many other names under the Soviet supervision, and finally to ISIS, which required a special research.

8. *ISIS - final creation of the Russian Stalinist Intel in 2009-2010. The foundation of the terrorist state is its leadership. The field commanders of ISIS consist of many former Soviet trained operatives: They are former Sunni Saddam Hussein's secret service members, trained by the Soviets, former Soviet citizens from the Muslim republics (Turkmens, Chechens, and others), who were trained by Russian Intel. Like Hamas and Hezbollah, they all have an immediate connections with Russian military and intelligence. When you are talking about the solidarity of these dictators, it is the same solidarity of the current terrorist groups and ISIS leadership with Moscow. There is no surprise for me about a very effective ISIS propaganda online—the Soviet actors of 1970-80s have returned to their dirty profession in ISIS.*

And like in the time of the Soviet Union, oil is playing a significant role. Neither al-Qaeda nor Boko Haram had a constant source of income to manage terrorist activities. ISIS has a huge arsenal of oil and enough territory for the training terrorist camps and centers. As my book has already been completed, I'd like to remind you here about my knowledge of terrorist activity. In one of my books, I told about the conversation with a client of mine in the past. It was in the late 1960s or in the beginning of the 1970s. The man visited my office before returning to Syria, where he worked as an instructor in the Soviet terrorist training camp. Has anything changed in Russia since? No.

A special information on ISIS by a Soviet military expert, living in the U.S, Mark Shteinberg:

The Islamic State we called ISIS or ISIL is well organized socially and has quite educated military and intelligent leadership. After the defeat of Saddam Hussein, the Iraqi army was dismantled: hundreds of officers and many Sunni Generals were left without means of existence. The al-Maliki Iraqi government employed only the Shiites, leaving the huge Sunni military throng unemployed. They constituted *The Insurgency,* the heart of the leadership structure in the Islamic State today.

They all got their education in Soviet military institutions, some speak Russian. Do not be surprised by the military success of ISIS, the military leadership is highly educated in the Soviet Military Colleges and Academia. Like in the Soviet territory, the military field in ISIS is divided into two Filaret and small mobile groups.

Speaking Russian, Mark Shteinberg named some Generals and Colonels of the military and Intel leadership in ISIS. I'll give you their names, but I can't guarantee a correct spelling: Mohamed Dulliny, Turkish men, al-Suleiman, and other. As a matter of fact on the border with Turkey, ISIS has a caveat of ethnic Turkish people. Two of the men from this area are ISIS military leaders in Syria and Iraq today. I have warned the West for the last twenty years about the real threat—Soviet Fascism, disseminated by Russia across the world. We are witnessing globally the clear symptoms of this dreadful ideology. As you know several Sunni Generals from Saddam's security apparatus had been trained in Russia. They still have direct contacts with Russian military and Intel. Recent information disclosed what that connection has meant in terms of WMD.

It has been reported ISIS is now in possession of 40 KG (188 pounds) of nuclear material that they took from Mosul University. The Guardian newspaper of Sunday July 13, 2014 in the article *The Mosul Mystery: The Missing Uranium and where it came from* states that the 40 kg of nuclear material is thought to be low grade, consisting of uranyl acetate, yellowcake, ammonium diuranate, uranium trioxide, and possibly gram-quantities of uranium tetrachloride. But, what if they were wrong?

In his February 22 radio broadcast Mark Shteinberg reported that Russia had built highly-explosive nuclear devices—portable nuclear charges or cartridges or bombs 40 kg. each, which could be placed at a target and blown up there. Russia had 8-9 such portable nuclear devices in the 1990s. President Yeltsin ordered the inventory of nuclear weaponry to be carried out by the Chairman of Russian Security forces, General Alexander Lebed. General Lebed found that three nuclear charges had disappeared from Russia. It happened in the 1990s.

As we know the history of those years, the KGB and other communists in Russia did not like Genera Lebed and his discovery during the inventory. General Lebed was later assassinated by the KGB. Mark Shteiberg further states that Saddam bought three portable nuclear devices from "Russians" in the 1990s. The material held by ISIS was transferred to them by former Sunni Generals from Saddam's security apparatus that are now field commanders for ISIS.

These devices are far more dangerous than the low grade material now assumed to be their hands. The danger was underlined by Bennett Seftel of the Center for Strategic and International Studies at the August 2014 Project On Nuclear Issues (PONI) Fall Conference. In his presentation, *Al Qaeda's Nuclear Quest* he gives a history of Al Qaeda's terrorist track and early nuclear efforts, and states that in 2003 the US picked up an Al Qaeda message regarding plans to obtain three stolen Russian nuclear devices! Mr. Shteinberg gives us the link between those plans and the devices in ISIS hands today. Very chilling information.

In the same broadcast, Mark pointed out something very treacherous that is happening in Russia. He spoke of a break down inside the FSB, (the former KGB) and between FSB and the Russian military. As a result of that something strange has occurred: Two well- known Russian Generals have committed suicide, shooting themselves, another General hanged himself, and two other Generals died not by natural causes. The subject of disagreement could be the pro-Putin leader of Chechnya, Ramzan Kadyrov—a real criminal and fascist. He promises to quit at end of term. The next election is on April 5, 2016. After the murder of my friend Boris Nemtsov, this series of deaths reminds us all of Stalin's assassinations when fighting political opponents. Nothing seems ever to change in Russia, does it? I have written about the different methods of assassinations employed by the Soviet/ Russian regime for the last 20 years. You can dig deeper into this in my book *What is Happening to America?* Pp. 133-144.

The confirmation of my efforts regarding ISIS and some ideas just came from a German journalist Jürgen Todenhoefer, who visited ISIS for several weeks and published a book Inside ISIS. Here is the confirmation: *Author's journey inside ISIS: They're 'more dangerous than people realize'* **Frederik Pleitgen, CNN** Updated 9:58 AM ET, Sun January 4, 2015

Yes, they are extremely dangerous, because behind all terrorist groups stands Russia, the notorious KGB and its twin- brother German Stasi. Knowledge of Soviet Fascism is a MUST for Western civilization to survive. You are now watching Russia destabilize the world by playing the game and faking the history in the 21st century. Look at how Russia seduces Extreme Muslim Jihad by the memory of the Caliphate—their past Glory in Islamic history…

Tectonic Weaponry – Wikipedia says the following - A tectonic weapon is a hypothetical device or system which could create earthquakes, volcanoes, or similar events in specified locations by interference with the earth's geological processes. It was defined in 1992 by Aleksey Vsevolovidich Nikolayev, corresponding member Russian Academy of Sciences: "A tectonic or seismic weapon would be the use of the accumulated tectonic energy of the Earth's deeper layers to induce a destructive earthquake".

My editor, an electrical engineer by training, took a special interest in this aspect of the book and did some research of his own into the phenomena that could produce such a weapon and found the following:

The following information was put online by Tom Bearden, Ph.D., LTC U.S. Army (Retired) illuminating the subject further:

On April 28, 1997 U.S. Defense Secretary William Cohen made the following statement:

> *"Others [terrorists] are engaging even in an eco-type of terrorism whereby they can alter the climate, set off earthquakes, volcanoes remotely through the use of electromagnetic waves… So there are plenty of ingenious minds out there that are at work finding ways in which they can wreak terror upon other nations… It's real, and that's the reason why we have to intensify our [counterterrorism] efforts."*

Secretary of Defense William Cohen at an April 1997 counterterrorism conference sponsored by former Senator Sam Nunn. Quoted from DoD News Briefing, Secretary of Defense William S. Cohen, Q&A at the Conference on Terrorism, Weapons of Mass Destruction, and U.S. Strategy, University of Georgia, Athens, Apr. 28, 1997.

Note that the Secretary did not speak the words in square blocks; these were added by the writers later, probably to "soften the tone" of the Secretary's information release. So the Secretary confirmed that some nations of the world — not just some ragged terrorists, as the writers tried to imply for spin control — do possess novel electromagnetic weapons and are using them to induce earthquakes, engineer the weather and climate, and trigger volcanic eruptions.

In Russia, these weapons are totally under the control of the KGB, including research, development, manufacturing, deployment, and manning and firing the weapons. The weapons are not in the conventional Russian armed forces at all.

The weapons referred to by Secretary Cohen are longitudinal EM wave interferometers (LWIs). Longitudinal EM waves easily travel through the ocean and earth with very little loss. In a distant interference zone, there appears real EM energy again, of the kind we have in our textbooks. However, the energy arises from space- time itself in the interference zone, as proven by M.W. Evans, P.K. Anastasovski, T.E. Bearden et al., "*On Whittaker's Representation of the Electromagnetic Entity in Vacuo: The Production of Transverse Fields and Energy by Scalar Interferometry*," Journal of New Energy, 4(3), Winter 1999, p. 76-78. (That entire issue of JNE contains some 60 papers by the Alpha Foundation's Institute for Advanced Study (AIAS), dealing with the kind of higher symmetry electrodynamics needed to understand such weapons).

Though tested in prototype in the 1950s, the first strategic LWIs were deployed in Russia in April 1963, and were used to kill the U.S.S. Thresher nuclear attack submarine, underwater off the East coast of the United States, in April 1963. The signatures of the kill are 100% decisive. One day later, the same weapon placed an enormous electromagnetic burst (explosion) deep underwater, 100 miles north of Puerto Rico. From the surface of the ocean there arose a giant cone of water, rising a half mile into the air, turning into a mushroom, and falling back into the sea. This was the second test of the new Russian strategic LWIs, under KGB control. By this test and the fact that the West did not even recognize what killed the Thresher, Khrushchev managed to stay in power another two years or so, after his Cuban Crisis fiasco where he lost face in front of the entire world.

World-wide weather engineering started in earnest by the Russians on July 4, 1976 — as a quirky sense of humor and "bicentennial gift" to the United States.

The weapons have been used to shoot down aircraft, etc. worldwide also, mostly as tests, and have also destroyed ICBMs shortly after launch. Aircraft shot down included the TWA-800, e.g. and others.

The world is actually a secretly armed camp, armed to the teeth with unpublicized highly secret weapons, waiting to explode like a powder keg at the touch of a match. These developments have eluded most of the scientific communities of the Earth (who are still mostly using a decrepit, hoary old U (1) electromagnetics theory put together in 1864, which is totally a material fluid flow theory and riddled with known errors, omissions, and curtailments). The developments over several decades also completely eluded the news media of the world, who are more concerned these days with yellow journalism than probing and investigating news. As an example, not a single news agency even reacted to the astounding revelation of Secretary Cohen, which merely shows how well the news media have brainwashed themselves with their own "formula news" and propaganda.

What is being prepared worldwide is a "mix" of all sorts of weapons and attacks — everything from terrorists armed with incredibly developed pathogens and already inserted in various nations, etc. — worldwide. Every major nation is also already "seeded" with clandestine nuclear weapons placed in its large cities, ready to annihilate them. E.g., the highest ranking GRU defector to the U.S. is Lunev. In his book (passed by the CIA), Lunev even tells some of the ways that the Russians secretly brought such nuclear weapons into the United States, easily. Quoting Stanislav Lunev and Ira Winkler, *Through the Eyes of the Enemy: Russia's Highest Ranking Military Defector Reveals Why Russia Is More Dangerous Than Ever*, Regnery, Washington, D.C., 1998, p. 22:

> *"Though most Americans don't realize it, America is already penetrated by Russian military intelligence to the extent that arms caches lie in wait for use by Russian special forces — or* Speznaz."

Quoting p. 26:

> *"It is surprisingly easy to smuggle nuclear weapons into the United States. A commonly used method is for a Russian airplane to fly across the ocean on a typical reconnaissance flight. The planes will be tracked by U.S. radar, but that's not a problem. When there are no other aircraft in visual range, the Russian airplane will launch a small, high-tech, stealth transport missile that can slip undetected into remote areas of the country. The missiles are retrieved by GRU operatives. Another way to get a weapon into the country is to have an 'oceanographic research' submarine deliver the device—accompanied by GRU specialists—to a remote section of coastline. Nuclear devices can also be slipped across the Mexican or Canadian borders. It is easy to get a bomb to Cuba and from there transport it to Mexico. Usually the devices are carried by a Russian intelligence officer or a trusted agent."*

Quoting p. 30:

> *"Other instruments of destruction the Russians have had success with are seismic weapons. Spitac and other small towns in the Transcaucasus Mountains were almost destroyed during a seismic weapons test that set off an earthquake. This would have obvious applications on America's west coast and other areas of the world prone to earthquakes."*

As you can see from the latter quotation, Lunev was actually referring to the LWIs and their use to initiate earthquakes, precisely what Secretary Cohen confirmed in 1997. Again, the news media are completely asleep.

PART II

Socialism/Communism: The Enemy of Mankind

Articles Written 2018 - 2022

2008
K150
MALAWI

CHAPTER 15

The Ideological Battlefield in Washington D.C.

May 27, 2018

The term "the Soviets" correctly exists today—the Soviets materialized Socialism for the first time in history. To understand today Stalinist Socialism, you have to know how Stalin built the first Soviet Socialist State. I dedicated this topic to four books and over eighty columns. Please read *Socialist Lies, Chapter: The Soviets* to understand the significance of the term. It was a beginning of the colossal global ideological fraud . . .

In short, Stalinism was a bloody, compulsive and forceful way directed against the will of Russia people with the main activities and help of the police—the KGB. By preaching Marxist slogans, Stalin actually implemented system of Stalinism, using his own arsenal of lies, deception, fraud, and obfuscations, making a system of incredible corruption. Moreover, the system was spread throughout the globe, bringing millions of deaths and injuries to populations, destroying and harming the land of all inhabited continents . . . Perhaps, this is the reason, I named Stalinism—Soviet Fascism.

Today the media uses with ease the terms socialism, communism, and Marxist ideology, they have become popular topics for discussion on radio, TV, and the internet without awareness of reality. Their words are often misleading, and to really understand socialism, you must have lived through it. I am a survivor of Stalinist Socialism and I know what it truly means. To prove it, I'll give you only one feature of Stalin's Socialism to grasp the reality, and it is not Gulag, Great Purges or Show Trials, you have already heard about. I'll give you the picture of real human disaster of life under Stalinism.

The Face of Stalinist Socialism—A Communal Apartment

I got married and moved to Estonia, my entire life since childhood had taken place in a communal apartment (*kommunalka)* first in Moscow and then in Leningrad. It was the very famous Pertsov's building, biggest in Leningrad, if I am not mistaken, 10,000 people lived there. Pertsov was a successful Russian businessman dealing with railroad transportation, particularly with the first Russian railroad from St. Petersburg to Moscow. It was the famous Imperial Government of Russia Nicolas Railroad built in 1869 in honor of Czar Nicolas I. After the 1917 Socialist Revolution all Real Estate of the country, including the Pertsov's building was confiscated and nationalized, thus becoming the property of the State.

As thousands of 2 to 7 room apartments had become property of the government, they were remade to be communal ones, where each family received one room. My family got a room in the apartment on the second floor. Although it was a pretty big room, there was not enough light—the only window at the corner, looked out at the building's wall. We had to have electrical lights on all the time. There were seven families in the apartment, which had one kitchen, one bathroom, one lavatory next to the kitchen. Can you imagine what was going on at seven o'clock in the morning in our apartment??? A long corridor had never been empty—each family had the right to locate some old items and boxes with laundry next to a door off their room.

The kitchen was big and comprised of seven tables with seven *kerosinka* (an oil or paraffin-stove), one on each table. We had a table with our own *kerosinka* to cook. The women in the apartment were spending hours in the kitchen preparing the meals for the family. Our kitchen became the place to socialize and exchange the views. The big kitchen also had a back door to take the garbage out. All the neighbors threw their garbage down stairs to the back yard, where the big wooden boxes were constructed for garbage. I am talking about the time of the 1950s.

If you are a woman and have some imaginations, you can perceive the life of a Soviet women for all 24/7, let alone the empty shelfs in the supermarket, and limited incomes to buy food in a farmer's market. It was hard life for everybody in the Soviet Union, especially for the women. Suddenly we got interesting news. In late 1958, the Soviet Union and the United States agreed to set up national exhibitions in each other's nation as part of their new emphasis on cultural exchanges. Vice President Nixon was bringing a model of the modern American kitchen to Moscow . . . Now you can't imagine what happened in each communal apartment behind the Iron Curtin . . . The American kitchen in Moscow!?

The apartments with an individual kitchen had been a rarity in the country, only 3–5 percent of the population had them—the Communist leaders. The rest had lived in communal apartments in a country spread across eleven time zones. After hearing the news over the radio, the entire female part of the country wanted desperately to see the American kitchen. The air and soil behind the Iron Curtin were boiling and buzzing by women's whisperings, desires, and preparations. There were no barriers the women couldn't overcome to go to Moscow to see the American kitchen. Women and men traveled by horses, by the contingent trucks, by ships, by trains, often walking miles to get some means of transportations, in the country of eleven time zones.

The men were also concerned, especially the men in power, the Communists, they had never seen such active women's movement. The exhibition of the American kitchen had occupied the minds of the population and the KGB had not been ready to react adequately. The significance of the event, had scared them, they had known about a desperate housing situation in the country and did not know how to respond to "capitalist propaganda." "During the grand opening ceremony of the American National Exhibition in Moscow, Vice President Richard Nixon and Soviet leader Nikita Khrushchev engage in a heated debate about capitalism and communism in the middle of a model kitchen set up for the fair. The so-called "kitchen debate" became one of the most famous episodes of the Cold War."

In front of an army of reporters and photographers who followed them around, Nixon and Khrushchev continued their argument in the kitchen of a model home built in the exhibition: "For a few moments, in the confines of a "modern" kitchen, the diplomatic gloves had come off and America and the Soviet Union had verbally jousted over which system was superior—communism or capitalism." The KGB and all Communists hated Nixon, because they were helpless, being exposed by the presence of the American kitchen . . . Yet, the enemies of democracy have a long memory and use it when the circumstances presented them the opportunity . . .

I have visited this exhibition, met a lot of women, talked to them and I know the dramatic effect of the American individual kitchen on the Soviet human mind in 1959. The KGB also recognized the dramatic effect the Soviet people had experienced and they used the opportunity of revenge to Nixon in the 1970s. It is a huge story that requires a different column to tell you how the KGB organized the Watergate and ousted President Nixon with the help of some Democrats. Ironically, history repeats itself and we are dealing with the same KGB and the same set of techniques today, fifty years later. Now the KGB works with the entire Democrat Party against President Trump, confronting his family and the people working for him. You are witnessing this every day, yet you don't know who is really behind anti-Trump campaign . . . Stay tuned . . .

A Hundred Years War: Communism vs. Capitalism

If you read documents about the famous "kitchen debate," you will have the big picture arguments about Capitalism and Communism, which in fact continues between America and Russia today, in 2018. It is an "epidemic of disinformation" produced by Russia today, using the old Stalinist arsenal of lies, fraud, deceptions, and obfuscations to fool and deceive you. Writing for the last thirty years and giving you a detailed anatomy of this war, I was calling it the asymmetrical war against capitalism and Western civilization. Actually, it is the same war against the Truth, waged by the Russian Intel against the Republicans fifty years later.

Knowledge is Power—Richard Nixon had known the Truth of the housing disaster in Russia. He had exposed the biggest problem of a totalitarian State—misery conditions and quality of life under Stalinist Communism/Socialism. . . . "The communal apartment became the predominant form of housing in the USSR for generations, and examples still exist in "the most fashionable central districts of large Russian cities." *Wikipedia*

Telling the truth is a powerful method to expose the "epidemic of disinformation" that has continued since the victory of 1917 Socialist Revolution in Russia. Knowledge is the best disinfector! Do you remember who help Stalin to maintain his Socialism? The carrier of this epidemic had been then and still is the Russian Intel, which I have written about for thirty years. To be precise—the KGB (currently Putin's FSB) and GRU with Stalin's skillful propaganda techniques. President Nixon had known the true Housing disaster in Russia. His courageous actions cost him the presidency. The enemy of America had prearranged, connived and manufactured the activities against him with the help of some Democrats. It was open season on the Republicans and they had not defended their President—they surrendered. They did not know about a deep infiltration of the Soviets into our political system, and they have never heard about the ideology of Soviet fascism . . .

Fifty years later we see something very similar to the past: the attempt to oust another American President—Donald J. Trump. The predicament in America is even worse today, due to erroneous American foreign policy, especially during the last thirty years. Up to now, America is still unaware of the ideology of Soviet fascism, which to survive will never stop fighting successful capitalism. The last thirty years have given Soviet fascism the time and opportunity to enhance Russian military and its intelligence apparatus to continue its expansion to the world. Today we have a global political forces confronting a sitting American President . . .

Soviet fascism is an International Scam to fight the American political system designed and left to us by our Founding Fathers. The rule of Law is a determining factor in American exceptionalism and the agenda of Soviet fascism was and is trying to delegitimize our political system by infiltrating it and destroy it from within. The Soviet infiltration started with the socialist-professors, camouflaging Socialism by inculcated our youth and teaching a cosmetic version in the Colleges and Universities since the 1950s. The infiltration was spread into other areas of social activities: Academia, Media, Sport, our security agencies, and so on. I dedicated many pages of my books to Russian Intelligence institutions to inform you about them. Just read my latest columns to know the KGB Chairman Yuri Andropov and his *Operation Barbarossa* against America.

The war against the American system of government is in its apogee today to oust American President Donald J. Trump for a very simple reason—he plans *To Make America Great Again.* The negative politics derived from this war, from two distinct philosophies of Evil in the world and it is the major political distinction between the Republican and Democrat Parties. For many decades the Democrats have been soft on the Soviets—history records it. The last three decades they were appeasing Russia and its satellites North Korea, Iran, Hamas and Hezbollah in the Middle East becoming the real Soviet Socialists. They are using all Stalin's political methods and imitating the issues of opposition to fool and deceive you, like Stalin taught them in his Doctrine of Political Correctness. I recognized consistent patterns of Soviet fascism, its deliberate propaganda and rhetorical spins in defense of Obama used by the Democrats.

Republicans have a completely different philosophy and approach to this Evil–peace through strength: the policy of Presidents Ronald Reagan and Donald J. Trump has testified to that. Rush Limbaugh is the smartest and savviest man in the world after Winston Churchill: he defines the Democrats as Socialists on his show every day and doing that brilliantly. I can't compete with him. He is right, yet, I am analyzing politics due to my own experiences: The Democrat leaders, working with the KGB for decades, have inherited the Evil ideology of Soviet fascism and are trying to implement it in our country today. I catalogued it in my book: *Socialist Lies: From Stalin to the Clintons, Obamas, and Sanders*, XLIBRIS, 2016

Yes, Soviet fascism is the Evil ideology spread throughout the world. It is confirmed that Russia launched missiles and brought down Malaysian plane MH-17, killing 298 victims—there is no respect for human life in Russia. People who adhered to this Evil ideology have assassinated human beings with Polonium-210 and other nuclear agents in England, the moto is to assassinate the opposition leaders by all means possible to implement the ideology of Soviet fascism and *One World Socialist Government under Kremlin's rule.* If you still unaware of the ideology of Soviet fascism, to convince you, I'll try to address the topics discussed by all media outlets today to show you a predominant subject:

1. North Korea, a Stalinist State, was founded personally by Stalin. North Korea is holding its twenty-five million inhabitants in Gulag conditions. Both the Gulag and North Korea are the production of Soviet fascism. Though the Summit in Singapore

has been canceled, I have a warning to President Trump: the security apparatus of North Korea is inextricably tied to Putin's Intel, therefore we can expect provocations and fabrications, complaints, blame, protests, and delays to slow expectations and deprive President Trump of clear victory. Besides, China has a tremendous fear of a unified Korea. So, ahead of us lays a long diplomatic choreography with so-called Communist/Socialist camp. Yet, the Summit will take place—Trump has a new strategic thinking to prevent the war . . .

2. Iran is also a satellite state built by Putin's Intel for the last three decades. Remember: Putin is a devoted disciple of Yuri Andropov and Stalin. The agenda of invasion of Iran was started by Stalin and was completed by Andropov in cahoots with Ahmadinejad. Their collaboration ousted the Shah of Iran in the 1979 Revolution and built the Revolutionary Guard and Quds Force imitating the KGB structure. If you know the last two, you can also understand the inextricable ties of Iran to Russia. For your information, it was Putin, who designed *Iran Nuclear Deal* and got a chunk of our money. The same hostile-to-America country is Socialist Venezuela, built by Soviet fascism. People are dying from hunger there. Read about Stalin, Andropov's *Operation Barbarossa*, Iran and Venezuela in my books and latest columns.

3. Shooting in the American Schools is also a continuation of the asymmetrical war waged by Soviet fascism. I have been writing about the shooting in our schools since Columbine. It was the first then in 1999. I was stunned by the failure of the FBI and local police to investigate the case with the consideration and knowledge of Soviet Fascism. I have written about this failure consequently in my two books: *The Russian Factor*, XLIBRIS, 2006 and *What is Happening to America?* XLIBRIS, 2012, *Chapter 7, WWIII: Recruitments and Drugs, Infiltration and Assassinations*. The absence of response from the FBI, drove me to address the Soviet crime again in my column, describing "the Soviet Medicine." The shooting in the schools will continue until the ideology of Soviet Fascism is learned.

4. The MS-13 gangs. I've lived in New York City for many years. Long Island was the most peaceful part of the city, while Republicans ran it. Everything has changed when the Democrats Barack Obama became President and Bill de Blasio mayor of New York City. As my main issue is American National Security, I am sure that the MS-13 gangs are the continuation of Andropov's *Operation Barbarossa* in the asymmetrical war against America and the Republican Party. MS-13 encompasses all crimes committed by the Soviets in 1950-1990: human trafficking, cruelty in killing, drug trafficking, and so on.

Soviet fascism has no nationality or race, the unhuman brutality and nefarious nature of the gangs indicates the Evil ideology of Soviet fascism. I have been writing about the Democrat's collaboration with the KGB since 2008, pp. 337-338, *What is Happening to America?* You can read about the Obama/Putin Alliance in my columns as well. The Obama/ Putin Alliance I called sometimes the Obama/Putin Joint Venture, but the essence of the conspiracy and its reprehensible, evil agenda is still there. A treacherous conspiracy from within caused deaths of thousands of young boys and girls in uniform and a great deal of wealth to the United States of America.

The Ideological Battlefield in Washington D.C.

We are dealing today with "the criminal Deep State," espionage and treason, I have been writing about this for many years. Therefore, knowledge of the enemy is a MUST. To learn how much the Soviets/ Russian "have achieved," you have to start with the famous Soviet document dated a year 1955. The document is the factual act of war, unknown to the FBI and to the vast majority of Americans. My books and columns will help you to learn, too. But the information about both is suppressed by the FBI to deprive you the real knowledge of the enemy—FBI submitted my name to the FISA court to have a probable cause to block information about my writings in 2002. It was done by the Democrat Party in power, the way they demolished the Russian Studies in many Universities, the field of Sovietology and Kremlinology to suppress the Truth.

Today we have a paradox of incompetence in Washington D.C. The rank-and-file Democrats are not familiar with the information in my books and columns—they are fooled and deceived by a group called by Judge Pirro a "criminal cabal." I like this term. To your surprise, the Republicans are not well informed either. And all those people have the audacity to talk about Russia every day! This paradox of incompetence allowed "a criminal cabal" in cahoots with Putin's KGB to successfully go fishing in the murky waters of the DC Swamp. Of course, it was a spy program for information from Trump's team, the same way Putin's KGB has used the unmasked name of Americans and information, trying to recruit them: Andropov's teachings . . .

In fact, the anti-Trump Investigation is a cover-up of Obama's and DNC's crimes committed during many years collaborating with Putin' KGB. Obama weaponized our entire security apparatus CIA, FBI, DOJ, to fabricate Trump's crime. It was triggered by the KGB production of a fake Dossier. Then investigation had become a perjury trap to convict President Trump for crime committed by the Democrats a typical injustice of Soviet fascism. Do you have an idea about the force running "a criminal cabal?" Yes, Vladimir Putin and his KGB in collaboration with the Democrat Party. Actually, the fate of the Democrat Party is at stake and some Democrats knowing that will defend Obama by all means possible, by hook or by crook, with rhetorical spins taught by Stalin. Just watch them!

Former Federal Prosecutor Joe Genova told The Daily Caller, "There are agents all over the country who love the bureau and are sickened by Comey's behavior and McCabe and Holder and Lynch and thugs like Brennan-who despise the fact that the bureau was used as a tool of political intelligence by the Obama administration thugs." Knowing Andropov's design against America, I would suggest to look for the members of family working in CIA, FBI, DOJ—Andropov liked to use family. I would also add several more names to the list: Bill Clinton, Terry McAuliffe, Barack Obama, and all people of Clinton's Mafia, if you read my books and know them . . .

America has two types of people committing betrayals: those who do not like the system established by our Founding Fathers and trying to transform it—they are currently collaborating with the KGB to destroy America the Beautiful, and those politicians who haven't a clue about the KGB infiltrations, hence becoming their accomplices. Current security people won't be able to identify them without reading my books and columns. One thing history as taught us that we cannot let up until the enemy is completely defeated. It is especially important in the day of memory for our soldiers who did not return home.

Good luck America!

CHAPTER 16

The Gripping Control of Soviet Fascism on the Democrat Party

June 12, 2019

Anatomy of the Treason

Knowledge comes with life and years of experience. It was not enough for me to know Soviet Socialism and rename it what it is, Soviet Fascism. Listening to Nancy Pelosi's press conference on May 23, 2019, I realized that Soviet Fascism has not only come to my America the Beautiful, but it deeply rooted within the leadership of the Democrats' Socialist mafia. Pelosi accused President Trump of being engaged in "cover-ups." I couldn't believe how fast my prediction had come to political reality by the traitors in the Democrats' leadership. Three days prior to Pelosi's accusation of Trump's "cover-ups," I published a column with these words: To save their skin, the Democrats are using Stalin's teaching—"Offence is the best defense, never admit the crime committed, *but accuse the opposition of that exact crime*." Pelosi just exhibited Stalin's teaching in her presser.

Many are right to call the Democrats in the House of Representatives—Socialist Lawmakers. I would specify and call them—Socialist mafia members using abusive investigative overreach against their political opposition, resembling activity of the KGB. There is no possibility to repeat friendly collaboration like under Reagan. The Democrats have fundamentally changed. I have been analyzing the changes within the Democrats for several decades, talking about the KGB's political-operatives working within the Democrat Party nationwide, infiltrating, and corrupting all major government institutions. Look at the state of Virginia, where three top Democrats are in deep scandals. This is also no coincidence. A former Governor, Terry McAuliffe was Bill Clinton's lieutenant, and I suspect a leader of the Socialist mafia, forcing the entire state to adopt the ideology of Soviet Fascism. He was working with FBI's corrupt Andrew McCabe to manufacture a protest by white supremacists at a rally in Charlottesville, Virginia. I am not sure that the connection was known. The case was investigated and two trivial actors convicted. The names of Terry McAuliffe and Andrew McCabe were left in the dark . . .

It is also not a coincidence that 43% of Americans and 57% of Democrats prefer Socialism. The inculcation of "cosmetic Socialism" has been going on for decades. Therefore, our political predicament in the US is extra complicated—we have overseas rival-actors running and coordinating activities of the Democrat Party for the last several decades. They are the carriers of the ideology of Soviet Fascism. This is the crux of the matter—we are dealing with an adversarial ideological force within, whose agenda is total destruction of the American Republic. You saw this gradual destruction during Barack Obama's disastrous regime, but you couldn't see the enormous extent of harm, but we will find it out in the future. President Trump stopped that destruction and to some degree reversed it. Yet, I know the rival-actors, they will never halt doing damage and harm to us—we have an obligation—knowledge of our enemy is a must.

It is not a coincidence that Russia is in the center of recent events, the paradox is that only a few know the real Russia and its security apparatus. It is for that reason that my latest 20-25 columns have revealed the real face of the KGB, as a global terrorist agency. Nothing has changed in Russia and I am using the term KGB, uniting the images of all Russian agencies—as the term is familiar to Americans. AG Barr performing the real investigation on origins of Russia probe and the crime committed against the American Republic should evaluate this international ideological force, invading, and damaging our national security, economy, and our value system. In my opinion, we are dealing with the united force of the KGB in cahoots with the leadership of the Democrat Party—they are executing an evil international espionage operation against the American Republic. The Russia probe was only a part of it, the industry of treason is much wider . . . In his statement on May 29, 2019, Robert Mueller confirmed my view. Be ready for Anti-Trump Fishing Expedition No. 2, performed by the Socialist mafia goons in the House of Representatives.

Fascism Never Sleeps

There was plenty of sufficient evidence for Robert Mueller to investigate the industry of treason, if he knew Russia and its ideology of Soviet Fascism. Unfortunately, he didn't. As a devoted disciple of Stalin and Andropov, Putin has continued an expansionist policy of Soviet Fascism even with bigger parameters. That same Russian policy forced on Venezuela was expended in Iran, Syria, Afghanistan, and the Middle East as a whole. The agenda stays the same, left by Stalin and Andropov—a *War Against Western Civilization*, capitalism, and our value system by all means, methods, and tricks possible. We have been dealing with a [known to me] KGB *Disinformation Campaign* responsible for holding us hostage with a fraudulent KGB-produced Trump/Dossier for three years. It is a very sophisticated KGB international operation, involving different countries, against the American president and against the American Republic. We have been so penetrated by Socialist operatives that even the top of our Intel has participated in the operation!!

Yes, the agenda stays the same, left by Stalin and Andropov—a war against Western civilization and capitalism by all means, methods, and tricks possible. The KGB is first and foremost a terrorist agency, I have evidence to call them that—the story of the Olympics in Russia in 1980. Haven't you noticed a lot of severe extreme weather, massive storms, and tornadoes, and constant ecological disaster, not in Russia, but in the outside world and America? I've been familiar with the hoax of "climate change" since 1980. Here is a quotation from my book *Socialist Lies, Xlibris, 2016, p. 59*:

> "I can add an example of how the Soviet Mafia uses natural forces for its own purposes. On the day the Olympic Games opened in 1980, the sky over Moscow was covered with heavy clouds. A member of the Politburo called the KGB. By the time the opening got underway,

> the sun was shining and the sky over Moscow was blue. As I found out later, KGB scientists used an extremely powerful mega-laser to disperse clouds. In the same way, they also could create rain and storms. "Conquering nature" is the creed and agenda of the Soviet Mafia. Stalin's experiments inside the Soviet Union cost the country billions, destroyed the natural ecology, and killed millions. Now the Soviet Mafia is destroying countries around the globe. I would suggest our American scientists research the nature of the recent tornadoes and flooding in America keeping an open mind to the possibility of human intervention."

Knowing the regime's political agenda and strategy and its technological ability to mimic the nature, I was very attentive to natural disasters in the world when I came to America. That menacing Fascist regime has one desire—to destroy as much as possible and to kill as many human beings as much as possible. Fascism is fascism and that political agenda is the Must for the KGB . . . Aware of that, my first suspicious were the repeated eruptions of volcanoes—a small nuclear device can provoke this . . . If I had doubts about earthquake in Indonesia, I did not have doubts when the disaster happened in Japan, the Pacific 3/11/2011, an earthquake in Fukushima with several aftershocks after a huge catastrophic tsunami . . . I like Japanese people—Putin mortally hates Japan . . .

"Following a major earthquake, a 15-metre tsunami disabled the power supply and cooling of three Fukushima Daiichi reactors, causing a nuclear accident on 11 March 2011," according to the World Nuclear Association. As I understood, the tsunami is a major factor to watch and a future possibility for use by the KGB's Technological Department. Then, a couple of days ago, I found an interesting quotation by a Russian specialist about tsunami in America:

> "For big earthquakes, the tsunami is going to be the big destructive factor," said Vasily Titov, director of the National Oceanic and Atmospheric Administration's Center for Tsunami Research in Seattle, Washington. "But if the nation is prepared, warning and education

> definitely saves lives. Compare the human lives lost in Sumatra and Japan. It's about 10 times less." Think about it. Haven't you noticed a lot of severe weather, massive storms, extreme flooding, and tornadoes, constant disaster in America? Last week a monster tornado has ripped 20-mile trail of destruction through the Missouri capital. It was almost a mile wide. This week a devastating tornado, severe flooding in Oklahoma, and other devastation across Ohio, Arkansas as the center of the country grapples with aftermath of 200+ tornadoes. Maybe that special international espionage operation against the American Republic is even bigger than I suspected?

There is a spectacular ignorance pertaining Socialism in America—people do not understand basic civics. Socialism is a system of a big, centralized government within a mafia-like police state, which runs all means of production, and assumes absolute control of the people, and all methods of productivity. There are no freedoms, no personal liberty, nor First Amendment rights. I can testify that in any courts, because I lived half of my life under real Socialism. Tom Palmer, in *The Morality of Capitalism*, proves that Capitalism is beneficial for people: "Capitalism is not a system of government, it is the practice and philosophy of transforming resources into capital goods for the purpose of producing consumer products."

Capitalism is the basis and foundation of liberty and America has all the elements of a responsible democracy: Social Justice, Social Equality, and Social morality. *Social* and *Socialist* are two completely different words with different meanings. The global Socialist mafia deceives the public by using the term Social Justice, but factually promoting and agitating to establish Socialist Justice, which is a fraud, known to the entire world. Just look at Venezuela and read my books about Soviet Socialism. Millions have run from Socialism during the last decades. The Socialist mafia goons use this fraud to deceive and fool people. Look at what a dictionary has to say about it:

Social

/ˈsōSHəl/
adjective

1. relating to society or its organization.

"Alcoholism is recognized as a major social problem"

synonyms:

communal, community, community-based, collective, group, general, popular, civil, civic, public, societal; More

needing companionship and therefore best suited to living in communities.

"We are social beings as well as individuals"

noun

an informal social gathering, especially one organized by the members of a particular club or group.

"a church social"

Unlike *Social,* the word *Socialist* is a political term, here is the dictionary:

Socialist

/ˈsōSHələst/
noun

1. a person who advocates or practices socialism.

synonyms:

left-wing, Fabian, syndicalist, utopian socialist; More

adjective

1. adhering to or based on the principles of socialism.

The History of Socialist Movement

The Democrats have been using this fraud to sucker our population for decades. The so-called Democrat Party in our Congress consists of three major parts: members of Socialist mafia, Progressives that collaborated with the KGB for decades (read my columns), and a new faction, the Islamists. All three parts are infiltrated by the KGB and inculcated in the ideology of Soviet Fascism. The Democrats in Congress keep manufacturing crises just like the real Soviet charlatans of the past. The Democrat Party is a political fraud like any other Socialist entity. Moreover, Vladimir Putin and his KGB now control the Democrats and the anti-Trump *criminal cabal.* If you want to see the ideology of Soviet Fascism, look for lies, deceit, and a fraud across the world. Do you know that 96 people indicted for an illegal immigration *Marriage Fraud Scheme* lately? And the Democrats in Congress failed to fulfill their obligations by not acting to prevent invasions of one million illegals to our country . . . What a shame!

Fascist Tactic Used Against Me

I had been writing about Russia and its KGB for many years. Somewhere in the 1990s, I noticed some abnormalities in my mail and computer, but I did not have time to investigate the cause. In 2002, I published my first book and those abnormalities doubled. Since then I have experienced all sorts of violations of my Constitutional rights from wiretaps to arresting my mail, like it was in the Soviet Union. I recognized this to be the KGB. To silence me and ban my writings, the KGB, through the infiltrated FBI or CIA submitted my name to the FISA Court and made me a foreign agent in 2002, the year my first book was published.

Just listen to the story of my third book . . .

In the spring of 2012, I had completed and published my third book titled: *An Agony: Face to Face with Soviet Fascism* with Intermedia Publishing Inc. in 2012. I identified the ideology of Soviet Fascism and described the KGB's tactics, methods, and tricks in the book. With joy, I sent immediately several copies of the book to my friends and got the alarming news: "Everything is up-side-down in your book with a lot of grammar mistakes." I was in shock. When I opened the book . . . it was obvious the KGB had gotten access to the manuscript, because the Trojan Horse has become a Trojan House in the entire book with many similar changes—the internet allows these mischiefs very easily.

The 2012 election was around the corner, I had critically short time to correct the harm and my friends helped me. But the next news did not wait, they made me speechless—Intermedia Publishing Inc. was forced to file for bankruptcy and my book was killed . . . I was again in shock . . .

When I got over the shock, I had to act and the only choice was Xlibris, the publishing house that produced my first and second books. I understood that I couldn't use the same title, I had to change it. I did. Xlibris accepted the book under a new title: *What is Happening to America? The Hidden Truth of Global Destruction,* Xlibris, 2012. A fantastic and alarming Press Release was written and published. But . . . suddenly everything was stopped . . .

"Honorable Attorney General William P. Barr! The entire decent world is looking at you with hope and the desire to see the sworn enemy of the American people exposed. Knowledge of Soviet Fascism is the only means to do so and expose the enemy within. America the Beautiful and her people deserve to know the Truth and to see what Democrats have done to us and our American Republic!" There was no response...

To confirm my ideas and views, please watch a warning of the KGB defector about the silent war which is being waged against America.

Editor's Note: Special thanks to Dr. Rich Swier. The original version of this article appears here.

Simona Pipko is a contributing author for NRN and former Soviet attorney. Pipko practiced law for 25 years in Tallinn, the capital of Estonia, and immigrated to the US in 1981. She is the author of five books and over 100 columns and essays.
www.simonapipko1.com

CHAPTER 17

The Enemy Within

July 21, 2019

"The weak grow strong by effrontery—the strong grow weak through inhibition." Henry Kissinger

Watching what is going on in American House of Representative and social media, Vladimir Putin and his KGB cronies are laughing and chuckling at America's incompetence. Three Directors of the FBI were unable to identify the Trump/Dossier as a KGB hoax-production and, nobody in the American Security Apparatus exposed this Russian fraud—Falshivka produced by the Russian Intel. What a Shame! I wrote about it for about three years. I recognized this fraud in two seconds, warning you constantly about a paralyzed American Intel, unwilling at the highest level to identify our foremost enemy—the KGB. I am using these three letters as they are familiar to vast majority of Americans, I have combined under this term the entire Russian Intelligence.

In addition to the shameful condition in our Intel, the laughing in the Kremlin become even more hysterical after "the squad" identified America as the worst place to live in the world, run by the occupant of the White House, who they scream is a racist. The Kremlin is in frantic hysterical laughter, because 90% of their agenda is completed. The rest 10% is coming—the preparation for a Socialist Revolution in the 2020 presidential election in America going on at full speed . . . And this is not news for me, I am writing about the political operatives of the

KGB, fishing in the murky waters of the Washington D.C. and treason committed by the Dems for the last three decades.

Don't be surprised that "the squad" is insisting on Trump's impeachment, it has nothing with the "color" of four radical women, it is ideology. This is also Putin's agenda; he mortally hates Trump and his political operatives illustrate it. Read my columns written in 2017-2018, discussing Putin. Don't be surprised that all 2020 Dems candidates for the U.S. presidency end up praising "the squad." Unlike them, look at the strong reaction of Senator Graham to "the squad" as he goes nuclear: *Graham RIPS "Anti-Semitic, Anti-America" Dems; Says They "Hate Their Own Country"* posted by Hannity staff. Senator Graham stated: *"They are running on an agenda that is disgusting . . . They're socialist, they're anti-Semitic, and they stand for all the things most Americans disagree with."*

Andropov's Legacy: A Fraudulent and Phony Democrat Party

Sen. Graham is right, every person, who loves America is disgusted, watching those four radical liar-provocateurs. I did, too. Listening to their hateful speeches, trashing America I was stunned by four radical women, who were returning me to my past in the Soviet Union, where the policy "to blame America first" had indoctrinated us in the Stalinist ideology, with an arsenal of different devices: lies, fraud, deceit, distortion, fabrication, perjury, and so on. Mocking America and praising Russia was the central part of the ideology, a modus operandi in our lives, in a time when perverted truth was turning logic upside down for all 24/7. That way Russia became a model of goodness and America became a rotten country with an illegitimate political system. We knew they were deceiving us, but Russia was a totalitarian state and we were intimidated into silence . . .

Now, in America, listening to those four Representatives of the Congress, I was scared, my entire body has become covered with goose bumps and a cold snake crawling along my spine has frozen me—Stalinist Political Correctness is reigning and with arrogant effrontery they demonstrated it here on American soil. I was terrified, but continued listening, analyzing the familiar handiwork of the KGB . . . I couldn't believe it was happening in America! There is a third reason for Putin and his "criminal cabal" to enjoy and laugh, watching their several people participating in the Dems debates as the candidates for the American presidency. We can expect a third Manchurian President . . .

Moreover, none of Dems had reacted to terrorist attacks in Colorado and Washington where Antifa has raised the Mexican flag over the ICE facilities and our flag up-side down. It was a typical fascist putsch by the criminals with masked faces. The same crime had been perpetrated by these fascist Antifa thugs in Berkeley, California several years ago with no lawful penalty for their fascist ferocity. Just look at the whole Democrat Party's policies, actions and agenda. They don't respect our flag and pledge of allegiance. They want to abolish ICE and DHS and install a policy of open borders, giving healthcare to all illegal migrants, Medicare for the rest of us, and "Green New Deal," which costs $93 trillion. Everyone who disagreed with them is a "Racist"—a typical Soviet approach to politics. CNN, their mouthpiece, mentioned the word "Racist" 22 hundred times during one day . . . Watch their language—they redefined the words and actions, like Stalin has taught them by his Political Correctness . . .

Truman's Democratic Party has dissolved into the current American Socialist Party in July 2019. Look at Washington D.C.—the term "Racist" is customized by the Dems and has become the worst possible crime committed in America. In fact, our Founding Fathers created a self-reappearing system that restored and mended the mistakes of the past. America has NO problem of racism any longer—we all have equal rights and enjoy living in the most humane and well-developed democracy with capitalist economic system in the world.

We have been at war for a long time, an asymmetrical war waged by the Socialist mafia against Western civilization and its successful capitalist economy during the last hundred years. Yes, it began after the victory of Socialists in the Russian Revolution in 1917 and became extremely effective in the middle of the 1960s. *The infiltrated Democrat Party brought this war to our soil . . .*

I have been writing about this war in all my books and columns for over thirty years—the war is the main topic, to me it is WWIII—its definition: "WWIII: Recruitments and Drugs, Infiltration and Assassinations." I am writing about this war, because I am a witness of how this war was executed and perpetrated by the KGB, which is the major culprit in the propaganda of Racism in America . . . Please, read an Epilogue of my book *What is Happening to America? The Hidden Truth of Global Destruction*. Xlibris, 2012. In this book, I am describing Soviet fascism and giving you the definition of the ideology on p.159. Yes, the Epilogue addresses the recent topic of "Racism" and its roots . . .

Epilogue

"Dear Reader,

I owe you an explanation. With some American participation, the year 2011 has brought so many violent events in the world that you are confused—who are we fighting against and who are we helping? No other author talks about or confirms the brand new terms I gave you: Soviet Fascism and WWIII. By reading my book you have already gotten basic knowledge of Soviet Fascism; however, it has recently changed its tactics—WWIII has taken a new spiral. As a result the Democrats, Republicans, and Independents are deceived and misled. Writing the Epilogue at the end of 2011, I am taking this opportunity to present my analysis and commentaries of the new spiral of WWIII, waged by the Kremlin.

If you have any doubts in my identification of Soviet Fascism and WWIII, the first person to confirm the identity of both will be the Chairman of the KGB, 1967-1982, Yuri Andropov. I will give you a conversation of Lt. General Ion Mihai Pacepa, the highest-ranking KGB officer ever to defect to the U.S, with Yuri Andropov:

"In 1972 the Kremlin decided to turn the whole Islamic world against Israel and the U.S. As KGB Chairman, Yuri Andropov told me a billion adversaries could inflict far greater damage on America that could a few millions. We needed to instill a Nazi-style hatred for Jews throughout the Islamic world, and to turn this weapon of the emotions into a terrorist bloodbath against Israel and its main supporter the United States. No one within the American/Zionist sphere of influence should any longer feel safe." ("*Russian Footprints*," by Ion Mihai Pacepa, *National Review Online*, August 24, 2008.)

General Pacepa wrote in the same article: "According to Andropov . . . the Muslims had a taste for nationalism, jingoism, and victimology. Their illiterate, oppressed mobs could be whipped up to a fever pitch. Terrorism and violence against Israel and her master, American Zionism, would flow naturally from the Muslims' religious fervor, Andropov sermonized." What can better confirm both of my terms Soviet Fascism and WWIII than those words? They summarized my entire book. I remind you that under Andropov the infiltration into Western civilization had tripled. Under his watch occurred the bloodiest terrorists' attacks in the world, from the Munich murder of Israelis in the Olympic Village to the *Johnstown* tragedy in America.

Now you can see the personality and character of the KGB Chairman Yuri Andropov targeting America in different aspects. Yes, the Muslims mobs were "whipped up to a fever pitch" by the Andropov KGB. Moreover, the same races policy was targeting our Black population by the KGB document designed to instill and inflame the racial division in America in the 1960–70s, titled *Message to the Black Movement, A Political Statement from the Black Underground.* Please, read the document to see clear the propaganda of racism in the ideology of Soviet Fascism . . .

I am writing about the time of Yuri Andropov, the KGB Chairman, because I was a member of the legal community in USSR at the time of his tenure and familiar with all of the KGB's criminal activities. The Epilogue is only a part of that to introduce you the personality of the KGB's Chairman, under his leadership more sinister and nefarious crimes took place against America. The mentioned above *Message to the Black Movement* was flooding America to divide and conquer the black communities in the best Stalinist traditions in the end of the 1960s. For you to understand where the term "White Oppressors" came from, please read the *Message*, I don't want to describe it, you won't believe me, and you have to read it for yourself to grasp the direct effect of it on the Black Caucus in our Congress and on recent events . . .

Do you remember what Khrushchev promised to you? "Your children will live under Communism!" He had in mind the socialist platform and leadership of "the squad" that is guiding the entire Socialist mafia to a direction of Socialist revolution against the system designed by our Founding Fathers. We have it today. The last 3–4 decades the Dems have been infiltrated by the KGB, a Socialist mafia has been created within the Party, nothing left from Truman's Party. The current House of Representatives demonstrates its movement towards Socialism and definite action against capitalist economy, "the squad" is leading the movement. My conclusion: The Dems Party is a political fraud like any other Socialist entities. Moreover, Vladimir Putin and his KGB now control the Dems and lead the Anti-Trump *criminal cabal*.

By the way, a recent study from the University of Pennsylvania has found that America is actually **LESS** racist under President Donald Trump than it was under Barack Obama. The study was conducted by researchers Danial J. Hopkins and Samantha Washington, who found that anti-Black and anti-Hispanic prejudice *declined* after the 2016 campaign and election. "Racism is dying, as people become more educated, bigotry and hatred will become a thing of the past." My conclusion: Knowledge is Power! President Donald J. Trump is not a "Racist!" Donald Trump is fighting Soviet Fascism!!!

Knowledge of Russia and its Intelligence is a Must

I am repeating this refrain for over thirty years, writing about Russia and the KGB, because most of the trouble in the world is derived from and caused by Russia. It is not a coincidence that my latest two columns were dedicated to Political Correctness in the column *Soviet Socialism in the 21st Century*. As you know, I have renamed Soviet Socialism to Soviet Fascism lately. Political Correctness and Social Engineering are two sides of the same coin of Soviet Fascism. Stalinist PC was aimed at hiding or masking the Truth and replacing it with Stalin's ideological Dogma. You can read official definition in my latest column, here is my definition of Political Correctness:

> *" . . . Political correctness is a Stalinist policy, driven by the political agenda, a skillfully crafted design of a quintessential system of lies, fraud, and a long-term strategy of war against Western civilization to create of One World Socialist Government under Kremlin's rule."*

To achieve the result Stalin needed a force, a mind-control mechanism or apparatus to implement his PC and the KGB became that very force. This is the reason I write about the KGB in my books and columns for thirty years. Soviet Fascism had been alive for 70 years due to the force provided by the entire Intelligence apparatus working in collaboration with the lies and fraud of Political Correctness. It is the Soviet Socialist economy that collapsed in 1991—the Soviet System, the regime and the KGB survived and not a lot has changed in Russia since, where Putin and his KGB are running the country. Knowledge of the regime, its methods, tricks, and diabolical Political Correctness is a Must!

Political Correctness is Stalinist social engineering within semantics, to use and affect a human emotional core, with touching scenes that play on your emotions, while deceiving you. Returning to "the squad" of four women who were blaming America, their agenda is clear to me—to replace our political system left to us by our Founding Fathers. They were acting by the protocol PC requires—they aimed at hiding and masking their real agenda while deceiving you with their "love" for America. They are the Islamist part of the Socialist mafia aimed at replacing capitalism with Soviet socialism, which I renamed Soviet Fascism. Moreover, Socialist mafia has its combined military force to achieve the goal—Antifa and several other fascist gangs are comprising that force. They don't wear black shirts, they wear black masks. The Socialist Revolution is in progress in America! Be ready for 2020! The Dems will use all methods and tricks of Soviet Fascism to win!

Knowledge of Russia is a Must in foreign policy as well, as we are dealing now with *"the Axis of Evil"* a coalition of the countries under Kremlin's umbrella adhered to the ideology of Soviet fascism. To know how to deal with Iran, you have to know Soviet fascism, to deal with North Korea, China or Syria, you have to know the KGB and the ideology implemented by Russia in the countries of the *"Axis of Evil."*

In front of you is a typical repetition of the 1980s Russian game, trouble and confrontation with the West. Iran, a member of *"the Axis of Evil"*, illustrates this game in the international waters now in 2019. Never forget: It took 29 years for Stalin to create a Chinese Communist State. Read *What is Happening to America?* Xlibris, 2012. This book was sabotaged by the corrupt FBI twice to prevent its publication—Soviet Fascism doesn't tolerate the Truth!

Stalinist policy of distributing the ideology of Soviet Fascism throughout the world is strongly sustained by that devoted disciple of Andropov—Vladimir Putin. Do you know that people from former Soviet Republics are joining ISIS? The field commanders of ISIS are Chechen or the former Saddam's security operatives, both were trained by the Russian security forces. There are some documents accusing Russia in designing the attacks of 9/11 and bombings in Kenya and Tanzania. Yet, this topic should be discussed separately.

Knowing the Russian methods, agenda, and its proclivity to mold Soviet style charlatan-leaders around the world to engineer cadres of fifth columnists, I believe there are two types of people committing betrayals: Those who do not like the political system established by our Founding Fathers and are trying to transform it—they are currently collaborating with the KGB to destroy the country, and those people who haven't a clue about the KGB infiltrations, hence becoming their unwitting accomplices. Both groups are the enemy within, they constitute a huge help to President Putin, who is continued running the anti-Trump show today . . .

My fellow Americans!

God gave us this last chance to save our county—President Donald J. Trump! Don't allow Soviet Fascism to take over the American Republic. Now you can recognize all so-called socialists, "the squad," the Trojan Horse Bernie, AOC, Beto, Pete, other Soviet Socialists, and their leader Tom Perez. They are lying, fooling and deceiving you for decades. Be vigilant! Some of them are sponsored by the KGB. Fight the ideology of Soviet Fascism and save the legacy of our Founding Fathers and the American Republic!

Knowledge is Power!
Good Luck my beloved America the Beautiful!
P.S.

For the last twenty years, I have been warning Americans about the Russian spy network threatening the USA from within and abroad. In this book, I introduced the ideology of Stalinism, I called it Soviet fascism and named the main components of WWIII waged against Western civilization for the last 7–8 decades. Yet I have never worked inside the KGB and wasn't able to totally expose this enemy of Western civilization. Konstantin Preobrahzensky had done just that. His words are the logical completion and confirmation of the events in my books.

A former lieutenant Colonel in the KGB who defected to the United States in 1993, he is an intelligence expert and specialist on Japan, about which he has written six books. The information he conveys in his other writings was so extremely important that I felt it is my duty to share it with you. Please read three pages of the Truth, published by Gerard Group International, Intel Analyses, Friday, August 31, 2007.

These three pages tell you more than many political pundits combined have told you for the last ten years. I hope you remember the tragic death of former KGB agent Alexander Litvinenko in London. He told Konstantin Preobrazhensky the information he obtained during the years working within the KGB.

Konstantin Preobrazhensky is quite a prolific writer. His article titled "Putin's Espionage Church" says Russia gained a historical victory over America when Russia opened its province in America, which is called the Russian Orthodox Church Outside Of Russia.

Those who read my book know my writings about infiltration into our culture by the KGB, and a constant fight against our traditional values and our foundation in Judeo-Christian philosophy. Reading the article titled: *Putin's Espionage Church* you will find the real enemy, an enemy waging a war against Christianity in America. I would add that this culprit is waging a war not only against America, but against the entire Christianity and Western civilization.

As you know, FSB means the old KGB. The book is revealing the following:

— How the old KGB has returned and infiltrated the Russian Orthodox Church
— How Russia is still today spying in the United States.

Reading my book, you became acquainted with my favorite refrain that knowledge is power. Yes, it is true. For example, I often referred to George Soros and the 187 social organizations he sponsors. Using the information conveyed in my books, we could have exposed this man for what he is. Alas, for several decades, that hasn't been done. Watch cartoons and other mockery of the Republican candidates for the US presidency, sponsored by Soros. We can also expect waves of paid protest agitators against the Republicans, sponsored by George Soros.

Konstantin Preobrazhensky's next book is *FSB's New Trojan Horse: Americans of Russian Descent.* I like the title, yet I called them all socialist charlatans.

As terrorism is an integral part of WWIII and its consequences, absence of the reality of the war is shaping an illusory picture of the world conditions, keeping the vast majority of the population uninformed. Americans love their country, yet they do not know the real story of Libya's invasion and many other events described in this book. A current disruption within the Republican Party frustrates all the members and is the direct result of a tremendous absence of the knowledge about our enemy and crucial information of the war itself.

The grievances within the Republican Party can be only solved by knowledge of Soviet Fascism, exposed in this book. Become acquainted with the works of Konstantin Preobrazhensky, I can conclude my opinion: All above-mentioned works of Konstantin Preobrazhensky signifies a vivid and total conformation of my book *Socialist Lies: From Stalin to the Clintons, Obamas, and Sanders* (Xlibris, 2016).

CHAPTER 18

Slavery Has No Color: Karl Marx, and Stalinist/Socialist Charlatans

Senator Tim Kaine gave a speech on the Senate floor on June 16. He said "The United States didn't inherit slavery from anybody. We created it." Read the transcript here. *Tim Kaine Speech Transcript: Says US Created Slavery, Didn't Inherit It*, June 16, 2020

I watch his speech and when I heard those words, my jaw dropped. I have followed this man for several years and found him radically anti-American. Since American's haven't been taught American History for decades, he could say ridiculous bromides like that and get away with it. I didn't like him then and I don't like him now! I am a former Soviet attorney and in addition to Soviet Law, I studied history and Marxism for four years at Law School and know that slavery is a global phenomenon of our world—no country escaped slavery. Unfortunately, in America, the issue of slavery provided Socialist Charlatans with a narrative to exploit the division between whites and blacks—ignorance has become a radical force fighting the political system designed and left to us by our Founding Father . . .

My Response to Senator Tim Kaine

Studying in Leningrad Law School at the time of Iron Curtain, I loved Marxism—it was the only information from the West. Any literature, books, magazines and newspapers from the West were forbidden under the Soviet Socialist regime. Marxism was a mandatory subject and we studied it for all four years of Law School. I knew Marxism pretty well. Yet, I didn't like Marx for his militancy, though all his words had become axioms for me. Coming to the West, I found out a different assessment of his personality and his legacy. Of course, as the historical figure Marx was very controversial. Judge for yourself:

Karl Heinrich Marx was a German philosopher, economist, historian, sociologist, political theorist, journalist and socialist revolutionary. Born in Trier, Germany, Marx studied law and philosophy at university. Wikipedia.

Karl Marx (1818–1883) is best known not as a philosopher but as a revolutionary, whose works inspired the foundation of many communist regimes in the twentieth century. It is hard to think of many who have had as much influence in the creation of the modern world. *Karl Marx (Stanford Encyclopedia of Philosophy)*

The ***Communist Manifesto***, originally titled ***Manifesto*** of the ***Communist*** Party (German: Manifest der Kommunistischen Partei) is a short 1848 book written by the German Marxist political theorists Karl Marx and Friedrich Engels. It has since been recognized as one of the world's most influential political manuscripts.

Marx's theory of *history* is centered on the idea that forms of society rise and fall as they cause progress and later impede the development of human productive power. *Historical* materialism, also known as the materialist conception of ***history***, is a methodology used by some communist and ***Marxist*** historiographers that focuses on human societies and their development through ***history***, arguing that ***history*** is the result of material conditions rather than ideals. *Wikipedia*, *Historical Materialism.*

The last quotation from *Wikipedia* is exactly correct: ***history*** is the result of material conditions rather than the theory of such ideas as Socialism and Communism. As a historian and economist Marx had produced a very valuable study of history and the economy of capitalism. My first acquaintance with capitalism came from his Das Capital, we had to read and discuss it at Law School. The book was written in a very dry language was quite difficult to read, but I got an elementary knowledge of capitalism from it: capital, labor and money. The historical part of his theory and four stages of development civilization were also logical, understandable and clear to me then. Today, I see something discussible in his presentation if not wrong and dishonest.

Slavery has no Color

I never read this document in Law School—Modules on Stages of Economic Development. Soviet professors had taught me and Marx's four stages of economic development were an authority for me. Now living in America, and having the document in front of me gave me the opportunity to discuss it. I agree with the quote from *Wikipedia*—human productive power is the force that develops civilization rather than fallacy, a fraud with utopian concept of Socialism/Communism. Here is the document:

*Introduction to **Karl Marx**, Modules on **Stages** of Development.* ACCORDING TO ***MARX***, human ***civilization*** has manifested itself in a series of organizational structures, each determined by its primary mode of production, particularly the division of labor that dominates in each ***stage***. 1) The tribal form . . .

The document lists four stages of socio-economic development of civilization: 1) The tribe form, 2) "primitive communism, 3) Feudal or estate property, and 4) Capitalism.

The tribe form . . . ". . . During this stage, it is also possible to see a slave culture established, particularly as the population increases, leading to "the growth of wants" and the growth of relations with outside civilizations (through war or barter). With slave culture, we see the beginning of class society." The given part of the first tribe stage clearly presents the ties of the tribal form to slave culture, indicating the beginning of economic development of civilization. Considering Marx's design to show the changes in the human productive power of the stages, doing that, in fact, Marx verifies slavery as a beginning of socio-economic development of civilization and in this he was right.

Slavery has no color—there is no country in the world that has escaped slavery as economic development of civilization. Slavery is a global phenomenon. For your information, slavery was abolished in Russia at the same time that it was abolished in America. Republican President Abraham Lincoln signed the Emancipation Proclamation and payed a dear price for that—he was assassinated. Yet, the Republican Party has been fighting for freedom and liberty of the black community since.

Race and Policing in America

Policing in America is a hot topic all over the country. The conversation is even considering completely defunding the police. Yet, nobody talks about the history of black race. This is the reason I deliberately started a conversation about development of our civilization in the preceding paragraphs. In this part of his early study, Marx was right—civilization was developed in four stages. It took five hundred years to develop Western civilization in Europe. America is a part of European civilization consisted of a homogeneous population. *African-American* migrations—both forced and voluntary—forever changed the course of *American* history. It is not a matter of color it is a matter of civic literacy brought to us by four stages of civilization for centuries. These developments were not experienced by the black community in America and as a result both sides are suffer.

There were both white and black slave owners and the black slaves were brought from the first stage of civilization to the third or fourth stage into American society. As a result, they missed the centuries of civic literacy teaching and economic development. I am surprised by some talented black individuals who did succeed, but the vast majority of blacks had not, they had missed the centuries to learn and experience the socio-economic development of our civilization . . .

Moreover, the black community had been attacked by Socialist Charlatans since the 1960-1970s. It was another obstacle to prevent them from succeeding—the ideological inculcation "to divide and conquer" by the Russian Security operatives-agitators. Writing about them, I use the term KGB. Don't be surprised by "Black Lives Matter," using propaganda, full fledge force and intimidation, the major methods of Socialist Charlatans. Please, read here my two preceding columns with documents to understand the dangerous predicament in America today.

Under these circumstances to hear the Democrat Sen. Kaine's statement: "The United States didn't inherit slavery from anybody. We created it" made me sick. It is a sign of deep ignorance if not treachery.

To expose some Stalinist Socialist Charlatans in America, I need a separate column, there are hundreds of them confronting our political system to implement what we know as fraudulent Socialism. I'd rather continue Marx's presentation as I found dishonesty and some wrongs in it. For your information Karl Marx was a correspondent on the New York Tribune. Marx's principal earnings came from his work as European correspondent, from 1852 to 1862, for the New-York Daily Tribune.

The man who is writing for an American newspaper is supposed to know American history. If you go to his second stage "primitive communism" you wouldn't find even an elementary knowledge of history. For me "primitive communism" was established by the Plymouth Colony and William Bradford (1590–1657) a founder and longtime governor of the Plymouth Colony. "For many years, the story of the first failed commune of Plymouth Bay was part of the collective memory of American students. But Progressive Education found that story unhelpful and it has fallen into obscurity." Jerry Bowyer, Forbs, *Occupy Plymouth Colony: How A Failed Commune Led To Thanksgiving.*

Jerry Bowyer is right, we are dealing with Dems-Progressives—an army of Stalinist Socialist Charlatans who infiltrated our Universities and created one-party campuses. Unfortunately, nobody is doing anything to stop it. They are using Marx's name with no knowledge of the utopian theory itself. They have been inculcated since the 1960-70s and are not interested in truth, but instead fight for power—they are the leaders of Antifa and Black Lives Matter-terrorist organizations. They can be exposed only with knowledge of the fallacy of fraudulent Marxism, Socialism and Communism. **We must do it, otherwise the American Constitutional Republic is doomed . . .**

I have no direct answer to why Marx did not use the Plymouth Colony. There are two explanations why he didn't use the failed communism of Plymouth Colony in his Modules. He didn't know America's history, or he invented a fraudulent theory for his personal agenda, to become famous and get married to the rich girl he was in love, Jenny von Westphalen. As the theorist of the utopian future Socialism and Communism, Marx has waged a war against mankind, which is going on today in America and across the world . . . Maybe Karl Marx was the first Socialist Charlatan?

Living under American capitalism for over thirty years, I have learned that the word "job" is a very respectable term in America. It was just the opposite in the Soviet Russia, and the Russian saying had emphasized it: "The Government is pretending to pay us and we are pretending to work." This saying is a crux of the matter, the truth of the difference: Capitalism respects Labor. Those are the moral standards of capitalism and labor with dignity accepting those moral standards. There is a peace between the two—Marx was wrong. If I was suspicious about Marx's "class struggle" before, now, I believe it is his pure speculation to give a foundation for utopian socialism; and our academia should analyze my ideas.

Watching Conservative blacks, I came to believe that they are the force for good in America—their personal experiences and incredible achievements in America is the best proof of the Founders' brilliant, if not genius, politico-economic design of our Constitutional republic. As it's declared by our Founding Fathers, "We have been a property holders' democracy."

Conservatives of all colors white, black, and brown due to the freedom and personal liberty are approaching their JOB with dignity; they appreciate and value the system that provides them with respect, justice, and responsibility. The dignity of work leads to American Dream! The statistics of the four years of Trump's presidency is the best evidence of that. I believe that "the Force for Good" will save our constitutional republic.

The Conservative blacks, Latinos, and whites will reignite patriotic confidence in AMERICA!

CHAPTER 19

Criminals Are Now Destroying Our Country

June 27, 2020

When historical monuments and buildings are vandalized; when citizens are killed and injured by various groups of criminals in the big cities of the country; and when one Party in the parliament is behind all of that, promising to defund the police, Vladimir Lenin called the predicament—a "revolutionary situation". He was right—the 1917 Socialist Revolution in Russia followed that exact predicament very quickly. If you know modern history and its tragic result, the entire world has endured since—as Socialist regimes forcefully implemented Socialist mantra globally . . .

You're witnessing a Socialist Revolution in America in your midst. Yes, that revolution is taking place **now!** We cannot remain complacent as our historical monuments are being demolished, with looting and arson in the streets of big cities bringing billions in damages. It is all about power over your life, to take away your freedom, your guns, and your lives if you do not bend the knee to their demands. I know how the Russian Socialist Revolution was manufactured by Socialist Charlatans in 1917 Russia and we are now experiencing in America a carbon copy of the events of a hundred years ago in Russia—Socialism has its patterns, regardless of nationality, ethnicity or race. A strong forceful response by the Republicans holding the levers of power is a must to stop these counter-revolutionary efforts, a thuggery by so-called Democrats fighting all American patriots and the system designed by our Founders.

Socialism is a lawless and criminal regime. Under Socialism criminals are taking over our passive population. I don't need to give you my experience under Socialism, you can see it in Seattle, Minneapolis, Chicago and other big cities in America. I have no words to describe my frustration and anger watching chaos in our cities and the mob demolishing our history and traditions to erase our culture and memory. The events at Lafayette square is a repetition of an earlier attempt to take over the White House in June 1, 2020, like the Winter Palace had been taken in 1917 Russia by the mob. The Democrats have placed themselves in the pockets of the looters and other criminals who create the "revolutionary situation" in America—it is insurrection, if not treason . . .

Lately, I deliberately introduced you to the term Socialist Charlatans, they are manufacturing Socialist Revolution in America. The entire leadership of the Democrat Party consists of the Progressive's Socialist Charlatans using the methods and tactics of Russian Security apparatus. In writing about them, I use the term KGB. There are variety of gradations of Socialist Charlatans acting throughout the midst of the society to destroy our way of life: they occupied all strata of our society inculcating Americans in their fraudulent ideology, instigating violence. They are no longer small groups of infiltrators. No, they are now presenting themselves in large numbers. You are watching today an accumulation of the access of inculcation by the evil mindsets of Marxism, Socialism, and Communism in America . . .

Putin's KGB within America's Midst

Several months ago, I warned you that Antifa and "Black Lives Matter" are the product of the KGB and trained by them. The leader of the group has admitted: Black Lives Matter co-founder Patrisse Cullors said in a newly surfaced video from 2015 that she and her fellow organizers are "trained Marxists." . . . BLM leader proclaimed: If change doesn't happen, "we will burn down this system . . ." Do you remember the International used by the Bolsheviks in Socialist Revolution in Russia? The words of the BLM leader are equal to words from the International: "We will destroy old world and build a new . . ." In fact, that ideology destroyed the USSR—the country collapsed economically in 1991 and the criminal agency the KGB took over . . .

A 2015 video clip has surfaced of an interview with Black Lives Matter founder Patrisse Cullors in which she assures her interviewer that the group has an underlying ideology, saying, "We're trained Marxists." Responding to the interviewer's concern that the BLM movement might not have enough of a "clear ideological structure," Cullors responded by saying that she and another co-founder "in particular" are dedicated to the ideology of Communist leader Karl Marx: "We actually do have an ideological frame. Myself and Alicia in particular, we're trained organizers. We are trained Marxists. We are super versed on ideological theories."

Please, read here my column; *Slavery Has no Color: Karl Marx, Slavery, and Stalinist, Socialist Charlatans*, June, 23, 2020.

When another leader of BLM Hawk Newsome promises to burn the system and replace it with the new one, it is the real threat of counter-revolutionary forces, an insurrection to destroy the system designed and established by our Founding Fathers. A recent interview of the acting FBI Director shows that he is still not aware of the destructive forces that ideology stands for:

> *The FBI is "looking carefully" at the possibility that foreign actors are influencing the sometimes-violent nationwide protests in the wake of George Floyd's in-custody death, FBI Director Christopher Wray exclusively told Fox News' Bret Baier.*
>
> *Wray also revealed that "the FBI has over 2,000 active investigations that trace back to the government in China," marking "about a 1,300 percent increase in terms of economic espionage investigations with the Chinese nexus from about a decade ago."*
>
> *"We have certainly seen in the past a variety of foreign adversaries looking to amplify controversy in this country," Wray said. "And they use state media. They use social media. Some of that is through propaganda, some of that's through disinformation, some of that's through just fake information. And we are looking carefully at the prospect of foreign influence or foreign interference in all of the protests and activities that have occurred over the last few weeks."*

[Source: Fox News] FBI Drops Bombshell: Investigation Proves "Planned Destruction" Of America, National Insiders' June 25, 2020

This interview testifies to my two points, just look at the words which characterize the adversary's activities: propaganda, disinformation, fake information, and protests—all of that are typical goings-on of the arsenal of KGB tactics. In addition to that China now joined the KGB. When the FBI Director doesn't know history—History repeats itself. In order to save the American Constitutional Republic it is vitally to know the enemy and the enemy No. 1 is the current Democrat Party—a criminal cabal of Progressives' Socialist Charlatans. Let me prove it.

A Criminal Cabal of "Progressives"—Socialist Charlatans

The infiltration into American society by the KGB' forces began many decades ago. I'll give you two examples to identify the time the infiltration began. The Windy City, Chicago, is currently a war zone, people are killing each other every day there for decades. Don't be surprised a killing field in Chicago. I know one of the leaders in Chicago who is responsible for the killing—Rahm Emanuel, the Mayor of Chicago. I knew him when he was in Israel. He had a friendly relation with Yasser Arafat. To my knowledge the latter was recruited by the KGB in 1957—friendship with Arafat speaks for itself—Arafat initiated a war in the Middle East, it is still going on. Besides, Rahm Emanuel was a right hand of our first American Manchurian President, Bill Clinton, his chief of staff. Read here my column *Revelation*, April 26, 2018.

Yes, we are at war waged against Western civilization and American capitalism by the KGB and the forces of Marxism, Socialism, and Communism. The destruction of America is planned by our adversaries and the criminal cabal of the "Progressives" Socialist Charlatans of the Democrat Party have been implementing it in America for many decades. You can find additional information on Rahm Emanuel in Israel. The second example is the State of Virginia.

If you read my books or columns you know that my work in the legal community of the USSR coincides with the tenue of the KGB Chairman Yuri Andropov. I knew him pretty well. It was Andropov's idea to invent a "control opposition." The KGB had practiced it in Russia for many years. It is very simple to achieve, just infiltrate the opposition with a couple of people, promote them to the leadership and program them to act in a way beneficial to you. That exact move to create White Nationalism was realized and implanted by the KGB in America. The result you saw in August 2017, in so-called Unite the Right, the violent white supremacist rally in Charlottesville, Virginia.

Nazi slogans and violence at the march were manufactured in the best traditions of the KGB. The BBC commented the following: "Aug 13, 2017—The deadly violence on the streets of Charlottesville, Virginia, comes at a time of a dramatic rise in prominence of far-right movements in the US. The election of Donald Trump to the White House has been cited as a factor in the re-energizing of activists . . ."

It was clear to me that the entire event of violent white-supremacy was manufactured by the anti-Trump "criminal cabal" run by the Clinton/KGB mafia. Terry McAuliffe was governor of Virginia and his deal with McCabe is known in its monetary aspect. Yet, it was more than only that—McAuliffe was a Clinton long-term lieutenant. This event is also known to the McAuliffe's staff— staff involvement was needed, as the preparations to organize a "control opposition" takes time. For your information—this exact staff is working now under the new Governor of Virginia. Don't be surprised by what is going on in Virginia 2020—people feel undefended and neglected there. If the case investigated professionally by DOJ, we can find McCabe in a link in a long chain of criminal activities within the Democrat Party.

I've been writing about Terry McAuliffe for many years. He was a prominent member of Clinton's mafia, Socialist Charlatan, inculcating and corrupting everybody around in the State of Virginia for many years. Today, I saw him acting and speaking like a typical mafia apparatchik, lying, cheating, always harming the American interests, as designed by Andropov. A year ago, I reacted on the same protest in Charlottesville, writing the column, describing how it was orchestrated and enflamed by the members of the Clinton mafia, Terry McAuliffe, Governor of the state in cahoots with Andrew McCabe. I knew well the members of Clinton's mafia and their cooperation with the KGB. While President Trump was signing an American spending bill for 1.3 trillion for the year 2017; I would say that half of the money was caused by the KGB' criminal activities in cahoots with Socialist Charlatans. What a spectacular failure of our Intel!

Don't be surprised by the media in America, it was recreated by the first American Manchurian President, including making the KGB's political operative George Stephanopoulos a journalist. Today there are hundreds of them, poisoning America's minds. **Guard your minds America!** Propaganda is insidious, deceiving you into believing its narrative. The anti-Trump crusade was begun by Russia and the KGB's production of the Trump/Dossier under the second American Manchurian President, who was giving Aid and Comfort to the enemy. All of that was done to cover-up the crime committed by them—a real collusion, collaboration with the enemy for decades. This is the tide of the times. Read here my column *The KGB: A Global Terrorist Agency*, March 11, 2018.

The second American *Manchurian President* doubled the infiltration of the ideology. Even further infiltrating the American Congress by the "Squad." You saw the events pertaining to Rep. Ilhan Omar and Rep. Rashida Tlaib. They are using our freedom and liberty to subvert both, talking about White Nationalism as a threat to humanity. Just listening to their statements will convince you who you are dealing with—they are agitators advocating both Islamism and Marxism/Socialism to fight Capitalism. For your information the KGB feels free acting through them to take action in America and manufacturing another narrative to fight Capitalism, aiming at President Trump—now it is the *White Supremacists.*

President Trump is right: "White nationalism is not a rising threat to humanity." Marxism/Socialism continues its threat to humanity! It is threatening the entire world as it has been spread by the KGB globally and especially to our country. Tom Fitton of Judicial Watch, is also right. It was: "Attack on our Republic . . . . spying, coup, sedition, impeachment, ballot harvesting, open borders, looting, Anti-American propaganda on secession, and open violent insurrection . . ."

My fellow Americans!

It is time to think seriously to save the country we have and prevent the repetition of Treason . . . Remember Joseph Stalin—a famous murderer of the 20th century in Russia…

P.S. I'd advise you to read the comments on this original column at www.drrichswier.com/author/spipko/

CHAPTER 20

Treason: Two "Manchurian" Presidents

July 2, 2020

"You can avoid reality, but you cannot avoid the consequences of avoiding reality."— Ayn Rand

When the historical monuments were tumbled from their pedestals, many Republicans were surprised by how quickly such a thing could take place here. They haven't read my warning about the American Manchurian President and the Obama/ Putin Conspiracy. During all eight years of his presidency, Barack Obama openly showed his conspiracy with Putin for those who know Putin's methods, tactics, and dirty tricks. I did and I warned you, but a corrupt Obama FBI sabotaged and banned my writings.

The current debates involving the strange behavior of Justice Roberts and Russia, the Taliban, and war in Afghanistan have been discussed by me years ago clearly showing Russia's treacherous policy against America. The answer to both issues is Knowledge of Russia and her Security apparatus and to demand security from our government. And this is one of the reasons we don't understand what is happening to America and the predicament that is tearing apart America the Beautiful. Listen to me, writing in 2016–2017 in this e-magazine:

The Russian Connection

As a matter of fact, a lot of Socialist and KGB methods have been implemented in the U.S. during the last three decades, especially the last eight years of Obama's administration. The Democrat Party has become America's Socialist Party embracing the KGB's methods of implementing Soviet Socialism. To prove my point I'd like to present the part played by the Obama/Putin Conspiracy—a military collaboration, which I described in my preceding columns. The following list represents military collaboration within the Obama/Putin Conspiracy during all eight years of Obama's presidency:

1. Killing of bin-Laden
2. Invasion of Libya, conspiracy of Obama, Putin, and French Pres. Sarkozy.
3. Benghazi, murder of the U.S. ambassador Stevens to provide arms to Assad's Syria and Iran.
4. "On 6 August 2011, a U.S. Boeing CH-47 Chinook military *helicopter* was shot down while transporting a quick reaction force attempting to reinforce an engaged unit of Army Rangers in Wardak province, west of Kabul, *Afghanistan*. The resulting *crash* killed all 38 people on board—25 American specialists . . . Fifteen of the *Navy SEALs* that were killed were members of the Naval . . ."
5. The return of the war-deserter Bergdahl from Afghanistan for the release of five Taliban commanders.

The Afghanistan story, I have explained in my preceding columns, Russia was working with the Taliban and needed the return of several famous commanders imprisoned in America. The deal was manufactured by the Obama/Putin Conspiracy using the family of a mentally unstable individual." The idea of Obama/Putin collaboration was introduced completely in my two books, talking about ongoing WWIII. And that war is the crux of the matter—Obama has brought the war waged by Soviet Socialism to our American soil, by allowing his party to become a Socialist one.

Those Who Forget History Are Doomed to Repeat it

Recent reports have alleged that the Russian government offered monetary bounty-rewards to Taliban terrorists for killing American soldiers. I don't know whether Trump was informed of that or not, at any rate I don't trust the FBI nor any of Obama's Intel. I was writing about the Soviet collaboration with Taliban and the dirty tricks against American military for years. My writings was banned to cover-up both a corrupt FBI and the Obama administration over one particular reason to prevent the Truth about Evil-Treason by the Dems' leadership to be exposed. And today Queen-of-Socialist Charlatans Nancy Pelosi continues covering up the Dems leadership and Treason committed by them, by playing with Americans lives in Afghanistan for decades . . . In the best traditions of Stalinism: "never admit crime committed, instead accuse the opposition in that exact crime," she is lying and accusing Trump in the crime committed by the Democrats . . .

The Soviet invasion in Afghanistan began as the war against Western civilization and American capitalism. Yes, the Russian government offered monetary bounty-rewards to Taliban terrorists for killing American soldiers. It has been doing that since its invasion to Afghanistan—a very sophisticated operation against America. I had described that exact Russian operation against the American Military in my column *The KGB's Roots and Pedigrees*, October 19, 2017. Reading that column will educate you in term of the KGB/Menace, it'll open your eyes on the Obama/Putin Conspiracy and the Treason committed by the Democrats' leadership . . .

Do you really believe that the 9/11 terror attack of the twenty-first century came from Afghanistan? I do not. Do you think that the spread of terrorism across the globe to sixty countries also came from the Taliban or al-Qaeda? No chance. We are in the historic struggle of the twenty-first century against criminals of the twentieth century. And that is my main point in WWIII—the Russian Connection. It began many decades ago and continues with the Clinton Mafia—my book, *Socialist Lies,* presents the Truth in details. Reading it you will grasp my point of knowledge and memory discussed in the book, which is connected to the article below:

The National Review, *Did Britain Fall into Putin's Trap in Prosecuting a Russian Dissident? By* **CLAIRE BERLINSKI, May 11, 2016.** The author has a legitimate point describing the current predicament in the world: "Having failed to finish off conclusively the Communist system, we are now in danger of integrating the resulting monster into our world. It may not be called Communism anymore, but it has retained many of its dangerous characteristics . . . *Until a Nuremberg-style tribunal passes its judgment on all the crimes committed by Communism, it is not dead and the war is not over."*

From my experience this is correct and also the reason I am identifying "the resulting monster" that has become post-Soviet Russia and writing about Soviet Fascism for the last twenty years. Several writers have caught the scent of Fascism about the regime, but nobody researched the issue and identified the ideology I have presented. *The Russian Connection* October 14, 2016 and *Warning: The Russian Connection II,* October 18, 2016

A leader of the Socialist Revolution, Vladimir Lenin has left advice for the leaders building a Socialist system— government-controlled Health Care system must be enacted first. Don't attribute to Lenin any benevolence to mankind; health care is a matter of life and death, every citizen needs a well-functioning health care. Lenin's socialism had a precise target, the entire population—it enslaved all citizens in this one shot. And this is not the first nor the last example of Soviet Socialism. Unfortunately Obama's administration left more unknown yet obscure attributes of Socialism, set up in our system.

If you know the literature written by Vladimir Lenin and his Socialism, you will understand that Obamacare has little to do with health. Its main target was an existing system of health care—to destroy it. Then it planned to establish a Socialist model, which according to Lenin was supposed to be deeply connected to the budget and other monetary links of the government—the second Obama agenda to bankrupt the entire system. The GOP's fiasco happened because they didn't know Socialism. Like some dissenting Democrats, they also don't know Joseph Stalin's Doctrine on One Socialist World Government, well known to Barack Obama. If you want to know what is ahead of us, please read my conversation with Rush Limbaugh, pp. 571–574, *Baltic Winds: Testimony of a Soviet Attorney*, Xlibris, 2002.

Gain Wisdom and Speak the Truth!

Taking Crimea was the usual behavior of an aggressor who senses the absence of punishment. Russia has never stopped its aggressive, criminal behavior since the Socialist coup date in Russia, 1917. After the Reagan presidency Russia resumed its behavior, something I have written and reported on for the last twenty-five years, while our media kept largely silent on such matters, practically withdrawing from the discussion and depriving Americans of the strange, tragic events within the Putin administration.

This lack of Russia's knowledge was the primary reason the news from Moscow was misinterpreted—causation and linkage to past behaviors had been lost in the minds of middle class Americans. Nothing substantial has changed in Russia: failed Soviet Socialism has been substituted by Crony capitalism under the KGB's leadership. Yet the killing of innocents, war crimes, and the destruction of the land continued globally for all those years, without a proper definition of the ideology, causing suffering and grief to millions . . . The time was lost, the situation has changed dramatically lately in the direction I had predicted. Alas . . . Knowledge is power!

The recent headlines about Russia and its meddling in our election should not be surprising. The fact of the matter is that Russia's aggressive posture attempts to overwhelm all aspects of human life—**it is a Global War for power of the Mafia-State of Stalinism against Capitalism and Western civilization.** The war resurrects all of Stalin's methods, tricks, and devices that are so familiar to all former citizens of the socialist states. They have been given a foothold in America. Today Russia, China, Iran, and North Korea are together attacking Western civilization and America . . .

This war intensified when the leadership of Democrats took up the banner of Socialism, created by Stalinist dogma and openly entered social conflict against capitalism in America. And despite the fact of socialism's inability to produce, it became a legitimate political and economic theory in America due to the effort of Bernie Trojan Horse Sanders. That was the reason I started my latest book *Socialist Lies*, presenting and identifying Marxism and Stalin's dogma as a fallacy, fraudulent utopian concept. The term *Con Man & Criminal,* I have read in *Barack Hussein Obama,* by BRADLEE DEAN, Freedom Outpost, AUGUST 3, 2018.

His description of Obama as Con Man & Criminal reminded me my description of Comrade Stalin: "Marxist theory, which opened Pandora's Box in the 19th century marched across the globe to the 20th century. It was used by thugs, charlatans, and criminals to acquire power, to fool, mislead, manipulate, and then to abuse and exploit people around the globe. The leader who had all the negative human characteristics mentioned above was Joseph Stalin." He left us his Doctrine of Soviet Socialism, used by the Socialist Mafia forces in America today. I called his Doctrine the Ideology of Soviet Fascism, implemented by the Obama/ Putin Conspiracy in America . . .

Look at another announcement about the book titled *The Manchurian President.* "Aaron Klein has unmasked the most radical—and therefore dangerous—president by far this country has ever seen. The radical forces that shaped Obama, as revealed in this telling investigation, were not the best of the radical sixties, but the very worst—the anti-American, communist-supporting, terrorist fringe."—David Horowitz, bestselling author. Yet, there had been two Manchurian Presidents in America, I have been written about the first for the last thirty years: Bill Clinton. Both had been chosen by the anti-American, communist-supporting, terrorist fringe, run and coordinated by the KGB. The critical issue for America is the investigation of both Manchurian Presidents to save the American Republic and show the incredible damage done by Socialist Mafia and Socialist Charlatans to our America the Beautiful over the last several decades.

If you want to know the Socialist Mafia, just pay attention to Socialist Charlatans: Nancy Pelosi, Tom Perez, James Clyburn, Dick Durbin, Donna Brazil, Debby Dingle, Keith Ellison, Comrade De Blasio, and many others. Watch them and their speeches, they haven't read 1984 by George Orwell—they live in Oceania and Vladimir Putin is their Master . . . **American Patriots should rise up against fraudulent Socialism . . .** My friends it is time for us to speak the truth openly. We are people of worth, not to be ignored nor thrown under the bus for our opinions. Meantime, I am waiting for the DOJ's investigation to see how it investigates the crime against the political system of the American Republic without reading my books and columns . . . We will see it soon . . .

Be ready for July 4th protests, riots and chaos by Socialist Charlatans in cahoots with street mobs in the Dems-run states.

CHAPTER 21

Stalin Planned America's Collapse—It's Under Way

"America is like a healthy body and its resistance is threefold: its patriotism, its morality, and its spiritual Life. If you can undermine these three areas, America will collapse from within."—Joseph Stalin.

I believe that Joseph Stalin made the statement about America seventy years ago in Moscow. What Stalin had in mind, I experienced seventy years later in America, when immigrating in 1981. And I am horrified, because Stalin's design has almost come to fruition in 2019 due to this incredible "achievement" of the KGB. I am emphasizing the significance of the KGB, because it represents Russia today and I am using the term KGB meaning the entirety of Russian Intelligence Apparatus. The Ukrainian scandal is an intimate Russian one.

Ukraine and Its Socialist Mafia

Ukraine is a beautiful country with vast areas of very fertile land and plenty of hard-working and freedom-loving people. The country was under the regime of the Stalinist Socialist mafia for seventy years and the Ukrainians suffered enormously all those years. In the 1930s Stalin prosecuted a man-made starvation in Ukraine in which 7-to-10 million people perished: every family was devastated and memory of this tragedy has been confirmed by the history. Ukraine proclaimed its independence immediately after the collapse of the Soviet Union and thus started the fight with the Stalinist Socialist mafia . . .

My colleague, a defense attorney in Moscow, Arkady Vaksberg, wrote a book-documentary and titled it—The Soviet Mafia, St. Martin Press 1991. He details the organized, systematic corruption and crime institutionalized in the Soviet Union since Brezhnev's day, and how it involved the Communist Party leadership and organized crime. You would not want to read this book, as there are thousands of murders described and thousands of unpronounceable Russian names. Here are my analyses on the book taken from my book: *What is Happening to America? The Hidden Truth of Global Destruction* XLIBRIS, 2012, p. 153:

There are three main concepts in the book. First, the evil empire may be dead, but not the evil that drove it—the Soviet mafia. Second, the book gives us a new definition of political forces and their leaders previously known as the Communists, the KGB, and the Soviets. Vaksberg redefines those old terms with a new collective identity: the Soviet mafia, the nucleus of an organized crime syndicate. Third, the Soviet mafia is a multinational political force, not limited to any ethnicity, religion, or race. Considering the arguments presented above, I believe that Islam and Jihad are instruments of the Soviet mafia used against the West—it unites all the countries of holding to Soviet Fascism with a common agenda aimed against the West . . .

The book was written in the 20*th* century, I have learned a lot since. It was the Soviet mafia spreading Soviet Socialism across the globe and creating Socialist mafia worldwide. Today we are dealing with the result of that: *The Axis of Evil* under Russian supervision with a common agenda aimed against Western civilization-a very dangerous united force. Ukraine is part of this war: the Socialist mafia was in power for a long time in Ukraine and it will continue its dirty deals under new Ukrainian government until exposed. Remember the definition of the Soviet mafia left by Arkady Vaksberg—it is today Socialist mafia spread worldwide including the United States of America . . .

Biden's Influence-Peddling

It is not the Biden Probe, it is the Washington Swamp, the Deep State, where America's Socialist mafia collaborates with Ukrainian Socialist mafia to accomplish the Russian design against Trump, which started with Trump/Dossier, produced by the KGB. Knowing the Obama/Putin conspiracy, a coup d'état against Trump, with the active participation of the CIA and FBI, the sought for resolution can be achieved, as it is the same anti- Trump Witch Hunt—round 2.0.

Obama delegated Joe Biden as a point man to Ukraine in 2014. Biden traveled to Ukraine with his son Hunter, whose activity deserves explanation. There is a direct connection between Biden's family and an oligarch in Ukraine—" ***Joe Biden's*** son, ***Hunter Biden***, joined the board of Ukrainian energy . . . According to The New York Times, ***Hunter Biden*** helped assemble the ***company's*** legal team, . . . Burisma is led by an ***oligarch*** named Mykola Zlochevsky."

Ukrainian ***Mykola Zlochevsky***, founder of ***Burisma*** Holdings Company, on whose board Hunter Biden in 2014 was appointed, while at the same time his father was leading the Obama administration's diplomatic dealings with Ukraine. Zlochevsky was a Minister of Energy in the Yanukovych government, which means he is the Russian asset, like Yanukovych himself, who fled to Russia to escape the wrath of the Ukrainian people.

Zlochevsky is the subject of several closed cases now under audit by the Ukrainian prosecutor general. "We are now reviewing all the cases that were closed or split into several parts or were investigated before, in order to be able to rule to reverse those cases where illegal procedural steps were taken." Americans can't even imagine the scale of monumental corruption in Ukraine, it is Soviet style corruption. There is a very peculiar situation within America's Socialist mafia, I mentioned in my column *Face to Face with Fascism in America*, in this magazine September 28, 2019:

"To investigate the Ukraine scandal, knowledge of Russia's KGB is a must. For your information the KGB loves to fish in a murky waters and pre-election Ukraine was that exact location of murky waters. Putin's desire to have Ukraine back will never change: the KGB has a lot of sleeper cells in Ukraine, a country of enormous corruption. This current scandal has very intriguing kinds of people involved: the top Dems Joe Biden, the KGB agent George Soros, four Dems Senators, and some even more questionable persons—a knot of possibilities that may even lead to uncover the long-term Obama/Putin conspiracy that I have written about for many years." I have already identified two possible conduits, perhaps Obama decided to create the third one in Ukraine: Biden-Burisma-Putin . . .

Obama/Putin force has initiated digging dirt on Trump in Ukraine in 2016 before his inauguration. Yes, to investigate the Ukraine scandal, knowledge of Russia's KGB is a must. Our Constitutional Republic is at stake, because 90 percent of pundits do not know the subject matter Russia or Ukraine and arrogantly discuss them anyway. I am not talking about CNN, I am talking about Fox News. What do Juan Williams and Chris Wallace know about Obama/Putin conspiracy and the ties between Putin's KGB and former Ukrainian President Yanukovych? What do they know about the ideology of Soviet Fascism to destroy Western civilization? They never read my books or columns, because the FBI's Socialist mafia submitted my name to the FISA Court to make me a foreign agent and ban my writings in 2002.

The KGB's Brotherhood American-Style

I had a reason, in my above mentioned column, in which I presented you with the Stalinist crimes in 1937 Russia. Stalin politicized and weaponized the entire Russian Intel and used it against the Russian people: Show Trails, Purges, investigations, and so on. In 21st century American-style, Socialist-Obama also politicized and weaponized the American Intelligence against the Republican Party and later against Trump. ". . . we did what Obama told us to do," a member of Intel had described the situation. And as we know now a Communist lover, the CIA's John Brennan is a key member of the Deep State, who actively helped Obama to dig dirt on Trump, and also traveled to Ukraine—it was America's Socialist mafia in action.

Look at the impeachment led by Socialist mafia of the House of Representatives—a total fraud and waste of time and money a-la Soviet Socialism, which corrupts everything it touches. The market is hurt by impeachment debates, yet American's Socialist Mafia reinforces the effort to get rid of Trump at any cost and destroy a unique political system left to us by our Founding Fathers. Obama Intel purposely or due incompetence did not inform Trump that Turkey President Erdogan is working with Putin for the last three years: watch now how *the Axis of Evil* deceives us. Who is the beneficiary of this political chaos in America?? The answer is Obama/Putin's Deep State, the KGB, and America's Socialist mafia—the KGB's Brotherhood American style . . .

All of this also reminds me of the Soviet Union's pattern of lies and fraud used by Socialist mafia there. The picture is so similar to contemporary America, that I constantly recall Stalin's order for Communists: *Never admit any crime you committed, but accuse the opponent in this exact crime.* You will see in the upcoming investigation of the Ukraine scandal how Joe Biden follows that exact recipe—he will accuse Trump in the actions he himself had committed. Stalin is very popular among leaders of Socialist mafia: I recognized the Soviet style of propagandist-manipulator Adam Schiff, the epitome of Stalinist Political Correctness: lies and fraud.

In the absence of due process, he is constantly lying using the essentials of Stalinist Political Correctness: He is a witness, investigator, and judge in the partisan impeachment circus, acting secretly like in Stalin's regime. I am not sure he knows that Stalin is the author of Political Correctness used by Dems' Socialist mafia.

Don't be surprised by the appearance of numerous Dems whistleblowers. They are being produced by our Intel and in the Soviet Union they were called informants. When I left the country in 1980, the KGB had over 20 thousand informants. Socialist mafia is a multinational political force, not limited to any ethnicity, religion, or race—mafia is mafia fighting for power worldwide using Stalinist Political Correctness. Let me remind you my definition of Political Correctness: "*. . . Political correctness is a Stalinist policy, driven by the political agenda, a skillfully crafted design of a quintessential system of lies, fraud, and a long-term strategy of war against Western civilization to create of One World Socialist Government under Kremlin's rule.*"

The GOP is missing the elephant in the room: Revolution is happening right now in America—*The Brain-Washing War on America's Mind and Soul.* We are dealing with the army of aggressive international Socialist mafia aimed at turning the Constitutional American Republic into the *Union of Socialist American States.* The Dems' are leading this fight not only to revenge a losing election, the main reason of the fight for power is to cover-up the sinister crime of TREASON that they have committed over several decades. This crime committed by the leadership of Dems' Socialist mafia should be a major topic in the November 2020 election.

CHAPTER 22

Putin's Counter-Intelligence Operation in America

August 31, 2020

History is the Mother of all sciences; and when a chunk of history is purposely erased from the mind of an entire generation, those people become confused and disoriented by world events. That chunk of history is Stalin's Russia and the ideology of Socialism/Communism. This tragic history is missing in the minds of today's American youth. In my books and columns I was describing and analyzing the history as a witness, delivering to you the real events in Russia. For thirty-five years I warned you that we are at war, in an asymmetrical war waged by an Evil ideology focused on destroying Western civilization, particularly American capitalism. This war is attacking the principles and values America was built on. I called it World War III, and gave the definition—WWIII: *Recruitment, Infiltration, Drugs, and Assassinations.*

You see this war has broken out on the streets of our major cities run by the Dems. Don't be surprised by the escalated violence. A radical mob wants destroy the unique American Constitutional Republic left to us by our Founders and to implement Socialism/Communism. Today this missed chunk of history is on display in Americans living in 2020, echoing the attempt to assassinate Republican Rep. Steve Scales. It was no coincidence—Republicans are being targeted nationwide, the tactics designed by Stalin's devoted disciples Andropov and Putin. The race card was their ace. Read here my column *Andropov's Legacy.* The war started in the 1960s has been reignited and explains the current chaos . . .

Putin's Socialist Revolution in America

Socialism is no laughing matter—it is an ideology of destruction, ideology of lies, deception and fraud: it is an infection like coronavirus, a political disease of incompetence and dishonesty spread by Socialist Charlatans. Alas, the American education failed to teach the criminal history of Socialism. Socialism is a culture of abuse and total corruption, becoming a system of slavery, depriving people of all rights known to humanity. Don't be confused with the two words Socialism and Communism—both are Marxist fallacies, a fraud with a utopian concept to deceive you . . . Yet, our Academia decided that discussing and analyzing the collapse of Soviet Union in 1991 was a waste of time.

As a matter of fact, the Soviet Union did not collapse in 1991—it was Socialist economy, unable to produce that collapsed. Yet, the other part of Stalin's Soviet System, all Intelligence services have survived. I use the term KGB talking about them. This force of the KGB helped Socialism to deceive and fool people. In 1991 the fraud had died in the country where Socialism was born and practiced. Yet, the Soviet System, established by Stalin continues functioning and controlling the population . . . Therefore it is a must to know two major Stalinist postulates:

1. Blame America First.
2. Never admit crime committed, instead accuse opposition in that exact crime.

You can see both postulates in actions taken by America's Democrat Party . . .

The people of the KGB and the bureaucracy of the Soviet System have usurped governmental power, prolonging the life of the fake ideology. Though Socialism had already collapsed and was dead, the KGB used the narrative to promote the fake ideology, wrapping themselves in the Russian flag and uniting religion and the force of the KGB together. Stalinist Soviet Socialism was restored by the KGB, and Vladimir Putin was catapulted to the Russian presidency. That entire process took place within all Soviet Republics, where the KGB had usurped all governmental power. Nothing substantial had been changed in Russia since: the failed Socialism was substituted by Crony capitalism under the same KGB leadership. That's it. The Stalinist postulates are used as ever today . . .

To understand the current events in America, knowledge of Russia's Stalinist Intelligence apparatus is imperative. The mistaken statements of winning the Cold War has mislead Americans, because the war against Western civilization had never ended. On the contrary, the KGB used the situation and a massive infiltration to all corners of our society: to the government, courts, media, business, sports, educational system, and Academia. Politicized recent sports events have confirmed the infiltration, they are more visible for all now. The army of Socialist Charlatans created America's Socialist Mafia within the Democrat Party. To successfully fight China we must know the KGB's methods, they are the same in China. Read here *America's Socialist Mafia: Putin's Revenge*, August, 12, 2020.

Socialism corrupts everything it touches, can you now see how America's Socialist mafia runs the Democrat Party? Besides, they have their armed forces destroying America: Black Lives Matter, Antifa, and many other anti-American formations. Ask Bob Woodson, he knows. BLM is the best example of the KGB's creation: Black Lives Matter Los Angeles: BLMLA

"Black Lives Matter Los Angeles is made of regular people who have committed our lives to Black freedom." This is a wrong assertion in form and substance! BLM are not regular Americans, they are "trained Marxists." Jun 25, 2020—Black Lives Matter co-founder Patrice Cullers said in a newly surfaced video from 2015 that she and her fellow organizers are "trained Marxists." I want to know what Marx's work they read about Black Lives and whether they read any of Marx's works. They didn't. As the usual ideological Charlatans, they are deceiving and defrauding you. They are a typical KGB's fraud, trained by the KGB.

They are not committed to Black freedom, it is a KGB cliché—America's Blacks are the freest people in the world. You saw many Black Americans talking about their freedom during Republican Convention. The narratives "Systemic Racism" and "Police Brutality" are fraudulent narratives created by the KGB and promoted by the ticket Biden/

Harris—Dems Socialist Charlatans. *Read Socialist Lies From Stalin to the Clintons, Obamas, and Sanders*, XLIBRIS, 2016.

This ticket needed and created the current violence in America. A couple of days ago, I heard Fox News, Bill Hammer interview a Linda from Kenosha. She knows the community and said that only a few people in the riots have been from Kenosha, the thugs from neighboring states were shooting looting, and burning. I believe her, because I know the KGB's methods and techniques of violence. Kenosha's three night of riots was organized by the Democrats, bringing the thugs from different states. Do you remember the thugs paid and organized by the Dems to disrupt Trumps rally's in 2016? History repeats itself: focus your attention on Trump's opposition—they are all creations of the KGB. This is Putin's last Hurrah to destroy America—Putin's Socialist Revolution in America—revenge for the collapse of USSR.

The KGB has brought all methods of Stalinist violence to our American soil. Provocation is one of them. If you want to know what real provocation means, just recall the scene of a musical attack challenging Christian boys who came to Washington to see the Lincoln Memorial. The musical Charlatans were accompanied by thugs drilled by the KGB in violence to provoke. It was an Evil scene, of provocation and we all watched how the Christian boy reacted honorably to the attack. What strong character he has displayed! His character and values are confirmed by the court. His name is Nicolas Sandmen. Remember, our children are the main target of the KGB and the subject deserves a separate article.

The research I have done over the past decades, shows the strategy that progressives have pursued, it is the destruction of what has made America great. Actually, the "Green New Deal" is an attempt to destroy American capitalism. This is a result of Putin's KGB working in concert with the progressive Democrats for decades—the war against American Capitalism is under way. With one political party, the Democrats, having converted to socialist ways, the war is now being fought between our main political parties! The fundamental difference between the parties is the level of knowledge of Russia and her Intelligence apparatus, I have presented as The KGB. The Anti-Trump Republicans do not know the KGB as well . . .

Treason: The Major Issue of the 2020 Election

The word journalism has been prostituted since the first American Manchurian President Bill Clinton injected George Stephanopoulos into the media. Read my books and columns about George. The consequences of his doings have been devastating for the name of American media and the real Truth. The recent example is August 23, 2020, CBS's 60 minutes presented a very misleading segment about Russia helping Trump in the 2016 election. What a shame! The word misleading is a very soft definition of the presentation. 60 minutes has tried to revive a farcical and fake Mueller Report. The 10-12 members of the GRU is a drop in the bucket of the monumental destruction inflicted to our country by the KGB for decades.

The Mueller group either didn't know Putin's KGB, or intentionally under leadership of John Brannon had covered up the crime committed by the Dems leadership, manipulating and influencing America's mind for decades. Though the FBI and CIA have a major duty to protect and defend American Interests—both have failed. As we know today, the FBI has treated differently two Presidential campaigns: Clinton and Trump's campaigns. I am not sure that current investigation by DOJ knows that the FBI and CIA had been infiltrated by the KGB and to prevent the truth, covered-up the Obama/Putin conspiracy. If you want to know about Obama/Putin conspiracy, read my book: *What is Happening to America? The Hidden Truth of Global Destruction*, XLIBRIS, 2012.

Here is my warning. Please, read two quotations from my columns to grasp extend of Putin's operation:

> ". . . Of 22 Dems candidates for the U.S. presidency, there are 6 candidates sponsored by the KGB and George Soros, the primary KGB agent attacking America. Those candidates have contempt for Americans, yet, they are lecturing us on Christianity, morality, democracy and purity. Do you recognize some of them? The FBI has been shown to be incapable of doing their job to defend us . . . God help us!!!" My column: *The Ideology of Soviet Fascism VS. Trump.*"

The second one: "The situation in America is even worse than we know today. From twenty-two Democratic candidates for the U.S. presidency, six were sponsored by the KGB and George Soros. They were preparing for you the third American Manchurian President. For your information, two from the six came to the finish line: "Trojan Horse" Bernie Sanders and Joe Biden. They deserve each other, yet there is one difference between two of them—Trojan Horse Bernie knows that his campaign runs by Putin's KGB, Joe Biden does not know it, Obama didn't tell him . . . "*Treason: The Major Issue of the 2020 Election or The Ideological Pandemic.*"

I don't need naming the six Democrats mentioned above, you could see all six, speaking on the show when Joe Biden accepted the party nomination . . .

Oh, Mighty God, help us!

Remember: The collapse of the Soviet Union has not changed Russia's internal security system; it is intact today in Russia. To learn it, read my article "The Soviet Internal Passport System" (*The International Lawyer*, Vol. 19, No. 3, Summer 1985). Putin plans to implement this system in the United States. Watch the FBI and CIA.

CHAPTER 23

Putin's Old Soviet Fraud in America!

To the memory of Manning R. Johnson,
a brave black man who learned the truth.

The best illustration of old Soviet fraud was made by a black writer, I had never heard about. It was a pleasant surprise to receive information from my friends about an American Communist, who had completely agreed with this former Soviet attorney. I knew about the race card as a main strategy used by the KGB in America and, knowing the war being waged against Western civilization, the KGB was a major topic of my writings for all thirty-five years in America. Yet reading the book *Color, Communism and Common Sense* Paperback—January 1, 1958, I was stunned by the information the author conveyed—it was a testimony about Soviet Fraud, from the personal experiences of a black man. Judge for yourself:

> "I saw communism in all its naked cruelty, ruthlessness and utter contempt of Christian attributes and passions. And, too, I saw the low value placed upon human life, the total lack of respect for the dignity of man, the betrayal of trust, the terror of the Secret Police and the bloody hand of the assassin, during and since, those fateful years when I embraced communism." Manning R. Johnson (December 17, 1908–July 2, 1959) was a Communist Party USA African-American leader

and the party's candidate for U.S. Representative from New York's 22nd congressional district during a special election in 1935.

The man definitely loved America and in a warning to the next generation, he tried to secure and enhance the goodness of the country. His book illustrated that, the way he has described "the highest level of the communist conspiracy in America." It is a precious book, conveying a real history of the infiltration of the Soviet/Russian Intel into the American Black social midst in the 1950s. His description of a gigantic network of Soviet communist-agitators is a fact—they represented all branches of the Soviet Intel and in my writing, I use the term KGB, covering them all. *Color, Communism and Common Sense* should be a mandatory reading in the High Schools, Colleges, and Universities of America.

Putin against America: Sixty Years Later

With all respect for Daniel Hoffman of CIA, he is wrong: the chaos, looting, burning, and killing were created, calculated and executed by the Russian Intel through the so-called Democrat Party. It is currently Putin against America. We are witnessing Trotsky's *Permanent Revolution* used by the Dems under the leadership of Putin and his KGB. The huge army of Socialist Charlatans and the KGB agents set up since the 1950s have executed the Permanent Revolution in American States run by the Dems. Protests are going on in day time to openly show the subject of the demonstration. Riots are going on at night—criminals don't want to show their faces while looking, stealing, and killing . . .

Don't ask me where riots come from. I have warned you for the last thirty-five years about this massive infiltration in our country to harm and divide us. I was not alone: "It took decades for the politically correct, progressive and insufferable swamp monsters to establish total control of our universities, our corporations, our special interests groups, Hollywood, our professional sports leagues and, most importantly, our federal, state, and local governments." Jeff Crouere, Canada Free Press, 2020-08-29.

History is the crux of the matter to grasp the predicament in both America and the world today. The knowledge of Russia and her Security forces is imperative to realize that they are here in 2020 America. History of the 20th century has put a spotlight on their subversive activities and helps to grasp the reality of the 21st century. Yes, China is our prime military adversary today, yet, Russia and China have identical agenda and the ideology that makes them both our principle enemies: it took Stalin, his KGB and military 29 years to build the Chinese Communist State. Hence, if you know that history you'll identify something very similar to Russian subversive activity going on in our country today—watch Biden's campaign and the people around him, and his stuffers . . .

It is my obligation to remind you my definition of the ideology: Socialism is an ideology of destruction, ideology of lies, deception and fraud: it is an infection like coronavirus, a political disease of incompetence and I was writing about the subversive doings of the KGB for years. The ideology of Socialism/Communism was successfully implemented in North Korea, China, Eastern Europe, Cuba, Nicaragua, Iran, and Venezuela by the Russian Intel. Due to two American Manchurian Presidents, the spectacular achievements of the KGB in the 20th century, had provided Putin with the opportunity to build on that Stalin/Andropov achievements into the 21st century. Due to the KGB's recruitments and infiltration in all locations and corners of our society, the Democrat Party was successfully transformed to a Socialist Party and ideology has become the basis for its unity with the KGB.

The pundits use different terms describing the enemy: Marxists, Socialists, Communist. In fact, it is an old Stalinist Soviet ideology and the collapse of the Socialist economy in 1991 had proven that. Marx, in his theory presented Socialism as a first base for future Communism. Hence, without Socialism there is no base to build Communism. In both current Russia and China we have Crony Capitalism within Police States. The buildup of Chinese Communism was impossible without a Socialist base, which doesn't exist any longer in Russia and had never been built in China. Socialism is DEAD, Communism is impossible to build: it is probably fascism . . . Yet, both countries use the old fake term Socialism and cover-up their Intelligence apparatus operations. Actually, the war against Western Civilization is executed by the Intelligence para-military forces of those countries and their proxies. Disguising themselves by the old fake ideology, the criminals are waging war against humanity.

Watch Democrats' behavior, their conduct, their naked lies, and the methods they apply and exercise in their fight for power and you can easily identify Socialist Charlatans. Grasp a simple, but sad fact: <u>we have</u>

enemies foreign and domestic and they act together today. The old coup against Trump is still going on and will not stop until this collaboration is exposed. It was a shame, but Pelosi was in a hurry to impeach Trump during the Christmas 2019, poisoning America's Christmas celebration. She had known that the Chinese/Wuhan virus was in its way to America; that is the answer to her rushed impeachment ploy in December 2019. Watch incredible fraud, a Soviet style arrogant dishonesty bordering on crime, demonstrated by Biden and other Democrats. Our FBI and Intel both are incapable to see the reality of the massive infiltration and indoctrination of Americans for the last sixty years . . .

And more shame is under way today—the Dems are using the pandemic to their advantage against Republicans though they could've stop it, exposing the criminals in December 2019, but they didn't. Chinese Covid-19 is a Chinese Counter-Intelligence Operation against humanity. It is biological warfare in the 21st century, similar to the biological war run by Russia, infiltrating the HIV virus to humanity in the 20th century. If you want to learn this history, please, read my book: *What is Happening to America? The Hidden Truth of Global Destruction*, XLIBRIS, 2012.

The Soviet/Russian Ideological Fraud

We are at war, an ongoing asymmetrical war with many different fronts, using a variety of tools, devices, methods, and tricks unknown to us before. Seemingly unrelated events, in fact, are inextricably connected—all events coordinated and directed from the Kremlin. An apparatus or engine of nefarious actions is waging a war against America. There are now over 100 days and nights of chaos in Portland and an Antifa supporter is running for mayor of Portland. This is a clear Stalinist/Socialist extortion: "vote for me or else," which means burning, looting and killings.

This is the KGB's violent insurrection and should be treated accordingly. The Dems created that in concert with a foreign power as possible calculated evidence to use against Trump. Putin is a mortal enemy of Trump and America. The calamity has been produced by the Dems! The recent riots, burning, and killing is a part of the coup, prolonged by the Dems for the last five years. Watch how Pelosi lies with eyes open. Read here my column *Revelation,* April 26. 2018

Fraud is in the bloodstream of all Charlatans. I've already described Rahm Emanuel. I believe he is a KGB agent. As Mayor of Chicago he presided over the destruction of a black community in the city. He also helped the second American Manchurian President to win in 2012. He, together with then Governor of Pennsylvania, Ed Rendell committed a fraud in the Philadelphia election and Barack Obama won. Something similar will be done by the Biden's campaign 2020. Jesse Waters' suspects: "There are not only lies, lies, and lies, something is more sophisticated behind all lies." Jesse is right. It is old Soviet Propaganda Machine brought by Putin to America and the main attributes of the media mob are lies, deceit, and fraud . . . You will see all of that in action of the Biden campaign' promises, read on prompter by careless Joe Biden, imitating President Trump's manners and gestures . . .

Next to the Swamp and Deep State of Washington D.C. there is another center—the State of Virginia. For many years Virginia has been run by Terry McAuliffe, the Clinton mafia's lieutenant and I suspect a KGB agent. Terry McAuliffe and Andrew McCabe organized and orchestrated the White Supremacy rally in Charlottesville Va. in 2017. This couple must be investigated very toughly to expose deep infiltration in our midst by the KGB. Remember the Manning Johnson story—the KGB race card continues dividing American. The DNC and KGB now accusing Trump, using the narrative of White Supremacy, the division they themselves had created in the 1950s. Remember Stalin's major postulate: *Never admit crime committed, instead accuse opposition in that exact crime. . . .*

I believe there are other KGB's agents playing the race card to pay attention to: Soros, Sanders, Lopez, Farrakhan, and thousands in disguise that harm and damage America with impunity. You can read about six of them, sponsored by the KGB, in my preceding column—they were the Dems' candidates for U.S. presidency. Wow! Pay attention to the Biden campaign and you will discover old Soviet Propaganda Machine brought by Putin to America. Today we are dealing with Socialist Charlatans and Obama's holdovers: they will stop at nothing to lie, deceive, and defraud to remove Donald J. Trump—the endless Socialist vengeance has no borders . . .

My fellow Americans!

God and the memory of a brave Manning R. Johnson gives you the choices in the 2020 election. It is the second term of Donald J. Trump presidency, or Putin's Permanent Revolution in America.

Now it is your term to decide . . .

CHAPTER 24

America's Socialist/Fascist Party = No Peace!

The recent death of Justice Ginsburg will intensify the battles between America's Socialist/Fascist (Democrat) Party and Republicans. Our national security is at stake as in fact you are witnessing Putin's war against the Republicans and all patriotic Americans . . . It is more than an Anti-Trump war, it is Putin's war against the American Constitutional Republic to transform Capitalism to Socialism, a war against the unique political system designed by our Founding Fathers. Knowledge is Power! Knowledge of Russia and her Security—Intelligence apparatus is a MUST to expose the traitors in our midst—the leadership of America's Socialist/Fascist Party.

The History of the Socialist War Against America

It had happened at the end of 1940s or in the beginning of the 50s when Comrade Stalin gave a secret order to his military and Intelligence—Security forces to involve the U.S.A. in Middle East wars. He explained his order: "the Sectarian Wars in the Middle East will never end . . ." Both the Soviet Military and Intelligence forces executed that order. Writing about the Soviet/Russian Intelligence agencies, I use the term KGB. So, the KGB contacted its agents in the Muslim Brotherhood and gave them the assignment to find a reliable Muslim leader. They had found the man and Yasser Arafat was recruited by the KGB in 1957—Russia thus entered the wars of the Mideast.

For decades the Middle East bloody war was a primary concern of the world and humanity's desire to create peace there. To grasp the unique and historic magnitude of Israel-UAE-Bahrain Abraham Peace Accord, you have to be informed of the war waged by the Socialist/Fascist regimes against Western civilization for many decades. The Abraham Accord is the first dove of peace in that bloody neighborhood. This is a remarkable twist of history—President Donald J. Trump has reversed Stalin's war to initiate peace in the Middle East. Isn't it something astonishing! Yet, Stalin's war has intensified in the rest of the world, especially in America . . .

Writing about Stalin's war, I called it WWIII and identified as *WWIII: Recruitment and Infiltration, Drugs and Assassinations.* You can see all of it in the 2020 America. I deliberately called those regimes Socialist/Fascist. As a matter of fact I was writing about Soviet Socialism for the last thirty-five years and renamed it to Soviet Fascism after the attack on 9/11. I felt that the 14 Saudi Arabian students were recruited by the KGB and the attack was engineered and executed under the supervision of the KGB. At the time I had only my feeling, but later I found evidence in the writing of a Russian defector Konstantin Preobrazhensky. Both Socialism and Fascism are totalitarian ideologies and the terminology depends of the one's knowledge of Russia and her Intel apparatus. Read *What is Happening to America? The Hidden Truth of Global Destruction*, XLIBRIS, 2012.

Andropov's Legacy in America

Stalin also gave guidance to the war against America: "America is like a healthy body and its resistance is threefold: its patriotism, its morality, and its spiritual Life. If you can undermine these three areas, America will collapse from within."—Joseph Stalin. To grasp the menace of that war, let me show you how Stalin's devoted disciples continued his war for decades. The Chairman of the KGB, Yuri Andropov, was Stalin's devoted disciple. I knew him well. My work within the legal community coincided with his tenure as the KGB Chairman. If you have any doubts in my identification of Soviet Fascism and WWIII, the first person to confirm the identity of both will be the Chairman of the KGB, 1967-1982, Yuri Andropov. It is an irony and a paradox of the time, but a fact—his words exposed his Socialist/Fascist ideology and behavior . . .

Here is a conversation of Lt. General Ion Mihai Pacepa, the highest-ranking KGB officer ever to defect to the U.S, with Yuri Andropov:

> "In 1972 the Kremlin decided to turn the whole Islamic world against Israel and the U.S. As KGB Chairman, Yuri Andropov told me a billion adversaries could inflict far greater damage on America that could a few millions. We needed to instill a Nazi-style hatred for Jews throughout the Islamic world, and to turn this weapon of the emotions into a terrorist bloodbath against Israel and its main supporter the United States. No one within the American/Zionist sphere of influence should any longer feel safe." ("*Russian Footprints*," by Ion Mihai Pacepa, *National Review Online*, August 24, 2008.)

In the same article General Pacepa wrote: "According to Andropov . . . the Muslims had a taste for nationalism, jingoism, and victimology. Their illiterate, oppressed mobs could be whipped up to a fever pitch. Terrorism and violence against Israel and her master, American Zionism, would flow naturally from the Muslims' religious fervor", Andropov sermonized. What can better confirm both of my terms Soviet Fascism and WWIII than those words? I remind you that under Andropov the indoctrination and infiltration into Western civilization had tripled. Andropov had designed *Operation Barbarossa* to infiltrate simultaneously American Intel and media. Under his leadership there occurred the bloodiest terrorists' attacks in the world, from the Munich murder of Israelis in the Olympic Village to the *Johnstown* tragedy.

Vladimir Putin's War on America

Vladimir Putin is a devoted disciple of the KGB Chairman Yuri Andropov, his student. It is Vladimir Putin who brought Stalin's war to the 21st Century, and he is not alone. The ideology united him with Chinese Communists as they have the same agenda, strategy, and methods in fighting humanity. Technology developments have widened their criminal activities in the 21st Century and they use it to quadruple their crimes. The Chinese Wuhan-virus is a warfare missile of the Communist ideology against humanity. Don't you smell fascism in attacking citizens of the world, even their own citizens, with a deadly disease without gas chambers? If you want to know the details of infiltration and indoctrination by this ideology, please read my books and read here my column: *Putin's Old Soviet Fraud in America*! September 10, 2020.

Knowing the history, tactics and methods of the Russian Socialist Revolution, I predicted events in America. Look at my definition of Soviet fascism made in 2012 and compare it with the current predicament in America:

> "Now, many years later, I can see the overall dynamics of the events in the world—the Stalinist ideology is moving from one country to another like a plague. It contaminates the land and the human psyche. I saw it with my own eyes. I felt it. And with time a more complete idea and identification of Soviet Fascism had been growing and ripening in my head. Soviet Fascism[i] has become the ideology of various political groups, an amalgamation of Marxists, Communists, Socialists, Anarchists, radical Islamists, and other left-wing groups around the globe, united under the Kremlin's umbrella to fight Western civilization. Be prepared—different types of violent extremism even a revolution will become an instrument of official policies of the countries adhered to Soviet Fascism . . . WWIII is marching across the globe . . ." *What is Happening to America*? p. 159, XLIBRIS, 2012.

Don't you see the carbon copy of the quandary described above in 2020 America? This mess was created by two Democrat American Manchurian Presidents. They, in concert with the KGB transformed the Democrat Party to the Socialist Party and Socialist mafia we are dealing today. The actual example of the Socialist mafia in action is the Biden campaign, run by Socialist Charlatans. Besides, a demented Biden speaking and acting according to a prescribed script, the entire campaign is operating by the Socialist methods and tactics and Stalin's major postulate: *Never admit crime committed, instead accuse opposition in that exact crime*. . . . Listen to Biden and his Charlatans, it will be lies, deceit, disinformation and fraud—the essence of any Socialist/Fascist regime. Read here *The Origin of Washington Spy Ring and the Swamp,* March 30, 2018.

Warning to the 2020 Election

Do you feel the rising political temperature in the country? We are super divided! *Socialist/Fascist Party* of America has "achieved" a great deal to create this division during the last couple of decades. Two American Manchurian Presidents executed that division from within then and today. Abraham Lincoln was right, we are committing suicide. Here are the doers of the division the Clinton mafia: George Stephanopoulos, John Podesta, Tony Podesta, Terry McAuliffe, and Sidney Blumenthal. Those people have been a totalitarian force of Socialism/Fascism, undermining the American Republic for decades with impunity, and continuing it today. The recent Trump interview by Stephanopoulos was a set up in the best traditions of the Stalin's KGB. Read here my column Revelation, April 26, 2019.

The racial division created by Obama is unprecedented, yet the country bought into his cult of personality and nobody dared to criticize him. His holdovers doubled undermining America. Don't blame Millenniums they were purposely deprived of knowledge. I'd like to talk about Obama's long-range policy, keeping America ill-informed, deaf, mute, and naked. . . . I am an Alumni of the Kennan Institute. The Kennan Institute was the premier U.S. center for advanced research on Russia and Eurasia and the oldest and largest regional program at the Woodrow Wilson International Center for Scholars. My colleagues were really knowledgeable people in their subjects. I knew George F. Kennan and he loved listening me and the Russian poetry I was reciting.

I was shocked hearing that "Resigning from Congress in February 2011, Jane *Harman* became President and CEO of the Woodrow *Wilson* International *Center* for Scholars." Her knowledge of Russia was equal to zero during this time of Putin's war against America. Her appointment stopped real information about Putin's Russia for several years, making America ill-informed, deaf, mute, and naked . . . . Obama had achieved his goal, in addition to that he depleted our military. This and other analogous actions of TREASON has mobilized the Democrat Party to save their future and fight Trump to divert the people's attention from the TREASON the Democrat's leadership has committed for several decades.

The Grand-Conspiracy Operates Undercover

The Anti-Trump prolonged coup was manufactured and executed by three Presidents: Bill Clinton, Barack Obama, and Vladimir Putin to cover-up the crimes they committed. You are witnessing a global war-room aggressively attacking the government system of the American Constitutional Republic!!! Read here my column *Watergate 2.0: The KGB's Global Spy Ring*, November 8, 2020.

My fellow Americans!

America's Socialist/Fascist Party is ready to implement in America a totalitarian regime similar to the Soviet Union and China. Expect an enormous voter-fraud by the Socialist/Fascist Party to take over POWER. Be ready for hate, intimidation, threat and violence . . . Defend your country, your freedom and personal liberty!

Vote Republican!

CHAPTER 25

From Soviet Socialism to China's Covid-19 Pandemic

May 1, 2020

President Trump once used the word "plague" with disgust on his face talking about Covid-19 at a WH coronavirus task force briefing. He reminded me of my Father, who often used the word "plague" with the same disgust on his face talking about Soviet Socialism. There is an inextricable chain of events in the world we live in and as a student of history, I have found a striking similarity in human behaviors in the events of the 1980s and 2020. I'd like you to be a judge.

It was in the 1980s, around the time I was about to immigrate to the West and visited my father in Leningrad to say goodbye to him. We had a conversation that I recalled in my first book *Baltic Winds: Testimony of a Soviet Attorney,* pp. 315–316 and in my third book: *What is Happening to America?* pp. 164–165. I'll give you the essence, a short transcript of the conversation between three of us my Father, my son Roman and me:

> "Separation from you will be one of the most difficult experiences of my life. It's even more painful that I can't help you. But the thought that you and your children will be free at last gives me some comfort. Yet you have to promise me one thing." He glanced at me and waited as I dried me eyes.

"What should I do, Papa?"

"I want you to promise me that no other country will ever seduce you—not England, not France. You must go to America . . . there won't be peace in Europe . . . you're entering an unfamiliar world, and I want you to understand the transformation going on in it. Have you heard about the American hostages in Tehran?"

"Well, I've heard something." Roman said

"It's not *something!* Young people . . . students brainwashed by Marxist ideology, took those Americans and humiliated them. The only crime of those hostages is that they're *American.*

Do you know who's behind that ordeal?"

"No, I don't."

"The Soviet bandits, who are spreading the plague of hatred against America because they can't destroy it the way they're destroying Europe."

"What do you mean, destroying Europe?" Roman asked.

"I mean just what I said. In our age, ideas run the world, and the wrong ideas destroy it. You . . . are leaving because the country adhered to a wrong idea. That's why I want you to go to America. . . . Did you meet the KGB agents recruiting students in your law school?"

"Yes, we had them every year. They asked for cooperation."

"You see how easy it is—first indoctrinate and then recruit. Remember, the KGB uses the same strategy in major universities around the world. It gets its payoff when youngsters become professionals. In the

Middle East some of them join terrorist groups trained by the Soviets, in Europe they join the government. Let me tell you about the results of that. In the thirties, the KGB recruited five students from Cambridge in England, and later on it had the entire British counterintelligence in its pocket. You are not staying in Europe . . . you must do your utmost to get to America."

What a short lesson of real history! What an analogous use of the word "plague" with disgust in different continents, different countries, and forty years apart. What an incredible connection of times in human feelings! My father knew well Soviet Socialism and Communist ideology. What an ideological tie of times! Don't you see a direct similarity between coronavirus in 2020 and conversation about Soviet Socialism with my Father in 1980? I do and that drives me to present some explanations:

The Ideological Ties Between Times

Yes, what an ideological tie of times forty years later! Today, we are blaming Chinese Communist regime of the crime of spreading the global coronavirus pandemic. Do you know where the Chinese Communist regime came from? It came from Soviet Socialism and was implemented by Joseph Stalin. It took Stalin twenty-nine years to achieve the result by 1949. Russian Intelligence and military have built Chinese Communist State and implemented the entire Soviet governmental structure and institutions, which means placing the Soviet system within the Chinese State with the Communist Party on the top, like in the USSR. Mao had accepted the Soviets leadership of the Socialist Camp after the KGB attempted to poison him. You can read the details on the Chapter 5 *Tell me Something I Don't Know, What is Happening to America*? By Simona Pipko, Xlibris, 2012.

Moscow had been running all Soviet Republics and having identical departments for all involved—it had eased the control. Asian experience of implementing Soviet Socialism in Mongolia, North Korea, and China also helped Stalin to implement his Soviet Socialism within Eastern Europe. Under the Warsaw Military Pact it was done the same exact way—replicating the Soviet governmental structure with all its negative features of total secrecy, fraud, disinformation, stealing technology, nepotism—the entire Soviet System to all countries of the Eastern

Europe. That was a simple way for the Kremlin to run the Socialist Camp from Europe to Asia and all mentioned countries had received from the Kremlin the Project of 1955 to study and follow it. To grasp this recent pandemic, read here my column *Covid-19: A Fascist Act of Terror Against Humanity*, April 12, 2020.

Don't be confused by the different terms Marxism, Communism and Socialism—all three are a fallacy—a fraud with a utopian concept. In fact, we were dealing with Stalin's Soviet Socialism, which began killing Americans in the 1950 Korean War, when Soviet pilots were shooting down American planes. The Vietnam War of 1962–1975 with Chinese volunteers had brought another killing of over 50 thousand American military. After that the Soviet killing field moved to Middle East: in the Beirut barracks bombing 243 U.S. military men were killed in 1983. The collapse of the Soviet Union has changed the world temporarily, yet, by the end of the 20th century and Putin's presidency, Russia has obtained power again; close relations with China resumed and a new group of the Chinese leaders has been trained and drilled by Moscow. The killing of Americans was also resumed in the attack of 9/11/2001, near 3 thousand Americans killed in New York . . .

Yes, there is no more Soviet Socialism, it was replaced by a new criminal cabal—*the Axis of Evil* under Russian umbrella. Russia is there again in a new century, because Putin and his Security apparatus are still running this criminal cabal and the war against American capitalism. Only people who know Russian Intelligence agencies are aware of Russia's power in the world through the agents of influence, designed by the Project of 1955, I called then the Soviet Charlatans. We also should consider a great "success" of the Russian/Chinese Intel, infiltrating all corners of our society: the governmental institutions, especially the House of Representative, business, sport, academia, and the media . . .

Agents of Influence or the Soviet Socialist Charlatans

History is the Mother of all sciences. In this time of crises, stress, anxiety, and fake news, history is the only way to find the Truth. We are at war, in asymmetrical war. It was the Soviet Russia that injected viruses in the war, opening a new sinister front against Western civilization and American capitalism. Though today, with all eyes on China, we should remember: China has the same counterintelligence apparatus that Russia has, (under different names), the same institutions, agenda and methods against us. Knowing Chinese politicians, their connection to Russia, their incompetence and dishonesty using lies, fraud, intimidation, and deception, I don't expect a word of truth from them—they are all Socialist Charlatans. So, I have found some objective materials. Here is one of them:

Nature, *WUHAN, CHINA,* by David Cyranoski, 22 February 2017. It is a big column and I give you one paragraph, where I found three Red Flags:

> "The Wuhan lab cost 300 million yuan (US$44 million), and to allay safety concerns it was built far above the flood plain and with the capacity to withstand a magnitude-7 earthquake, although the area has no history of strong earthquakes. It will focus on the control of emerging diseases, store purified viruses and act as a World Health Organization 'reference laboratory' linked to similar labs around the world. 'It will be a key node in the global biosafety-lab network,' says lab director Yuan Zhiming."

Three Red Flags:

First: The wet market is the Asian primitive medieval tradition in the times of plague and cholera. The Wuhan lab was built in the 21st century. Why was the location of the lab chosen in proximity to a wet-market, known for its anti-sanitary conditions? I suspect it was done purposely with mischief reasoning to have a current explanation. Besides, the bat-virus was researched miles apart from the wet-market . . .

Second: The Wuhan lab ". . . will . . . act as a World Health Organization 'reference laboratory' linked to similar labs around the world." This is telling me the Soviet agenda to run a global organization through their agents—I have no doubts the W.H.O. General-Secretary Theodor is a KGB agent, recruited in Ethiopia and has been promoted since . . . Besides him, Bill Gates is also closely connected to the W.H.O. sponsoring it. The KGB agents serve an ideological agenda, regardless of their race and ethnicity, it doesn't matter he or she is Russian, American, Chinese or Ethiopian—they are all the Soviet Socialist Charlatans confronting the U.S.A. The tendency to infiltrate the world organizations was and is the ultimate Communistic agenda to have a global control.

Third: Who is the Director of the Wuhan lab? His name is familiar to me. I am not a biologist, but I know Chinese politicians, and especially China's Presidents. The Wuhan lab construction started under President *Jiang Zemin in 2003 and I suspect that he and the Wuhan lab's Director are relatives. Their last name spells a bit differently, yet, I still suspect. Look at this former Chinese President:*

Jiang Zemin is a Chinese retired politician who served as General Secretary of the Communist Party of China from 1989 to 2002 as Chairman of the Central Military Commission of the Communist Party of China from 1989 to 2004 and as President of the People's Republic of China from 1993 to 2003 . . . I still suspect the relation, which will testify to the lifeblood connection between ideology and virology in the world of Communism.

Russia/China: The Biological Connection

I believe there is not only an ideological connection between Russia and China, but a criminal bio-chemical connection as well. It was Soviet Socialism that injected viruses in this war for Global control. I've told you the story of my client who worked by the Soviet government assignment in researching HIV in Africa. Having the same Soviet System, and common agenda, the Russian virologists provided Chinese scientists with needed techniques to use viruses in this current war. As a result, we have several types of the viruses connected to HIV, besides coronavirus—a new one. Please, listen to a respected contemporary scientist:

Professor Luc Montagnier, who was the 2008 Nobel Prize winner for Medicine, claims that SARS-CoV-2 is a manipulated virus accidentally released from a lab in Wuhan. Chinese researches are said to have used the coronavirus in their work to develop an AIDS vaccine. Fragments of HIV DNA are believed to have been found in the SARS-CoV-2 genome. Indian researchers have already tried to publish the results of the analyses that showed that this coronavirus genome contained sequences of another virus, the HIV virus (AIDS virus)" *Man Who Discovered HIV Makes Explosive Comments About Origins Of The Coronavirus,* The Patriotic Voice, April 22, 2020.

I am talking about Russia/China ties for a reason—both are totalitarian states, both our mortal enemies working hand in hand. Nothing substantial has changed in Russia since a devoted disciple of Stalin/Andropov Putin become the President—runs by the KGB's officer the Soviet system was revived in Russia. Here is a Russian journalist's opinion today: "Putin's pyramid has no system of checks and balances other than Putin himself. Neither the parliament, nor the court, nor the press can become a truly serious obstacle to those influential groups that seek to maximize their income by any means. . . . This kind of standard procedure results in two types of abuse: bribes and kickbacks." *Will the Putin System Exist Until 2042?* By DMITRY TRAVIN

As you can see, very little has changed in Russia during last forty years. Perhaps only the titles have changed: Stalin had a Socialist Camp, Putin has the *Axis of Evil* under his Russian umbrella. Of course, China is still the most dangerous economically and militarily to the West, but it is worth remembering the criminal cabal of the Socialist Charlatans in America and around world. Iranian boats are provoking our military ships at the time of global pandemic. Look at the chorus of Russia, China, North Korea and Iran how they are covering up the real number of Covid-19 victims, lying and deceiving the world, while the pandemic kills 60 thousand Americans.

Be ready for several bombshells about America's Socialist Charlatans, yet the story requires a separate column. At least, I hope now you understand the reason I renamed Soviet Socialism to Soviet Fascism. History is the Mother of all sciences and we can expect a very challenging time ahead. North Korea is a Stalinist police state. Knowing the events in March 1953 in Moscow after Stalin's death, I can predict a power struggle in a highest echelon of the North Korean authority, like it was in Moscow in 1953 . . .

CHAPTER 26

Treason: The Major Issues of the 2020 Election and the Ideological Pandemic

May 11, 2020

A global pandemic requires a global response and solution. This time it is more than just virus—it is ideology as well. Yes, a virus is invisible, but the criminals who unleashed it are very visible and well-known. That is the reason, publishing my latest column on April 12, 2020, I titled it *Covid-19: A Fascist Terror Act against Humanity.* I did it deliberately to remind you the history of the global crime committed by a Socialist/Communist regime—The Project of 1955. The Soviets sent the Project to all Socialist Camp countries to study and to follow the Soviet order. The covid-19 pandemic illustrates this ominous order. Only people who read or know the Project of 1955 can objectively assess origins of China's covid-19 pandemic and the force we are up against. The Project bared its evil nature and the agenda of Socialism/Communism to achieve global control—a total destruction of capitalism, Western civilization, and its leader, the American Constitutional Republic.

That menacing agenda drove me to warn you for the last thirty-five years to be informed and ready for a disaster ahead of us. I have introduced you to a Soviet defector Yuri Bezmenov, who introduced the *Soviet Ideological Subversion of America in Four Stages,* a plan to destabilize Western civilization and destroy the global system of capitalism. Even more, I showed the infiltration of the Dems Party by the KGB, and its transformation by the traitors who led it. I did all of that, because I knew the Project of 1955, its methods and the tricks it used to succeed. Here is the latest example:

> "While watching the so-called Trump/Dossier documentary in the 2017, it did not take me even ten seconds to realize that it was Russian "fallshivka" a fraud in front of me. Everything in the Dossier exposed the KGB's handwriting: its arrogant manner of presentation, method, character with an aggressive and salacious tone to denigrate President Trump, the Republican Party, and to influence American opinion. It was a vivid picture of the incredible dirt being dumped on Trump, a typical Stalinist legacy of demonizing and attacking the opposition leader, used by the KGB." I wrote that in my column *The Global Spy Ring*, January 1, 2018.

The History of Treason

The term KGB applies to the entire Russian Security Apparatus in my column. For me, the Trump/Dossier was the first sign of the KGB's big scheme to fight personally President Trump from the first day he had announced his candidacy for the U.S. presidency. This successful capitalist had then become a very comfortable target to destroy and with him a political system designed by our Founding Fathers. In the KGB alliance with the DNC, everything that followed had been coordinated and calculated by the Obama/Putin Conspiracy. Our weaponized Intel has participated in the conspiracy. I had figured out that years ago. Look here at my column *Failed American Intelligence*, on August 1, 2018:

> **First:** Anti-Trump "criminal cabal" was manufactured and organized by Russian Intel through Democrats' leadership and the Clinton Mafia.
>
> **Second:** Anti-Trump "criminal cabal" consists of two groups: the leadership of the Deep State and the leadership of the Clinton Mafia. Today, Rod J. Rosenstein of the DOJ is a connective link of the two groups.

> **Third:** Anti-Trump "criminal cabal" is run by three individuals: Barack Obama, Bill Clinton, and Vladimir Putin. The three are working together for decades . . .
>
> **Fourth**: Investigation of this huge case of international espionage and treason requires deep knowledge of Russia and its Intel. The current FBI Director, Christopher Wray did not read my books, he doesn't know that it took Stalin twenty-nine years to create and establish the Chinese Communist State. The structure, agenda, and ideology were identical in Russia and China. The two National Intelligence Agencies executed the same strategy, tactics, methods, and tricks, working hand in glove. Yet, there is a difference today: a billion hardworking Chinese people have achieved substantially more than the alcoholic and drug addled Russians . . .

AG Barr is not "Disrupting Justice in America"

President Trump wasn't the only one accused by the Dems of being a Russian agent. Three other Republicans have also been accused of the analogous crime with a common narrative: collaboration, connection or helping Russia in disrupting the 2016 election. It was the second KGB stage of confronting the Republican President Trump that I noticed a familiar KGB behavior. The abuses of power, methods, and dirty tactics used against General Michael Flynn, Carter Page, and George Papadopoulos testified to that—the FBI created crime, like Stalin did in Russia . . .

General Michael Flynn went through hell for three years of FBI investigation. As we know now, Flynn was entrapped, which is a deliberate act of crime, not err of judgment on the part of the FBI investigators. Unprecedented corruption and abuses of power by this Law-Enforcement agency had been used against all four Republicans. Maybe the cruelest prosecution of General Flynn took place, because he knew something about Obama/Putin conspiracy??? Yet . . .

There was the third stage of the KGB's scheme—the manufactured Mueller Report. I watched Robert Mueller testifying before the Congress. It was a tragic spectacle—I was ashamed for my country. The Mueller

Report is a fraud perpetrated by someone, not by Robert Mueller. He didn't know the major elements of the report and his mental capacity was at question. The KGB, as usual were using mental deficiency to its own benefit. I have an idea of who committed the fraud and fabricated the report. Read here my columns, *Origin of the Washington Spy-Ring and the Swamp*, March 31, 2018.

The Covid-19 pandemic and its catastrophic impact on our economy reminds us that we are still dealing with *The Global Spy Ring*, where the Democrat Party and DNC are a part of the ring. Don't be surprised that the Dems and DNC are the part of the ring. During the last 3–4 decades Truman's Democrat Party was infiltrated by the KGB and suffocated, a new Socialist Party was born with leader's hell bent on damaging the free market while building Socialism in America. This utopian ideology has become a major divide between the current Democrats and Republicans, a war you are witnessing every day . . .

> This war is known to me, but it is not a Cold War with China. Warning you for the last two decades, I called it WWIII. It is waged by the ideology of Socialism/Communism against Western civilization and the American Republic. The current Democrats joined the war on the side of Socialism against the Republican Party. Don't be surprised that Democrats don't want to hold China accountable for the covid-19: they are sharing the same ideology, first with Russia and then with China in the 21st century. The Russian/Chinese Intel runs the ideology in both countries and has infiltrated all corners of our society and its elite: from Hollywood to the media, from Harvard University to the House of Representatives.

Unfortunately, most Americans have no idea of the massive, deep, and ubiquitous infiltration by the KGB into American institutions in the 20th century. They do not know that two U.S. Presidents had been chosen for them by the KGB.

Stalinist Postulate in the 21st century America

Offence is the best defense—this was the slogan and policy of the Soviet apparatchiks taught by Stalin. "*Never admit the crime committed, but accuse the opposition in that exact crime*" Stalin's Postulate. This policy helped the Soviet system to survive for a hundred years, and under Putin's leadership the current apparatchiks are flourishing in Russia today. Yes, nothing substantial has changed in Russia. The KGB is still running the country with a crony capitalism instead of failed socialism. That's it. The agenda is still the same—*One World Socialist Government Under Kremlin's Rule* and for Putin to be a President of the world. This is the answer to what is happening in America in the 21st century.

The Obama/Putin conspiracy and its massive cover-up had required action to save the Democrat Party from accountability for treason. The Stalinist postulate was successfully used to blame the Republicans for collaborating with the KGB, like Stalin taught. The Russian meddling in the 2016 election and the accusation that Trump colluded with them, is the KGB's maneuvering trick to cover-up their real collaboration with the Democrat Party for decades. It is not a coincidence that 20 30 of my latest columns had been describing the KGB and its Chairman Yuri Andropov. We are witnessing the disastrous result of failed American Intelligence in May 2020. The FBI Director is an empty suit or dupe of the enemy, he doesn't understand Russian Security Agencies and allowed them to undermine the American Constitutional system from within. What a shame!

The situation in America is even worse than we know today. From twenty-two Democratic candidates for the U.S. presidency, six had been sponsored by the KGB and George Soros. They were preparing for you the third American Manchurian President. For your information, two from the six came to the finish line: Trojan Horse Bernie Sanders and Joe Biden. They deserve each other, yet there is one difference between two of them—Trojan Horse Bernie knows that his campaign is being run by Putin's KGB, Joe Biden doesn't know it, Obama didn't tell him . . .

CHAPTER 27

A Spy Ring: Putin-Xi-Obama-Biden

October 8, 2020

Russia's *Operation disinformation* cost us an enormous waste of human energy, waste of time, and waste of millions dollars during the last five years. The inability of the CIA, FBI, NSA, and DOJ to know and detect the modus operandi of Russia's Intelligence is the result of it. The war waged by Socialist/Communist forces of Russia against Western civilization during several decades were exacerbated by the forces of China's counter-intelligence application of a biochemical agent to commit a colossal crime against Humanity. The situation in the world has risen national security concerns and required urgency to focus on Russia's and China's responsibility in revealing their ideological regimes which have committed this crime against mankind. The first presidential debate emphasized and exposed our obligation and necessity to hold those regimes accountable.

The Socialist-Democrat Party Connection

A week prior to the first presidential debate, I sent an email to Chris Wallace with a warning: "I am a former Soviet attorney and don't trust you. To grasp a dangerous predicament in America, please, read my must read column: *America's Socialist/Fascist Party = No Peace*! September 22, 2020." He probably did not read it and the debate became chaotic for Chris Wallace, who has been ignoring political history. I am not sure that he and Commission on Debate are politically well informed and know that we are dealing with the political Charlatans, America's Socialist Party and a *Putin-Xi-Obama-Biden Spy Ring* in the 21st century.

History is the Mother of all sciences; and when a chunk of history is purposely erased from the mind of an entire generation, the people become confused and disoriented by the world events. That chunk of history is Stalin's Russia and her Intelligence apparatus forces' a crime against humanity. Writing about them, I use the term KGB, as knowledge of the KGB is missing in the minds of today's Americans. Those forces run Russia today. An undetected massive infiltration of those forces into all corners and locations in the midst of America, turned out to be very beneficial for Putin and Xi, but tragic for America.

To grasp the significance of the events in the 21st century one should know that Truman's Party is dead, it was transformed to a Socialist Party by the collaboration of the party's leadership with the KGB. America's Socialist Party doesn't like the American political system designed and implemented by our Founding Fathers and wish to dismantle it. America's Socialist Party is combating and undermining the American Constitutional Republic for the last several decades. I am not sure that Chris Wallace knew that Biden was representing America's Socialist Party covered-up by the name Democratic. Nothing democratic left in the current America's Socialist Party. It is not a coincident that Biden and China identically mocking Trump—Communists and Socialists are always working together and . . . Wuhan-Covid-19 infected America to help America's Socialist Party to get rid of President Trump . . .

Decorum and Civility in Debates

Debate is a process that involves formal discussion on particular topics. The rules of debate can be changed, but not decorum and civility. They are imperative under democracy. Wallace violated that decorum and civility. When Biden called Trump a liar and clown, in the best tradition of Stalinist character assassination, insulting Trump, Wallace didn't stop him. Instead he debated Trump, who expressed his ideas. It was two-on-one debate, where Biden told the President to "shut up." Wallace suffered the Napoleon complex-inferiority complex and he demonstrated his ego. Wallace is a Democrat, successfully maneuvering in the Republican channel. He is the most ill-informed man in terms of Russia at Fox News. Recently he gave an opportunity to two Dem Party Communists to agitate America with their ideas in his show. For me, both individuals were KGB agents. Wallace is unaware of Socialist Charlatans' destructive activities in America . . .

Joe Biden a Socialist Charlatan-Traitor

From the first day of Obama's presidency the war against the American Republic began to transform our country to a Socialist Administrative State. Socialist-Obama did not hide his real agenda, openly calling for this transformation. And he began fighting the unique political system left to us by our Founding Father. The Socialist/Communist's *brain-washing war on America's mind and soul was started by Socialist-Obama, lying constantly, using Stalinist Political Correctness. The train-engine of the coup against Trump has been moving ahead, combating Western civilization and you, the American people. Surrounded by Obama's holdovers, some are KGB agents helping Biden to run that coup today—the agenda is one-party-system as in Russia and China and as it used to be in the USSR.*

We know Biden as a liar and plagiarist, yet there is more: he is a weak man, who naturally follows a stronger one. Being in the Washington D.C. Swamp for 47 years he didn't produced any key legislature or vital law—he followed. In the 1980s he followed his mentor, leader of Ku Klux Klan, Sen. Robert Byrd and Biden's High-Tech-Lynching of a really decent and honorable Judge Clarence Thomas is documented by history. The face and the sound of the offended Judge's voice is still in my head . . . As a follower Biden was chosen as VP by Obama. Recent revealed actions by Obama's Deep State have proven Biden's total participation in the coup against President Trump. To learn a real story of Ukraine and Biden, please read here: *Soviet Style Impeachment In America,* November 20, 2019 and *Stalin Planned America's Collapse—It's Underway* October 10. 2019

Tom Fitton is right: "Americans weren't generally aware of Joe and Hunter Biden's shenanigans in Ukraine, but Obama's State Department was, as was Ukraine." I'd add that Biden's assignment by Obama was aimed at the destruction and suffocation of the young democracy in

Ukraine to help Putin, like Obama helped him by erasing the Red Line he had established in Syria. Obama had several conduits to Putin, but Putin needed "help" in Ukraine, as he had known that his man, President of Ukraine Victor Yanukovych would be defeated in the upcoming 2014 Ukrainian election. That was the reason Putin annexed Crimea in February 2014 and that was the reason for Obama to assign Biden as a point man to Ukraine. Obama designed the scenario of Biden's activities there including his son Hunter.

At the time Biden was in good health and right mind—he accepted the plan aware of its criminality. From that moment on Joe Biden became a traitor, working for president Putin. Don't be surprised by Hunter's connection in Moscow. For your information all leaders in Russia are connected to the KGB and definitely the wife of a former Mayor of Moscow, Elena Baturina. Chinese nationals from the Communist government in China are also connected to their counter-intelligence apparatus like in Russia. This is also the identical scenario of Hunter's connections in Ukraine with the oligarch in Kiev being connected to Putin—the way KGB operates the International Spy Ring.

America is not a Raciest Country

I wasn't surprised when Biden brought an old Trump accusation of "White Supremacy" in his nomination acceptance speech. "White Supremacy" is a narrative of the KGB playing the race card for several decades. This twist of fate indicates at last the same thinking process, of Biden's campaign and the KGB. But I believe in the direct connection of the two. I have written about that connection thee columns since the 2017. Here is two paragraphs from the third one:

> Putin's Old Soviet Fraud in America!
>
> "For many years Virginia has been run by Terry McAuliffe, the Clinton mafia's lieutenant and I suspect a KGB agent. Terry McAuliffe and McCabe had organized and orchestrated the White Supremacy rally in Charlottesville Va. in 2017. This couple must be investigated very toughly and thoroughly to expose the deep infiltration in our midst by the KGB . . . The DNC

> and KGB are now accusing Trump, using the narrative of White Supremacy, the division they themselves had created. Remember Stalin's major postulate: *Never admit any crime committed, instead accuse opposition in that exact crime.*

I believe there are other KGB agents continuing to play the race card, we must pay attention to: Georg Soros, Stephanopoulos, Sanders, Tom Lopez and thousands in disguises that harm and damage America with impunity. Pay attention to the Biden campaign and you will discover the old Soviet Propaganda Machine brought by Putin to America. Today we are dealing with Socialist Charlatans and Obama's holdovers: they will stop at nothing to lie, deceive, and defraud to remove Donald J. Trump—the endless Socialist vengeance has no borders"

The White Supremacy will be the main argument against Trump by the KGB. This is an Andropov's design in action-a race card. I have sent all three columns with details on the subject to AG William Barr personally—no result. The FBI Director is dysfunctional—he doesn't know the KGB's modus operandi and the KGB have free hand destroying America by using their armed forces BLM and Antifa, which are not an "idea", but the KGB's in America. We are living in an era when Communists and Socialists are coming out of the underground to take over our country and delegated Joe Biden to complete that takeover for Vladimir Putin and Xi.

I deliberately gave you a picture of Chris Wallace—knowledge of Russia and her Intelligence forces is a must—the KGB is on our soil and through the American Socialist Party they have free hand to destroy our America the Beautiful. There are people who continue dealing with China regardless of the Communists' common agenda and threat to our national security. Arizona Dem candidate for Senate, Mark Kelly has the audacity to both deal with China and run for the U.S. Senate. What an obnoxious and dangerous behavior! This is the face of America's Socialist Party!!! Even more: the Dems are painting a false picture making a weak Biden a strong leader—as usual they are deceiving and defrauding YOU! The RINOS have followed them—the arguments of Ms. Fiorina are illogical and laughable. The Biden/Harris ticket is the focal point and apogee of fraud.

There are two kinds of traitors: people who collaborate with the KGB and those who don't know the KGB, becoming accomplices. An unprecedented harm and destruction have been brought to our country by these two groups. Obama has politicized the entire society, dividing even the medical community. You saw it. At the time of the threat of the Chinese coronavirus we have become mute and defenseless, as different groups of "experts" couldn't produce one professional decision. Moreover, some C.D.C. workers are now political activists: Socialist Charlatans are playing with numbers to confuse you in this critical time.

I've written about Communist subversion for thirty-five years so the current news about Obama/Clinton treachery in 2016 didn't surprise me. My opinion stays the same: Watching the Trump/Dossier in 2017, I knew it was the KGB's fraud—Falshivka. The anti-Trump cabal is led by the trio: Bill Clinton, Barack Obama, and Vladimir Putin.

We are dealing with an army of aggressive international Socialist mafia, a Spy Ring to turn the American constitutional republic into the Union of Socialist American States. The Democrats are leading this fight, their main reason is to take over the power and to cover-up the sinister crime of treason that they have committed over several decades. This crime, committed by the leadership of Dems' Socialist mafia, should be a major topic in the November 2020 election.

CHAPTER 28

Wake-Up Suburbia! Soviet/Socialist Inspired Insurrection!

October 19, 2020

"Insurrection is an art, and like all art it has its laws" Leon Trotsky

I have already focused your attention on Putin's old Soviet fraud and his counter-intelligence operations in America, yet, even I was stunned watching how Lenin's and Stalin's grandchildren are manufacturing and executing a Socialist Revolution in America. It is a real insurrection and I recalled the design of the KGB Chairman Yuri Andropov. It is the one I have shared with you in at least a dozen of my columns. All the troubles in America today are happening because of his plan, which has been implemented and executed since the 1960s in America. In my columns I named it *Andropov's Operation Barbarossa*. The design was a simple one: infiltrate simultaneously the media and all the Security apparatus of America.

Sixty years ago in Russia I heard about his design while talking with my friends from the Law School, who worked in different Russian Intelligence agencies, people close to Andropov. I didn't believe in the project, but just listened to them. Sixty years later I see it in America . . . The predicate of all current troubles in America are the dysfunctional FBI and Intel who had been missing Russia's counter-intelligence operations in America for the last decades (perhaps because they have been infiltrated?). The latest revelations show team Obama invented the whole Russia Gate Scandal. "In mid-2016, the FBI got word that Russian intelligence believed Hillary Clinton's campaign was planning to frame Donald Trump for colluding with Russia's Vladimir Putin." Obama's team allowed the fraud to go forward. I called this corruption the Obama/Putin Conspiracy and published it in my column *Watergate 2.0: The KB's Global Spy Ring,* 11.8, 2019.

That is a fact. Yet, for me the fraud was created and produced much earlier by the KGB in 2015. I recognized it in 2017, through watching the Trump/Dossier. It took me a couple of seconds to realize the KGB Falshivka, while three incompetent FBI's Directors couldn't or wouldn't. They didn't know the modus operandi of the Russian Security apparatus and had missed a massive infiltration of those different agencies into the soil of America and their destructive activities in indoctrinating America's minds, infiltrating all democratic institutions, businesses, sports, and changing our culture and criteria for moral standards. It was Russia's counter-intelligence operations aimed at implementing the Stalinist agenda—One World Socialist Government under Kremlin's rule. Now insurrection is going on with impunity . . .

Watergate 3.0: Biden's Family–Mafia Clan

Secret Biden E-Mails were sent to the FBI in 2019. There was no answer. Where is Mr. Wray? In my book Putin is a mortal enemy of Trump and he is using Joe to defeat Trump while the FBI remains silent, subverting our national security. Putin knows the money-family business, where all family members share money with Joe—a mafia clan. Putin is a devoted disciple of Andropov and the Biden campaign is Putin's KGB counter-intelligence operation in the realm of *Andropov's Operation Barbarossa*. Like many other KGB agents Biden is Putin's Trojan Horse for Socialism—the vessel for Putin's KGB working in his campaign and using the Democrat leader to destroy America's political system and to bankrupt capitalism: To continue the old Stalinist, Socialist/Communist idea to create *One Word Socialist Government under the Kremlin rule . . .* here is no doubt in there being an Obama/Putin conspiracy—Biden has been used by Obama to help Putin to suffocate the young democracy of Ukraine.

Putin's lust for power over Ukraine has no end. With it he will build the Russian Empire again. There is no European Empire of Russia without Ukraine, and the Obama/Putin conspiracy was supposed to change the map of Europe. I was writing about this conspiracy for years.

Biden should have been impeached due to the Ukrainian case and his support of Putin. Everything in Biden's campaign, his advertisements, his cynical lying during the Stephanopoulos Town Hall, and Biden himself is a totally tacit and outrageous FRAUD.

Listen to him, he is not only a compulsive liar, accusing Trump of the crime he himself committed. Biden at the same time plagiarized Trump—A typical Socialist Charlatan-Traitor. *Surrounded by Obama's holdovers, some are KGB agents helping Biden to continue running the coup against Trump today—the agenda is a one-party-system as in Russia and China and as it used to be in the USSR. To learn about Biden and Ukraine,* read New York Post, Oct. 14, 2020 and my columns about Biden and Ukraine–*A Spy Ring: Putin-Xi-Obama-Biden,* October 8, 2020, *Soviet Style Impeachment in America*, November 20, 2019, *Stalin Planned America's Collapse—It's Underway*, October 10, 2019, *Stalinist Political Charlatans in America*, 12, 15, 2019.

Socialism corrupts everything it touches. Socialism is an amoral ideology of total corruption and abuse of power, a regime with the modus operandi of lies, deceit, and fraud, and a regime that I lived under for half of my life. The regime is only beneficial for the top. You can see it in the behaviors of America's Socialist Charlatans lying and defrauding you for decades. They are fighting the American Constitutional Republic, the political system left to us by our Founding Fathers. Don't be surprised by Biden, Trojan Horse Bernie Sanders and George Stephanopoulos. They've been destroying America for decades and so has George Soros, who is for me, a KGB agent. There are thousands of them in disguises that harm and damage America with impunity. Some of them are sitting in our Congress.

A recent Senate Judiciary Committee Hearing confirming Judge Amy Coney Barrett to the U.S. Supreme Court showed two Senators familiar to me. Sen. Cory Booker was running for the U.S. presidency among some 22 other Democratic candidates. I was closely following them all and found out that six of them were sponsored by the KGB, Cory Booker was one of the six. It is not a coincident that Cory Booker tried to engage Judge Amy Coney Barrett in the race discussion mentioning

White Supremacy—Andropov's race card in America. Read *A Spy Ring: Putin-Xi- Obama-Biden,* October 8, 2020.

The second is Sen. Kamala Harris. Yes, socialism corrupts everything it touches. From the first I saw Kamala Harris, I didn't like her: she reminded me of a Soviet apparatchik with her radical hatred and rudeness. Then I found out about her relationship with the Soros family. You have to know the KGB modus operandi to grasp the crux of the matter—the KGB's tentacles are in the midst of our soil. We are dealing with a well-organized and calculated global Russian counter-intelligence operation in America where Biden is a center-point . . . There were a lot of Democrats' cheap-shots against Judge Amy Coney Barrett, who strongly defended freedom of speech and religious freedom. There is more evidence of a crucial infiltration and indoctrination of the minds and souls in America that have been exposed during the hearing. Here is another example:

As Karl Marx rebelled against the divine, he wrote,

> "I long to take vengeance on the One Who rules from above. The idea of God is the keynote of a perverted civilization. It must be destroyed."

And Stalin obliterated the idea of God; by his Purges and Show Trials he annihilated the Russian clergy throughout the country. For your information the Catholic Church in Russia was totally destroyed and ceased to exist. Only a few Catholic churches had survived in Ukraine. When I heard Sen. Feinstein talking about a "Catholic Dogma," it reminded me of that aspect of Stalinist Russia. It is not a coincidence that I was writing about the death of Truman's Party and a birth of America's Socialist Party run by Socialist Charlatans for the last thirty-five years. We are watching the result of their activities now.

Probably you haven't read my books and columns, where I was constantly warning you about the failed FBI and Intel apparatus and the methods and tactics of the KGB infiltration on America's soil. As a matter of fact, the KGB doesn't want the Truth about Russian Security agencies to be exposed and when my first book was published in 2002, the corrupt FBI submitted my name to the FISA Court, which made me a foreign agent in 2002. That is the reason you couldn't read my books and columns, they were sabotaged and blocked by the FBI to cover-up the TREASON being committed by the Dems' leadership. All of that had been done while Putin was spreading his criminal forces in the midst of America . . .

There are hundreds of groups created by the KGB in America and even the RINOS were used by the KGB. Look at The Lincoln Project-a bunch of RINOS who are responsible for all troubles we have experienced in the last decades. It was this group of RINOS that hibernated during three last decades giving Russia and China an incredible opportunity to infiltrate all corners and locations of our society: the government, businesses, our democratic institutions, courts, and academia, sports, and to brainwash and over indoctrinate Americans minds and souls. They saw the soul in Putin's eyes, but they haven't seen that massive infiltration. What a shameful bunch of RINOS and they have the audacity now to continue deceiving and defrauding America! Now they have a singular mission: To defeat Donald Trump and Trumpism . . .

Yes, it was Russia's counter-intelligence operation that cost us an enormous waste of human energy, waste of time, and waste of millions of dollars during the last five years. The inability of the CIA, FBI, NSA, and DOJ to know and detect the modus operandi of Russia's Intelligence is the result of it. Knowledge of Russian Intelligence agencies and their modus operandi is a MUST. As a matter of fact, Chinese Intelligence agencies are the carbon copy of the entire Russian Security apparatus—a tandem working against America. It is the Chinese Counter-Intelligence Security Services that had launched a missile of a deadly Covid-19, a disease killing the citizens of the world. "The $16 Trillion Virus": Economists Estimate Financial Toll of COVID-19 on US. We are at war waged by Socialists and Communists against Western civilization and humanity.

Don't be surprised by the censorship in America, an assault on freedom of the press, the endless attacks on the First and Second Amendments, the lower moral standards, and the degradation of American culture—traitors, Socialists, and Communists want to establish the Union of American Socialist States. We are at war and the 2020 election will be the apogee of this war. Putin's KGB and the Chinese Intel are working in tandem with America's Socialist Charlatans and attacking our political system to implement here the fraudulent Socialism which collapsed in 1991 Russia . . .

We the People! Wake UP!

Putin in concert with America's Socialist Party are going to steal the election from you. Be ready to defend our Constitutional Republic!

Vote Republican!

CHAPTER 29

Infiltration and Subversion—Communist-Inspired Insurrection!

July 29, 2020

A nation can survive its fools, and even the ambitious. But it cannot survive treason from within . . ."—Cicero

The BBC radio news informed us that a recently released report states that successive governments failed to deal with Russia's long term infiltration of all areas of Britain's' society. Object? To destroy democracy. Sound familiar? I've warned you about that for the last thirty-five years. Yes, this chaos we witness in all corners of our society has been primarily caused by the failure of our FBI and Intel. Though Communist China is our immediate military foe in the 21*st* century, the Marxist, Socialist/Communist ideology spread by Russia in the 20*th* century laid the blueprint for the chaos, killing, and cultural changes. The infiltration and indoctrination was ignored by the FBI. Both agencies also did nothing to stop the Dems Party's ideological transformation to Socialist Party and its long-term collaboration with Russia . . .

Secretary of State Mike Pompeo gave a key policy speech on the Chinese Communist Party (CCP) in which he said "the free world must triumph over this new tyranny." Everything in the speech absolutely correct, but the last two words in the mentioned quotation. It is not a "new tyranny," but the well-known tyranny of Socialist/Communist ideology implemented in the USSR and aggressively spread across the globe in the 20*th* century. The annexation of Hong Kong by China in the 21*st* century is a carbon copy of the Soviet occupation of the Eastern Europe in the 20*th* century. The Soviet Bloc occupied Eastern Europe and established the *Warsaw Military Pact.* Expansionist and aggressive Communist regimes in Asia followed the Soviet order and the bloody Vietnam War began, involving Kampuchea, Laos and others . . .

Infiltration: The Features of Socialism on American Soil

History is the Mother of all Sciences and Knowledge of the past will open your eyes to the future. I've been writing and warning you about Soviet Socialism, describing the Concentration camps and the menace of the Gulag in Russia. China has established a system quadruple the size of the Gulag and those Concentration camps—an unavoidable indication of China's Socialist/Communist regime in 2020. The spying and theft of secrets and intellectual property is the lifeblood of the criminal regime. You can see another feature of the ideology: the spread of violence on our streets in New York, California, Oregon, Minnesota, Washington D.C. and others. "We are at war, an ongoing asymmetrical war with many different fronts, using a variety of tools, devices, methods, and tricks unknown before. Seemingly unrelated events, in fact, are inextricably connected—all geopolitical events coordinated and directed from the Kremlin." Read here my column *Revelation*, April 26, 2018.

It is not a spontaneous movement: the crusade was designed and calculated by Marxist, Socialist/Communist Charlatans in 20th century Russia, where Soviet Socialism was born, practiced, and spread throughout the globe including China. Though the USSR's Socialist economy is dead, it collapsed in 1991, nothing substantially has changed in Russia and instead of failed Socialism it is now Crony capitalism. Yet, Russia still is being run by Putin's KGB using the old and fraudulent terminology of Socialism. If you do not know Soviet Socialism, you can't see its infection around you. I have lived through such a regime a half of my life. I see all the familiar features of the Socialist regime in America today. Judge for yourself . . .

For the most visual example of the Socialist/Communist infiltration and violence I present—the clans of Antifa, BLM, and the Squad—a militant face of the protest, promoted by the Dems. They are openly calling for the destruction of our political and economic systems—their goal is changing America, they want Communism. They are the armed forces of a so-called Democrat Party and America's Socialist mafia, creating the chaos, killings, and vandalizing our history: the Squad in the Congress is agitating for the same destruction of the political system, designed and left to us by our Founding Fathers. Please, read *Black Lives Matter" and the Camouflage for American Marxism*, by Gary Gindler, the FrontPage Magazine, 7, 22, 2020.

At every level of government in the Dems' states, they are stripping away freedoms and rights from the people. COVID-19 was not a surprise for them, it had brought what the Democrats needed—OPPORTUNITY—power to cement their control over the people as they forced them into a lockdown that has now been months long. It wasn't an instantaneous transformation of the Dems Party to a Socialist Party, it took decades of Socialist infiltration and spying. A major role in that was played by Bill Clinton and his mafia. When I saw the name Strobe Talbot President of Brooking Institution, my antenna went up I knew that the Russian connection is there, and the famous Trump/Dossier could've been concocted under prestigious name of the Institution.

Subversion—Socialist Media-Mob

Commenting on the highly publicized resignation of New York Times editor Bari Weiss, evangelist Franklin Graham is warning Americans not to let the far left sway this year's election. Her resignation letter, Graham wrote Thursday on Facebook, "confirms what many people already have known—the New York Times is biased to the left, socialist, radical agenda of the Democratic Party." *Franklin Graham warns Americans not to let socialists sway election*, By WND Staff Published July 16, 2020. *"Media powers are putting forth every effort to spin the story."*

I agree with every word written above, and in my writings I was warning you to learn the enemy, because Socialism/Communism is our mortal enemy with one agenda—destruction of American capitalism and implementation of Socialism. I was stunned reading Weiss' description about publishing in the New York Times, it was a carbon copy of the Soviet newspaper businesses in Pravda. The only difference was the name of the beneficiary party. I lived under one-party system of Communist Party in Russia, writing today in America Weiss was mentioning "progressive causes" of the Democrat Party. She wrote:

"It was very difficult to get anything published that did not 'explicitly promote progressive causes' and if something was published, it could happen only 'after every line is carefully massaged, negotiated and caveated." She just described the operation within the media in the government of the one-party system, like it was in Soviet Russia.

Conservative writer Andrew Sullivan announces resignation from New York magazine July 15, 2020. Sullivan subsequently expressed support for Weiss on Twitter. "The mob bullied and harassed a young woman for thought crimes," he wrote. "And her editors stood by and watched. I'd say Bari's future is a lot more promising than the NYT's." He is absolutely right, considering NYT's systemic anti-Trump publications confirm the ideological Marxist, Socialist/Communist brainwashing of America's media . . .

Guard your Freedom: The Enemies Within

At the same time Queen-of-Lies Nancy Pelosi called our law enforcement agents—"Nazis." What a shameful statement! Her words forces me to remind you the main Stalin's postulate of the 20th century: *"Never admit crime committed, instead accuse the opposition in that exact crime."* As a matter of fact, the ideology of Socialism/Communism is based on lies and deceit, treachery and fraud, intimidation and disinformation. Knowing the Russian methods, agenda, and a proclivity to mold Socialist style charlatan-leaders around the world to engineer the cadres of a fifth column, I was stunned when seeing them on America's soil. Pelosi's behavior calling China Covid-19, the "Trump-virus" has stunned me again, driving my memory to the past. It was a Red Flag.

Do you remember the Christmas Season on 2019? The Christmas Season is a wonderful time in America—with charming music, people are happily busy with preparations for Christmas. I have always enjoyed those several weeks in America: they were time of celebration, delight, pleasure, and happiness. The Christmas Season in 2019 was the opposite of that—Nancy Pelosi brought Impeachment against President Trump to Christmas 2019. It was an awkward and very unusual Christmastime in America. Moreover, she was in a hurry doing that, in real hurry as if she was afraid to be late to something extremely important. The inquiry was so flimsy that even Stenny Hoyer, the Democrat House Majority Leader, cautioned against the impeachment. In December 2019 nobody knew what was coming and why Pelosi was in such urgency. Do you have an idea why Pelosi was in such a hurry?

I believe that the puzzle can be solved if you are familiar with the global network of Socialism, its methods, and general agenda, which is the destruction of capitalism. The Dems' anti-Trump war had several phases and steps. It started with Obama's weaponized Intel and FBI to go after the president. Both had known that there was no Trump/Russia collusion, so they invented it, to cover-up the real Dems' collusion with Russia—a treasonous one. Then the farce of Mueller Investigation, the Christmas Season Impeachment, and so on. Though all that ended in fiasco, the subsequent corona virus changed the predicament by freezing and crippling people's lives in our country.

I presented at the beginning of this column the Global Network of Socialism for a reason, its methods, and dirty tricks so you could grasp the monumental implication and significance of the events going on before your eyes. In my opinion **Nancy Pelosi was in a hurry to Impeach Trump because she knew that Covid-19 way on its way to America from its home in China**. She and America's Socialist mafia were ready to use it as the next step of the anti-Trump war. Look at Dems officials—they are intentionally caving to the mob. Marxist, Socialist, Charlatans are devouring Democrat-led cities. The events in the Blue states indicate a long-term preparation with the calculation of unified actions against Trump and America's interests. In fact, the Democrats are engaged in a counter-revolutionary putsch against the American Constitutional Republic and against you!

My fellow Americans!

Before your eyes, it is an ideological confrontation waged by global Socialist forces against American Capitalism, Western civilization, and your way of life. That Socialist-aggressive force will fight until a total destruction of our country. The Republican Party is the only political force pursuing American interests and defending a political system designed by our Founding Fathers. In this warfare, there is no choice for us-"we the people" and Republican Party, but to win this war . . .

CHAPTER 30

The Death of the American Republic—the American Spirit Is Next

What you saw on the morning of November 7, 2020 were the convulsions of America the Beautiful before her death. A massive voter-fraud has been going on within our electoral system to make the U.S. into a Venezuela or USSR. The credibility of the entire electoral process was poisoned. On the afternoon of November 7, 2020, Joe Biden was declared 46th President by the media that abetted his candidacy. No one had understood nor been aware why Joe chose November 7, 2020, no one commented on the date. I got it the moment Joe proclaimed his winning. I knew the reason because I am a former Soviet attorney, writing about Russia and Putin's KGB for the last thirty-five years. It was all a part of Putin's vendetta against America for the collapse of the Soviet Union to make a demented Biden as President and a giggling twit as VP. Oh boy! Putin will play his puppet Biden like a Stradivarius!

Writing about Russia and her Intel for years, I warned you by my refrains: Knowledge of Russia and her Intel is a MUST. I also warned Republicans to learn, because I saw the Democrat Party's transformation from JFK's to Lee Harvey Oswald's and knew the result. Then in Russia, I worked within the legal community at the time of the KGB Chairman Yuri Andropov and had known his plan to subvert and take over America. Then in the 1960s I didn't believe his design would succeed, and was stunned to see its gradual implementation when I immigrated to America. Before my eyes the CBS *60 minutes* was transformed by

Socialist propaganda, the Universities and Colleges are unrecognizable, Newsweek and Time lost their objective attitude to events, and Truman's Party died. I knew why it happened: Vladimir Putin was a devoted disciple of both Stalin and Andropov and continued their legacy.

If you think that the Collapse in 1991 of the Soviet Union has changed Russia, you are wrong, you don't know Russia and her Intel. As a matter of fact, it wasn't a collapse of the USSR, it was a collapse of the Socialist economy that couldn't produce and compete with capitalism. Yet, the collapse didn't touch the security apparatus (the real power in the country)—the KGB. Using the instability and chaos in Russia during those days, Socialist KGB took over and catapulted Vladimir Putin to presidency—and the circle of authority was established. Today Russia is run by the KGB apparatus. The old socialist economy was replaced by a crony capitalism under the secured KGB's total control . . . Considering the political setting worldwide, an awareness of the Russian leader's shenanigans is imperative. Putin, armed with the legacy of Stalin's postulates and Socialist modus operandi has achieved a great deal across the world. *Socialist Lies: From Stalin to the Clintons, Obamas, and Sanders,* XLIBRIS, 2016

Vladimir Putin and the Political Setting of Socialism/Communism

Had you read my books and this column, you would be familiar with Putin and his career. Putin, a counter-intelligence officer of the KGB, had never changed his political view. As a lawyer with a major in the International Law, he has instilled Socialist mentality throughout the world since 1975. Socialism has its modus operandi: lies, deceit, and fraud combined with symbols and slogans. Socialism is a lawless system, a cult, a religion. The Soviet Socialist economy collapsed in 1991 because it was built on lies, deceit and fraud. Yet, Putin's vendetta continues running the Socialist ideas. There is an axiom in political philosophy: peaceful coexistence between Capitalism and Socialism is a myth—they are absolute mortal enemies and one of them must be defeated. It is a law of survival hence, Russia and China will be together fighting capitalism. The major role in this fight for now belongs to the devoted disciple of Stalin and Andropov—Vladimir Putin.

Andropov's Project: Operation Barbarossa

Andropov's design was a simple and arrogant one: to infiltrate simultaneously the media and all-American security apparatus. In my writings I called it—*Operation Barbarossa,* because I didn't believe in its validity. I was wrong. Fixing America was begun with the first American Manchurian President elected in 1992. He created the Dems/apparatchiks and delegated George Stephanopoulos (in my opinion the KGB agent) to culminate the changes that had been occurring in America's media. Bill Clinton has polluted the courts system and Socialist propaganda machine indoctrinated majority of Americans. The second American Manchurian President was elected in 2008 and continued to build up the process of transformation to Socialism. Barack Obama did it openly before your eyes. All of that was possible due to a massive infiltration of Putin's KGB in the midst of our entire society. Read my book *Socialist Lies: From Stalin to the Clinton's, Obama's, and Sanders, XLIBRIS, 2016.*

History is the Mother of all sciences and I knew the Russian history of Socialist Revolution. It occurred hundred years ago November 7, 1917 at the time of the deadliest pandemic in history—the Spanish flu which infected an estimated 500 million people worldwide. It took the Socialist/ Communist forces a hundred years to develop the similar conditions of the events in the world. And here we are. Don't be surprised by the Chinese COVID-19 Pandemic launched by Socialist and Communist forces to inflict psychological desperation and fear to intimidate and paralyze you. We are dealing with the hundred-year agenda to transform the American Constitutional Republic to Socialism. Vladimir Putin is the major force to achieve the result.

November 7, 2020: Putin's Vendetta

When Biden spoke as President-elect on November 7, 2020 I was the only person realizing that Joe Biden is Putin's puppet. The date itself proved the fact. For the entire 2020, I was warning you in dozens of my columns about Putin's Socialist Revolution in America. It is here today executed by the cartel of a Deep State-Biden-KGB in America. It is Putin's symbolic vendetta to emphasize the significance of the Socialist ideology and the Russian Socialist Revolution November 7, 1917. It is

Putin's vendetta for the collapse of the Soviet Union in 1991. Do you grasp now Putin's mentality and the crimes committed by him against America for years? Read my book: *What is Happening to America? The Hidden Truth of Global Destruction,* XLIBRIS, 2012

The Socialist ideology has its modus operandi and I was stunned by finding that Biden has followed its exact modus operandi in his speeches: lies, deceit, and fraud. Biden by himself was a total fraud, a demented old political crime family boss (the Big Guy). Moreover, there was a main Stalin's postulate. *Never admit crime committed, instead accuse the opposition in this exact crime.* It was incredible to watch Joe Biden exercise that precise Stalin legacy. Obama and Biden have released a cascade of accusations and witch hunts during last five years, trying to make Trump an enemy of the American people. Analyzing all charges against Trump you will find that exact crimes had been committed by the Democrats. Trump had never teamed up with Putin, dishonest Charlatan, Joe Biden did work for Vladimir Putin. Here are some evidence:

Obama delegated Joe Biden as a point man to Ukraine in 2013–2014. Biden traveled to Ukraine with his son Hunter. Neither Biden nor his son Hunter speaks Ukrainian or knows Ukrainian Law, which is completely different from American Case Law. Nevertheless, Hunter became connected to pro-Russian oligarch Zlochevsky-Burisma Holdings. Burisma Holding is the appendix of former Ukrainian President Yanukovych, a close friend of Vladimir Putin, who ran to Russia to escape the Ukrainian's people wrath for destruction of the Ukrainian Republic . . .

Hunter Biden in 2014 was appointed to Burisma's board, while at the same time his father was leading the Obama administration's diplomatic dealings with Ukraine. Zlochevsky was a Minister of Energy in the Yanukovych government, which means he is the Russian asset, like Yanukovych himself.

How could this happen and how did Hunter Biden get an immediate connection to pro-Russian oligarch Zlochevsky? There is only one answer to the question: the Obama administration had cooperated with the previous pro-Russian administration in Ukraine; that way Hunter Biden had been tied with pro-Russian oligarch. But that also means that the American Embassy in Kiev had been working towards the same direction providing Aid and Comfort to Putin's KGB . . . which is Treason against

America . . . My conclusion: Joe Biden has worked for Putin, helping Putin to destroy and end the young Ukrainian democracy . . . Read *A Global Spy Ring: Obama, Putin, and Biden*, July 9, 2020.

By the way, Joe Biden himself had emailed Vadim Pozharskyi, a top executive from Ukrainian gas firm Burisma (in my opinion a KGB agent). Secret Service logs include a travel entry for Biden on April 3-6, 2014.v. We the People Daily, **The Secret Service Just Won The Election For Trump**, 10.24.2020. Tony Babulinsky's credibility and his testimony have confirmed Biden's long-term help to Putin. Do you remember Biden's quid pro quo? Biden's threat to Ukrainian government about $1 billion to fire the Ukrainian prosecutor is also a vivid evidence of his work in Putin's behave to cover-up Biden's entire involvement.

Aware of that, let me give you my ideas of how it was done by Putin's KGB in America. 20 years ago, I gave you the realization of WWIII being waged by Socialist forces against Western civilization: Recruitment and Infiltrations, Drugs and Assassinations. All of that was successfully implemented by Putin and his Intel in America. We have the KGB agents on a powerful posts in all Dems states. In Minnesota we have AG Keith Ellison, in Texas we have Beto, in New Jersey Cory Booker, let alone the Squad in the Congress and seventy Socialists counted by Alan West. The election 2012 was a fraud committed by the Governor of Pennsylvania Ed Rendell and the KGB agent Rahm Emanuel. Kamala is Soros's close friend!!! Add to that Obama's weaponized Intel. Knowing Socialist's modus operandi just imagine massive fraud committed by them against Trump to cover-up the Dems' Treason! The coup against Trump is still underway in 2020 . . .

Introducing the term Socialist Charlatans, I hoped to show you the enemy within. Listen to Sen. Schumer and Stacy Abrams to realize the meaning of the term Socialist Charlatans. The chaos in America is made by them in concert with Putin. The Socialist fraud in this election, implemented by the Dems/KGB cartel, has enormously undermined and weakened our country for decades. **It must be stopped** to expose the criminals. The remedy is knowledge of Russia, her Intel, and Socialist's modus operandi. Authentication of the mail-in-ballots and certification of them is imperative. We must save the American Republic today! Tomorrow will be late!

P.S. I'd advise you to read the comments on this column by Sherry M. Kerr. www.drrichswier.com/author/spipko/

CHAPTER 31

America and the Global Communist Conspiracy

November 24, 2020

The political turmoil in America is not accidental it has been rising and growing for decades, but you may not have noticed it, because you don't know the enemy behind the turmoil. The corrupt FBI deprived you of knowing the enemy by sabotaging and banning my books and columns. When my first book was published, the FBI submitted my name to the FISA Court making me a foreign agent in 2002. Since then you have not being able to get the key knowledge—this was the time when the enemies prepared their plot against our American Republic. They did and you are now witnessing it in the 2020 political turmoil in America's election . . . There is a causation missed by many pundits . . .

Russian *Operation Disinformation* existed as a part of a monumental Russian project, the outline of a design to destroy the American Constitutional Republic and the pundits missed the elephant in the room for the past four years. The anti-Trump forces had the task of diverting, and dissuading your attention from the DNC, who had been collaborating with Russian Intel for decades, to cover-up the crimes they committed, the crime of TREASON. There has never been a Trump/ Russia collusion, in fact, there was a DNC/Russian Intel collusion. The entire ordeal of various witch hunts against Trump for years has been a fraud to cover-up the crime committed by the DNC/Russian collusion . . . Read here my column: *The Global Spy Ring*, January 1, 2018

I don't agree with Mark Thiessen and Victor Davis Hanson suggesting that Trump should concede to focus his forces on the 2024 election. A very incompetent advice-the two hadn't read my books and columns. Both still don't realize that the government of the KGB is coming to Washington D.C. to run America. Trump won't have any opportunity to do anything, even if he is not in prison (a possible reality). Considering the integrity of our election process and the challenges to our national security, Trump must do the most in the time left to him to expose the worldwide Communist fraud . . .

Socialist/Communist/ Subversion of America

I am a former Soviet attorney, writing about the subversion of America, by the Global Communist Conspiracy and a Global Spy Ring of America's enemies for thirty-five years. To grasp my ideas, you have to know at least three elements of reality: First: Truman's party is dead, it was infiltrated, contaminated and converted into America's Socialist Party by the Russian Intel and the Party simultaneously populated the "Swamp". As in the USSR, they are going against the dissent, be prepared for growing violence. Don't take my word, just look at the platform, policy, and projects the Dems entertain and follow today. This is the reason I have introduced you to the term Socialist Charlatans.

Second: There is no more Classic Liberals, they had been annihilated by Stalin in the 20*th* century. We are dealing with the Radical Left, which has a more appropriate name—Socialist Charlatans. These people have been indoctrinated, brainwashed and programmed for decades. Third: Understanding the power and reach of the KGB and the status quo of Russia. Using the term KGB, I mean the entire Russian Intel—it is a collective image—those three letters are familiar to the vast majority of Americans.

If you think that the Collapse in 1991 of the Soviet Union has changed Russia, you are wrong, you don't know Russia and her Intel. As a matter of fact, it wasn't a collapse of the USSR, it was a collapse of the Socialist economy that couldn't produce and compete with capitalism. Yet, the collapse didn't touch the security apparatus (the real power in the country)—the KGB. Using the instability and chaos in Russia during those days, the Socialist KGB took over and catapulted Vladimir Putin to the presidency—and the circle of authority was established and closed. Today Russia runs by the same KGB apparatus. The old socialist economy was replaced by a crony capitalism under the secured KGB's total control . . .

There is an axiom in political philosophy: peaceful coexistence between Capitalism and Socialism is a myth—they are absolute mortal enemies and one of them must be defeated. It is the law of survival hence, Russia and China will be seen together fighting capitalism. The major role in this fight for now belongs to the devoted disciple of Stalin and Andropov—Vladimir Putin. He has the arsenal of a KGB Army in America built for decades. This Mafia-Army has infiltrated all corners of our society, courts, business' sports, democratic institutions, and created a Socialist mentality within the minds of vast majority of the Americans, corrupting and secularizing the society. Remember the Communist modus operandi to hide the Truth with lies, deceit, cheating, and fraud.

Putin's KGB Mafia/Army in America

I have already listed some Communists, soldiers of the KGB Army, they are in positions that allow them to subvert our political system. I am not surprised by the massive fraud identified in Michigan, Communist Debby Dingle deceived and defrauded people with her eyes open for years. I can't stand her. In the latest episode Republican Monica Palmer refused to certify the election, so she was called racist, intimidated, her life was threatened the names of her children published by the Dems. This is a Communist tactic, which reminded me of the 1992 election, when the life of Ross Perot's daughter was threatened. Perot forsook his candidacy and Bill Clinton became the American President. The same criminal method had been used to change Justice Roberts', political judgement. Knowledge of Russian Intel is a Must! Read: *The Soviet Mafia*, by Arcady Vaksberg, St. Martin Press, 1991, and my column: *Fascist Evil is at Our Door*, 24, 11, 2018

In Minnesota we have a Communist Attorney General. Let alone Gorge Soros, Bernie Sanders, and the Socialist apparatchik Stacy Abrams. They were undermining American Republic for years. It is hard to be openly against First and Second Amendments: Socialist Charlatans know that Trump ties by umbilical cord to the American Republic. So they use Stalin's policy of personal destruction against Trump for four years. You saw it. I also believe that the George Floyd-riots were organized, calculated and coordinated by the Dems as a beginning of the putsch against the American Republic and President Trump—today we having the result. The KGB has already given us two American Manchurian Presidents. I am afraid that the third one is coming . . .

Please, look at this document:

> *The Transition Integrity Project* is a document worked out by Putin's KGB with the leadership of the Democrat Party. In fact, it presents the well-organized stages of Socialist Revolution in America, the tactics of game-play to secure the Biden victory. Don't be confused by the words integrity, bipartisan, and a peaceful appearance to convince you. The title is crap to hide the Truth and instead to create chaos, a constitutional crises by design to topple the American Constitutional Republic.

Actually it is a continuation of the witch hunts against Trump, the screed type of Impeachment against Trump. Do you remember Pelosi being in a hurry during the Impeachment farce on the eve of Christmas 2019? The rush can be explained: she was informed by China that Covid-19 was on its way to America—Socialists and Communists are always working together. Analyzing the documents plus the events presiding them and following Pelosi's actions gives you the real picture of the well-crafted plot, a coup against President Trump. The Chinese Communist COVID-19 is a deadly missile launched to help the Dems' coup to destroy the American Republic. The subject of COVID-19 has required a separate column.

Remember it is the war against American capitalism. That is one of the reasons Biden from Delaware had been chosen by the KGB. Let me remind you of my definition of WWIII: recruitments, infiltrations, drugs, and assassinations. This process was going on for decades in America. Mafia loves the money. Don't be surprised that the financial sector supports Joe Biden, he is from Delaware and he is the existential thread to the American Republic. Here are some statistics:

"The *total number* of LLCs *registered* in the First State crossed the one million mark and continue to be the domicile of choice for members of the Fortune *500.* Over a million businesses—publicly traded **companies** in the U.S. and more than 60 percent of **Fortune 500 companies**—are incorporated in **Delaware.** More than half of U.S. publicly traded *companies* and fully of the *Fortune 500* were among *that number*, according to the states, 68.8 percent of all *Fortune 500 companies* are incorporated in *Delaware.*" *Considering the written above, the next step is Corporate Fascism in America.*

Communist Patterns of Subversion

When I am writing this column, Rudy Giuliani and his group of lawyers speak about a fraud in the election 2020. Sidney Powell outlined what could be the greatest crime in American history. As many as 2.7 million votes were said to have changed in swing states, where Trump was winning, to favor Joe Biden and were key in Biden winning those states. Time will tell, but I know that some kind of interference and manipulation took place. Maybe Sidney Powell was right. I was watching the Washington State for a decade, every Republican winning the election was defeated by Dem ballots that appeared after the election. That was a typical sign of the Communist fraud—the leadership in the state definitely has ties with the KGB Mafia-Army . . .

As a former Soviet attorney I ask you to read my column: ***The Fascist Putsch in America.*** The centralized infiltration into our midst by the foreign governments in concert with the Dems is much bigger and more sinister than you think. The putsch is run and coordinated by three Presidents: Bill Clinton, Obama, and Putin to implement Socialism in America. Read my columns on the KGB: Venezuela's or Serbia's electronic machines count our election with the aid of "communist money": both are Russia's puppets. The KGB' Mafia-Army is going around our checks and balances and converting American electoral system into the Soviet one! Knowledge of Russian Intel is a Must.

Don't listen to the pundits who don't know Russia and her Intel, like Jonah Goldberg and Chris Christie, they will confuse and deceive you. Knowledge of Russia and her Intel is a MUST.

But what outraged me the most is the silence of the FBI and DOJ, they have disappeared from the Earth, providing the KGB Mafia/Army with free hand to undermine and destroy the American Republic. The names of Christopher Wray, William Barr, and Michael Blumberg will go to history as the people who help the KGB to destroy and extinguish the American Republic. And another outrage: Harvard University raises the possibility of preventing any Trump representative from entering Harvard territory. Professor Dershowitz called it McCarthyism. I don't agree—it is Soviet Socialism or Chinese Communism, which is the same totalitarianism. I have an impression that it is not America I live in, but I have been returned back to the Soviet Union.

The upcoming Senatorial runoffs in Georgia are critically important, it can prevent the Dems from having the Senate. Just look at the Dems' candidates and you will be stunned by their anti-American views and connection to the Socialist/Communist ideology—they are typical Socialist Charlatans of America in Georgia—the cadres of Stacy Abrams. Look at their anti-American views and connection with China. Senator Kelly Loeffler faces a Socialist Charlatan, who hosted Fidel Castro, He wants to change America, which is the substance and goal of the Communist conspiracy!!! Ukrainian-born GOP Congresswoman-elect Victoria Spartz, of Indiana, warned that the American left is now "building socialism" like she saw in the Soviet Union. Political Insider, November 16, 2020.

There will be the protests in Atlanta, watch Antifa and BLM, both are for the Dems' candidates against Trump's supporters. Read my columns about Antifa and BLM, they are the Dems' armed forces, trained by the KGB . . .

It was a Communist global scheme! Fight back to save the world and win! The Republicans must expose Socialist Charlatans of America and show their real faces . . . God help us!

P.S. After this column has been written and edited, I received this document about a Communist voting machine:

APPALLING: Videos Prove Hacking E-Vote Machines Easy, Knowable, Training by YouTube, by Kelly O'Connell, Canada Free Press, *November 22, 2020* INTRO: E-Vote Machine

Hacking is Like an Olympic Sport. It's so easy on the internet a teen & smartphone can master it! The 2020 election was hijacked by electronic fraud. Yet, a staggering number of articles and videos detail the simplicity of hacking E-Vote machines. Many stories come from mainstream media, now pretending elections can't be rigged. Yet a communist voting machine is a handy companion for a day chock-full of fraud. See 2 Min Vote Hack. (8/16/18)

CHAPTER 32

Soviet Style Counter-Revolution in America

December 1, 2020

Two decades ago I warned you "we are in a war waged by Socialism and Communism against Western Civilization and American Capitalism." I described that war as WWIII: Recruitment, Infiltration, Drugs, and Assassinations. Twenty years later we can observe the result: Russia was very successful in achieving all of that in concert with the so-called Democrat Party, which they and their comrades transformed into America's Socialist Party. Many Dems were recruited, they infiltrated all corners of society right in our midst: courts, businesses, sports, media, and our democratic institutions. China has provided a deadly disease-COVID-19. Now, in concert with these two, the Dems have waged a counter-revolution in America. What's left for them to accomplish? The assassinations . . . ? Read further to see how those Evil forces have managed to become successful.

Sidney Powell has presented a credible case of massive and centralized foreign infiltration in the 2020 election. She has revealed an unknown to me company that produced an international voting-fraud named Dominion. I went to computer and find the definition of the Dominion:

> "Dominion, now the Largest or Second Largest Voting System Company, is Foreign Controlled and Depends Upon Secret Source Code Created and Owned

by Smartmatic, a Foreign Controlled Company With Ties to The Venezuelan Government Led by Hugo Chavez."

I was immediately suspicious, reading the name Hugo Chavez, a Communist asset of Russia, who ran Venezuela from 1998-2013. The normal mind can't perceive a Soviet/Russian fraud—Socialist, lawless regime.

Socialists/Communists have always won elections by 85%-91% in the Soviet Union, in Russia, North Korea, China, Cuba, and Venezuela. In those years we didn't know the name of the fraud, today we know its name–the Dominion electronic System. As a former Soviet attorney, the picture of Venezuela tells me a huge story of the Russian Intel and their Global conspiracy for these fifteen years. You have to know Russia, her Intel and their modus operandi—lies, cheating and fraud to see the picture. They do criminal acts by using their assets, their Communist cadres around the globe. The Republicans must know this modus operandi—a discovery of the Dominion fraud-scandal is possible only through awareness of Russia and her Intel's activities . . .

Yet, additionally, Sidney Powell is investigating and reporting all kind of massive voter-frauds committed in six swing states by mail-in ballots, illegible people voting, dead people voting, the military votes for Trump dumped, 91% of people voted in Minnesota, where MN AG is a Communist, 85% of people voted in Wisconsin. Those numbers are testimony to the Fraud—an incredible fraud. But a corrupt FBI is intentionally ignoring all of that. The incompetent FBI and DOJ have taken no action against the Socialist Revolution that America has been undergoing for decades—they haven't fought the enemy and thus allowed overwhelming foreign infiltration in all corners on our society. We are witnessing the result of that incompetence in the 2020. Those people who told you that the election had been secured are deceiving you. They don't know Russia, her Intel, and Communist China with its Intel . . ., but are they really that stupid or is something else going on?

To grasp my ideas, I have to repeat again at least three elements of reality: First: Truman's party is dead, it was infiltrated, contaminated and converted into America's Socialist Party by the Russian Intel and the Party simultaneously fomented and fueled the "Swamp". As in the USSR, they are going against the dissent—be prepared for growing violence. Don't take my words, just look at the platform, policy, and projects the

Dems entertain and follow today. This is the reason I have introduced you to the term Socialist Charlatans.

Second: There are no more Classic Liberals, they had been annihilated by Stalin in the 20th century. We are dealing with the Radical Left, which has a more appropriate name—Socialist Charlatans. These people have been indoctrinated, brainwashed and programmed for decades. Third: Understanding the power and reach of the KGB and the status quo of Russia. Using the term KGB, I mean the entire Russian Intel—it is a collective image—those three letters are familiar to the vast majority of Americans . . . Do you remember Putin's KGB Mafia-Army?

If you think that the Collapse in 1991 of the Soviet Union has changed Russia, you are wrong, you don't know Russia and her Intel. As a matter of fact, it wasn't a collapse of the USSR, it was a collapse of the Socialist economy that couldn't produce and compete with capitalism. Yet, the collapse didn't touch the security apparatus (the real power in the country)—the KGB. Using the instability and chaos in Russia during those days, the Socialist KGB took over and catapulted Vladimir Putin to the presidency—and the circle of authority was established and closed. Today Russia runs by the same KGB apparatus. The old socialist economy was replaced by a crony capitalism under the secured KGB's total control. Only knowing those components of reality, you can analyze the current events . . .

The Failed FBI and American Intel

The FBI and our Intel have missed a critical causation to prevent the stealing of election. That causation had been missed by historians like John Mitcham, by many Republicans and other pundits. As a matter of fact, the Russian *Operation Disinformation* known for years has existed as a part of a monumental Russian project, the outline of a design to destroy the American Constitutional Republic and many Republicans missed the elephant in the room—Russia, her Intel, and the Chinese Communist advertising propaganda campaign by bribing the American media, sports, and universities. Remember, Russia and China are in tandem working against America like a hand in glove . . .

To cover up the crimes of Treason the Dems had committed, the anti-Trump forces had the task of diverting, and dissuading your attention from the DNC, who had been collaborating with Russian Intel for decades. There has never been a Trump/Russia collusion, in fact, there was a DNC/Russian Intel collusion. The entire ordeal of various witch hunts against Trump for years has been a fraud to cover-up the crime of Treason, committed by the DNC/Russian collusion. The epitome of this fraud is the state of Georgia, where the Republican leadership not knowing the causation allowed Socialist Charlatan, Stacy Abrams to work for years to produce that fraud. You have now her crop—two Dems' candidates, who want to change American system designed by our Founding Fathers by supporting the core-task of the Global Communist Conspiracy. Read: *America and the Global Communist Conspiracy*, November, 24, 2020.

Sean Hannity is right in general, yet, he repeats to us every day that he respects 99% of the FBI agents as doing the right things. In this respect, Sean Hannity is wrong, critically wrong! The FBI has dramatically changed during the last thirty years: the experienced in Cold War agents have retired and young ill-informed, brainwashed and indoctrinated young agents have come into the agency. All our security and Intel's agencies were transformed and some like CIA had been, in fact, collaborating with our enemies under John Brennon's leadership. Read here my column: The Global Spy Ring, January 1, 2018.

Afghanistan: Knowledge of Russia and her Intel is a MUST

Don't be surprised by an incredible, massive fraud in the 2020 election. Two American Manchurian Presidents Bill Clinton and Barack Obama made and left us naked, mute, and deaf to their Treason, depleting our military. But this was only a part of betrayals, the entire society was manipulated and conditioned by the Dems' Socialist Transformation, implementing Stalin's motto of Divide and Conquer for years. It is no coincidence that we have a divided science and medicine, which was unable to find a unified remedy to fight the Chinese COVID-19 in the critical first hours of the Pandemic. It is a result of the Dems' Socialist Transformation. The Obama era has left disastrous consequences; the vaccine was approved by FDA on November 22, but planned to distribute December 11. This is Socialism! While capitalist-Trump oversaw development of the COVID-19 vaccine in an unprecedented nine months.

The motto of "Divide and Conquer" came from the ancient world and has been used many times and mostly successful by the ideology. You saw it in the 1950s—Stalin's war against Korea and as a result Korea was divided. Then Vietnam, it was divided, Afghanistan and so on—the wars against Western civilization went on for the entire 20*th* century. It was brought to America by the global Communist conspiracy and Russian Intel. Sen. Cotton is right: "Afghanistan is the place from which the 911 attacks were launched and the place that has the largest concentration of terrorist organizations than anywhere else in the world, the reason we're in Afghanistan is to protect our own citizens here at home." I can add to that:

> We are in Afghanistan because of Russia and her Intel is there. Please, take a map and see a large extend of the border of the former USSR's Muslim Republics and Afghanistan. Also, please, remember that all those Republics are still run by the KGB. The hatred of Jews and Western civilization united all Muslims and the KGB has used it. As in all other places, the KGB has infiltrated the Taliban movement with its cadres speaking all the languages in the area . . . and the killing of Americans continues—Taliban is tied to the KGB . . . . Like in Afghanistan, multiple terrorist attacks across the world are coordinated in the Kremlin . . . Read my books, columns, and remember Putin's KGB Mafia/Army . . .

I never thought that I would quote Oliver Stone, but he was right in Oliver Stone exclusive with Jesse Watters. When asked about the job of our Intel, he went to the history of disinformation and many mistakes and failures by our Intel. In this connection Jesse asked him: Does Putin win? Stone didn't answer or did not have the answer. I can answer:

Dear Jesse, yes, Putin and his KGB are winning up to now and this is the reason I am writing the columns to stop a vicious cycle of fraud that the Republicans can't free themselves from. They lost Hollywood, then our educational system, then the media, and now the election . . .

Socialist/Communist ideology is pushing us out of existence. There is the time to wake up, fight back and save the American Republic from the Global Socialist and Communist Fraud . . .

God Bless President Trump! God help President Trump!

CHAPTER 33

Russian/Chinese Intel: Carousel and COVID-19 in America

December 21, 2020

When Karl Marx published his Specter of Communism in the 19th century, even he couldn't imagine that Specter in our midst in the 21st century. Yet, we have it . . . A compromised House Intel guy, Rep. Erik Swalwell sleeping with a Chinese communist spy is the latest revealed activity of the Specter. It didn't surprise me—I am writing about Socialist/Communist Intel activities and have been for the last three decades. To be precise about the Russia/Chinese Intel, it has spread its propaganda globally and even owns the Democrat Party. This triangle is fighting our Constitutional Republic on a variety of fronts for decades. Whatever the name of the ideology—Marxism, Socialism, Communism or Fascism, all of them have the same nature, origins and agenda-control and power. To survive you first need to identify it, because it is a war by an aggressive Specter against Humanity.

Russia's Global Agenda

For Russia, this Specter became a reality in the 1917 Socialist Revolution and Russian leaders ever since have been directed by the Specter. If the Global Domination was first imagined by Marx, the structural format, methods and arrangements of the war have been worked out by these Russian leaders: Stalin, Andropov and Putin. Those three have spread the ideology globally. It took Stalin 29 years to create the Chinese Communist State. I am constantly repeating that knowledge of Russia and her Intel is a Must, because both Russian and Chinese Ministries of State Security are identical—they have been built by Comrade Stalin with the same ideology, strategy, methods, and dirty tricks.

Though equally abused and subordinated to the malignant Communist regime yet, there is a distinction between the two populations: a billion hard-working Chinese people with entrepreneurial spirit have achieved much more than sick, alcoholic, state-dependent Russians. It is a matter of quantity and quality, plus the tremendous world technological advancements in the 21st century that have been appropriated by the Chinese CCP. Neither Intelligence service use their money for research and development—they rely on stealing the secrets from us. Writing about Russia's Intel I use the term KGB—it is a collective image—those three letters are familiar to the vast majority of Americans . . . Do you remember Putin's KGB Mafia/Army spread globally, BLM and Antifa infiltrating the midst of the American society?

Seventy years later we are dealing with a Global Spy Ring of multi-national forces subverting their target peoples: primarily Western civilization and American capitalism. The Russian leaders have chosen to act by destroying their enemy, us, from within and they have. The main target was American capitalism and in prior articles, I have shown you how the infiltration and destruction was done in the 20th century. The KGB Mafia-Army has interfered in all corners of our society, courts, business, sports, democratic institutions, and created a Socialist mentality within the minds of Americans, corrupting and secularizing the society. The Democrat Party was infiltrated, contaminated and converted into America's Socialist Party by the Russian Intel, a party of Socialist Charlatans. Their modus operandi: deceiving and confusing the opponents by lies, institutionalized fraud, and cheating—propaganda, symbols and slogans, intimidation, manipulation, provocation, and threat.

The Dems have weakened and undermined our political system bit by bit, destroying traditional culture and creating a chaos in America. As a result we have some of the Washington Establishment married to Russian spies. Don't be surprised by Eric Swalwell, he is just the latest example. Obama's Ambassador to Russia was sleeping with a KGB Alumni in Moscow (you can see their picture in my column). The KGB's Mafia-

Army has had a free hand to damage us from within in concert with the Dems. It was the KGB that trained the Chinese Intel to do the same. Years ago, I was warning you about the so-called Romeo-Department of the KGB. The tragedy of America is that the Republicans do not have the in-depth knowledge of Russia and her Intel and never fought back the real COLLUSION: Dems/KGB—the criminal cabal that committed TREASON. You witnessed the resignation of two Republican Attorney Generals—both did not know Russia, her Intel, and allowed the Dems-criminals to sell America . . . Read my books and columns about *"the Axis of Evil"* under Kremlin's umbrella.

Putin's KGB "Operation Disinformation"

Coming to power in the 21st century, Vladimir Putin used this confusion with his usual dirty tricks. Trump was his mortal enemy by declaring America First and Putin's coup against Trump began on the day Trump announced his candidacy—Trump/Dossier. It took me two seconds to see this KGB production—a Falshivka, a Soviet-style fraud—the "operation disinformation" has started. American politicians called it "Russian Disinformation,"—wrong—we were dealing with a long-term KGB practice "operation disinformation." Words matter. For four years media pundits and social justice types were discussing Russia, it is a paradox of incompetency—none of these people knew Russia and her Intel and for four years they were wasting our time, energy, and $40 million of taxpayer money.

"*The Russian Disinformation*," known for years, has existed as a part of a monumental Russian project, the outline of a long-term design to destroy the American Constitutional Republic—*The Operation Disinformation* (you should know the Soviet style KGB play-book.) Many Republicans sadly ignored the elephant in the room—Russia, her Intel, and the Chinese Communist advertising propaganda campaign which bribed the American media, sports, and universities. Remember, Russia and China are in tandem, a pair working against America like a hand and glove . . . To cover-up the crimes of Treason the Dems had committed, the anti-Trump forces had the task of diverting, and dissuading your attention from the DNC, who had been collaborating with Russian Intel for decades.

Hang on to the task of diverting the attention from the crime committed by the KGB—this is *the control mechanism* used since Stalin's postulate: *Never admit crime committed, instead accuse the opponent in this exact crime.* Coming to power in the 21st century, Vladimir Putin has developed further Stalin's dirty trick. Putin's dirty trick was supposed to kill three birds in one shot: To cover-up the crime of treason committed by the Dems, to divert attention from China, and to support anti-Trump forces. Maneuvering, Putin's three-pronged policy were enhancing each other, they were connected, calculated, coordinated and executed by the Dems criminal cabal and Socialist Charlatans.

There has never been a Trump/Russia collusion, in fact, there was a Dems/Russian Intel collusion. The entire ordeal of various witch hunts against Trump for years has been a misdirected fraud to cover-up the crime of Treason, committed by the Dems/Russian collusion and divert attention from China . . . In persistent unity Pelosi, Swalwell, and other Dems have overplayed Russia, Russia, Russia to dissuade your attention from the Dems and China. The trick was obvious: focus America's negativity toward Russia so that nobody suspected the Dems of Treason. All three task-tactics exercised by Putin had been swallowed by the Republicans. Once again I'd repeat: Knowledge of Russia and her Intel is a Must!

Russian Carousel (Roundabout) in America

Encouraged by his success, Putin and his criminal cabal began designing the final assault on the political system of the American Constitutional Republic—the 2020 election. To grasp my ideas you have to know the KGB Mafia/Army, Putin's KGB government, and certain events going on in Russia. In my preceding column. I have tried to show you massive infiltration in the 2020 election by several foreign governments, in particular Putin's KGB, because I was afraid that Russian hackers would outwit Americans. Maybe the Dominion machines produced fraud, maybe **David Sanger NYT is right researching software**, I am not an expert in computer and software technology, but an expert in Russia. The events of multiple fraud were not only obvious visually, but they have been very familiar to me, as it happened in Russian election years ago. And I have described them in my books. The Navarro Report is accurate: the stories of the illegitimate ballots in suitcases and ballots driven by truck from New York to Pennsylvania happened exactly the way it occurred in the Russian 2007 election. Please, read a fragment from my book at the time:

> "Have you heard the term *carousel* (roundabout) used in the election to Duma? Do you know what it means? Hearing this word in Russian, I did not understand its application at first. The events that followed had given me the meaning of the word. The United Russia party together with the Kremlin's administration had organized the youth movement's groups providing them with a caravan of buses. The vast majority of youngsters were called NASHISTS. I watched them on Russian TV. Young people, wearing shirts with Putin's portrait, singing with enthusiasm bordering on euphoria, occupied the buses and moved along the streets to the voting precincts one after another. The voting ballots were waiting for them and they all voted for United Russia. Then they left for other voting places where they voted again and again for the United Russia (Party).
>
> I will give you another example so you can fully comprehend what is going on in Russia. A couple of months before the election, the Kremlin had issued an order to all enterprises and offices throughout eleven time zones. The order requested all the workers of the above mentioned plants and offices, students and teachers to take the absentee ballots from their places of residence and vote in their place of work or study. The heads of all offices were told to watch how people were voting and provide United Russia with the victory. Moreover, the policy of infiltration from the Soviet past became clear in the present Russia." pp. 191-192, *What is Happening to America? The Hidden Truth of Global Destruction*, XLIBRIS, 2012.

Socialist Charlatans vs. the Western World

The Republicans still don't understand that there is no patriotic Democrat Party any longer, a multi-national cabal of Socialist Charlatans are fighting Republicans and our Constitutional Republic. Until Republicans call Socialist Charlatans their real names, Republicans will lose . . . language matters . . . Socialist Charlatans have camouflaged themselves by the name Democratic, though nothing democratic is left in the so-called Democrat Party. Biden is using the name of democracy and lying to you by talking about American democracy, because people didn't grant power to Joe Biden—the KGB did. The Republicans in Georgia's runoff election need to learn and use an appropriate terminology. Language is a major factor in debates!

Not surprisingly Biden was chosen as a leader of the Dems—he has been working for Putin under the Socialist, Obama, for years. Biden was chosen by Obama to suffocate the young Ukrainian democracy to help Putin to resurrect the Russian Empire again. As a matter of fact, without Ukraine it cannot be Russian Empire again. Do you remember quid-pro-quo and a $billions to fire a prosecutor who investigated Hunter and the Burisma controlled by Russian asset? Biden himself is a part of the fraud within "operation disinformation," but . . . hang on . . .

Today a demented Biden is a vessel to make Kamala the U.S. President. Yes, this is Putin's agenda to make this close friend of the Soros family, the U.S. President, and to demolish completely the American Constitutional Republic. Kamala is more of a threat to our Republic than anybody else. She is Putin's asset to make another American Manchurian President . . .

Though Tony Babulinsky credibly reported Biden's family monetary ties with China, I'd recommend you to read my book mentioned above to see for yourself the Russia/China ideological bonds against Western civilization. You will also learn why Justice Roberts changed his political affiliation. All of that had started years ago with the infiltration of the KGB onto our soil—a political operation to take over our Constitutional republic, the way the Socialist Revolution in Russia took over that country a hundred years ago. This operation in America has been done by the KGB in concert with the Dems' leadership and it is going on today in 2020. Here are two recent examples:

The term "White Supremacist" is not the new one: it is an old one, as the KGB's major agenda of "divide and conquer" using the race card has never changed. The KGB Chairman Yuri Andropov had designed the terms "White Oppression" and "White Privileges" in the 1960s. The term "White Supremacist" has the same agenda—"divide and conquer," it is a continuation of 1960th. Read my columns describing Andropov's Legacy and indoctrination of the Black communities by Andropov's KGB in the 1960: Chapter 25, *Stalinism and Destabilization of America*, pp. 135-142, *Socialist Lies: From Stalin to the Clintons, Obamas, and Sanders*, XLIBRIS, 2016. Keep in mind also that the Dems have their armed forces Antifa and BLM and, (obsessed with Trump) Nancy Pelosi knows it and uses them under Putin's supervision against the Republicans . . .

The second example of the KGB infiltration is The Lincoln Project. I have already express my opinion about the Project in my column October 19, 2020 *Wake-Up Suburbia! Soviet/Socialist Inspired Insurrection!*

> *"Insurrection is an art, and like all art it has its laws"*
> *Leon Trotsky*

However, focusing your attention on Putin's old Soviet fraud there, here is also a caveat—the KGB was trying to infiltrate both parties. Yes, Trump is Putin's mortal enemy and so are all famous American Presidents, including Abraham Lincoln. Knowing the KGB agenda to discredit all of them, I suspect an infiltration of the Project by the KGB to disgrace the name of Lincoln. I won't be surprised by crime being committed by a member of the Project. I don't know the name of the individual, but I know well the KGB. Whatever you call the ideology: Marxism, Communism, Socialism, or Soviet Fascism (they all constitute a totalitarian one-party system), the terminology depends on ones' knowledge of the KGB and Russian/Chinese Intel. Read my column *Nationalism, National-Socialism, and Soviet Fascism*, November 19, 2020.

A Man-Made Chinese COVID-19

To achieve his monumental agenda, Putin needed Chinese help and got it. The deadly missile of COVID-19 was launched. The Chinese preparation for the deadly virus has been going on since the 20th century. The KGB has a network of secret laboratories dealing with man-made viruses. One of them had invented HIV and spread it throughout the globe in 1970–1980. That entire experience was taught to the Chinese scientific agency within the Ministry of State Security by the Russian Intel. Besides, Chairman Xi learned a lot from Putin. Having his internal problems-millions of the Chinese elderly—a burden to Chinese economy. He needed to get rid of them as I have already reported in my columns. And he did. In my opinion "The Maximum Security Biolab in the Wuhan Institute of Virology" had deliberately produced man-made COVID-19 to kill, like the KGB secret lab had produced HIV in the 1960s also to kill . . .

Chairman Xi has declared his support for Biden whose family had commercial ties with China. Besides, he learned a lot from Putin and like Putin, he, by one shot killed three birds. First: as I prior reported the COVID-19 killed from 21–30 million people in China. Second: Chairman Xi promised to expend Chinese economic power and challenge the U.S. economically and he did—a part of American capitalism, small business, was devastated by COVID-19. Third: COVID-19 helped anti-Trump forces, and many Socialist Charlatans openly admitted it. I also recognized the W.H.O. Director Dr. Tedros, who often visited China as he is a KGB agent. A man-made Chinese COVID-19 promises a lot of negative surprises for the citizens of America and the globe . . .

Remember: Russian/Chinese Intel is waging a war against Western civilization and American capitalism for global Control and Power.

My conclusion:

The recent Russian cyberattack on six departments of the American government is equal to a declaration of war in the 21st century. The Specter's criminal ideology is fighting Humanity by all means possible, including the use of cyber and biological weaponry. A global response is required to save the lives of living beings. The criminal ideology must be exposed, intellectually defeated and judged with a world verdict. This global threat needs a vital global response and reparations.

CHAPTER 34

From Uncle Joe #1 to Uncle Joe #2

"America is like a healthy body and its resistance is Threefold: its patriotism, its morality, and its spiritual Life. If you can undermine these three areas, America will Collapse from within."—Joseph Stalin

Surprisingly the immigrants from Socialist countries discovered in America the man named Uncle Joe, whom they had known as Comrade Stalin. They were shocked and stunned, but didn't understand how that could happen in America, how the famous murderer of the 20th century could be named Uncle Joe. Yet, years later these immigrants were even more shocked by the destruction of traditional monuments, historical buildings, along with a rewritten history of America. All of which they had experienced in their native Socialist lands. They love their adopted country and are terrified by the events in America today, it has become a reminder of their abysmal past . . .

The Dynamics of America's Transformation

History is the Mother of all sciences. Awareness of past events and a knowledge of past experiences is critical for the projection and building of a successful future. Alas, the American public has missed this crucial history, which has resulted in a deep divide in our country between the Democrats and Republicans today. This perilous knowledge is the history of Russia and her Intel, the history of Stalin, his Soviet Socialism and the brutal force in implementing his Formula of Power around the world in the 20th century. I realized that Stalinism had finally come to America, when Speaker Pelosi labeled all Republicans "the enemies within," it reminded me of Stalin's calling all Russian dissent "the enemies of the people," then he began the Purges, deporting, imprisoning, and killing millions of people . . . As I see, political thoughts in America were criminalized to eliminate all opposition as it was under Stalin . . .

Please don't forget the Soviet/Russian decision of 1955—a factual declaration of war against Western civilization and American capitalism designed by Comrade Stalin. His decision to wage the war by infiltration into all strata of the American society was to destroy it from within. This war has been going on since 1955, it is in its apogee today. To emphasize the significance of the war declared by Stalin today, we have to return to the ideology we are fighting against. Whatever we call it Marxism, Socialism, Communism, Fascism, or Soviet fascism, there is a caveat—Marxism is a theory, the rest became realities because of Stalin, who built the first Socialist Police State and disseminated his ideological creation throughout the world. That's the reason I've been writing about Stalinism for the last thirty-five years . . .

The lack of real information about Russia's crime against humanity and in particular against Western civilization and American capitalism has caused a deep partisan divide, division in American culture, American politics, including many senseless killings and degradations. Knowing that my books had been banned by the corrupt FBI, I continued being engaged in repeating the information in my columns to educate young Americans and decent people of all ages.

I am a child of Stalinism and a former Soviet attorney. Unlike Ayn Rand, who predicted America's future in her brilliant writings of prophecy-fiction, I am writing my books and columns with ultimate knowledge based on the real events in the 20th century Russia: I have lived half of my life under Stalinist police state. I am the facts witness and recognize the regime when I see it. I saw both sides. Knowledge of both sides has brought the understanding of a Global Spy Ring initiated by Stalin to destroy Western civilization and American capitalism from within. His devoted disciples Andropov/Putin developed the formula further throughout the years.

Yet, China is the existential military threat for us today, because Chairman Xi has not only further developed the Stalinist Global Spy Ring, but widened it by infiltrating the global capitalist economy to destroy it from within. It started with the help of Bill Clinton, the first American Manchurian President, continued with the second Manchurian President, Obama, and have never ended. Stalinist formula were transforming normal human mentality into a Socialist one and the globalist Democrat Party bought into those ideas. It has self-transformed into America's Socialist Party with no self-control nor any responsibility to we the people for their actions. Their allegiance is to the goals of the globalist elites. Socialist mentality is the engine of the Dems armed with Stalinist modus operandi: lies, deceit, and fraud, propaganda, symbols, and slogans, intimidation, manipulations, provocations, threat, and violence . . .

Socialist mentality

Don't be surprised when overwhelming fraud is revealed in 2021 America, I warned you about Russian infiltration in 2012: "Legitimacy of the Russian KGB's Government, a destabilizing force in the world, had opened a Pandora's Box—saboteurs, hackers, charlatans, speculators, money counterfeiters, swindlers, provocateurs, and other scoundrels and rascals, flooded our country and the world." All of them are here and Socialist mentality is here with them, too. One of Cuomo's aids, a victim of sexual harassment said it very clear: "it was expected." By that, she testified to the climate and culture of socialist mentality in New York. Cuomo won't resign, he like all Soviet apparatchiks thinks the Earth is revolving around him. Yet, New York Nursing Home's 15,000 deaths are deadly for Cuomo. All of that resembled what I encountered in Russia: arrogance and incompetence is a very dangerous combination! Don't be surprised by the venom against Trump coming out from New York . . . Vladimir Putin hates Donald J. Trump and Socialist mentality is everywhere within the Democrat Party machinery.

You will see very soon a silencing of, and a crackdown on Conservatives in America, which equates to Stalin's Purges and Hitler's corporate political monopoly to eliminate competitors. This is equal to political partisan control and power by Communists in Russia and Nazis in Germany. A planned American upheaval is aimed at empowering the powerful in 2021—the National Guard is defending them from us today in the Capitol. You can't find the truth without knowing Russia's Intel.

As a former Soviet attorney, I invite you to learn how Putin in concert with Speaker Pelosi, Tom Lopez, Bernie Sanders, George Soros, and other Communists has quietly implemented American Fascism. Watch the first segment of the *60 minutes* on 2.14.21 and read my column: http://bit.ly/2KrRBXj.

Here are several individuals with Socialist mentality fighting our political system: Rep. Ocasio-Cortes' *Green New Deal* is aimed at bankrupting our economy and destroying the system left to us by our Founders. She accuses Trump of putting "kids in cages." She is wrong: America is not running a Concentration camp on a South border yet, but the movement of the country to the radical left direction is obvious. AOC only heard the term "concentration camp," she doesn't know that the term is a main feature of all totalitarian regimes be it Marxism, Socialism, Communism, Stalinism, or Fascism. She is in the front line of propagandizing the ideology of Socialism in America. Besides, these are the same "facilities" on the border that were built under Barack Obama and Joe Biden, then utilized by Trump.

And she is not alone ill-informed pertaining the leftist philosophy. Joe Biden's recent pick for Attorney General, D.C. Circuit Court of Appeals Judge Merrick Garland has revealed himself to be another one with a lack of political awareness. On the confirmation hearing "Garland appeared to be the most uninformed man in America, saying he didn't know anything about John Durham's investigation into the origins of the Russian collusion hoax or Andrew Cuomo's scandal involving the cover-up of the true number of nursing home deaths from coronavirus in New York State." That didn't surprise me. As a Judge, he participated in the hearing of the Oklahoma government building blast in 1995 and rendered a wrong verdict . . . And this is the crux of the matter—he doesn't know Russia and her Intel . . .

Then, after that blast, I reacted immediately and wrote the story of the real criminals. The blast, in my view was orchestrated and executed by the Russian Intel in concert with Bill Clinton to manipulate public opinion and help to elect Bill in 1996. As a matter of fact, I expressed my judgement of Bill Clinton four years prior to the blast in Oklahoma by My Conversation with Rush Limbaugh October 29, 1992. You can read here this conversation in my recent column dedicated and published to the memory of Rush Limbaugh, February 20, 2021.

The recent FBI investigation of the January 6, 2021 violence in the Capitol has revealed more features of Stalinist police state: interrogation of people in the absence of an attorney, silencing them, and checking their bank accounts is not the American Law. It is the Soviet/Russian laws, one of the main features of Soviet Socialism, unknown to vast majority of Americans. They are not familiar with Stalinism and Russian Intel that sponsored the Dems' armed forces Antifa and BLM. The FBI Director didn't find the ideological motives in the Capitol Hill events January 6, 2021. He couldn't, because he doesn't know that ideology of Stalinism has infiltrated the Democrat party, and due that the KGB has a free hand to constantly harm America. The recent history of the FBI and our Intel have testified to their ignorance and corruption. I don't trust them and I am not alone. Look at this:

"Antifa and BLM are not civil action groups. They are terrorist groups looking to destroy America. The target areas where they know that they will not get much resistance. And it is these areas that are controlled by Democrats. The Republican Party is the one group that stands for law and order." Liberty Angle, January 30, 2021, *Ted Wheeler Gets a Taste of His Own Medicine.*

And another one: "A top member of 'Insurrection USA," which is allegedly linked to BLM was seen among the people who entered the Capitol this week." We the People Daily, January 7, 2021

History of The Truth

Over 75 million Americans voted for President Trump in the recent election. They were shocked by Joe Biden's win. I have some explanation for them to understand what has happened. There are several facts unknown to them:

First: The 9/11 Commission failed miserably . . .

As a devoted disciple of Stalin, Putin followed Stalin's design and began implementing his Formula in Iran, using the KGB in the 1990s. By the year 2000, the KGB had recruited 14 Saudi Arabian students and with help of Bill Clinton, and motivated to break down American relations with Saudis, the strategy of the plot was realized in the 9/11 attacks against our country. The truth of my view confirms by the KGB defector to America Konstantin Preobrazhensky, who found that the leader of the Saudi student Muhamad Attah had met with the KGB in Prague, the city where foreign agents meet with the KGB. The 9/11 Commission had failed to identify the main culprit of the attacks on 9/11—Russia. Tamerlan Tsarnaev was trained by the KGB for six months in Russia and the blast of Boston's Marathon was committed after the attacks on 9/11. Our Intelligence agencies don't know about Stalinism. That exact fact helps the KGB to reemerge through the connection with International Terrorism in the 21st century America.

Second: The deaths and blood of all our servicemen in Afghanistan is on the hands of Russia. Since the invasion in Afghanistan in 1979, Russia was collaborating with Taliban by using the KGB of all neighboring Muslim Republics with common languages. This criminal cooperation has gone on and never ended.

Third: Iran, like Syria, is Russia's provinces in Putin's mind. Nouri al-Maliki was recruited by the KGB, living in Iran and got an assignment to move to Iraq. Our war in Iraq was doomed from the start with Prime Minister Nouri al-Maliki taking commands from Vladimir Putin. At the time I had information that Jamal Khashoggi had connection to the KGB as well. He was implicated in the Iran-Contra affair as a key middleman in the arms-for-hostages exchange along with Iranian arms dealer Manucher Ghorbanifar in 1987.

Fourth: The race card was the Ace in the KGB's political strategy: indoctrination of the black communities by the "White Oppressors" began in the 1960s. The smart conservative Blacks didn't swallow it and the KGB changed the narrative to "White Supremacists" in 21st century and the Dems employed it at once to resurrect their failed policy to destroy you. I have been analyzing the changes within the Dems for several decades, showing the KGB's political-operatives working within the Dems Party nationwide, infiltrating and corrupting all major government's arteries, courts, sports, culture, democratic institutions, and so forth. It is not only Socialist California and Oregon, it is the Dems' corrupt machinery . . .

"Look at the state of Virginia, where three top Dems are in deep scandals. This is also no coincidence: a former Governor, Terry McAuliffe was Clinton's lieutenant, and I suspect a leader of Socialist mafia, making the entire state adhere to the ideology of Soviet fascism. He was working with FBI's corrupt McCabe to manufacture a protest by white supremacist group rally in Charlottesville, Virginia in 2017. I am not sure that the connection was known, when the case had been investigated and two trivial actors convicted." My column: *Anatomy of Treason*, May 31, 2019.

The Evil Empire is Alive and Well—The KGB's Plans for America

The election on 2020 has changed everything for the worse for America. It is not cancel culture, but a long-term Sovietization of America, a *Social Engineering* like it was in the Soviet Union. Yes, the Evil Empire is alive and with the help of Chinese COVID-19 is getting more aggressive in its infiltration into the Western world. At the same time, if you have eyes and ears, you understand that Joe Biden is unable to run our country. Reading this column you will get the reality of who does it and who runs the show. Educated like Putin by the Soviet Law, I know his next steps—his success in the 2020 American election spins his head and he will go straight ahead with the KGB's plans. As a stanch follower of the Stalinist formula he will use immigration and changes in America's Electoral System. To grasp both, you have to know Stalinist Formula:

In 2015, after the Muslim invasion in Europe, our Intel should've known the KGB's criminal design for Western civilization and America, and the methods the KGB uses inside and outside our country to fight Western civilization and capitalism. Europeans were shocked by the reality of the Invasion of the Muslims in 2015. The global elites in Europe were not shocked. They sponsored it. Do you know that now any criticism *of Islam in Europe* is treated as a form of racism, and "Islamophobia" is considered a crime or a sign of mental illness? "Europe has renounced force, so to many, it appears weak, vulnerable and easily able to be overpowered." *Muslim Invasion of Europe, by* ***Guy Millière***, October 22, 2015

I am giving you this paragraph, because we are at war with the forces that manufactured Muslim Invasion of Europe. It was orchestrated by Russia and its Intel. Read my columns at the time to learn how it was designed and prosecuted. I have been writing about an asymmetrical war against Western civilization for the last thirty years. The Caravans that approach the US southern border are a carbon copy of the Invasion of Europe that was orchestrated and well-organized by the same forces. Both cases are examples of an asymmetrical war against the West. Anti-Trump war is a part of this war. It is a carbon copy of the war waged against Nixon by the Soviet Intelligence machine—history of that treason has very deep roots. But this topic requires a separate column. I don't want to repeat many other reasons why Knowledge of Russia is a Must! Believe me it is!

To grasp the KGB plans for illegal immigration to America, you should know how the KGB uses children and read my column about the children of the Spanish-war 1936-1939. Those children boys and girls were indoctrinated in special schools called *Internat*, where children studied and lived. Thousands of Spanish children have been brought by Stalin to the Soviet Union and twenty years later used them to infiltrate the Central and South America. Do you know the origins of the Mexican drug cartel and MS-13 gangs? Now you know. We have a national security crisis today. The same plans Putin's KGB has for the current massive invasion of children, when 321 children are taken every day to the American border: the KGB plans to start the second cycle of the Permanent Revolution in the 21st century . . . .

The changes of America's Electoral System will be the next fight by the Dems under Putin's supervision to finally destroy our Constitutional republic and establish a one-party system in America. I hope Republicans are reading this column and ready to defend our Exceptional political system, left to us by our Founding Fathers . . .

Those people who have doubts in the authenticity of the Stalin's words in my epigraph, I invite them to look three decades back, today they will not recognize America the Beautiful we had then . . . The design of Uncle Joe #1 was and is being implemented by the Democrat Party leadership in America. Our Constitution is in jeopardy, our Bill of Rights will be shredded. And all leftist Charlatans like Kim Jong Un will announce more nukes, daring weak Biden to do something about it . . . The irony of two centuries is striking: Uncle Joe #1 started a war against humanity in the 20th century Russia. Uncle Joe #2 is completing this war in the 21st century America by joining a Global Spy Ring fighting against us. Some Republicans still don't grasp the horror, we are facing: They are calling Socialist Charlatans—The Democrats!

CHAPTER 35

A Global March by Putin's KGB Mafia/Army

February 21, 2022/in Commentary, Culture War, Elections, National Security, News, Policy, Politics /by Simona Pipko

I am writing about Vladimir Putin for three reasons: First, I belong to a few who know more about Vladimir Putin than others. Second, we are watching Putin's Socialist Revolution in America. Third: the recently revealed Durham's bombshell is not news for me, I was writing about the deep criminal conspiracy of Russia's Intelligence and the Democrat Party for thirty years. Durham is on the right path to expose it. Yet, for expressing my knowledge and sharing it with the American public, the FBI has submitted my name to the FISA Court and made me a Foreign Agent. That is the reason, you still have not read my books and articles: they have become banned …

All America's problems and troubles in 2022 are caused by Putin's KGB' Mafia/Army and that is the reason knowledge of Putin's KGB Mafia/Army is imperative. I am a political refugee from Russia and I know Putin. He and I lived in the same city and we both were Soviet lawyers. We studied Marxism-Leninism and Stalinism at the Law School for four years. My major was Criminal Law, Putin's International Law. He graduated from Law School twenty years later, when I had already been practicing law as a defense attorney. His mentor, a Chair of the International Law Faculty, was my close friend: a smart and very savvy man with broad political horizons, who gave Putin recommendation to the KGB after Putin graduated from Law School.

Vladimir Putin is a creation of the Soviet Socialist System. That means: Putin is a byproduct of Stalin's dreams of *One World Socialist Government under the Kremlin rule.* Putin is connected to Stalin by the umbilical cord of ideology. The same connection Putin has with China and Chairman Xi Jinping; they are both war criminals, the natural allies representing Socialist/Communist forces waging the war against Western civilization and American Capitalism... I have been writing about this war for the last thirty years and called it WWIII. Read my books and columns at www.drrichswier.com/author/spipko/ and http://www.simonapipko1.com/index.htm.

The Roots of WWIII: Putin's Socialist Revolution in America

It is not a coincidence that Peter Schweizer began his book *Red Handed* about China with a quotation from Vladimir Lenin and the Soviet times. That fact proves the real history of events—the war against American capitalism started a hundred years ago by Russia. Though China's military now is a great danger to the United States today, yet, Russia presents an existential threat to America, covertly destroying our republic from within. All America's problems in 2022 derive from the decades of real collusion between Russia's Intelligence and the American Democrat Party. Bill Clinton was the first American President recruited and drilled by the KGB under the Chairman, Yuri Andropov in 1969-1970. Read the details in my book: *What is Happening to America? The Hidden Truth of Global Destruction*, XLIBRIS, 2012.

Yes, all America's problems in 2022 are caused by Putin's KGB' Mafia/Army and that is the reason knowledge of Putin's KGB Mafia/Army is imperative. The second American President, Barack Obama has been educated and drilled also by the KGB mafia/Army. The above mentioned book details his story as well. The massive infiltration by the KGB Mafia/Army to American democratic institutions, courts, sports, and government took place during the time of Clinton's and Obama's presidencies. Biden's presidency has also been created by the Putin's KGB Mafia/Army and the first executive orders by Biden illustrated its anti-American essence: self-inflicting energy policy, inflation, and open borders have continued demolition of the American republic… Read my book: *Socialist Revolution in America, XLIBRIS,* 2021

There is a special and fundamental idea in my entire writings: a war against Western civilization and American capitalism by the totalitarian Regimes. That multi-faceted geopolitical war for world domination started by Stalin and developed at the time by his devoted disciples, the KGB Chairman Yuri Andropov 1967-1982 and Vladimir Putin. This war has never stopped. The tension of Russia's claim over Ukraine is that WWIII was waged by Vladimir Putin in the center of Europe today. His desire to have a Great Russia will impact the entire world and destabilize the globe.

Putin had thirty years to prepare, analyze, and calculate his war on Ukraine. The Democrat Party has given Putin those thirty years. Today, Putin practices coercive diplomacy along with intimidation and threat to the world order. Democracy is under attack and the dark future is looming. Modern Warfare has changed dramatically since WWII: there are now a quadruple opportunity to kill and destroy, let alone cyberattacks and electronic warfare, known well by the KGB Mafia/Army…

Please, remember September 1, 1939 when WWII had begun by Nazis with a false flag operation Glaives against Poland: the German soldiers disgusted in Polish uniform attacked Nazi Germany. Doesn't it remind you of Putin's preparation to attack Ukraine? Do you remember Hitler, Nazis and their war against Western democracies in WWII? This is the repetition and illustration of the aggressive and reckless behavior of the leaders in the global setting! Fascism never sleeps. Watch similar events in our hemisphere.

I have been writing about worldwide Russian/China's criminal activities for thirty years. Misinformation means in Russian—Disinformation. Planting a fraud is the usual Russian dirty trick and Putin is a master of provocation, dirty tricks, sabotage, and disinformation. I have deliberately focused your attention on the Soviet narrative-propaganda to lie, deceive, or defraud to advance the agenda—those are the tools. For that exact reason I was writing about *Socialist modus operandi* and describing it as lies, deceit, and fraud. Those verbs exactly portrayed the intent to misinform and mislead.

In fact, it was the exact task of *Socialist modus operandi* described by me based on Stalin's Political Correctness and aimed at masking the truth and substituting it with the Stalinist Dogma of Soviet Socialism.

The essence of Stalin's PC, those precise narratives, actions, and events you can see in Biden's 2021-2022 America. This *Socialist modus operandi* has been implemented in all countries of "the Axis of Evil" under the Russian umbrella, now run by Putin. Read my columns about "the Axis of Evil" to see the real division of the globe and the place the Democrat Party occupied.

I have already warned you that America looks very weak on the world stage in 2022 and as a result the criminal and aggressive "Axis of Evil" forces will act. You will see their real faces! In this respect, Hunter Biden's connection with Moscow's Mayor, which means the KGB and the weak personality of our President Biden is the crux of the matter. Watching and following Joe's family for the last decade, I found his direct ties with Putin and the KGB. He has been collaborating with Putin since 2013-2014 or maybe even prior to that. You saw Biden illustrating his interest in helping Putin to suffocate democratic Ukraine. Do you remember Biden's quid-pro-quo with $1 Billion of our money? He was against the democratic Ukraine!

Just look at Biden's first executive orders to undermine American energy policy, the major engine of our independence and success of capitalism. His un-American energy policy impacted the American economy, creating world crises and giving control and power to Russia... At the same time Joe Biden helped Russia with the Nord Stream 2 pipeline, providing Putin with psychological support, and enabling him to act aggressively further. Biden didn't "carry a big stick" he did the opposite! I don't trust Biden's team and don't believe a word from them: I suspected the KGB was running his presidency. Putin's aggressive plan to surround a defenseless Ukraine on three sides with almost 200 thousand troops is a threat to Humanity and world stability. That conduct required a stronger language against the Russian aggressor. Listening to Jake Sullivan, we heard the opposite. Wake up, America! Democrats keep failing you!

Watch the American administration's narratives and actions: censorship, control, self-defeating energy policy, inflation, and surge of crime. Those are anti-American events opposing moral principles of our Constitutional republic. Moreover, you can see a collaboration of the government with big-tech corporations censoring the descent. Pay attention to the recent policies of the Canadian and American administrations. Be aware: your political view has become the cause of freezing your bank account by the government. Socialism and Fascism are two sides of the same totalitarian coin and Fascism never sleeps.

Biden called Tridua to inspire him to apply more severe police force against truckers. Both administrations are deeming the Canadian Truckers and American parents to be the terrorists. For control and power they are expending the definition of terrorism, which is illegal. Recently, Justin Tridua is engaged in fascistic practicing, treating truckers as terrorists, arresting the leaders and their bank accounts. It is not law and order, but it is Martial Law against democracy.

Here is the right conclusion "Every day Americans need to wake up to how their own money is used to advance an ideological agenda that they find repugnant." Vivek Ramaswamy.

Special Counsel Durham and the Faith of the Democrat Party

Yes, if Special Counsel John Durham knows Russia and its Intelligence, he will be able to prove long-term treasonous activities of the Democrat Party leadership—a real collusion of the leadership with the KGB Mafia/Army. I was describing that exact collusion in my columns and books providing a reader with the names and events for thirty years. I had named six candidate-Democrats running for the U.S. presidency sponsored by the KGB. Some of them are now in the Biden administration. You see the result of the KGB' Special Operations during the decades...

I am warning you again: Our national security is at stake.

The entire Trump/Russia collusion narrative was a politically motivated scam, calculated, coordinated, and orchestrated by Russia's Intelligence in concert with the leadership of the Democrat Party to cover up the crime they themselves have been committing for decades. The leaders of that politically motivated scam were Bill Clinton, Barack Obama, and Vladimir Putin. We were witnessing the KGB Mafia/ Army Special Operation against the American Constitutional republic. The operation is still going on... Read about Stalin's postulates and Andropov's design to infiltrate America in my columns.

I think that Joe Biden and Vladimir Putin have a common agenda to save the Democrat Party from extinction; and that makes Putin's hands free for an arrogant aggression. Today you see Putin's psychological pressure on the West for concessions: he wants to have a Buffer-Zone and occupy Donbass in Eastern Ukraine.

Remember, the symbols played a big role in Putin's Soviet mind. The Soviet Union was established in 1922—a centennial is in 2022. February 23d is the Day of the Soviet Army.

Putin will act… Just wait…

To be continued www.simonapipko1.com
www.drrichswier.com/author/spipko/

CHAPTER 36

The Global Threat of Anti-Semitism: Fascism

The recent Putin's nuclear escalation, putting Russian nuclear forces on high alert is a sign of the existential threat to humanity. The world is threatened again like seventy years ago by another leader—Adolf Hitler. Ukraine is the victim-country in the center of Europe that knows that the best. Ukraine went through the hell of Stalinism, occupation by fascism in WWII, and now invaded for the third time by Putin's Soviet Fascism. We can expect millions of refugees! And the American President Joe Biden talks about minor incursion… What a shame!!! Wake up America!!!

I am a political refugee from the Soviet Union, I know their tremendous suffering. But it doesn't mean that I didn't like the Russian people. On the contrary, I loved these people and served them as a defense attorney in the Soviet courts for twenty-five years. Even more, I liked Russian literature, poetry and knew them well. Yet, I left the country along with my sick son. I left all my property, having only $90 in my pocket. I immigrated to the United States because we were Jews and my two children didn't have a future in the country of the anti-Semitic government. Knowing that the American mind can't perceive the term "the anti-Semitic government," I'll try to explain it, but don't be discouraged, our current corrupt Democrat government doesn't know it either.

You can start your education at this minute, by watching the TV and listening to the radio—we are in the beginning of WWIII, I have been warning you about for thirty years. Learn how civilians of Ukraine are dying, defending their country and thousands have already fled. Listen to the citizens of Ukraine, they don't want to live in a country like North Korea or Iran. They will fight for their freedom... Watch the brutal and meaningless destruction of land and everything alive... Remember the grandmothers with guns defending their homes! Remember a woman Olena with a sleeping child on her hands pleading to America for help!! The crime against mankind could've been prevented!!! The Democrat Party failed you! The Democrats betrayed us and Americas' moral principles! This war is a historical shame of America! The blood of the Ukrainian people is on the hands of the Democrat Party's leadership! This war will be catastrophic beyond Ukraine!

You should learn the lesson of life and death for freedom that has deep roots in our history. You should learn the history of the gigantic incompetence of the American officials who have brought our democratic country to that global crises of war by their incompetence and mismanagement—a geostrategic failure/fiasco. You are watching the Genocide of the 21st century in Ukraine! The tragedy of this war and agenda of the aggressor is clear: to change the regime and steal the Ukrainian FREEDOM! This is the crux of the matter! Putin wants POWER! The Ukrainian people are dying to defend their FREEDOM and reject his control! Those two words Power and Freedom are inseparable, they are the essence of world politics.

I began my story with the anti-Semitic government in Russia for a reason. The tyranny of the Soviet system drove me to emigrate to the U.S. You can read about the troubles and difficulties my son and I had to overcome to become Americans. *Baltic Winds Testimony of a Soviet Attorney*, XLIBRIS, 2002. Don't be surprised by the anti-Semitic voices around the world and in our American Congress by so-called Democrats and the "Squad." Please, remember that the United States Embassy was officially relocated to Jerusalem on May 14, 2018 by Republicans to coincide with the 70th anniversary of the Israeli Declaration of Independence...

Anti-Semitism is tied to the current war. Do you know that the President of Ukraine Volodymyr Zelenskyy is a Jew? Yes, he is a Jew and that fact is a bombshell for many in the world. Ukraine has the *Babiy Yar*, an International cemetery-graveyard for thousands Jewish men, women, and children—the mass graves known to the world. Read the poem

Babiy Yar by famous Russian poet Evgeniy Evtushenko. It is about a few Ukrainian policemen in collaboration with Nazis who were shooting those Jews, victims of anti-Semitism. It took place under the Nazis occupation of Ukraine in WWII. President Zelinskyy was democratically elected in Ukraine in 2019. I don't need more words—Ukraine has rejected and banned its Soviet-Communist past and elected a Jew as the President… You see his leadership and unprecedented courage today!

Religions and Politics

The definition of religion is a controversial and complicated subject. I am not going there. Yes, there are different denominations of faith, but I am not talking about organized religions. For me it is my faith in God. For many individuals, religion is their personal belief and connection with God. The tyranny is depriving you of that freedom. And that exact freedom of religion and personal liberty was forbidden under Soviet-Communist regimes in all countries, including Ukraine under the Warsaw Pact until the collapse of the USSR.

A totalitarian regime afraid of individual freedom, because it undermines totalitarian control and power over the population…

Judaism, perhaps, the most victimized denomination of human beliefs persecuted by politics. You know how the Gestapo was managing the Jews: by gas chambers and mass graves. In Russia, this persecuting force was multi-faceted. I am writing about that force and for your convenience using the term the KGB Mafia/Army. It is a very adequate term to grasp the reality of life under Stalin. The story of his death will illustrate the horror of anti-Semitism even better:

It was 1952 when my parents told me that we will move from Leningrad to another city. I was old enough to know that Jews will be deported from big cities to Siberia, the Far East, or Central Asia. The rumors of the *Doctors Plot* were spread and the usual propaganda machine was working: that Doctors attempted to poison and murder the leaders of the Communist Party. Those rumors were discussed between the youngsters, too. My parents were devastated, they didn't know what to do and how to react. In our life the walls had ears, my parents couldn't discuss the news with me. We were living under the Stalinist police-state regime…

Today, I know that it was the KGB Special Operation, manufacturing a threat that didn't exist—a pretext to deport all Jews. No Doctors had attempted to murder anybody. Stalin gave the order to the Politburo to prepare the law to execute his order, but thankfully Stalin died March 5, 1953 and we were saved… Anti-Semitism presents the worst form of racism to "divide and conquer" a white race. Anti-Semitism is a tool for politicians, thugs and charlatans to obtain Control and Power. That tool has given them the opportunity to create the additional force to secure their power: agencies like the KGB or Gestapo.

For your information, the next most prosecuted was the Catholic Church. Stalin proclaimed the Church the enemy of the country, destroying it and almost pushing it from existence in Russia. Only a few Catholic Churches survived in UKRAINE. All other houses of worship were penetrated by the KGB and controlled by the agency. Don't be confused: Putin used the Orthodox Church to come to power under the Collapse of the Soviet Union in 1991. Putin is a devoted disciple of Stalin and Andropov. He is a leader of Soviet Fascism today!

Here is a definition of Fascism:" a governmental system led by a dictator having complete power, forcibly suppressing opposition and criticism, regimenting all industry, commerce, etc., and emphasizing an aggressive nationalism and often racism." Thesaurus.com Please, remember European history and judge the events in Ukraine today. Fascism never sleeps…

Belarus is an accomplice in Putin's crime of spreading Soviet Fascism in Europe. They will go further by creating Stalin's agenda of *One World Socialist Government under Russian rule.* Belarus is a stage ground for Putin's invasion that means that President Alexander Lukashenko is an accomplice of the crime against humanity and deserves the same sanctions-punishment Putin's Russia receives. We must protect the world order and stop fascism in Europe!

Blood of Ukrainian People on the Hands of Democrats

Reading my books and columns, you will find the debates analyzing the identity of Soviet-Stalinism and German Fascism and their stunning similarity. Read my column *The KGB's Roots and Pedigrees*, Oct 19, 2017. You will learn that Stalin and Putin have the DNA of Genghis Khan.

Take it seriously. I have been warning America for thirty years about Putin's cruelty and agenda to defeat Western civilization and American capitalism. NATO should help Ukraine now, this minute, to prevent the upcoming Russian forces from reaching Kyiv. It is now or never... Ahead of us a long and bloody guerrilla war. If he needs to, Putin will bring the Chechen brigades to Ukraine and you will see his relation to Genghis Khan.

However, to know Putin as a leader is only half the answer for the solution; the other half is the awareness of his Intelligence apparatus. I use the term, the KGB mafia/Army—Putin and the KGB Mafia/Army are inseparable. The Dems don't have the remotest idea of the aggressive force and activities of the KGB Mafia/Army within America and globally. Our Intelligence and the FBI have missed that vital information: we have the current world crises as a result. They missed a chunk of Russian history of the 20th century. Russia is in partnership with the KGB Mafia/Army. Read my column: *A Global March by Putin's KGB Mafia/Army.* Here is a link: https://bit.ly/35cRMA2

The "climate change" Biden's policy is that exact old Soviet KGB's dirty trick Stalin had used in 1952 to deport the Jews from the Soviet Union. It is unprecedented, but NATO and the American Jews do not know Putin's regime of Soviet Fascism.

Today, in the 21st century, Biden's administration uses that old KGB dirty trick of "climate change" or "disinformation" to undermine and damage the American Constitutional republic and American capitalism. What a shame! Wake up America!

There is no compromise with the Dems, they are worse than hypocrites, they work in concert with the KGB. Joe Biden has been collaborating with Putin since 2013-2014. He was directly involved by helping Putin to suffocate the young Ukrainian democracy and personally participated in helping the old corrupt regime. You saw Biden's delaying sanctions strategy and slowing down help to Ukraine today. Personally he is incapable of grasping the seriousness of the world predicament. As I suspected, his staff is managing his presidency. Read about his staff: Threat to Our Freedoms and National Security, August 16, 2021/in Commentary, Culture War, Policy, Politics /by Simona Pipko

Putin's invasion of Ukraine could've been prevented had Americans known the Truth about Soviet Fascism, conveyed by my books during the last thirty years. It is not Marxism, but Soviet Fascism that wages the war in the center of Europe today. The Ukrainian people have revealed and demonstrated that Truth by their slogan: Putin=Stalin. Yes, Putin equals Stalin; both brought the ideology of Soviet Fascism to the world: Stalin in the 20th century, Putin in the 21st century. The crimes of Soviet Fascism must be exposed and stopped now! Russia must be condemned globally!!!

My fellow Americans!

Putin is a global threat! He is a war criminal! Putin understands only the language of force!

You are witnessing Putin's Socialist Revolution in America! The KGB Mafia/Army within our midst is helping Biden to demolish our Constitutional republic. Our national security is at stake. Educate yourself to stop the Democrats' treason! Read my columns. Stop the enemy of Humanity! It is now or never!

Save America the Beautiful!!!

The End

March 5, 2022

AUTHOR BIOGRAPHY

Simona Pipko was born in Moscow, USSR. A graduate of the Leningrad Law School, she practiced law as a defense attorney for twenty-five years in the capital of Estonia, Tallinn. Leaving behind her Communist husband, she immigrated to the United States with her two children in 1981.

While living in New York City and teaching at the New School for Social Research and New York University, she wrote a series of articles for various publications, including The International Lawyer ABA, Law and National Security Intelligence Report.

In 2002, Ms. Pipko published her first book *Baltic Winds; Testimony of A Soviet Attorney*. XLIBRIS, 2002. One of her readers, Director of the Center for Study of Popular Culture wrote:

> "Thank you for sending me your moving book. You are a very courageous woman..."
>
> David Horowitz

In 2006 Ms. Pipko published her second book: *The Russian Factor; From Cold War to Global Terrorism* XLIBRIS, 2006. The third book titled *What is Happening to America?* was published by Xlibris in 2012. In 2016 Ms. Pipko published *Socialist Lies: from Stalin to the Clintons, Obamas, and Sanders*. In 2021 Ms. Pipko published her book *Socialist Revolution in America*

Simona Pipko is the author of six books and over 100 articles published in the United States. She is an Alumni of the George F. Kennan Institute for Advance Russian Studies.

Other information at www.Dr.RichSwicr.com the articles written by Simona Pipko 2014-2016 *Soviet Fascism in the 21st Century* www.drrichswier.com/author/spipko/ --all columns published in 2010-2022

http://www.simonapipko1.com/index.htm--description of all books and columns.

www.simonapipko1.com Google images—all images of Simona Pipko books and articles.

Podcast: https://anchor.fm/right-now-podcast/episodes/Soviet-Spotlight--Interview-with-SIMONA-PIPKO--RIGHT-NOW-Podcast-e4k73n

Twitter: https://twitter.com/simonapipko?lang=en

Made in United States
North Haven, CT
20 October 2026

20740142R10261